Arab Conquests and Early Islamic Historiography

The Early and Medieval Islamic World

Published in collaboration with the Society for the Medieval Mediterranean

As recent scholarship resoundingly attests, the medieval Mediterranean and Middle East bore witness to a prolonged period of flourishing intellectual and cultural diversity. Seeking to contribute to this ever-more nuanced and contextual picture, *The Early and Medieval Islamic World* book series promotes innovative research on the period 500–1500 AD with the Islamic world, as it ebbed and flowed from Marrakesh to Palermo and Cairo to Kabul, as the central pivot. Thematic focus within this remit is broad, from the cultural and social to the political and economic, with preference given to studies of societies and cultures from a socio-historical perspective. It will foster a community of unique voices on the medieval Islamic world, shining light into its lesser-studied corners.

New and Forthcoming Titles

Cross Veneration in the Medieval Islamic World: Christian Identity and Practice under Muslim Rule, Charles Tieszen (Fuller Theological Seminary/Simpson University)

Power and Knowledge in Medieval Islam: Shi'i and Sunni Encounters in Baghdad, Tariq al-Jamil (Swathmore College)

The Eastern Frontier: Limits of Empire in Late Antique and Early Medieval Central Asia, Robert Haug (University of Cincinnati)

Narrating Muslim Sicily: War and Peace in the Medieval Mediterranean World, William Granara (Harvard University)

Female Sexuality in the Early Medieval Islamic World: Gender and Sex in Arabic Literature, Pernilla Myrne (University of Gothenburg)

Arab Conquests and Early Islamic Historiography

The Futuh al-Buldan of al-Baladhuri

Ryan J. Lynch

I.B.TAURIS

LONDON • NEW YORK • OXFORD • NEW DELHI • SYDNEY

I.B. TAURIS
Bloomsbury Publishing Plc
50 Bedford Square, London, WC1B 3DP, UK
1385 Broadway, New York, NY 10018, USA
29 Earlsfort Terrace, Dublin 2, Ireland

BLOOMSBURY, I.B. TAURIS and the I.B. Tauris logo
are trademarks of Bloomsbury Publishing Plc

First published in Great Britain 2020
Paperback edition first published 2021

Series design by www.paulsmithdesign.com
Cover image: Maqamat of al-Hariri; Bibliothèque nationale de France, manuscript
Arabe 6094, dated 1222-23AD. Folio 133 Verso: Abu Zayd before the governor.
(© World History Archive / Alamy Stock Photo)

A catalogue record for this book is available from the British Library.

A catalog record for this book is available from the Library of Congress.

ISBN: HB: 978-1-8386-0439-4
PB: 978-0-7556-4468-1
ePDF: 978-1-8386-0441-7
eBook: 978-1-8386-0440-0

Typeset by Deanta Global Publishing Services, Chennai, India

To find out more about our authors and books visit
www.bloomsbury.com and sign up for our newsletters.

For Jackie

Contents

Acknowledgements

The following research was my doctoral dissertation, originally submitted to the University of Oxford. It went through a great many changes between my original submission and its approval, and subsequently, its publication as this monograph. No research is perfect, and certainly, the remaining imperfections here are my fault alone. Should the reader find any form of insight or wisdom in the pages herein, however, the debt is largely owed to the direction of Robert Hoyland and Harry Munt. Both Robert and Harry were equally crucial in guiding me towards a study of al-Balādhurī, and I will be forever grateful for all that they continue to do to support me. Robert's masterful command of sources and his own intellectual curiosity are everything that a junior scholar needs from his teacher. Through Harry, I learned the fundamentals of what it means to be an Islamic historian along with my love of Arabic historiography.

A special debt is also owed to those who examined this research at various stages throughout the writing process, but especially to Christopher Melchert and Andrew Marsham, who helped to correct many (many) mistakes in the final drafts. Philip Booth, Julia Bray, and Marie Legendre examined this research at the earlier stages. The feedback from all of them was incredibly important in correcting errors and omissions and in guiding my writing forward towards completion.

I also owe countless thanks to the exceptional colleagues and friends that I made over the years of transitioning from student to scholar. Joshua Olsson was with me throughout the entire journey from graduate student to professor, constantly challenging my preconceived ideas about Islamic history and subsequently convincing me that remaining an academic was what I really wanted. No one has taught me more about being a historian than he has. Nicola Clarke nurtured my interests and always treated my ideas equally, yet critically, while helping me realize that I could study what I *wanted* to research. Nadia Jamil gave me the language tools necessary to work independently. Wahid Amin, Talal al-Azem, Antoine Borrut, Anna Chrysostomides, Nicholas Evans, Geert Jan van Gelder, Hannah Hagemann, Andy Hilkens, Marek Jankowiak, Taj Kandoura, Hugh Kennedy, Tom MacMaster, Michael Maher-King, Julian May, Roy Michael McCoy, Leyla Najaf-Zada, Nassima Neggaz, Salam Rassi, Adam Talib,

Luke Treadwell, Alison Vacca, and Edward Zychowicz-Coghill, all provided attention and insight at various times, whether in the classroom, at conferences, or through conversations over a drink. Umberto Bongianino was integral in assisting me on how best to describe the scripts of the manuscripts discussed in Chapter 1. I am indebted to Sarah Bowen Savant, Maxim Romanov, and the rest of the exciting *KITAB* Project's members for much of the data concerning *Futūḥ* reuse discussed in Chapter 6. I am thankful to Asma Afsaruddin, Michael Cook, and Stephen Humphreys for their comments on my chapter on genre during a brief presentation at the 2014 MESA annual meeting.

Additionally, there is a very long list of friends and family members who have supported me in various ways throughout my career: Ross Alexander, Hassan Ali Ahmad, Estara Arrant, Will Badger, Elissa Barche, Thomas Barche, Benedict Bernstein, Jim Cortier, Jo Cortier, DJ Deaton, Cara DeQuarto, Christine DeQuarto, Joann DeQuarto, Jon Hallahan, Sarah Hammond, Greg Hauenstein, Christa Heckman, Ishtar Hernandez, Dana Johnston, Casey Jones Toth, Jack Kelly, Eric Kurlander, Harry Long, Morgan Long, James Lynch, Janis Lynch, Jesse Napolitano, Dmitri Macmillen, Tom McLachlan, Charlie Mercer, James Morrow, Jeremy Papadinis, Rebecca Papadinis, Katie Perry, Katie Rash, Colin Ramsay, Kimberly Reiter, Anthony Salvatore, Matt Sherman, Kameron St. Clare, Hasnayn Syed, Kerri Taylor, Margaret Venzke, Isha Vicaria, and Linda Weser.

My research was generously supported by scholarships and studentships from Pembroke and Wolfson Colleges, Oxford, which were also my very welcoming homes throughout my years in England. I owe special thanks to the staff of both colleges as well as to the librarians at the Oriental Institute Library, but especially to my colleagues in the IT Team at Wolfson: Stephen Gower and Phil Nixon. Without their patience and support, I would not have been able to make the most of my time in Oxford.

Since arriving at Columbus State University, I have benefitted from the collegiality and supportive environment of my colleagues and students in the Department of History and Geography as I worked towards bringing this monograph to publication. We fail and succeed as a team, and I am thankful to have such great colleagues in Bryan Banks, Sarah Bowman, Patty Chappel, Dan Crosswell, John Ellisor, Brad Huff, Amanda Rees, Eric Spears, Gary Sprayberry, and Doug Tompson. I am also thankful for the support of the CSU Center for Global Engagement and the family of J. Kyle and Sarah Spencer, whose endowment of the Spencer House in Oxford has allowed me to continue my research at the Oriental Institute.

The greatest debt, however, is certainly owed to my family. My father, Raymond, was the catalyst for my love and appreciation of history. He set me on the path and gave me the skills to make my own way, although he did not live to walk that entire road with me. My mother, Florence, has sustained and believed in me at every step of this journey, and has ensured I worked hard to live up to the high standards she has always set for me. My brother, Shane, has always been what a younger brother should be: a wonderful distraction from work, and a reminder that life is more than just the job. My wife, Jackie, faithfully travelled across the world to support me and has brought so much joy to my academic life while equally bearing the burdens of frustration and uncertainty that come along with it. For that and more, she deserves the greatest praise and thanks of all.

Notes on primary source citation, translation, and transliteration

For references to *Futūḥ al-buldān* which will occur throughout this research, I have relied on the 1956-1957 Cairo edition of the text edited by Ṣalāh al-Dīn al-Munajjid listed in the bibliography. All of the citations to this edition will simply appear as "*Futūḥ*" with a corresponding page number.

The translation of primary source text occurs throughout this research. The overwhelming majority of these translations are my own, although in the case of the *Futūḥ*, the translation provided here will have been compared to the two-volume English translation of Philip Hitti and Francis Murgotten listed in the bibliography, and will in some cases be inspired by it. In the case of the translated poetry which appears in Chapter 4, the translation of this material is almost entirely Hitti and Murgotten's.

In a few rare instances, Arabic translation will be provided with only a citation to a published translation and not an Arabic edition. This signifies that the translation is entirely the work of the listed scholar.

For the benefit of the reader without any knowledge of Arabic, page numbers corresponding to western language translations of some of the texts used here will appear aside the references from the Arabic editions when available. In the case of the *Futūḥ*, I have included the page number to Hitti and Murgotten's translation in parentheses following the Arabic page number, with an "H" or "M" to denote in which volume of the translation that account can be found.

The transliteration of Arabic sources is provided here according to the standards of the *International Journal of Middle East Studies*.

Illustrations

Figures

Maps

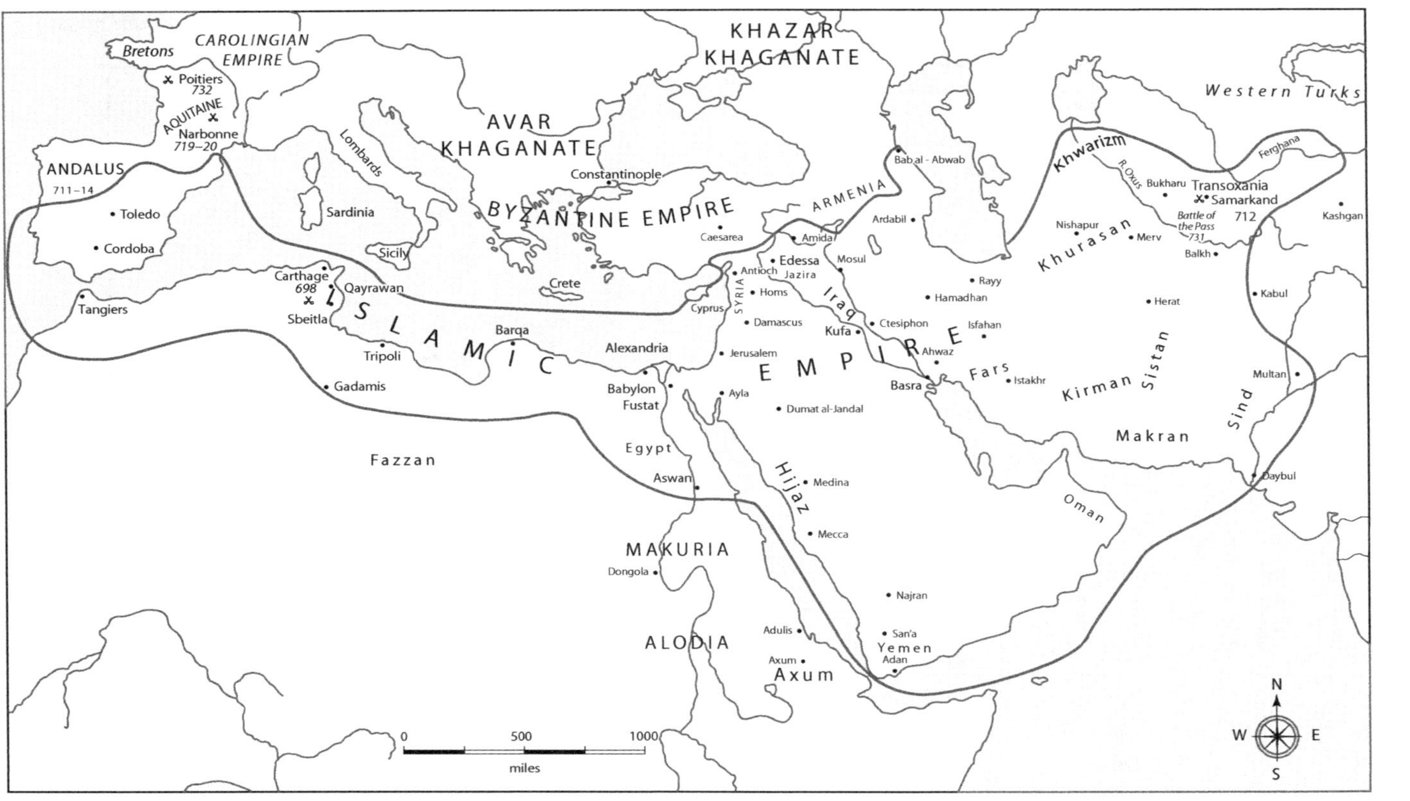

Map 1 Map of the Arab Empire ca. 750 CE, adapted from Robert G. Hoyland, *In God's Path* (OUP, 2015).

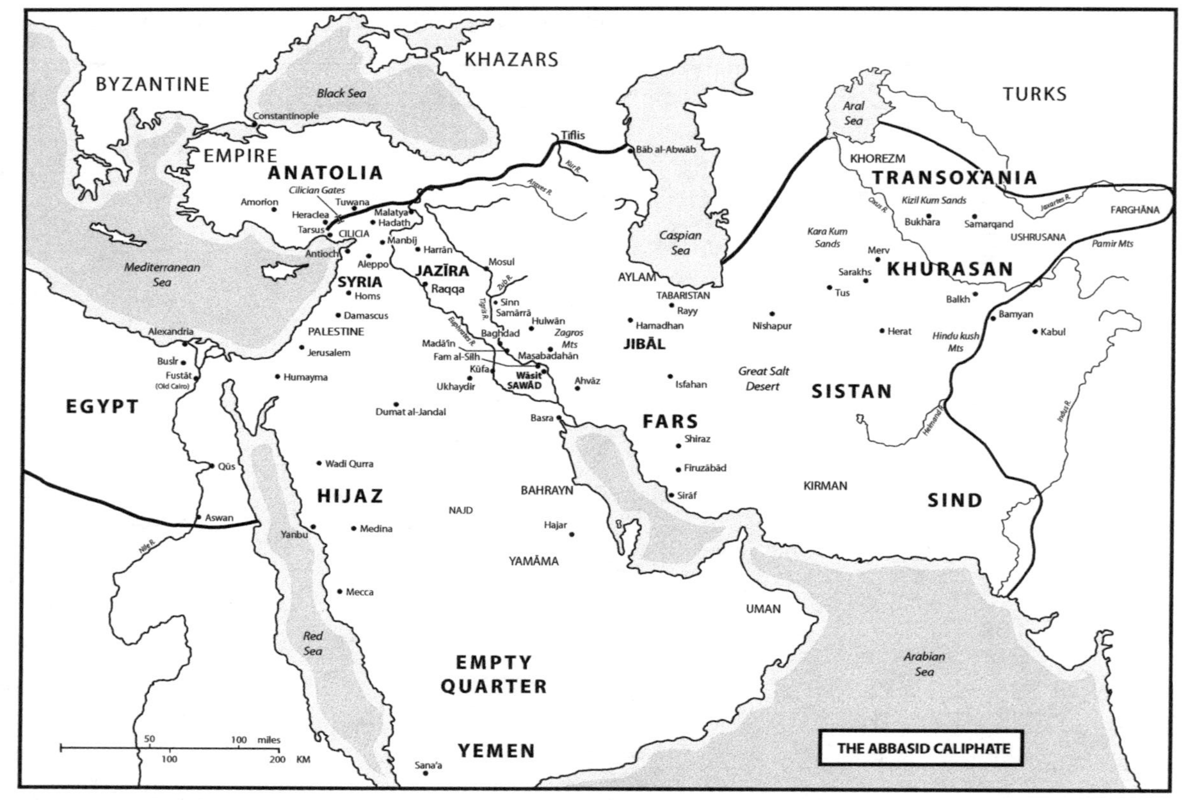

Map 2 Map of the ʿAbbāsid Caliphate, adapted from Hugh Kennedy, *The Court of the Caliphs* (Weidenfeld & Nicolson, 2004).

Introduction

> *The high estimation in which Balādhurī is held also by modern research may be due to his not suppressing the pro-Umayyad tradition. It is this circumstance that makes his rendering such a valuable historical source to us; but it cannot replace a real historiographical appraisal of his works.*[1]

Among the most vital sources of our information on the late antique and early Islamic Middle East are the works of the Muslim author Aḥmad b. Yaḥyā b. Jābir b. Dāwūd al-Balādhurī (d. ca. 892 CE/AH 279).[2] While among the earliest surviving Islamic sources, al-Balādhurī's two extant works – *Kitāb Futūḥ al-buldān* (*The Book of the Conquest of Lands*) and *Ansāb al-ashrāf* (*The Lineage of Nobles*) – are treasure troves of information on the Islamic conquests of the seventh and eighth centuries CE/first and second centuries AH, on early Islamic society, and on the formation and development of governance under Islamic rule. Both texts have played a crucial role in the modern reconstruction of the early Islamic period, although as will be discussed below, the attention that each text has garnered has been variable. Beyond this, both have immense value in enlightening readers on the development of early Arabic historical writing, early Muslim authorship, and the scholarly culture of the court in the time of the author's life, in addition to any actual historical insight they contain.

The present research will focus solely on the smaller of al-Balādhurī's works, *Futūḥ al-buldān* (which will henceforth be referred to primarily as the *Futūḥ*). When considering the available sources for Islamic history between the seventh and eighth centuries CE, there are few which can claim greater importance than al-Balādhurī's *Futūḥ*. Written in Arabic by a ninth-/third-century Muslim scholar working at the court of the ʿAbbāsid caliphs, the *Futūḥ's* content considers many important matters at the beginning of Islamic history. It details the major events of the early Islamic conquests, the settlement of Muslims in the conquered territories and their experiences therein, and the establishment and development of the early Islamic state under the first two dynasties of Islam, the Umayyads (661–750 CE/AH 41–132) and early ʿAbbāsids (750–1258 CE/AH 132–656). That a source from the ninth century CE is so vital to the reconstruction of events in the first two Islamic centuries is telling in itself, and yet few would doubt the importance of the *Futūḥ* for our understanding of early Islamic history.

In addition to the *Futūḥ's* important content as well as its (relatively) early date of composition, there are practical reasons for its widespread and near ubiquitous use by modern scholars of late antiquity, early Islamic history, and the medieval Mediterranean more generally, aside from just the rarity of contemporary sources.[3] Its popularity greatly benefitted from the efforts of Arabists Philip Hitti and Francis Murgotten, who in 1916 and 1924 translated the full text into English as *The Origins of the Islamic State*.[4] With the field of late antique studies established later and with the text's availability in a western language for researchers without a knowledge of Arabic, it became a vital data-mine for historians seeking easily accessible information – for comparison or otherwise – on the region during and immediately following the Islamic conquests. It has become commonplace to turn to the *Futūḥ* for information on a specific location or topic.

Despite the undoubted significance of the *Futūḥ*, there has been little attention paid to the nature of the text itself – its sources, genre, manner of composition, forerunners, and successors – as well as the identity of its author – his occupation, cultural background, colleagues, and students. For so long, these grander and, in many ways, more straightforward questions concerning the *Futūḥ's* creation have been almost completely disregarded. The present research looks to fill these gaps of knowledge by investigating the construction, content, form, and early reception history of al-Balādhurī's *Futūḥ* in medieval Islamic history. First, it attempts to illuminate the background of the author and his access to sources, correcting some of the previous incorrect assumptions about his life and training. It situates the author and his text in the ninth-/third-century milieu in which it was constructed, a transitional period for the ʿAbbāsid state while also the infancy of the early Arabic historical tradition's commitment to writing. It discusses his role at the court of several ʿAbbasid caliphs, including the influence his location had on both the inclusion of material in his text and his overall access to informants. This research has, at its centre, a desire to answer many of the questions of purpose and audience surrounding the *Futūḥ* through an analysis of not only its content and its author, but its legacy in the medieval Muslim world. Overall, it hopes to expand our knowledge of early Arabic historiography and, crucially, our understanding of the value and limitations of the earliest surviving ninth-/third-century Arabic sources and the use of the *Futūḥ's* material altogether.

The purpose of this study is to bring together previous research on *Futūḥ al-buldān*, the available information on al-Balādhurī the author, and these previously unconsidered questions about the text. At its core, it is hoped this research will provide some use to two different and distinct audiences: On one hand, non-Arabists or students who are engaging with al-Balādhurī's text for the first time or only tangentially as a part of their own larger research questions. On the other, it is hoped it will serve specialists of the Arabic historical tradition and early Arabic historiography who may find some benefit in a fuller discussion of a single early Muslim author and the processes, pressures, biases, and ambitions that were likely involved in the creation of a well-known and well-connected text. As the narrative of Islamic origins continues to be questioned and with our access to new sources of information – especially the material culture of much of the Middle East – unlikely to expand significantly in the near future,[5] confronting the challenges of the surviving Arabic sources is more necessary than ever before.

The early Arabic historical tradition and the problematic nature of the 'narrative sources'

There was an eruption of interest among Orientalist scholars in the history and traditions of the Middle East during the nineteenth century that resulted in prodigious work in the field of Arabic historiography. But it was a process, and one which many would argue was long overdue. The techniques of biblical and literary criticism were already hundreds of years old by the time that scholars began to apply similar techniques to the early Islamic historical tradition. The hazards of working with and within Muslim tradition have proven to be many. At times, the early Islamic tradition surrounding topics such as the codification of the Qur'ān, the transmission of *ḥadīth* (the sayings and actions of the Islamic Prophet Muḥammad and his Companions relied on as a major body of Sunnī Islamic law), and the beginning of the historical writing process seemed to be nearly impenetrable. In one camp, what Fred Donner referred to as the 'descriptive approach', many scholars of the early modern period proved unwilling to be overly critical of the sources they possessed, and, crucially, of the processes which bore them; they were all that was available, and western scholarship on Islam from the high medieval period through to the early modern had largely been driven by polemic that needed to shift.[6] To challenge the Muslim sources' problematic nature was to admit we knew very little. On the other hand, and spurred on by the works of those such as Ignaz Goldziher[7] and Joseph Schacht[8] in what Donner called the 'tradition-critical approach', fabrications of material within the early Islamic tradition by later generations became discernable – so what could be trusted? What could be said about texts like those of al-Balādhurī?

The entire process was turned on its head in the late 1970s thanks to the group who have come to be known as the *Banū* Wansbrough, which included John Wansbrough and his students Michael Cook and Patricia Crone. The publication of such works as *Quranic Studies: Sources and Methods of Scriptural Interpretation,*[9] *The Sectarian Milieu: Content and Composition of Islamic Salvation History,*[10] *Hagarism: The Making of the Islamic World,*[11] *Early Muslim Dogma: A Source-Critical Study,*[12] and *Meccan Trade and the Rise of Islam,*[13] did not simply shake up the field of Islamic studies, which had long begun to stagnate up to that point; it completely broke the previous model and forced even devout opponents of these new works, including the outspoken R.B. Serjeant, to eventually re-evaluate the state of the field and their own contributions within it.[14] This group and the subsequent generations they foaled – either directly or indirectly through their innovation and reinterpretation of Islamic history – came to derogatively be referred to as revisionists for applying the techniques of scepticism and source-criticism to the tradition. Yet, a revision of how these sources were being utilized and how the Islamic tradition as a whole should be navigated was exactly what was necessary. Although the reality was that the contributions of the *Banū* Wansbrough and their successors may have been viewed as merely modest in other fields of scholarship, their challenge and methodology proved to be revolutionary in a landscape ripe for intellectual change.[15]

Why was any form of revolution necessary when working with the earliest sources for Islamic history? Islamic tradition and the methods which had codified and canonized the most important historical sources, among them the 'narrative' histories, *ḥadīth*, *sīra* (biography, specifically of the Islamic Prophet Muḥammad), and the Qur'ān itself, had proven remarkably resilient to modern criticism or commentary. More than having a role as marks of faith and theology, much of this body of work also presents the reader with its credentials and expects to be accepted without demur: It purports to tell us where that information on the past came from, on whose authority it was transmitted, and why we should find it acceptable. The author (or compiler) expects the reader to understand and, importantly, accept these rules which the tradition itself has borne. These sources have had an essential role in explaining 'what really happened' during the foundational period of Islamic history, a period which saw not just the rise of the new religion of Islam, but the greater Arab-Islamic conquests, the establishment of the earliest Islamic state, and the communal dynamics which surrounded the later conversion of the majority of the population of the Middle East and North Africa to Muḥammad's message.

A fundamental issue regarding the Arabic sources like those of al-Balādhurī's, with the exception of the Qur'ān itself, is that while their role in the reconstruction of these processes has been essential, their commitment to writing dates from, in the best case, some 150+ years after the events they purport to describe.[16] The problematic late nature of these sources was at times noted by early Orientalist scholars of the nineteenth and early twentieth centuries,[17] but there was never the full inquiry that these problems required. The long-standing impenetrability of Muslim tradition did not properly give way until the publication of Crone and Cook's *Hagarism*, which argued that the late date of these sources and their religious partiality made them inadequate and unacceptable for a reconstruction of the early Islamic period. Instead, they advocated that the Islamic sources largely be discarded in favour of the limited non-Muslim contemporary evidence which survived from the region. While *Hagarism* failed to create a convincing narrative for Islamic origins, its impact in instigating greater analysis of the problematic early Arabic historical material cannot be understated.

Crone went on to famously write of early Islamic history that 'one can take the picture presented or one can leave it, but one cannot *work* with it'.[18] There have been very convincing recent contributions to the field of memory studies within the Islamic world which have demonstrated that the oral transmission of history – within which the early Islamic tradition resided during the bulk of the first two centuries – is far more reliable and interpretable than might have been previously imagined,[19] but the roles that time and circumstance play in the compilation of this material should not be underestimated, either. The building-blocks which make up the Arabic historical and legal traditions, *akhbār* and *ḥadīth*, need to be fully parsed, and the works in which they survived must be fully evaluated in an attempt to understand as much about their creation as possible.

To demonstrate the great problems of the pre-revisionist approach to early Arabic historical sources, one only need look to the scholarship surrounding al-Balādhurī's *Futūḥ al-buldān* itself. Philip Hitti, to whom we owe the long-utilized translation of the first part of the *Futūḥ*, was an extremely talented Arabist who, it can be noted, did not just lack scepticism of the sources he engaged with but was, at times, snide in his appreciation for Islamic historiography. Hitti's lifelong commitment to the study of classical Arabic literature should not go unappreciated, but nor can we simply pass over Orientalist comments like this one, concerning Arabic historians and their style: 'Once the words supposed to have been uttered by a contemporary or eyewitness are ascertained, the author feels his duty fulfilled, and his function as a historian degenerates into that of a reporter … the intellect is not brought to bear on the data.'[20] Throughout his preparation of the *Futūḥ*, he appears uncritical not just of who the author was, but of any of his processes in the creation of the text. The quotation above is indicative of an author writing before the postmodern revolution of Michel Foucault, Hayden White, and others, but as the introduction to arguably the most utilized form of the *Futūḥ*, it must be recognized as outdated. We read here an ignorance of the role the very selection of some material at the expense of others played in creating al-Balādhurī's narrative, which provides the fingerprints of the author's intentions that both Hitti and Francis Murgotten paid no heed to.

While there are some who still believe that the problems of the sources of the early Islamic tradition cannot be surmounted,[21] there are plenty of those in the field with a belief 'that conclusions reached about their usefulness, by the sanguine or the sceptical, have less to do with the evidence than with the approach'.[22] To this question, it is hoped the current research will contribute fully. While our textual evidence for the foundational period of Islamic history is unlikely to be further augmented by the revelation of great new narrative sources of information, this research hopes to provide a critical analysis and re-evaluation of one of the most vital Arabic sources on the early Islamic period by asking the key questions which have hitherto been ignored. In doing so, it is hoped that it will provide the greatly needed context for the *Futūḥ* and its author, al-Balādhurī, and make it a more useful source for any of those who hope to use it as evidence for the early Islamic Middle East.

Ansāb al-ashrāf and *Futūḥ al-buldān*

As for al-Balādhurī specifically, a number of scholarly works are attributed to him in the biographical record, of which only two survive into the modern period: *Ansāb al-ashrāf*, and *Futūḥ al-buldān*.[23] The two books are very different texts in their form and, likely, their function, and both represent a unique synthesis of historical information from the first two centuries of Islamic history. While the *Futūḥ* has benefitted from a longer history of availability to scholars in M. J. de Goeje's edition, the *Ansāb* has far more often been the focus of modern scholarly analysis of the text itself. The *Futūḥ* has more often served as a data-mine for historical titbits and been employed for historical reconstruction.

The *Ansāb al-ashrāf* is a massive genealogical compendium, which begins with a discussion of the lives and careers of the prophets and continues along a largely biographical organization into the reign of the mid-eighth-/second-century ʿAbbāsid caliphs. While it includes headings for certain major historical events during this period, the majority of information on early Islamic history is contained in genealogical entries on individuals and familial groups. Its substantial size and coverage of a period where little Islamic historical material survives in a written form has brought it considerable attention, but its publication in a proper edition was a very long time in the making. It was partially published in the early twentieth century by a team of researchers at the University of Jerusalem including S. D. Goitein and Max Schloessinger; only much later in the century was it published in a complete form, but by an entirely different team. For the *Ansāb*, a complete manuscript is held in the Süleymaniye in Istanbul, with several other partial manuscripts more recently discovered in Morocco.[24] Despite the gradual appearance of these editions, however, the *Ansāb* has benefitted from a great number of modern comparative studies and analyses of smaller sections of it.[25] In reality, more in-depth studies of the literary aspects of the *Ansāb* and its traditions have been conducted than the *Futūḥ* in spite of the latter's long-standing availability, but much more can still be done. Because of the *Ansāb's* immense size and different form compared to the *Futūḥ*, it will only occasionally be referenced in this present research when it can shed more light on al-Balādhurī's general technique as an author or on the *Futūḥ* specifically. An exhaustive study of the complete *Ansāb* is yet to appear because of these issues surrounding its publication, but it is similarly deserving of the great attention that al-Ṭabarī's *History* has received in recent scholarship.[26]

The centre of this present research, *Futūḥ al-buldān*, is a much more condensed text, which is primarily organized geographically into chapters, and then chronologically within those chapters. The vast majority of the *Futūḥ's* attention is occupied with the conquest period, especially the reigns of the first four 'rightly guided' (*rāshidūn*) caliphs following the death of the Prophet Muḥammad, as well as the reign of their successors, the Umayyads. Early Islamic tradition usually credits these first four caliphs with the consolidation of the Muslim community's control over the Arabian Peninsula and the entire Middle East, and the establishment of the institutions that constituted the earliest Islamic state. Al-Balādhurī's *Futūḥ* provides an image of this period which conforms to this idea. While al-Balādhurī was writing from the court of the second Islamic dynasty, the ʿAbbāsids, who had overthrown their predecessors the Umayyads in a civil war known as the ʿAbbāsid Revolution, the very large majority of al-Balādhurī's attention is focused on the rule of the Umayyads and not on the dynasty which employed him. While historical traditions from the ʿAbbāsid period and from al-Balādhurī's own lifetime are found in the *Futūḥ*, they are very limited in comparison to this material on the *rāshidūn* and the Umayyads.

At a glance, the title of the *Futūḥ* – *The Book of the Conquest of Lands* – might suggest a strong focus on historical reports discussing the success of Muslim armies and the defeat of the Byzantine and Sasanian states which had existed in the region. Such an explanation asserts only a part of its story, however. Al-Balādhurī includes an ample quantity of this information, but the narratives of conquest found at the opening of most of his chapters often serve as a context for the types of information the book tends to primarily focus on: the Islamization of the Middle East and the institutions and legal precedent surrounding the earliest Islamic state. In many ways, the title of the *Futūḥ* has served as a bit of a red herring for readers for some time, especially as it appears the book either did not have a formal title given to it by the author or, perhaps more likely, the title was simply *Kitāb al-Buldān* (*The Book of Lands*). Additionally, the author references himself several times in the *Ansāb*, making it seem fairly certain that the *Futūḥ* was completed before his larger genealogical work. Thus, we can speculate that al-Balādhurī is likely to have completed *Futūḥ al-buldān* before turning his attention to the work that would come to be known as *Ansāb al-ashrāf*.[27]

Because of the importance of the information contained within the *Futūḥ* on the conquests and the early Islamic period more generally, modern readers seem to have often passed over what was likely al-Balādhurī's original intention in creating the text. It will be argued here that al-Balādhurī was bringing together previously disparate traditions concerning the administration of the conquered lands that came to constitute the Islamic Empire, from both *muḥaddithūn* and *akhbāriyyūn*. He hoped to serve a version of that state which was undergoing a great deal of challenges during his own lifetime. He was creating, in essence, an 'administrator's handbook',[28] a synthesized text to be read by the secretaries working within the ʿAbbāsid capital. This 'synthesized text' contained material from a variety of sources – both written and oral – and from texts which would later be classified in a variety of different genres, including conquest literature, legal texts, and geographies. Al-Balādhurī's *Futūḥ*, in both its content and its form, shared many common features with texts contemporary and near-contemporary to it, and yet, with almost no direct correspondence.[29] Its synthesized nature also means that we find material from the *Futūḥ* in texts across time periods and across genre classifications. The form al-Balādhurī's text takes was likely born from a unique time and particular need by its audience of secretaries. This is likely a large part of the reason why – although its traditions remained relevant through to the present day – no other authors would imitate the style of the *Futūḥ* in succeeding generations.

Dating the text

The discussion of the unique form of *Futūḥ al-buldān* raises the problematic question of when exactly al-Balādhurī was likely writing his book. It is an important issue, and Chapter 2 will demonstrate that the Islamic world was a very different place at the beginning of al-Balādhurī's lifetime than at his death. To this point, there has never before been an attempt to definitively date the compilation of the *Futūḥ* within the lifetime of the author. It has therefore been accepted as a 'ninth-/third-century text' without much further thought aside from a brief mention by Norman Calder.[30] Yet, the likely date of creation of the text is of vital importance for deciphering precisely why al-Balādhurī created the *Futūḥ*, explaining why the work shares common features with works of *kharāj* and *amwāl*, and yet takes such a different form from others which came both before and after it. The context in which the work was created is vital to understanding both its form and content, and for positing an answer to why it was actually written.

Among the most important pieces of biographical information which survives to describe al-Balādhurī is his placement within the 'Abbāsid Caliph al-Mutawakkil's (r. 847–861 CE/AH 232–247) courtly retinue at some point during his reign. The reign of al-Mutawakkil itself would prove to be a watershed moment in the history of the 'Abbāsid state, as the caliph and the court more generally struggled to maintain its grip over the burgeoning military, which had begun to consume a significant proportion of the state's attention (and influence) between the middle and the end of the ninth/third century. The death of al-Mutawakkil ushered in the so-called 'Anarchy at Sāmarrā" and the power and influence of the 'Abbāsid caliphs was stretched even thinner. And yet, the state and its institutions still needed to be maintained. In these extraordinary circumstances and during what was likely the prime of al-Balādhurī's life, it seems that the author began the process of shaping *Futūḥ al-buldān*.

There are several signposts within the text that help to focus precisely on when the work was completed. Unsurprisingly, al-Mutawakkil is among the most regularly invoked 'Abbāsid caliphs within the *Futūḥ*, reinforcing the idea of a close relationship between the two, which is stated by a number of biographical sources. The caliph appears within a mix of information, with al-Balādhurī providing a number of events that occurred during his reign, important decisions the caliph made in various parts of the realm, and even an instance in which al-Mutawakkil himself was the informant for al-Balādhurī's information – the only 'Abbāsid caliph who appears as such.[31]

With all of this said, however, the *Futūḥ* cannot have been completed during al-Mutawakkil's reign. Within the work is a direct reference to al-Mutawakkil's death in Shawwāl 247 (December 861–January 862), followed immediately by a mention of his successor al-Muntaṣir's ascension and subsequent death within the year.[32] The latest explicit date that appears in the text is the year AH 253 (867 CE), where al-Balādhurī pens the following account:

> When the year 253 came,[33] the Commander of the Believers, al-Muʿtazz bi-llāh, sent Mūsā b. Bughā al-Kabīr, his *mawlā*, against the Ṭalibiyyūn who had appeared in al-Daylam and the regions of Ṭabaristān.[34]

No other caliph after al-Muʿtazz (r. 866–869 CE/AH 252–255) is mentioned in the text, nor is any explicit date provided later than 867 CE/AH 253. Elsewhere, al-Muʿtazz, his Turkic *mawlā*, and the problem of the Ṭālibiyyūn are mentioned again at the end of the *Futūḥ's* section on Qum.[35] While it is impossible to definitively state that al-Balādhurī concluded the text during the reign of al-Muʿtazz, the fact that there are no mentions at all of his short-lived successor al-Muhtadī, or the twenty-three-year reign of al-Muʿtamid which followed, convincingly lends itself to the belief that al-Balādhurī made no major revisions to the work after the 860s. Interestingly, this leaves a considerable length of time between the completion of the work and his speculated date of death ca. 892 CE/AH 279.

The limitations of the *Futūḥ* and this research

While the present research hopes to contribute to the greater study of early Islamic history and of Arabic historiography, there are a number of caveats and limitations that must be stated regarding my methodological approach in this endeavour. First, al-Balādhurī was almost certainly writing from a privileged position at the court of the 'Abbāsid caliphate and, in this way, we see only a limited subset of early Islamic history. Even if we accept the idea that al-Balādhurī made efforts to travel to a number of scholarly centres of the Islamic world in his day to compile the information that was included in the *Futūḥ* and the *Ansāb*, he was still learning primarily from an educated elite within these communities.

To those who already rely on the early Arabic tradition for discussions of this period, however, this will be of no surprise. As Konrad Hirschler and Sarah Bowen Savant have written:

> The sources that serve as the basis for dynastic histories, for example, tend to privilege the outstanding cultural and intellectual works of a narrow band of courtiers, jurists, and orthodox religious authorities. Such works may have served as classical references for their contemporaries' living, collective memory – but what of society beyond elite circles?[36]

Such is the case with regards to al-Balādhurī's writing. While the author may have worked particularly hard to take advantage of a wide variety of sources which informed the creation of his own work, the reader never sees more than a small glimpse of the actualities of Islamic history in those earliest centuries. Directly linked to this issue of al-Balādhurī's privileged position in the creation of the *Futūḥ* is the lack of detailed discussion of the 'on the ground' realities in the rural, resource-producing portions of the Islamic world. This particular issue only continues to grow clearer, as modern research on the surviving papyrological material – primarily from Egypt – continues to demonstrate that taxation in the provinces was never nearly as black and white as the courtly sources would have us believe.[37]

In terms of this research, comparisons between the *Futūḥ* and a variety of early Arabic sources contemporary and near-contemporary to its writing will be regularly invoked, but the focus will remain firmly fixed on the *Futūḥ* itself. Furthermore, the comparative analysis of the *Futūḥ* will consider almost exclusively Arabic texts, and the reason for this is twofold. First, this research will be absorbed with the early Islamic historical tradition which developed in the first three centuries of Islamic history; Persian and Turkish narrative sources dating from as early as the ninth/third century either never existed or are non-extant. While the work of al-Balādhurī has not hitherto had any form of in-depth comparison to Muslim works from the middle or later periods and might prove a fruitful vein for future analysis, it would provide little insight for one of the main efforts of this research: a greater understanding of the use and limitations of the early Islamic historical tradition. Second, the comparison of non-Muslim sources (from the Syriac and Greek traditions especially), while having already proven to be of great value to our understanding of the interconnected nature of the Muslim and non-Muslim traditions, still has many unanswered questions of its own that would similarly take us far beyond the source-critical inspired goals of analysing the *Futūḥ*. These questions are worthy of entire studies on their own, and remain only tangential issues for a discussion of al-Balādhurī and his text.[38]

Additionally, there are several important assumptions this research makes about the *Futūḥ* that deserve further note. First and foremost, it is assumed here that the *Futūḥ al-buldān* had a written form within the lifetime of al-Balādhurī. There are a great number of reasons this seems almost certain to have been the case: For one, and as will be discussed at length in Chapter 2, al-Balādhurī is remembered in the biographical record as having been a secretary (*kātib*), a professional class whose chief responsibility was writing. Added to this is the time that al-Balādhurī was living and working: While the early written Arabic historical tradition was still in an early development stage and the *Futūḥ* is among the earliest Arabic historical sources which survives, at least two generations had passed already since we can be certain Arabic texts were being committed to writing.[39] While the idea of publishing scholarship was still fairly young and not completely accepted within all disciplines of the Islamic sciences yet, al-Balādhurī was not the first to be doing it. Additionally, we have already by the lifetime of Ibn al-Nadīm (d. 987–988 CE/AH 377), mention of al-Balādhurī's oeuvre,[40] and the benefit of a very early manuscript, which will be discussed below. And then, as will be discussed in Chapter 6, there is the definitive reuse of portions of al-Balādhurī's compiled and/or authored accounts, which are found in a wide variety of sources and in the works of a plentiful number of authors, already by the time of Ibn al-Faqīh al-Hamadhānī (*fl.* late 800s CE/AH late 200s) and Qudāma b. Jaʿfar (d. 948 CE/AH 337), and possibly by the time of Ibn Khurradādhbih (*fl.* late 800s CE/AH mid-200s). Al-Balādhurī's traditions seem, by the beginning of the tenth/end of the third century, to have had a remarkable stability as demonstrated by their reuse in these other early texts. Finally, we have mention by the Andalusi scholar Ibn al-Abbār (d. 1260 CE/AH 658) that he used an autographed copy of the author's *Ansāb* as a source for his own work.[41] Thus, in the worst case, it seems likely that the *Futūḥ* could not have been committed to writing on his behalf by anyone even a full generation removed from his death,[42] and it seems very likely that it was completed by the author himself before his death.

Author, editor, compiler: The many professions of an early Muslim writer

Moreover, there is an issue of how al-Balādhurī and other early Islamic writers and their texts should be described and categorized.[43] The early Arabic historical and legal tradition relied almost exclusively on oral/aural transmission of information during the majority of the first two centuries of Islamic history. In recording the details of the past and crucial legal precedent relied upon throughout the medieval period, the Muslim scholars working with this material – both narrative historical accounts (*akhbār*) and the *ḥadīth*, which became the vehicle for legal material – began a process of compilation and codification. This material, transmitted from teacher to student in both formal and informal settings through recitation, repetition, and imitation, was passed down from the seventh/first century through the oral/aural chain until the end of the eighth/second and early ninth/third centuries.[44] Then, the process of selecting, organizing, and committing this information to writing had begun in earnest and, as mentioned, not without criticism. But what do we call the individuals who took up the pen (or employed others to do so on their behalf)? The narrative that they chose to weave into their own unique creations was known and long in circulation in one form or another. And so, while compiling and codifying this pre-existing historical information may make them seem to many as little more than compilers of what came before – al-Ṭabarī said so himself at the outset of his own *History*[45] – this is only a part of their role. In selecting this material, these compilers were breathing life into new creations – their very selection of material on the authority of some transmitters necessitated omitting others. Where and how they chose to organize (and reorganize) and deploy this material was one major act of agency. The amalgamation of older, established traditions into new shapes was the ultimate form of Arabic authorship. It was, as Hirschler has coined, 'authors as actors',[46] and what Stefan Leder has termed 'unavowed authorship'.[47] It is impossible to divorce this process of compilation of a vast historical tradition from the act of authorship – of creation – that was undertaken by those in the classical Islamic period who set about to give this material new form. Thus, while the process of compilation will be discussed at length here, so, too, will these individuals be recognized and described as authors of distinct books.

The deliberate intention of the author: Historical analysis through textual analysis

> In the field of Islamicate history, where scholars have tended to use historical narratives almost exclusively as unstructured, interpretive mines of factual information, the handling of sources has been particularly problematic. The criteria of validity for the facts obtained from historical narratives are largely external;

> rarely are they related to the internal dynamics of the work from which the facts have been taken or to the interaction of the author's mind with the material he has presented, matters that have long been important in European and American historiography. Systematic methods and categories of analysis through which such questions could be approached are virtually nonexistent. The usefulness of facts mined from historical writings is thus reduced and the relevance of the whole source to the history of ideas entirely neglected. Instead of asking what a premodern Muslim author was trying to do as a historian and how he accomplished his goals, the scholar of Islamicate history has usually been content to ask what information the source provides that can be useful in solving *his own* problems.[48]

Targeted studies on individual works in Islamic studies/ history largely went out of style over the last half-century, and contributions such as those on al-Masʿūdī,[49] Khalīfa b. Khayyāṭ,[50] and al-Bayhaqī, where Marilyn Robinson Waldman's statement above comes from, have become rarer. Returning to this narrow focus on individual texts and authors, however, can provide essential insight for modern readers working with these and similar texts, and there has been a recent return to this form that will hopefully prove greatly beneficial for continued work on medieval Islamic history.[51] This is especially the case if we hope to address the integral and linked issues surrounding the intention of an author in the creation of his text and the audience he likely had in mind when he set his pen to parchment. This question of audience and of al-Balādhurī's deliberate intention as an author in the creation of the *Futūḥ* is at the very heart of this particular study, and each of the chapters of this work will be presenting a portion of evidence in an attempt to fully address these issues.

Chapter 1 begins with a brief discussion of the available Arabic scholarly editions of the *Futūḥ*, before providing a definitive manuscript history of the text. It discusses the process involved in the creation of the two primary academic editions and the two manuscripts used in their publication: one manuscript held at the University of Leiden, and another now held in the collection of the British Library. It also discusses an as-yet unpublished manuscript purchased at the beginning of the twentieth century by Yale University, which proves to be the oldest of the world's surviving *Futūḥ* manuscripts.

Chapter 2 serves as a discussion of who the author al-Balādhurī was, based on both the surviving biographical material and an analysis of the text itself. This material suggests that al-Balādhurī was both a secretary (*kātib*) and a boon companion (*nadīm*) working from the court of the ʿAbbāsid caliphs in Baghdad. It highlights that the text was created during a particularly tumultuous period in early Islamic history, a period where the power (both political and financial) of the central ʿAbbāsid government was being seriously eroded away. With administrators in Baghdad tasked with the maintenance of the state's central infrastructure despite the turmoil of the era, I suggest al-Balādhurī created his text as an ʿadministrator's handbook'; full of legal and historical precedent, the author intended it to serve as a reference work for bureaucrats at the court who were attempting to keep the state running amid this upheaval.

Chapter 3 discusses the construction of the text through an analysis of its chains of transmission (*asānīd*, sing. *isnād*) and al-Balādhurī's selection of material. It identifies the background and training of his primary teachers, providing further insight into al-Balādhurī's own education and the resources he had at his disposal. It argues that the author of the text had access to a variety of different sources – both oral and written – and that he consciously chose to differentiate his use of this material based on the particular introductory words he uses at the beginning of each tradition. Furthermore, despite his training as a secretary, the analysis of his teachers demonstrates that a significant proportion of his informants were jurists with no particular secretarial background. It suggests that al-Balādhurī was intending to create a text which bridged the traditional training of the secretaries and the jurists on the issues of common interest to both – the administration of the state based on seventh-century precedent.

Chapter 4 discusses the overall foci/themes of the *Futūḥ* by considering the authorial hand of al-Balādhurī in the compilation of the text. As the text consists of a substantial amount of material transmitted verbatim from a variety of different informants without personal commentary, the primary means of seeing ʿal-Balādhurī the author' within the text is through an evaluation of the material he chooses to include and that which he omits. This is accomplished not simply by evaluating and comparing the traditions, stories, and chapters within the text itself, but also by comparing these accounts with the work of contemporaries in order to identify potential exclusions which did not fit his thematic focus. Furthermore, the text's key themes are discussed, among which are the issues over ownership rights concerning state-held/community land; the importance of seventh-century precedent and conquest settlement agreements in the financial expectations of the ninth-century ʿAbbāsid state over its outlying provinces; the qualities of *adab* in the *Futūḥ* which helped to make this relevant for an audience of administrators, including al-Balādhurī's use of poetry; and the overall role and purpose of the *Futūḥ* as a site of memory (*lieu de mémoire*) for the unified and authoritative Islamic state of the past.

Chapter 5 considers the purpose of the *Futūḥ* against the backdrop of previous scholarship and classification of the text. It challenges many of the preconceptions that have developed surrounding its genre, and discusses the issue of medieval genre theory more generally. It looks at the intersection of the *Futūḥ's* interests with the genres of conquest literature (*futūḥ*), judicial texts on fiscal administration (*kharāj, amwāl*), geographical texts, and secretarial texts (bureaucratic/grammatical works) by comparing the text to similar contemporary (and near-contemporary) works of these types. In particular, it discusses the problems associated with considering the text solely in the genre of 'conquest literature', as has been done by much of modern scholarship. It advises that genres did not yet have firmly established boundaries in the ninth-/third-century Arabic tradition, and it questions the validity of attempts to characterize early Arabic historical works fully within the confines of categories, which were not well defined until a later period. Finally, it identifies that while al-Balādhurī's text shares many common features with texts usually classified within different genres, there are no other texts which provide a one-to-one comparison, suggesting again that the *Futūḥ* was created in a unique time and place and to fill a specific need for its audience.

Chapter 6 focuses on the reception of the *Futūḥ* within the medieval period through a comparison of the quotation and reuse of al-Balādhurī's traditions in later sources. Six texts which include a large amount of reused material from al-Balādhurī's texts are discussed, as are the forms this reuse could take and the techniques involved in emplotting al-Balādhurī's traditions in texts of different styles and genres. This chapter briefly identifies some of the types of material later scholars valued, reused, and/or augmented from al-Balādhurī's work, while confirming that the high esteem al-Balādhurī is held in by modern historians of the Islamic world was also an opinion held by his peers throughout the medieval period.

Notes

1 Erling Ladewig Petersen, *'Alī and Mu'āwiya in Early Arabic Tradition: Studies on the Genesis and Growth of Islamic Historical Writing Until the End of the Ninth Century* (Copenhagen: Munksgaard, 1964), 136.

2 He is also known, according to the various surviving biographical sources, as Abū Ja'far, Abū al-Ḥasan, Abū 'Abd al-Ḥamīd, and Abū Bakr.

3 An exhaustive list of modern secondary studies that have used al-Balādhurī's *Futūḥ* for a reconstruction of the early Islamic period would be exceptionally long. Suffice it to say, however, that the *Futūḥ* is cited as a major source of information in many of the seminal and standard narrative historical works in these fields, including Leone Caetani's *Annali dell'Islām* (Milan: Ulrico Hoepli, 1905–1918), Fred Donner's *The Early Islamic Conquests* (Princeton: Princeton University Press, 1981), M. J. de Goeje's *Mémoire sur la conquête de la Syrie* (Leiden: E.J. Brill, 1864), Marshall Hodgson's *The Venture of Islam* (Chicago: University of Chicago Press, 1974), Walter Kaegi's *Byzantium and the Early Islamic Conquests* (Cambridge: Cambridge University Press, 1992), Hugh Kennedy's *The Prophet and the Age of the Caliphates* (London: Pearson, 1986), Ira M. Lapidus, *A History of Islamic Societies* (Cambridge: Cambridge University Press, 1988), and many more.

4 Philip Khuri Hitti and Francis Clark Murgotten, *The Origins of the Islamic State: Being a Translation from the Arabic Accompanied with Annotations Geographic and Historic Notes of the* Kitāb Futūḥ al-Buldān *of al-Imām Abu-l 'Abbās Aḥmad b. Jābir al-Balādhurī* (New York: Columbia University Press, 1916 and 1924), two volumes.

5 Aside from papyrological material coming from Egypt, it is worth noting that many brief inscriptions have been discovered in the Middle East in recent years that have aided our understanding of the early Islamic period. See as an example Robert G. Hoyland, 'Epigraphy and the Emergence of Arab Identity', in *From al-Andalus to Khurasan: Documents from the Medieval Muslim World*, eds. Petra M. Sijpesteijn, Lennart Sundelin, Sofía Torallas Tovar and Amalia Zomeño (Leiden: Brill, 2007), 219–42.

6 Fred M. Donner, *Narratives of Islamic Origins: The Beginnings of Islamic Historical Writing* (Princeton: The Darwin Press, 1998), 5–13.

7 See especially Ignaz Goldziher's two-volume *Muhammedanische Studien*, translated into English as *Muslim Studies* (Chicago: Aldine, 1967).

8 See, for instance, his *The Origins of Muhammadan Jurisprudence* (Oxford: Clarendon Press, 1950), as well as *An Introduction to Islamic Law* (Oxford: Clarendon Press, 1964).

9 John E. Wansbrough, *Quranic Studies: Sources and Methods of Scriptural Interpretation* (Oxford: Oxford University Press, 1977).

10 John E. Wansbrough, *The Sectarian Milieu: Content and Composition of Islamic Salvation History* (Oxford: Oxford University Press, 1978).

11 Patricia Crone and Michael Cook, *Hagarism: The Making of the Islamic World* (Cambridge: Cambridge University Press, 1977).

12 Michael Cook, *Early Muslim Dogma: A Source-Critical Study* (Cambridge: Cambridge University Press, 1981).

13 Patricia Crone, *Meccan Trade and the Rise of Islam* (Princeton: Princeton University Press, 1987).

14 For Serjeant's scathing reviews of the work of Wansbrough, Crone and Cook, see R. B. Serjeant, 'Review of *Quranic Studies: Sources and Methods of Scriptural Interpretation* and *Hagarism: The Making of the Islamic World*', *Journal of the Royal Asiatic Society*, Vol. 110, No. 1 (1978), 76–8.

15 On the important legacy of these scholars from those within the field, see Carlos A. Segovia, 'John Wansbrough and the Problem of Islamic Origins in Recent Scholarship: A Farewell to the Traditional Account', in *The Coming of the Comforter: When, Where, and to Whom? Studies on the Rise of Islam and Various Other Topics in Memory of John Wansbrough*, eds. Carlos A. Segovia and Basil Lourié (Piscataway: Gorgias Press, 2012), xv–xxiv and Chase F. Robinson, 'Crone and the End of Orientalism', in *Islamic Cultures, Islamic Contexts: Essays in Honor of Professor Patricia Crone*, eds. Behnam Sadeghi, Asad Q. Ahmed, Adam Silverstein and Robert Hoyland (Leiden: Brill, 2015), 597–620.

16 Here, I refer to *Sīrat Rasūl Allāh* (*The Life of the Messenger of God*) by the Prophetic biographer Ibn Isḥāq (d. ca. 767 CE/AH 150), which does not survive on its own, but only in later recensions. The issue of whether a 'text' existed in a written form from the date of these earliest authors or simply as a body of memorized material passed down to students orally before being committed to writing by a later generation and ascribed to an earlier author is discussed in Harold Motzki, 'The Author and His Work in the Islamic Literature of the First Centuries: The Case of 'Abd al-Razzāq's *Muṣannaf*', *Jerusalem Studies in Arabic and Islam*, Vol. 28 (2003), 171–201.

17 Many of the great Arabists of this period penned contributions – large and small – to the discussion of Arabic historiography, but all of them have largely been superseded. See, for instance, Franz Rosenthal, *A History of Muslim Historiography* (Leiden: E. J. Brill, 1952 and revised second edition in 1968).

18 Patricia Crone, *Slaves on Horses: The Evolution of the Islamic Polity* (Cambridge: Cambridge University Press, 1980), 4.

19 See especially the discussion on communal memory and the power of place in Antoine Borrut, *Entre mémoire et pouvoir: L'espace syrien sous les derniers Omeyyades et les premiers Abbassides (v. 72–193/692–809)* (Leiden: Brill, 2011) and Sarah Bowen Savant, *The New Muslims of Post-Conquest Iran: Tradition, Memory, and Conversion* (Cambridge: Cambridge University Press, 2013).

20 Philip Hitti, 'Introduction', in *The Origins of the Islamic State* (New York: Columbia University Press, 1916), Vol. 1, 7.

21 See, for instance, Herbert Berg, 'Competing Paradigms in the Study of Islamic Origins: Qur'an 15: 89-91 and the Value of *Isnāds*', in *Method and Theory in the Study of Islamic Origins* (Leiden: Brill, 2003), 261–2.

22 Nancy Khalek, *Damascus After the Muslim Conquest: Text and Image in Early Islam* (Oxford: Oxford University Press, 2011), 32.

23 The additional books attributed to him by the biographical sources, as well as the confusion over these attributions, are discussed in Chapter 2.

24 Süleymaniye MS ʿAshir Efendi 597–8. On the additional manuscripts from Morocco, see Hugh Kennedy and Ihab el Sakkout, 'Book Review: The *Ansāb al-ashrāf*, Vol. 6B. By Aḥmad b. Yaḥyā b. Jābir al-Balādhurī, edited and annotated by Khalil Athamina,' *Journal of the Royal Asiatic Society of Great Britain & Ireland*, Vol. 5, No. 3 (1995), 410.

25 Many of these works will appear as references throughout this present research, but they include the contributions of Khalil Athamina, Fred Donner, Steven Judd, S. D. Goitein, Isaac Hasson, Michael Lecker, Ilkka Lindstedt, Stefan Leder, and Erling Petersen, that are listed in the bibliography.

26 See, for instance, aside from the impressive 40-volume English translation conducted by the State University of New York Press, the edited volume *Al-Ṭabarī: A Medieval Muslim Historian and His Work*, ed. Hugh Kennedy (Princeton: The Darwin Press, 2008); Boaz Shoshan, *Poetics of Islamic Historiography:* Deconstructing Ṭabarī's *History* (Leiden: Brill, 2004); and Håkan Rydving, *Al-Ṭabarī's* History*: Interpretation and Challenges* (Uppsala: Uppsala University, 2007).

27 This was a claim previously made by Khalil Athamina, as al-Balādhurī makes comments such as 'we have mentioned his information in the *Book of Lands* (*wa-qad dhakarnā khabarahu fī kitāb al-buldān*)'. See Athamina, 'Introduction,' 8.

28 The first person to use this phrase to describe al-Balādhurī's *Futūḥ* was Chase Robinson. His description was apt, even if he spends only very limited time explaining what he means or why he refers to it as such. Chase F. Robinson, 'Islamic Historical Writing, Eighth through the Tenth Centuries', in *The Oxford History of Historical Writing*, Vol. 2, *400-1400*, eds. Sarah Foot and Chase F. Robinson (Oxford: Oxford University Press, 2012), 244–5.

29 Aside from, as will be discussed in Chapter 5, the surviving portion of Qudāma b. Jaʿfar's *Kitāb al-Kharāj*.

30 Calder mentioned in passing that he believed the *Futūḥ* to be from the 'middle decades of the third century'. Norman Calder, *Early Muslim Jurisprudence* (Oxford: Clarendon Press, 1993), 150.

31 Al-Mutawakkil appears as al-Balādhurī's direct informant for information in the *Futūḥ* once, recalling an elder of the tribe of the Banū Ṣāliḥ speaking to al-Muʿtaṣim in the year his father invaded ʿAmmūriyya in Syria. *Futūḥ*, 173 (H 225).

32 *Futūḥ*, 364–5 (H 461).

33 Strangely, al-Munajjid has chosen to render this year in Arabic numerals (٢٥٣) in his edition, clearly breaking from his usual practice of spelling the date out completely as it appears in the manuscripts. This seems likely to have been influenced by de Goeje's decision to also render the numerals, although in his

edition, he does this for all dates. It is a strange decision for al-Munajjid to have made, however, as the surviving manuscripts all have the year spelt out in the traditional form.

34 *Futūḥ*, 398 (M 14).

35 *Futūḥ*, 386 (H 489). Interestingly, the wording here seems to describe al-Muʿtazz's reign in the past tense, as the account reads 'They [the people of Qum] revolted (*naqaḍū*) in the Caliphate of Abī ʿAbd Allāh al-Muʿtazz bi-llāh b. al-Mutawakkil ʿalā Allāh,' but this likely reads too much into the simple Arabic. It seems more likely that al-Balādhurī was just aware that the work may be used in posterity.

36 Konrad Hirschler and Sarah Bowen Savant, 'Introduction – What is in a Period? Arabic Historiography and Periodization', *Der Islam*, Vol. 91, No. 1 (2014), 16.

37 See especially Petra M. Sijpesteijn, *Shaping a Muslim State: The World of a Mid-Eighth-Century Egyptian Official* (Oxford: Oxford University Press, 2013).

38 See, for instance, Robert Hoyland's reconstruction and discussion of Theophilus of Edessa's lost *Chronicle* and its use in the medieval Middle East across traditions, and Lawrence Conrad's discussion of Theophanes Confessor's possible use of Muslim sources for his *Chronographia*. Robert G. Hoyland, *Theophilus of Edessa's Chronicle and the Circulation of Historical Knowledge in Late Antiquity and Early Islam* (Liverpool: Liverpool University Press, 2011); Lawrence I. Conrad, 'Theophanes and the Arabic Historical Tradition: Some Indications of Intercultural Transmission', *Byzantinische Forschungen*, Vol. 15 (1990), 1–43.

39 Here, I refer to the Arabic chronicle, *al-Taʾrīkh*, by Khalīfa b. Khayyāṭ, written at the beginning of the ninth/end of the second century, although there are reasonable cases to be made for even earlier sources that survive in later recensions or with challenging manuscript traditions, such as the surviving portion of Sayf b. ʿUmar's *Kitāb al-Ridda wa-l-Futūḥ*, Ibn Isḥāq's *Sīra*, and the various works attributed to al-Wāqidī.

40 Ibn al-Nadīm, *Kitāb al-Fihrist*, ed. Riḍā Tajaddud (Tehran: Maṭbaʿat Dānishgāh, 1971), 125. Although this by itself would not be demonstration of the fact that al-Balādhurī's books existed in a written form already, as the mention of a book (*kitāb*) may have referred to the collective, accepted, and taught knowledge of a scholar rather than a physical, written book.

41 Ibn al-Abbār writes: 'I read in the writing of Ahmad b. Yahyā b. Jābir al-Balādhurī, in his *Book of the Lineage of Nobles*, from his own writing…' (*Qaraʾtu bi-khaṭṭ Aḥmad b. Yaḥyā b. Jābir al-Balādhurī fī Kitāb Ansāb al-ashrāf min taʾlīf…*). Ibn al-Abbār, *Kitāb al-Ḥulla al-siyarāʾ*, in *Beiträge zur Geschichte der westlichen Araber*, ed. M. J. Müller (Munich, 1866), 173.

42 Here and elsewhere, for consistency's sake, I follow the suggestion of Richard Bulliet that a generation be considered approximately thirty-four years. See Richard W. Bulliet, *Conversion to Islam in the Medieval Period: An Essay in Quantitative History* (Cambridge, MA: Harvard University Press, 1979), esp. 21.

43 The concept of authorship and the varying definitions of an author regarding the earliest classical Islamic texts is something that has had surprisingly limited published research. The many contributions in *Concepts of Authorship in Pre-Modern Arabic Texts*, eds. Lale Behzadi and Jaakko Hämeen-Anttila (Bamberg: University of Bamberg Press, 2015) are going a long way to correcting this across different Arabic genres, but there is still much more work to be conducted.

44 This process is discussed at length by Gregor Schoeler in *The Genesis of Literature in Islam: From the Aural to the Read*, trans. Shawkat M. Toorawa (Edinburgh: Edinburgh University Press, 2009) and *The Oral and the Written in Early Islam*, trans. Uwe Vagelpohl, ed. James E. Montgomery (London: Routledge, 2006).

45 'The reader should know that with respect to all I have mentioned and made it a condition to set down in this book of ours, I rely upon traditions and reports which I have transmitted and which I attribute to their transmitters. I rely only very exceptionally upon what is learned through rational arguments and produced by internal thought processes. … This book of mine may (be found to) contain some information mentioned by us on the authority of certain men of the past, which the reader may disapprove of and the listener may find detestable, because he can find nothing sound and no real meaning in it. In such cases, he should know that it is not our fault that such information comes to him, but the fault of someone who transmitted it to us. We have merely reported it as it was reported to us.' Al-Ṭabarī, *The History of al-Ṭabarī*, Vol. 1, *General Introduction, and From the Creation to the Flood*, trans. Franz Rosenthal (Albany: State University of New York Press, 1989), 170–1.

46 Konrad Hirschler, *Medieval Arabic Historiography: Authors as Actors* (London: Routledge, 2011).

47 Stefan Leder, 'The Literary Use of the *Khabar*: A Basic Form of Historical Writing', in *The Byzantine and Early Islamic Near East*, Vol. 1, *Problems in the Literary Source Material*, eds. Averil Cameron and Lawrence I. Conrad (Princeton: The Darwin Press, 1992), 277–315.

48 Marilyn Robinson Waldman, *Towards a Theory of Historical Narrative: A Case Study in Perso-Islamicate Historiography* (Columbus: Ohio State University Press, 1980), 3–4. The emphasis is Waldman's.

49 Ahmad Shboul, *Al-Mas'ūdī and His World: A Muslim Humanist and His Interest in Non-Muslims* (London: Ithaca Press, 1979).

50 Originally written as a PhD dissertation in 1977, Karl Wurtzel's work on Khalīfa has recently been updated and reissued as Karl Wurtzel, *Khalifa ibn Khayyat's History on the Umayyad Dynasty (660-750)*, ed. Robert G. Hoyland (Liverpool: Liverpool University Press, 2015).

51 See, for instance, Shoshan, *Poetics of Islamic Historiography*; Michael Richard Jackson Bonner, 'An Historiographical Study of Abū Ḥanīfa Aḥmad ibn Dāwūd ibn Wanand al-Dīnawarī's *Kitāb al-Akhbār al-ṭiwāl*' (DPhil diss., University of Oxford, 2013); Andreas Görke, *Das* Kitāb al-Amwāl *des Abū 'Ubaid al-Qāsim b. Sallām: Entstehung und Überlieferung eines frühislamischen Rechtswerkes* (Princeton: The Darwin Press, 2003); and Sebastian Günther, *Quellenuntersuchungen zu den* Maqātil aṭ-Ṭalibiyyin *des Abū 'l-Farağ al-Isfahānī (gest. 356/967)* (Hildesheim: Olms, 1991).

1

The text of *Futūḥ al-buldān*

To begin a discussion of al-Balādhurī and his *Futūḥ al-buldān*, there are some essential comments that should be made on the current critical editions presently available to readers, as well as on the manuscripts used in their creation. *Futūḥ al-buldān* was one of the first texts to have a critical Arabic edition created by E. J. Brill publishers in the middle of the eighteenth century, and it has had many subsequent editions produced in the 150 years since. This chapter will begin by focusing on the two primary scholarly editions of the text, those of M. J. de Goeje and Ṣalāḥ al-Dīn al-Munajjid, before moving on to discuss the history of the manuscripts, which have survived to the present day. As will be shown, for such a familiar work as the *Futūḥ*, the manuscript tradition of the text has remained understudied, with only al-Munajjid publishing any in-depth analysis of this material previously. Furthermore, there is an additional manuscript that was not utilized in the creation of either modern critical edition. It has remained unpublished until now, and provides significant insight in demonstrating the stability of the *Futūḥ* even in the early medieval period while providing important opportunity for future research.

The modern scholarly editions

The original edition of the *Futūḥ* was published by M. J. de Goeje in 1866, and given the title *Liber Expugnationis Regionum*.[1] De Goeje would go on to have one of the most important careers of any Arabist in the modern period, creating the standard edition of a huge number of early Arabic historical works. The creation of his edition of the *Futūḥ* was actually among the first texts he set out to edit, predating his monumental efforts in the editing of al-Ṭabarī's *Ta'rīkh* and his series of early geographies, which he titled the *Bibliotheca Geographorum Arabicorum*, and unsurprisingly, his experience with editing the *Futūḥ* pre-publication played a major role in developing his own understanding of history in his *Mémoire sur la conquête de la Syrie*.[2] For many, de Goeje's edition remains the standard version used by students and researchers of the text, and it remains a competent version that has been fairly accessible in its 150+ years since publication. De Geoje provides a useful index, as well as footnotes, which usually indicate when he is transliterating an Arabic word which originally lacked diacritics or when he is providing alternate renderings for words. The use of Latin in the preface and in the references, however, limits its usefulness to many researchers, and its early date of conception means that not only had there been little modern research on al-Balādhurī which could be integrated in some way into his text, but de Goeje himself also did not yet have the experience (and expertise) of editing the many other historical and geographical texts that he would engage with in the future. Thus, the references are useful, but there are few noted connections between the *Futūḥ* and other early texts that his later works take advantage of, and there is little to no commentary.

More recently, Ṣalāḥ al-Dīn al-Munajjid created an edition in 1956–7, which has several drawbacks, but remains the preferred version of the text that has been relied on for references throughout the present research.[3] Al-Munajjid, himself very experienced in the creation of critical editions for classical Arabic texts from the original manuscripts, benefitted from integrating de Goeje's and others' previous scholarship in the completion of his publication. Among this edition's most positive features is that al-Munajjid was able to reintegrate de Goeje's list of *errata* and those corrections into the core of the text; he has provided a wealth of basic information about the text, its previous publications, and background on the author and his sources in his introductory sections; and he parcelled out individual traditions introduced with phrases such as 'they said' (*qālū*) or introduced with a full chain of transmission (*isnād*). This allows the reader of his version greater clarity in identifying the different pieces and processes which al-Balādhurī brought together in making the *Futūḥ*. Among this version's drawbacks, however, are its complete lack of footnotes (although concordance with other early Arabic texts are occasionally noted in the text in a fairly vague manner) or in-text commentary, and, quite importantly, its lack of availability outside of modern research libraries. With all of this said, however, although al-Munajjid had access to almost another century's worth of scholarship on al-Balādhurī and his *oeuvre* when he set about to plan a new edition, he relied on the same two manuscripts de Goeje used for his edition, and hence passed over what would have been his greatest contribution in this process: the use of a previously unknown and unstudied manuscript of the *Futūḥ* which was discovered between de Goeje's and al-Munajjid's work.

The surviving manuscript tradition of the *Futūḥ*

The remarkable achievements of nineteenth- and early twentieth-century orientalists such as de Goeje who worked from the original manuscripts to create such valued editions of many Arabic texts should not be downplayed. Their selection of texts has had an extraordinarily long-lasting effect on the field of Arabic and Islamic studies, as the availability of these texts in critical editions has heavily predisposed modern scholars working on various aspects of the medieval Islamic world to look first to these texts before – if ever – turning their attentions to the huge amount of unedited and uncatalogued Arabic manuscripts which reside in collections around the world. It has also had a decidedly negative effect, however, on the researchers who have come to rely on these well-known texts – especially the earliest available Arabic sources – seeking opportunities to view the original manuscripts themselves. With regards to the skeleton of the texts themselves, they are often very well edited, but many factors led to the interpretation of these texts by their editors during the editorial process, whether conscious or otherwise. Especially concerning manuscripts of the early Arabic tradition, often the surviving copies will be unpointed or only partially pointed, leaving the editor to rely on his own knowledge and judgement when selecting the word which appears in the edition. Whether that interpretation is correct or not is an entirely different matter, but the readers of the edition will often be blindly led to that interpretation without ever seeing for themselves an unspoken dispute, unless they choose to seek out the manuscript tradition of the text itself.[4] Often, these important early editions of texts such as the *Futūḥ* will include little if any comment on the manuscript tradition involved in the text's transmission or its use in the creation of a printed edition, which further muddies a sea whose depths already leave the reader largely unaware.

Additionally, new manuscripts are sometimes found which can augment our understanding of a text and its transmission, and the methodological approaches to working with manuscripts as documentary sources have evolved a great deal since many of these texts were codified.[5] While these early editors of Arabic texts have done an admirable job in bringing to a larger audience the main content of the text, detailed attention to marginalia and so-called 'reading certificates' (*samāʿāt*) which can provide targeted and extremely valuable insight into who actually owned and/or engaged with a text were often passed over. For the benefit of the reader of the *Futūḥ*, it is worth attempting a definitive discussion of the surviving manuscript tradition.

For such a well-known text as al-Balādhurī's, there has not existed a full discussion of the surviving manuscript tradition of *Futūḥ al-buldān.* Fuat Sezgin's important *Geschichte des arabischen Schrifttums* has often proved to be the most definitive depository of catalogued Arabic manuscripts around the world outside of the handlists of individual manuscript collections,[6] but it proves far less useful on its own for al-Balādhurī's work, as will be noted below. In the Latin introduction of his *Liber Expugnationis Regionum*, de Goeje notes that he used two manuscripts of the *Futūḥ* in the creation of his edition: a manuscript held at the University of Leiden, which he labelled 'A' and serves as his base for the creation of his edition, and a second manuscript held previously in the collection of the British Museum, which he has labelled 'B'. De Goeje discusses the quality of these two manuscripts only momentarily during his preface, and includes a mention of an even earlier opinion on the quality of the Leiden MS by H. A. Hamaker, which he was correcting.[7]

Manuscript A, held in the Oriental collection of the University of Leiden, was used by de Goeje as the basis for his edition. While previously bearing the shelfmark MS Warn 430, today it bears the shelfmark MS Or 430, and it remains in Leiden.[8] That de Goeje used it as his primary manuscript was more due to its availability rather than the greater quality of this manuscript over the other, as de Goeje – living and working from Leiden for the majority of his life – only had access to facsimiles of Manuscript B while he had ready access to A. There is a certain amount of confusion over this manuscript, as al-Munajjid misunderstands the Latin of de Goeje's preface and incorrectly believed that there were two manuscripts held in Leiden that were used in the creation of the Brill edition, separate from the British Museum manuscript that de Goeje actually labelled B. Al-Munajjid also mentions that in the creation of his updated edition of the *Futūḥ*, he had written to the keeper of the Oriental collection in Leiden at the time, Petrus Voorhoeve, 'asking him about these two manuscripts', but Voorhoeve could only send him a facsimile of Manuscript A, noting that there was not a second manuscript held in Leiden at that time.[9] The reality, ofcourse, was that there never was, and because of this, al-Munajjid's otherwise vital introduction to the manuscript history of the *Futūḥ* is incorrect and bears the improper manuscript labelling.[10]

The Leiden manuscript is written in a standard *Mashriqī* bookhand on vellum, with a very consistent size and spacing throughout. It is made up of 274 folios, and is the largest of the surviving manuscripts owing to the size of its script and its large spacing. The majority of diacritics are missing, although some are included for the benefit of the reader when words might otherwise be confused; this is not always the case, however. Individual traditions (*khabar*, pl. *akhbār*) are marked with a cluster of three red dots, which serve as dividers (*fawāṣil*), while breaks within these traditions and within lines of poetry are punctuated with a single red dot. Chapter headings are clearly marked and written in red, and occasionally the introductory phrase *qālū* ("they said") is similarly highlighted. While the text itself is written by a single hand, there are occasional marginal notes throughout: Some of this marginalia is written in the same hand as the main text, and merely denotes an omission from the main text (such as, in one instance, blessings for the Prophet);[11] in another instance – especially in the case of *bilād al-Shām* – a different hand has written separate subheadings in red ink for topics which may have been of interest to the reader (such as 'the conquest of Caesarea', *futūḥ Qayṣariyya*);[12] finally, a third hand in a darker black ink has made fairly rare and much cruder occasional comments, which also appear to serve as signposts for information which may have interested that particular reader.

The Leiden MS is the only surviving manuscript to include any form of illumination. It contains a detailed title page written in black and red ink, adorned with a flowery motif and accented by a gold leaf that is written in the same hand as the rest of the manuscript (Figure 1.1).

It bears a brief colophon at the end of the text, stating that it was written by Aḥmad b. Niʿma al-Maqdisī on 10 Muḥarram AH 613 (29 April 1216 CE).

Here, too, there is further confusion, as both de Goeje and al-Munajjid believed that this date reads 10 Muḥarram AH 623 (11 January 1226), but this is likely due to the extended final *lām* at the end of the final word *al-wakīl*, which mistakenly connects to the end of the word *ʿashar* above it, and can be seen in Figure 1.2. This is further confirmed by the differences in the colouring of the ink between both lines, something which would have been exceedingly difficult for al-Munajjid to have noticed in a mid-twentieth-century facsimile.

Manuscript B, previously held by the British Museum at the time de Goeje created his edition, is now held in the same collection and accessible through the British Library in London. It bears the shelfmark Add 23264, and its details were included by William Cureton and Charles Rieu in their original catalogue of the pre-1871 collection of Arabic manuscripts owned by the Museum and

Figure 1.1 The illuminated title page of Leiden University Library MS Or 430. Photo credit: Author.

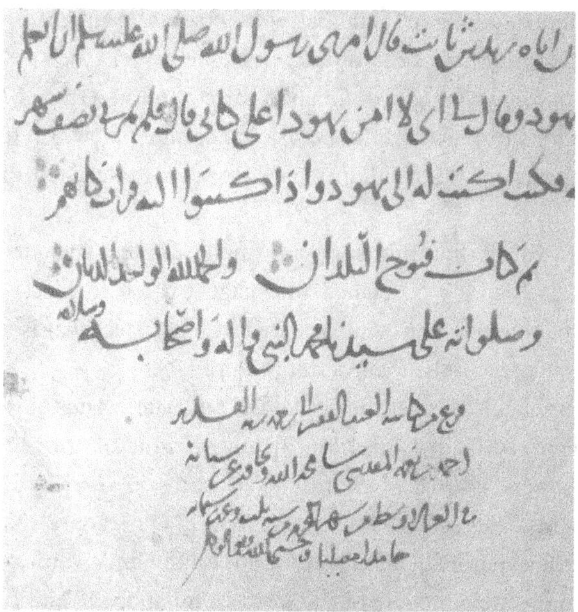

Figure 1.2 Leiden University Library MS Or 430 folio 274A, including a part of the final tradition and the colophon. Photo credit: Author.

its trustees.[13] De Goeje described the British Library manuscript as having been written in minuscule, but it would be better to describe it as rendered in a diminutive *Mashriqī* bookhand. It is made up of 101 folios, and is not completely pointed, although it more regularly includes diacritics than the Leiden MS. Of the two manuscripts (A and B) used by de Goeje, he comments positively on the quality of the British Museum manuscript over the one held in Leiden, and also notes its later provenance. The British Library manuscript is the latest of the surviving *Futūḥ* MSS, and it bears an additional subscription as part of its colophon detailing that it was copied from a slightly earlier codex, dating from the beginning of the year AH 851 (1447 CE) (Figure 1.3).

Uniquely, the colophon of this MS provides an ownership connection to a distinguished late medieval Muslim scholar, Ibrāhīm b. ʿUmar al-Biqāʿī (d. 1480 CE/AH 885), a *ḥadīth* scholar and popular preacher who was a student of the renowned Ibn Ḥajar al-ʿAsqalānī (d. 1449 CE/AH 852). The note reads that the earlier codex this surviving MS was copied from 'was owned by Ibrāhīm b. ʿUmar al-Biqāʿī' (*qāla dhālika Ibrāhīm b. ʿUmar al-Biqāʿī ṣāḥibuhu*). Al-Biqāʿī's interest in early books which concentrate on the conquest period can be seen in his own work, and he quotes from Ibn ʿAbd al-Ḥakam's (d. 871 CE/AH 257) *Kitāb Futūḥ Miṣr wa-akhbāruhā* (*The Book of the Conquest of Egypt and Its Reports*).[14] To take this even further, the section of al-Balādhurī's text in this manuscript concerning 'The Conquest of al-Andalus' is filled with marginalia and additions directly from *Futūḥ Miṣr's* section on the conquest of Spain in a style very unlike the rest of the manuscript – seen here in Figure 1.4 – and this is likely due to al-Biqāʿī's interest and ownership of the earlier codex.

The third manuscript of the *Futūḥ* is, strangely, the only one noted by Sezgin in his *Geschichte,*[15] and is held in the collection of Arabic manuscripts at Yale University's Beinecke Rare Book and Manuscript Library. As remarked by Sezgin, it is catalogued with the shelfmark Landberg MSS 33. As part of the Landberg collection, which contains some 800 manuscripts collected by

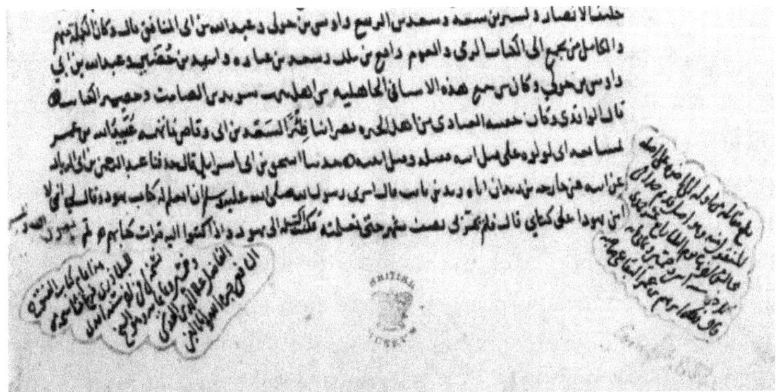

Figure 1.3 British Library MS Add 23264 folio 101B, including the final tradition and the colophon. Photo credit: Author.

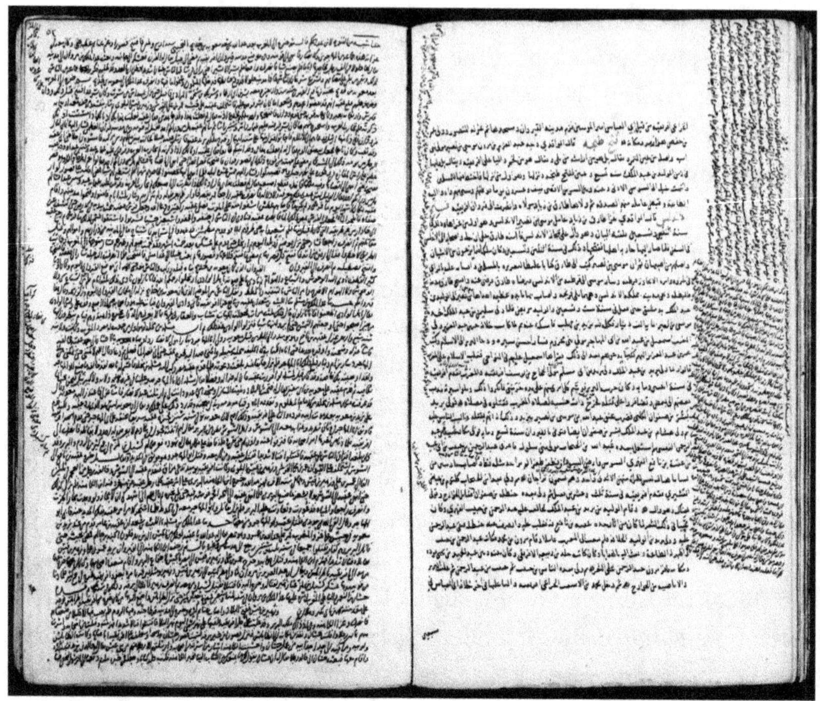

Figure 1.4 British Library MS Add 23264 folios 51A and 52B, showing the change in style in the section on al-Andalus. Photo credit: British Library Board.

the Swedish Orientalist count Carlo Landberg, it was purchased by Morris K. Jessup and bequeathed to Yale in the summer of 1900, where it has since remained. In briefly summarizing some of the major works held in the newly purchased Landberg collection, Charles Torrey noted of this *Futūḥ* manuscript: 'The Landberg collection contains the oldest and best manuscript known of Belādhurī's "Conquest of Lands" … the Arabic text has already been published, it is true; but a new edition is soon to be issued, and for this our manuscript will be indispensable.'[16]

Torrey probably did not imagine that it would take such a long time for anything proper to be written about Yale's important purchase. Not coming to public attention until 1900, the manuscript was part of neither de Goeje's nor al-Munajjid's editorial process in the creation of either critical edition, and because of this, it holds exceptional comparative value for modern researchers who might be using the *Futūḥ* as a critical piece of evidence in their work. The text is undoubtedly early – and certainly earlier than the British Library MS – but unlike the manuscripts of Leiden and the British Library, it bears no formal

Figure 1.5 Yale Landberg MSS 33 folio 1A, the line above the title page bearing the name of al-Farghānī. Photo credit: Beinecke Rare Book and Manuscript Library, Yale University.

colophon. Leon Nemoy's *Arabic Manuscripts in the Yale University Library* postulates a '12th(?) century' date in its brief entry with no further comment,[17] but the evidence of the manuscript itself suggests that it is indeed older than this. Landberg and de Goeje briefly corresponded about the text in January of 1894, and de Goeje speculated on the potential date of the manuscript based on a brief note from the top of the title page that states, 'this portion by the hand of al-Farghānī, (*hādhā al-ḥadd bi-khaṭṭ al-Farghānī…*)',[18] but inexplicably, he has passed over the most important part of this statement: "the author of the appendix of al-Ṭabarī' (*ṣāḥib dhayl al-Ṭabarī*) (Figure 1.5).

This al-Ṭabarī would appear to be none other than the famous jurist Muḥammad b. Jarīr al-Ṭabarī (d. 923 CE/AH 310), the author of the monumental *Ta'rīkh al-rusul wa-l-mulūk* (*The History of the Prophets and Kings*) and arguably the medieval Islamic world's most famous historian. This would make the named al-Farghānī – the author of the non-extant 'appendix', a continuation of al-Ṭabarī's work – his student, Abū Muḥammad 'Abd Allāh b. Aḥmad b. Ja'far (d. 972–973 CE/AH 362).[19] Thus, the Yale MS is likely considerably older than the other two surviving manuscripts of the *Futūḥ*, and probably dates from the mid-tenth/fourth century.

Landberg MSS 33 is written in an early, *Mashriqī naskh* script in a very compressed form that takes up the majority of the surviving page. It is made up of ninety-six folios, many of which are damaged. It is largely unpointed with the exception of verses, but the scribe has included occasional diacritics for clarification of certain words and, in the case of uncommon names or locations, has included vocalization, too (this can be seen in the case of the discussion of the mosque of Qubā in Figure 1.6 below).

While the manuscript is clearly legible, the compact nature of its script gives a considerably less 'polished' look to the text. Additionally, the script maintains a certain amount of angularity, again hinting at its very early date. Poetry is clearly segmented separate from the prose, and chapter headings can at times appear as afterthoughts.

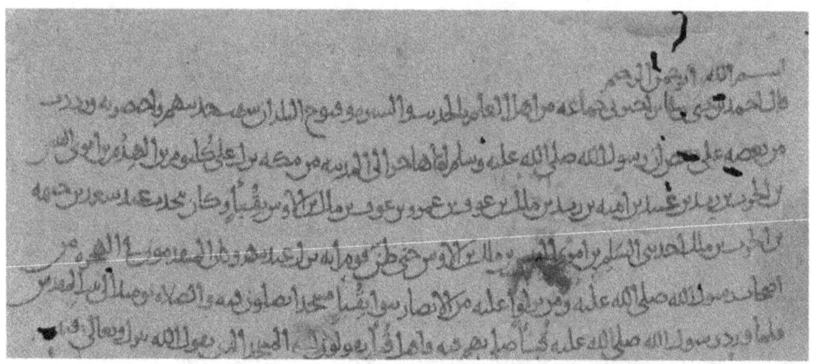

Figure 1.6 Yale Landberg MSS 33 folio 1B, including the opening tradition of the *Futūḥ*. Photo credit: Beinecke Rare Book and Manuscript Library, Yale University.

As exciting as the publication of a new manuscript of such an important text is, there are not any immediately recognizable variants between the Yale MS and those of Leiden and the British Library. Chapters appear in the same order and with the same titles, and the content of the text appears largely the same. This manuscript's great value lies, primarily, in reinforcing the point that al-Balādhurī's text was already remarkably stable within a century of the author's purported death, while allowing further comparison of questionable phrases or passages that may be discovered by researchers using the *Futūḥ*. Should a new edition and/or translation of *Futūḥ al-buldān* appear – and there is certainly opportunity for one to be commissioned considering the deficiencies of the available options – Landberg MSS 33, as Torrey imagined, will undoubtedly have an important role in that process.

Finally, al-Munajjid notes in his discussion of the manuscripts that there is another manuscript titled *Futūḥ al-buldān* that is located in the *Dār al-Kutub al-Miṣriyya* in Cairo, the Egyptian National Library and Archive, belonging to the collection of Taymūr and with the shelfmark 2627. With easy access to this manuscript, al-Munajjid was able to examine it and immediately recognize that this was not al-Balādhurī's text, but he was not aware of what this text was.[20] In fact, this incomplete manuscript held in Cairo is incorrectly titled, and is in reality *al-Iktifāʾ fī maghāzī rasūl Allāh* (*The Sufficiency of the Campaigns of the Messenger of God*) by Sulaymān b. Mūsā al-Kilāʿī al-Ḥimyarī (d. 1236–1237 CE/AH 634). It does not contain any section of al-Balādhurī's text.

Notes

1 Al-Balādhurī, *Kitāb Futūḥ al-buldān*, ed. M. J. de Goeje as *Liber Expugnationis Regionum* (Leiden: E. J. Brill, 1866).

2 de Goeje, *Mémoire sur la conquête de la Syrie.*

3 Al-Balādhurī, *Kitāb Futūḥ al-buldān*, ed. Ṣalāḥ al-Dīn al-Munajjid (Cairo: Maktabat al-Nahḍa al-Miṣriyya, 1956–1957), originally published in three volumes.

4 As just one example, see J. H. Kramers' discussion of de Goeje's (almost certainly incorrect) reading of the Arabic terms *al-Siyāsijiyya/al-Siyāsījīn* in early Arabic texts concerning the Caucuses. I am greatly indebted to Alison Marie Vacca for originally drawing this particular example to my attention. J. H. Kramers, 'The Military Colonization of the Caucasus and Armenia under the Sassanids', *Bulletin of the School of Oriental and African Studies,* Vol. 8 (1936), 613–18, but esp. 615.

5 See, for instance, the many contributions in Andreas Görke and Konrad Hirschler, *Manuscript Notes as Documentary Sources* (Beirut: Ergon Verlag Würzburg, 2011).

6 Fuat Sezgin, *Geschichte des arabischen Schrifttums* (Leiden: E. J. Brill, 1967–2000). It should be noted that Sezgin only includes works written prior to the mid-eleventh/fifth century.

7 de Goeje, 'Prefatio', in *Liber Expugnationis Regionum*, 8. Hamaker had begun a translation of the *Futūḥ* into Latin, which was never completed – his limited translation exists in Leiden under the shelfmark Or 1629.

8 I am very thankful to the University of Leiden and to John Frankhuizen for his assistance in providing me access to this manuscript and for allowing me to photograph it fully.

9 Ṣalāḥ al-Dīn al-Munajjid, 'Our Plan in Publication', in *Futūḥ al-buldān* (Cairo: Maktabat al-Nahḍa al-Miṣriyya, 1956–1957), 26. This is also confirmed (by omission) in the handlist of Leiden's collection that Voorhoeve created. See P. Voorhoeve, *Codices Manuscripti*, Vol. 7, *Handlist of Arabic Manuscripts in the Library of the University of Leiden and Other Collections in the Netherlands* (Leiden: In Bibliotheca Universitatis Lugduni Batavorum, 1957), 87.

10 This confusion over the labelling was also noted by Jan Just Witkam in his remarks 'Manuscripts & Manuscripts' in the very first issue of *Manuscripts of the Middle East* (1986), with the subheading 'The "Lost" Manuscripts of al-Balāḏurī's *Kitāb Futūḥ al-Buldān*.'

11 Leiden University Library, MS Or 430, folio 44A. I am grateful to the special collections librarians in Leiden, along with Leiden University, for permission to use these images.

12 Ibid., folio 82A.

13 William Cureton and Charles Rieu, *Catalogus codicum manuscriptorum orientalium qui in Museo Britannico asservantur: Pars secunda, codices arabicos* (London: Impensis cutatorum Musei Britannici, 1846–1871), 545–6.

14 See, for instance, Ibrāhīm b. ʿUmar al-Biqāʿī, *Naẓm al-durar fī tanāsub al-āyāt wa-l-suwar* (Hyderabad: Dār al-Maʿārif al-ʿUthmāniyya, 1969–84), Vol. 7, 45–6. I am grateful to Roy Michael McCoy for drawing this quotation to my attention, and his own work on al-Biqāʿī can be found in Roy Michael McCoy, '*Scriptura Scripturam Interpretatur:* An Analysis of the Arabic Bible as Used in the *Tafsīrs* of Ibn Barrajān and al-Biqāʿī' (DPhil diss., University of Oxford, 2018).

15 Sezgin, *Geschichte,* Vol. 1, 320.

16 Charles Cutler Torrey, 'Special Collections in American Libraries: The Landberg Collection of Arabic Manuscripts at Yale University', *The Library Journal*, Vol. 28 (February 1903), 53–7, esp. 55.

17 Leon Nemoy, *Arabic Manuscripts in the Yale University Library* (New Haven: Yale University Press, 1956), 135.

18 This correspondence between de Goeje and Landberg is written in both German and French, and is also held in Yale's Beinecke Library with the shelfmark Arab MS 69.

19 Franz Rosenthal, 'al-Fargh̲ānī', *EI*[2] and Rosenthal, *Muslim Historiography*, 83, esp. n1.

20 Al-Munajjid, 'Our Plan in Publication', 25.

2

The author and the context

[The Secretary] should be friendly to the subjects, and refrain from harming them. He should be humble and mild in his office, in handling the tax (kharāj)*, and in calling in outstanding claims.*[1]

The biographical information which survives detailing al-Balādhurī's life is extremely limited, and yet does provide some vital information which can be used to explain who he was and the environment in which both *Futūḥ al-buldān* and *Ansāb al-ashrāf* were created. Within the modern period, there have been a great many assumptions about precisely who he was, and many of the most recently published biographical sketches of the author have latched onto these assumptions with little to no challenge regarding their validity. In addition, there have rarely been attempts to augment knowledge of the author using perhaps the most important resource which could aid that understanding: the texts themselves.

The context of Islamic history in the period during which al-Balādhurī lived and worked is vital for a fuller understanding of the usefulness and limitations of his surviving works, his intent in their creation, and the audience whom he intended to address. These topics will be discussed at greater length in the individual chapters of this work, but all engage with the identity of the author himself. As will be discussed throughout this work, the context in which I suggest al-Balādhurī was completing the *Futūḥ al-buldān* – namely, the so-called 'anarchy at Sāmarrā'' period of the mid-ninth/third century CE/AH – made the construction of his work of vital importance for the administrators within the 'Abbāsid court who were attempting to keep the state and its institutions from collapsing. This was especially the case regarding the astronomical expense which had been committed by ninth-/third-century 'Abbāsid caliphs to an overhaul of the standing army, primarily the integration of a new military system to replace the so-called *abnā' al-dawla* (sons of the state) that had served the Islamic world since the success of the 'Abbāsid Revolution in 750 CE/AH 132. Categorizing the period and the significant expense attached to these military changes was the outbreak of revolts throughout the realm, and the overall deterioration of central authority which coincided. Al-Balādhurī thus set out to create a text that would allow these bureaucrats to keep the state functioning, all the while coping with decreasing revenue streams and the increased autonomy of Muslim governors outside of Iraq.

The Biography of al-Balādhurī

Classical Islamic civilization had a love of biographical and genealogical information, and this is evinced by the considerable amount of biographical dictionaries and traditions which survive from the early period in a number of different forms. Despite this, the explicit biographical details on al-Balādhurī available to the modern scholar are imperfect, and even the most fundamental information on his life and background requires extensive decipherment. Additionally, the challenges to a fuller understanding of his life, influences, and legacy have been exacerbated by insufficient attempts to interrogate this information we 'know' accordingly. Many modern scholars have, perhaps understandably, opted to simply rely on the incomplete information collected by early Arabists such as M. J. de Goeje and Philip Hitti, and their original assumptions of the biographical material, and have therefore – wittingly or unwittingly – perpetuated this false sense of understanding of who al-Balādhurī was. Even Chase Robinson may have fallen into the pitfall of false security regarding the biography of al-Balādhurī, classifying the author at the outset of his 1997 progress report on Islamic historiography as a 'much better known' historian – although in this case, he may have been referring to his texts rather than his background.[2] While his texts are certainly much better known and more relied upon by historians of the eastern Mediterranean than others, the author's life still remains clouded in uncertainty.

The earliest surviving biographical reference on al-Balādhurī is found in *Kitāb al-Fihrist* of Ibn al-Nadīm (d. 987–988 CE/AH 377). His entry here informs us of his full name, Abū Ja'far Aḥmad b. Yaḥyā b. Jābir al-Balādhurī, and describes that he was 'from the people of Baghdad', while calling him 'a poet and reciter' (*wa-kāna shā'iran rāwiya*) before recounting his death in a hospital (*bīmāristān*) as he 'consumed the marking nut (*thamar al-balādhur*)[3] without knowing'.[4] Ingesting the marking nut has been highlighted in modern times as an antioxidant and anti-inflammatory, and is most commonly known for – as its name implies – its use in the creation of dark-coloured dyes.[5] It has been speculated by Becker, Rosenthal, and others that al-Balādhurī consumed the nut to help his aged mind, which appears a reasonable assumption.[6] In the medieval period, there is a plentiful amount of evidence within the Arabic medical tradition to suggest the marking nut was used as a useful agent for this, including in the *Firdaws al-ḥikma* of al-Balādhurī's contemporary, 'Alī b. Rabban al-Ṭabarī (*fl.* mid-ninth/third century).[7] The language of the passage, though, suggests that the author's consumption of the nut was unintentional, and he may have intended to take an agent more in line with his physical disposition.

The problematic nature of the biography of al-Balādhurī is best encapsulated by the issues surrounding his *laqab*, the very title of 'al-Balādhurī' by which he is known best. While Ibn al-Nadīm clearly advances the theory that Aḥmad b. Yaḥyā, the author of the *Futūḥ*, was driven mad by the consumption of the marking nut, other sources express uncertainty. The report of al-Jahshiyārī (d. 942 CE/AH 331) in his *Kitāb al-Wuzarā' wa-l-kuttāb* (*The Book of Viziers and Secretaries*) mentions a man who bears the same *laqab*, al-Balādhurī, named Jābir b. Dāwūd. Ibn al-Nadīm writes that 'his grandfather, Jābir, worked as a secretary for al-Khaṣīb, the governor (*sāḥib*) of Egypt', and most have reasonably assumed that the two Jābirs are one and the same.[8] The problem develops, however, from al-Jahshiyārī's decision to describe his grandfather with the same *laqab*. While an 'earned' *laqab* can often descend through a family for several generations – the famed Persian secretary Ibn al-Muqaffa' is a well-known example of this – it is far stranger to see a name applied to a preceding ancestor. There is no notice by al-Jahshiyārī of a connection between the two men, nor of why Jābir was given such a unique name. In his entry on Aḥmad, Yāqūt (d. 1229 CE/AH 626) obviously struggles with the same conclusion, citing al-Jahshiyārī's mention of Jābir before writing that 'it is not known which of the two consumed the marking nut', although he makes clear that the scribe working in Egypt was Aḥmad's grandfather and not Aḥmad himself.[9] While there is no real evidence to demonstrate it, it seems that there must also be a possibility that *balādhur* was a place – perhaps in Iran – that was little known and eventually forgotten, and the story of the nut was invented at a later time to explain his strange name. If this were the case, it would help to explain why both grandfather and grandson were known by this same *nisba*.

Owing to the nature of many classical Arabic biographical dictionaries and their interest in scholarly circles, the transmission of religio-historical material, and the authentication of that material, this information in the biographical entries provides firmer ground. We can more easily be confident, for instance, of some of the teachers al-Balādhurī heard (*sami'a*) information from directly, and, as will be demonstrated later, this biographical material can be matched through an analysis of the citations within his own surviving writing. We are informed, for instance, that Yaḥyā b. al-Nadīm,[10] Aḥmad b. 'Abd Allāh b. 'Ammār, and Abū Yūsuf Ya'qūb b. Nu'aym Qarqāra al-Arzanī were all students of his, and a number of his primary teachers include Abū 'Ubayd al-Qāsim b. Sallām, Muḥammad b. Sa'd, Alī b. Muḥammad al-Madā'inī, Hūdha b. Khalīfa, and Hishām b. 'Ammār.[11] The biographical information also provides a list of those who learned traditions directly from al-Balādhurī. Aside from this information, however, there is little more that can be said with certainty about the author's life.

On the date of his death, there is more uncertainty. The date often cited for al-Balādhurī's demise is 892 CE/AH 279, but no source actually attests to this exact year. Ibn al-Nadīm, as our earliest source, only makes mention of the means of his death, but is silent on its dating. The earliest biographical comment on al-Balādhurī's death comes from Ibn 'Asākir, who comments only that 'he met his end in the days of [the Caliph] al-Mu'tamid (r. 870–892 CE/AH 256–279), and he spoke deliriously/confusedly (*waswasa*) in the last of his life'.[12] There is no specification of a precise year, and al-Mu'tamid's twenty-two-year reign provides an ample range of time wherein his death may have occurred. The next surviving biographical entry, that of Yāqūt, is surprisingly more specific, writing that 'he died in the days of al-Mu'tamid 'alā Allāh, in the last of it'.[13] It is this entry by Yāqūt that seems to have provided modern scholars with the suggested death date of ca. 892 CE/AH 279, but there must remain some flexibility owing to this entry never naming a particular year. Moreover, Yāqūt's entry relies on the biographical notices of earlier scholars (al-Jahshiyārī, Ibn al-Nadīm, Ibn 'Asākir), which are clearly cited but do not include this information within their own biographical notices, with the only named source of information whose own work only partially survives for comparison being that of Abū Bakr al-Ṣūlī (d. 947 CE/AH 335).

There is almost nothing known of al-Balādhurī's early life. No date or location of birth is provided, although a number of modern assumptions have been made on this period in his life. It has been suggested that he was born between 786 and 796 CE/AH 170 and 180, but this suggestion is unlikely owing to his suggested period of death, which would place him upwards of one hundred years old.[14] It would seem that ideas such as this spawned from the conflation over al-Jahshiyārī's mention of the scribe of al-Khaṣīb during the reign of Hārūn al-Rashīd (r. 786–809 CE/AH 170–193) with the author of the *Futūḥ*.[15] If he did die around Yāqūt's suggested date of 892 CE, however, he would have died at a considerable age, regardless. A comparison of the age range of a number of his most important teachers demonstrates that he would have reached an age of scholarly maturity already by the early 830s CE/mid-210s AH, or else certain teachers he is remembered as having studied under – namely Abū 'Ubayd (d. 838 CE/AH 224) – would have already been deceased. With such limited information providing few definitive events in al-Balādhurī's life, significant caution must be expressed about the author's lifetime. While many scholars have been comfortable to cite 892 CE/AH 279 as the year of his death, it is equally plausible to imagine that al-Balādhurī died much earlier in the reign of al-Mu'tamid, which would also make greater sense of why the *Futūḥ* seems to have been completed and not amended after the late 860s CE.

Aside from the mistaken identification of al-Balādhurī with his grandfather, it seems probable that he spent the bulk – if not the entirety of – his life in central Iraq, with a sustained stay in Baghdad. The biographical material clearly describes him as a Baghdadi, although this alone does not dictate it was his home for the entirety of his life. It has been common to attribute to al-Balādhurī Persian ancestry, owing to his skill in the Persian language as evinced by his translation of Persian poetry and stories into Arabic, but there is little to demonstrate this with any certainty. His grandfather's presence already in the service of the Arab bureaucracy in Egypt during the late eighth-/mid-second century makes it likely that his family was of Arab descent or, if they were Persian, had assimilated into Muslim society outside of Iran prior to his birth. By the end of the Umayyad period, the employment of originally Persian-speaking administrators trained in the Sasanian bureaucratic traditions had already become popular, and a great deal of modern scholarship has discussed this adoption.[16]

Of his profession there can be more certainty. He is described by al-Ṣūlī as being among the boon companions (*nudamā'*, sing. *nadīm*) of the 'Abbāsid Caliph al-Mutawakkil (r. 847–861 CE/AH 232–247).[17] This status as a boon companion of the caliph was certainly prestigious, being a part of the caliph's most inner circle, and would have allowed al-Balādhurī a great amount of influence at the caliph's court for at least a time during his reign.[18] They were expected to be well educated, masters of etiquette, reliable, and trustworthy. They were also expected to be companions in the drinking of wine and entertainers of the highest order, capable of engaging in eloquent conversation, and often possessing skills in music, gamesmanship, and storytelling. The famed Seljuq vizier Niẓām al-Mulk (d. 1092 CE/AH 485), for instance, in his *Siyar al-mulūk* (*Rules for Kings*), recommended:

> A boon companion should be well bred, accomplished, and of cheerful face. He should have pure faith, be able to keep secrets, and wear good clothes. He must possess an ample fund of stories and strange tales both amusing and serious, and be able to tell them well. He must always be a good talker and a pleasant partner; he should know how to play backgammon and chess, and if he can play a harp and other musical instruments, so much the better. … Where pleasure and entertainment are concerned, as in feasting, drinking, hunting, polo and gaming – in all matters like these it is right that the king should consult with his boon-companions, for they are there for this purpose.[19]

Al-Balādhurī's training would seem to make him an apt fit for the role. He was a skilled poet and an able translator of Persian into Arabic, and his storytelling prowess is clearly manifest in *Ansāb al-ashrāf* while more rarely on display in the *Futūḥ*.[20] We cannot, however, say for how long al-Balādhurī was a *nadīm* during the reign of al-Mutawakkil's caliphate. Furthermore, there is no evidence that he remained in this position beyond the reign of al-Mutawakkil, and, quite the contrary, he seems to have fallen out of favour with the majority (if not the entirety) of the caliphs who reigned during the 860s CE.[21] This is, perhaps, foreseeable. Being a *nadīm* was a position that was heavily driven by personality, and the close individual relationship between caliph and his courtier. It would be strange to assume that a successor – particularly one coming during such tumultuous circumstances – would have wanted to keep around his predecessor's favoured people.

Beyond his role as a companion and friend to the caliph, however, al-Balādhurī was very clearly trusted in a formal role at the court. Ibn ʿAsākir states that al-Balādhurī participated in al-Mutawakkil's council,[22] and Yāqūt quotes a lengthy account on the authority of ʿAlī b. Hārūn b. al-Munajjim detailing an appearance of al-Balādhurī at a session of al-Mutawakkil's court. The caliph had commissioned a book by a certain Ibrāhīm b. al-ʿAbbās al-Ṣūlī and, despite the number of people present at the meeting, we are informed that al-Balādhurī was the only one who recognized the flaw in its scholarship and addressed its issues to the caliph in front of all present.[23]

Al-Balādhurī also served a formal role in the bureaucracy as a secretary (*kātib*), although no biographical source provides exact details for which caliph's administration he served in. Ibn al-Nadīm is the first to classify him as such, naming him with a number of others in a list provided by Ibn al-Ḥājib al-Nuʿmān (fl. mid-900s CE/early 300s AH)[24] entitled 'the names of the poets who were secretaries' (*asmāʾ al-shuʿarāʾ al-kuttāb*).[25] Being a *kātib* and a *nadīm* were not posts that needed to be clearly delineated, and Ibn Khaldūn's much later statements on the secretary demonstrate the commonality between the role and that of the caliph's companions:

> The ... [Secretary] must be selected from among the upper classes and be a refined gentleman of great knowledge and with a good deal of stylistic ability. He will have to concern himself with the principal branches of scholarship, because such things may come up in the gatherings and audiences of the ruler. In addition, to be a companion of kings calls for good manners and the possession of good qualities of character. And he must know all the secrets of good style, to be able to write letters and find the words that conform to the meaning intended.[26]

His training as a secretary is further reinforced by the examination of the works ascribed to him. Neither the *Futūḥ* nor the *Ansāb* are works which are purely focused on the office of the secretaries; they speak directly to the craft or skills that the secretarial class so valued, namely Arabic grammar, philology, or the art of writing more generally, only occasionally.[27] The *Futūḥ* largely limits this material to named sections at the end of the text, the so-called 'appendices', on issues such as 'the matter of the seal' and 'the matter of writing', although these sections are significantly truncated when compared with similar works.[28] There is also the matter of the author's attitude towards the construction of knowledge more generally, and the role that an extended presence at the court has on the shape of surviving works like the *Futūḥ*. As Paul Heck has written, 'Writers of history who were also in the employ of the state ... apparently strove to articulate a vision of Islamic history that was not the history of a tribal culture or a religious community [in contrast to authors such as Ibn Saʿd (d. 845 CE/AH 230), one of al-Balādhurī's teachers], but rather, the history of a state conscious of its prestige within the Islamic milieu as well as its place within imperial history universally.'[29] Statecraft, etiquette, and the skills of leadership that the secretarial class were so prized for at the court, however – the traits at the centre of the *adab* tradition – are present throughout both the *Futūḥ* and the *Ansāb*. They are highlighted not just in the actions and speech of the early caliphs, but exist throughout al-Balādhurī's traditions on military commanders and administrative figures like governors and judges, and his focus on the financial concerns of the state. As the Umayyad Secretary ʿAbd al-Ḥamīd (d. ca. 750 CE/AH 132) exhorted in his famous *Risāla ilā al-kuttāb* (*Epistle to the Secretaries*):[30]

> Acquaint yourself also with both Arab and non-Arab political events, and with the tales of (both groups) and the biographies describing them, as that will be helpful to you in your endeavours. Do not neglect to study accounting (*al-ḥisāb*), for it is the mainstay of the land tax register (*al-kharāj*).[31]

It might seem, at first glance, a strange juxtaposition: Be aware of the history and politics of your state, the biographies of your great people and those of others, and also be gifted in mathematics and the skills of accountancy because tax on produce is important. But both the *Futūḥ* and the *Ansāb* are admirable examples of these prescriptions by ʿAbd al-Ḥamīd in practice, although neither deals specifically with mathematics as opposed to the *records* of the land tax register. Both books detail these important events and the people involved across the region and in a variety of forms, not least of which is the biographical format of the *Ansāb*.

Furthermore, the final book Ibn al-Nadīm attributes to al-Balādhurī, the *ʿAhd Ardashīr* (*The Testament of Ardashīr*), was a Persian work of *adab* purportedly dating from the third century CE, which served to educate the elite by emphasizing the well-being of the realm through the roles of (and value in) social stratification.[32] It is recalled, above all, as a work known and regularly transmitted by the secretarial class, owing to its important lessons and value as a tale of good governance. The famous Muslim author al-Jāḥiẓ (d. 868–869 CE/AH 255), in belittling the work of the secretaries, even lists the *ʿAhd Ardashīr* as among the tedium all secretaries must know.[33] Al-Balādhurī, in an apparent twist on this popular text of his profession, is remembered for transmitting a version of the work in verse.[34]

Outside of these details, however, there is little additional information that can be gained from the biographical record alone. Ibn ʿAsākir is the first to provide small insight into the political stance of al-Balādhurī, writing that the author had ʻeulogized al-Maʾmūnʼ (*madaḥa al-Maʾmūn bi-madāʾiḥ*), the past ʿAbbāsid caliph and victor of the fourth Islamic civil war. Some modern scholars have interpreted this statement, which is repeated later by Ibn Kathīr, as meaning that al-Balādhurī had been a member of al-Maʾmūn's (r. 813–833 CE/AH 198–218) court.[35] This interpretation, however, may read too much into the brief Arabic phrase, and it may mean that al-Balādhurī merely composed positive reflections on the past caliph following his death, especially as none of the biographical sources explicitly mention that he served in al-Ma'mūn's entourage or as a part of the bureau during his reign.

Contextualizing the *Futūḥ*: Military transformation and the Turkish military crisis

Throughout much of al-Balādhurī's lifetime, the 'Abbāsid state faced a particularly chaotic period, which would have influenced not just his training and life experiences, but also his interest in writing a work concerned with the history of the Islamic state. This has largely been overlooked, and it is worth closely discussing the events surrounding his life and career which would have undoubtedly had an influence on his processes in the creation of the *Futūḥ*. At the centre of these events was a major civil war and consequent military reform, which came to consume much of the attention of the 'Abbāsid court during the author's lifetime, and which created a need for a work like the *Futūḥ* to be written.

Within the section on Khurāsān in the *Futūḥ*, al-Balādhurī writes of the development of the ninth-/third-century military system under the 'Abbāsids that would eventually force major long-term changes in the financial management of the empire:

> Al-Ma'mūn, the mercy of God be upon him, used to write to his officials in Khurāsān. ... He would send his messengers to enroll those, from among the people of those regions and their princes, who wanted to become members of the *dīwān*, and receive stipends. He won them over through favours. When they came to his court, he honoured them and presented them with their fine gifts and salaries. Then al-Mu'taṣim bi-llāh assumed the office of caliph. He followed the example of his predecessor such that the elite of this military were from the army of the people of Transoxania.[36]

The Central Asian military system first implemented by al-Ma'mūn and expanded substantially by his half-brother and successor, al-Mu'taṣim (r. 833–842 CE/AH 218–227), changed the shape of not just the military hierarchy of the 'Abbāsids, but the very trajectory of the state and its power over the Islamic world over the long term. Al-Ma'mūn's use of Turkish soldiers (*atrāk*) in the 'Abbāsid army proved successful in forcefully disassembling the rule of his brother al-Amīn (d. 813 CE/AH 198) and the old 'Abbāsid military hierarchy of the *abnā' al-dawla* (the 'sons of the state') during the fourth *fitna* (civil war), but it came at a considerable long-standing cost – both financial and otherwise – to the stability of the state.[37]

The fourth *fitna* (811–813 CE/AH 195–198) was yet another issue over succession of the caliphate, and was heralded by the Caliph Hārūn al-Rashīd's decision to divide the Islamic world among two of his sons, al-Amīn and al-Ma'mūn. Al-Amīn was the chosen successor of Hārūn to the title *khalīfa*, while his elder brother born of a slave woman, al-Ma'mūn, was given authority over the province of Khurāsān and the eastern portion of the realm.[38] That a succession crisis might arise following his death seemed to be an issue of which Hārūn was already aware, and his creation of the 'Meccan documents' and his dismissal of the Barmakid viziers, split as they were in their support of his children, seemed to emphasize this.[39]

Once the hostilities among the brothers had broken out into open warfare, al-Amīn found his support – and the elite of his army – in the *abnā'* of Baghdad, the descendants of the revolutionaries who had brought the 'Abbāsids to power originally. The revolutionaries had left Khurāsān and settled in Baghdad and its environs following their victory, and they were a unique amalgamation of the centre and periphery, which mirrored Umayyad Khurāsān.[40] Al-Ma'mūn, on the other hand, was in Marw, and had his military support primarily among non-Arabs – including Central Asian peoples settled in the environs of Khurāsān. As Patricia Crone put forward, it was a situation that could have resulted in a very different direction for the Islamic world had al-Amīn and the *abna'* been successful.[41] A decisive victory for a leader whose power and support lay in the periphery and with a substantial portion of Central Asian peoples, namely the primary commanders of his early armies, presented a turning point for the realm.[42] Al-Ma'mūn's support and personal preference was made clear throughout the conflict: during the *fitna* and through to 819 CE/AH 204, al-Ma'mūn did not even leave his stronghold of support in Marw for Baghdad despite the fact that his brother had been defeated in 813 CE/AH 198.[43]

The *fitna* and the unrest within the centre of the empire – specifically Iraq, and the traditional 'Abbāsid capital of Baghdad – created an intense necessity for consolidation of power by al-Ma'mūn and his successors. The *abnā'* and the Arabs of Iraq had been relied upon since the founding of Baghdad as the military strength of the regime. The *fitna*, however, had completely destroyed this support structure, leaving a vacuum in the military, which was filled by the integration of a Central Asian soldiery.[44] Al-Ma'mūn's decision to return to Baghdad to re-establish rule from there following numerous uprisings and untrustworthy governors only further emphasizes this point,[45] as the recorded *ahl al-Baghdad*, the *abnā'* corps which had been the basis of al-Amīn's power in the civil war, still maintained some power in the region and could not be relied on by al-Ma'mūn.[46] The available Arabic sources demonstrate that al-Ma'mūn exerted great effort in ensuring his support and power structure in Khurāsān before he departed the province for Baghdad,[47] and his time and relationship with the *umarā'* in the region were a driving force in his – and his successors' – acquisition of Central Asian warriors. As the old military hierarchy of the *abnā'* was shattered, its challenger – in the form of these Central Asian soldiers – would form the basis for their replacement. Al-Mu'taṣim would construct a purpose-built city to the north of the 'Abbāsid capital of Baghdad to serve as a new seat of power, and to provide a permanent barracks for the new soldiers – Turkish and otherwise. The site itself would come to be known as Sāmarrā', and its establishment seems to have been intended to quell the hostilities which were developing between the citizens of Baghdad and the outside soldiery.[48] To augment these changes in the makeup of the army as the military overhaul continued, the caliph and his successors also began to recruit a number of regiments from the west. The particular group which rose to prominence from the west in this military restructuring (but after the initial implementation of the Turks) were a group known simply as 'the westerners' (*al-Maghāriba*), who were also brought to Iraq and barracked in the city of Sāmarrā'.[49]

The Turkish guards were originally purchased and brought into service in more isolated numbers, becoming integrated as a significant part of a greater whole during the lifetime of al-Ma'mūn. Under his successor al-Mu'taṣim, their ranks only further ballooned as they became an increasingly more important part of the 'Abbāsid military apparatus, being purchased in far greater numbers and, importantly, in tribal groups. This is an important point that distinguishes the early 'Abbāsid use of this soldiery when compared with the period much later and, in many ways, better known systems of so-called 'slave soldiers' such as the *Mamluks* of Egypt and the development of the *Janissary* corps under the Ottomans. These were not children who were gathered and impressed into service, segregated completely throughout this process, and brought up within a walled garden to serve the state from childhood. Quite the contrary, as Étienne de La Vaissière has aptly demonstrated, these were full-grown warriors raised and groomed in the traditions of Transoxiana and Central Asia who not only were expensive but already had loyalties of their own before that of their employer.[50] Their increasing importance in and around 'Abbāsid courtly life similarly increased in stature as the ninth/third century went on.

They had become the major portion of the ʿAbbāsid standing army, and Iraq was now their home.

The economic crisis of the ninth/third century

That the financial struggles of the ʿAbbāsid state in the mid-ninth/third century were taking a toll on the bureaucrats attempting to run the state (and balance the budget) was first suggested by the late Norman Calder, during his discussion of the author of the important early *Kitāb al-Kharāj* (*The Book of Taxation*), Abū Yūsuf (d. 798 CE/AH 182).[51] Calder suggested that this first surviving work focused on taxation and land ownership belonged not to the late-eighth-century lifetime of Abū Yūsuf, but to the end of the Sāmarrān period, by way of a redaction by Abū Bakr Aḥmad b. ʿUmar al-Khaṣṣāf (d. 874–875 CE/AH 261), an assertion which is not unreasonable.[52] Furthermore, Calder importantly identified the problematic nature of the administration of the period that was later developed by Chase Robinson, Hugh Kennedy, and others, while further suggesting that Abū Yūsuf's surviving text be considered as 'roughly contemporary' to al-Balādhurī's *Futūḥ*, therefore from 'the middle decades of the third-century'.[53]

The political and economic issues aggravating the ʿAbbāsid state in the ninth/third century were deep seated. A great variety of revenue data from available historical sources compiled by David Waines demonstrates diminishing revenues for the empire from the turn of the ninth century. Waines considered a number of pressures which adversely affected the revenue stream of the period, including the political fragmentation of the empire, the internal disorder of the Sāmarrān period, and localized rebellions such as that of the Zanj. He primarily suggests that the falling revenue be linked to a decline in agricultural output, and rightly focuses some of his attention on the agricultural lands of Iraq collectively known as *al-sawād*.[54] These *sawād* lands, primarily consisting of the lands of central Iraq near the ʿAbbāsid capital of Baghdad, were among the most agriculturally productive – and therefore economically viable – lands of the entire Islamic world at the time. Their viability, however, was acutely attached to the regular attention and maintenance of the irrigation systems which fed the land, a reality that had existed since the time of the Sasanian Persian rule over the region. While *al-sawād* required constant investment in order to ensure the lands could provide full benefit, it was the breadbasket – both literally and economically – of the early ʿAbbāsid state.

More recently, Michele Campopiano has placed further emphasis on the role of the *sawād* lands in the economic crisis of the ninth/third century, as well as on the falling productivity of the lands and their decreasing grain production begun by Waines.[55] Campopiano compellingly ties the decreasing revenue stream in these lands to the problems of water management highlighted by a number of archaeologists working in Mesopotamia,[56] but also to the political and commercial interests of landholders given stewardship over these lands by the caliph under the developing system known as *iqṭāʿ*. It was these landholders, he argues, who were given land in *al-sawād* often in lieu of payment owed or as a reward for military service, who were far more interested in the short-term gain the land could provide rather than the long-term maintenance of irrigation systems, which made them consistently productive. Instead of the state providing an agreed-upon payment in coin to a creditor, these land grants (*qaṭāʾiʿ*, sing. *qaṭīʿa*) were awarded with the view that their surplus would pay off the debt. Alternatively, they could serve as a reward for loyalty and obedience to the caliph. They would also mean that a tax collector would not need to be employed to collect that land's revenue via tax farming.[57] For the military specifically, the award of a land grant was a common means for paying a portion of a soldier's stipend throughout both the Umayyad and early ʿAbbāsid periods.[58] By the end of the ninth/third century, three social groups are remembered as being eligible for this type of landed possession via tax farming: the merchant (*tājir*), the 'trustworthy officer (*ʿāmil wafī*)', and the wealthy landlord (*tān ghanī*),[59] all of whom, Campopiano argues, would have viewed the land as 'another source of revenue to integrate into their political, bureaucratic or commercial activities, or a limited resource that they could speculate on'.[60] As such, they were not interested in investing the resources in the infrastructure for irrigation that would have secured the long-term viability of this land.

This erosion of state-held (*fay'*) lands through the system of land grants was clearly an issue which deeply concerned Muslim jurists from the late eighth-ninth/second-third centuries. In order to accommodate the huge costs associated with the Sāmarrān military, viable lands which contributed to the overall state revenue (so-called '*kharāj* lands') likely found their way into direct administrative oversight of these Turks who needed to be paid.[61] The books concerned with land ownership that date from this period, that of Abū Yūsuf, Yaḥyā b. Ādam (d. 818 CE/AH 203), Abū ʿUbayd, and the *Futūḥ* of al-Balādhurī all include a substantial number of traditions regarding the nature of this land, which was intended for the collective benefit of the *umma* as a whole.[62] The issue seems to be of such clear importance that all three of these books, other than that of al-Balādhurī, place the discussion of collectively owned land, their status, and the state's responsibility over them as the first issue to be addressed.[63] *Al-sawād,* along with the Prophet's decision to take the lands of Khaybar and Fadak for himself, served as the primary precedent for the classification and use of *fay'* lands, and in each case, the Caliph 'Umar b. Khaṭṭāb (d. 644 CE/AH 23) himself is said to have chosen to classify the *sawād* land as collectively owned *fay',* rather than meting out its proceeds as the standard spoils of war for soldiers.[64] Making 'Umar the executor of such an important ruling served a clear purpose in protecting this land on behalf of the state, even though the case of the *sawād* itself broke the model; the land which was normally classified as *fay'* was land which was taken forcefully, and yet the *sawād* is always recognized as being appropriated peacefully. This was an important distinction, as it was this land taken peacefully by surrender and treaty that would normally be left in the hand of inhabitants and require the payment of the *kharāj* tax.[65] The traditions' regular inclusion in these collections of *kharāj* and *amwāl* likely demonstrate the need to protect and retain the 'Abbāsid state's stewardship over the *sawād* and its vital revenue. Its classification as such protected the most valuable land of the realm for the use of the state while making it unsellable and this reasoning is made explicit:

> Mu'ādh [b. Jabal] said to ['Umar]: By God, permitting this will lead to something objectionable. If you divide [the land], there will be a great revenue (*al-ray' al-'aẓīm*) in the hands of the people. Then when they die, it may pass on to a single man or woman. Those people who come after them in filling the needs of Islam (*yasuddūna min al-Islām masaddān),* they will not find any benefit. Consider instead a decision that will be equally beneficial for those present and those who will come after them.[66]

Hugh Kennedy was the first to demonstrate that the military reforms were closely tied to the steadily decreasing revenue of the 'Abbāsid state in this period, something which Campopiano does not spend enough time interrogating. Kennedy not only emphasized the extreme burden that implementation of the Turkish military had on the health and stability of the 'Abbāsid state, but dedicated more consideration to the breakup of 'Abbāsid political unity on the decreasing revenues, too.[67] With political fragmentation accelerating along with the subsequent loss of revenues from those provinces, the costs of the ninth-/third-century overhaul of the military left the scholar al-Ṭabarī to famously report that by the year 866–867 CE/AH 252,

> it was mentioned that the payments required by the Turks, the westerners (*al-Maghāriba*), and the Shākiriyya[68] for this year reportedly reached two hundred million *dīnārs*, which was [equal to] the entirety of the land tax (*kharāj*) of the kingdom for two years.[69]

The situation had become deeply troubling. As the new military system was implemented by al-Ma'mūn and further expanded by his successors, the costs of this standing army swelled to be far too high a proportion of the overall income of the state to be sustainable. Meanwhile, the most productive territory of the state which required constant investment for its maintenance – *al-sawād* – received less and less attention, resulting in the eventual breakdown of portions of the vital irrigation system. As portions of the irrigation system broke down, there was a decrease in the available cultivatable land and, therefore, a decrease in the overall revenue of the state from those lands. With the decrease in revenues, it would have been necessary to decrease the state's expenditure in order to 'balance the books' – but this was no longer an option, as the state's major expenditure – the military – was solely reliant on its stipendiary income. In the past, much of the army of the Umayyads and early 'Abbāsids could be viewed as a seasonal army, called into service during the seasonal raiding period or when otherwise necessary, and often returning to other professions when not in the service of the state. The portion of this early army which collected a stipend when in service was smaller, their positions were highly desirable,[70] and the number of commissioned soldiers could be decreased when necessary. This was far more difficult with the new military reforms. In addition, the central government would rely on the levy of troops from the governors of the provinces, which lessened the overall burden of the central state during this early period. The Turkish guard and other new regiments now employed by the 'Abbāsids following the fourth *fitna* consisted of professional troops who had been transplanted far from their native homes to a foreign land. They were completely dependent on their stipends, and their fortunes were therefore intimately tied to the regular revenue of the central 'Abbāsid state. Unable to easily scale back the size of the military and with revenue already decreasing, the military expense remained constant, while there were fewer funds available for the upkeep of the *sawād* lands, more of which were given as land grants or fell into disrepair. So it continued until the reign of al-Mu'tamid, when 'the size of the army was reduced and the budget brought back into balance'.[71] The ever-increasing cost of the military had a far-reaching effect on the ninth-/third-century 'Abbāsid caliphs' decision to provide an increasing amount of the important *sawād* land as land grants. They were granted as a means to alleviate the massive financial outlay already committed to the wages and overall upkeep of the changes to the military.

This economic downturn precipitated the so-called 'anarchy at Sāmarrā'. The Turkish guard, relied upon for the defence of the caliph, and the empire more generally, was not adequately paid and exerted their strength over al-Mutawakkil, killing him and plunging the state into a decade of chaos. The near-decade between al-Mutawakkil's death in 861 CE/AH 247 and the accession of al-Mu'tamid in 870 CE/AH 256 was characterized by political turmoil and a series of major revolts, including the appointment of four caliphs by the Turkish military and the execution of a number of these rulers.[72] Al-Mutawakkil intended to diminish both the authority and influence of the Turks following his ascension,[73] but in so doing, he provoked a portion of the Turkish guard to act against him. His assassination plunged the Islamic world into a period of turmoil where both the central administration's power and influence were significantly diminished.

The fracturing of central authority

> *Al-Mu'taṣim bi-llāh, when he raised up the Turks and humiliated the Arabs, made the Turks the defenders of his state and the banners of his claim* (wa-a'lām da'watihi) *... and while his dignity was made great by them and his behaviour was praised by them, they compelled him to serve them, and made him the fly on their testicle, and agents were appointed* (wa-qullida) *over the great regions of the periphery* ('an al-ḥaḍra)*.*[74]

The lack of stability and collapse of the financial might of the centre only further loosened the grip of Baghdad over both the outlying provinces and portions of Iraq. In particular, the reign of al-Mu'tazz (r. 866–869 CE/AH 252–255) – the final caliph mentioned plainly by al-Balādhurī in the *Futūḥ* – proved to be particularly tumultuous. It was the beginning of a period of increased autonomy for a number of important 'Abbāsid provinces: Egypt under Aḥmad b. Ṭūlūn (d. 884 CE/AH 270) and the Ṭūlūnids, itself a critical revenue stream for the state; much of Persia under Ya'qūb b. al-Layth; and Khurāsān under the Sāmānids. It was also a period of regional upheaval more generally, with challenges to 'Abbāsid authority also developing from Khārijī rebels, 'Alids, and the slave rebellion of the Zanj.

In North Africa, the process of devolution of power from the 'Abbāsids had begun at the beginning of the ninth/late second century with the establishment of the Idrīsids and the Aghlabid emirate during the reign of Hārūn al-Rashīd. Ibrāhīm b. al-Aghlab, the eponymous founder of the Aghlabids, rose to prominence in combatting a number of revolts in North Africa during the reign of Hārūn in an unofficial capacity, gaining power while an ʿAbbāsid-sanctioned governor of the region remained. While there was clearly tension between the ʿAbbāsid centre and Ibrāhīm's popular rise to prominence, this was alleviated with Hārūn's acceptance and confirmation of Ibrāhīm's power, with al-Balādhurī writing: 'al-Rashīd wrote to Ibrāhīm, notifying him that he had forgiven him his offense and excused his fault … and he expected to receive from him righteous conduct (*al-iḥsān*) and good counsel (*al-naṣīḥa*). Ibrāhīm was appointed [over] that frontier (*al-thughūr*), and managed its affairs thoroughly.'[75]

Governors already wielded a significant amount of power throughout the Umayyad and early ʿAbbāsid period, which included a certain amount of autonomy over their assigned regions. These positions, however, had long gone to family members of the caliph – whether by blood or through marriage – and their appointment traditionally stemmed from this close relationship with the central authority. It was a form of reward for loyalty to the caliph, and these positions were often sought after because of the opportunity and power they could provide. It is wrong to imagine that the central government exerted complete control over the affairs and decision-making processes of all of its territories. Some governors of the outlying provinces in the early ʿAbbāsid period benefitted from an amount of autonomy already, in exchange for loyalty and commitment to the mobilization of resources on behalf of the ʿAbbāsid authority. Ibrāhīm's appointment, however, was an example of a break with this previous tradition, forcing the hand of the caliph to provide official recognition to what was already de facto power over Ifrīqiyya. From the time of al-Maʾmūn, the process of relying on family members for provincial governorates had changed completely.[76] The Aghlabids and other successor dynasties, which were established during the ninth/third century, firmly broke tradition by choosing to appoint their own successors, who were normally their relatives, rather than leaving the issue to the caliph's discretion.

Following Ibrāhīm's appointment, this process of devolution only accelerated as ʿAbbāsid central power continued to be worn away. In Egypt, the province saw a number of Coptic and ʿAlid-led revolts that troubled Baghdad, as well as several major tax revolts.[77] They were followed by the arrival of Aḥmad b. Ṭūlūn, of Turkish origin, and his titular dynasty. While he was originally appointed to the post of governor of Egypt on behalf of the ʿAbbāsids, the series of troublesome events that developed in the 860s and 870s led Aḥmad to become increasingly more powerful. This, coupled with the displacement of the caliph's minister of finance (*ṣāḥib/ʿāmil al-kharāj*) who was responsible for the overall collection of tax and its remittance to Baghdad, robbed the already struggling central Islamic state of considerable resources, both liquid capital and in-kind goods. The importance of capable and loyal financial administrators in the provinces during the mid-ninth/third century, especially during the financial crisis of the period, cannot be understated. In *Kitāb al-Faraj baʿd al-shidda* (*Book of Relief After Hardship*), al-Tanūkhī (d. 994 CE/AH 384) provides us with a story of how the former minister of finance of Egypt under al-Mutawakkil, Sulaymān b. Wahb (d. 885 CE/AH 272) – himself a near-contemporary of al-Balādhurī[78] – was saved from the wrath of the caliph by a fellow administrator, Mūsā b. ʿAbd al-Malik, when the latter presented the caliph with a list of the proceeds brought from Egypt over the years, with Sulaymān's tenure in the post placed at the top of the list:

> [Mūsā said]: The minister [of finance] of Egypt (*ʿāmil miṣr*) sent in his [initial] statement (*al-kitāb*) for this year, surplus and expenditures totaled, with a detailed report to follow. ʿUbayd Allāh b. Yaḥyā b. Khāqān[79] read it to al-Mutawakkil, and he tasked my office to calculate Egypt's adjusted expenses (*fa-waqqaʿ ilā dīwānī bi-ikhrāj al-ʿibra li-miṣr*) in order to track the minister's performance. I took the figures from the bureau of land tax (*dīwān al-kharāj*) and from the estates (*al-ḍiyāʿ*), because Egypt currently comes under both bureaus and its accounts (*ḥisābuhā*) go through both, as you well know. In order to earn favour for your release, I placed the year when you were minister of Egypt at the start, with the years of deficit compared to your year after it. I stated my case by saying: 'The deficit in the year so and so, compared to the year so and so at the top, is such and such thousand'.[80]
>
> When ʿUbayd Allāh read the results (*al-ʿamal*) to al-Mutawakkil, the caliph asked: 'In this abundant year, who was appointed minister?'
>
> And so I replied: 'Sulaymān b. Wahb, O Commander of the Believers'.
>
> Al-Mutawakkil said: 'Then why was he not reappointed?'
>
> I replied: 'Where is Sulaymān b. Wahb to be found? Fined to death! The entirety of his wealth taken, and he has been made a pauper!'
>
> The caliph said: 'Remove the fine from him, and give him a hundred thousand dirhams for his expenses and send him to Egypt immediately'.[81]

The rise of the Ṭūlūnids in particular demonstrates both the gravity of the dissolution of ʿAbbāsid authority and the further exacerbation of the financial issues such dissolution caused for the centre. The Ṭūlūnids are remembered for significant financial reform within Egypt during the ninth/third century, first recovering from the financial mismanagement of the minister of finance currently in place when Aḥmad b. Ṭūlūn arrived, Aḥmad b. al-Mudabbir (d. ca. 883 CE/AH 270),[82] and subsequent Ṭūlūnid growth of the revenues within Egypt. The growth of autonomy over an important province such as Egypt, which was estimated to have a revenue of some 4.3 million dinars by the last year of Aḥmad's reign (883–883 CE/AH 270), resulted in a substantial decrease in the funds which actually made their way to the 'Abbāsid treasury.[83] One modern analysis of Ṭūlūnid expenditure, based primarily on information provided by al-Balawī (*fl.* early tenth century CE/late fourth century AH), suggests that only 100,000 dinars per year from the total 4.3 million were making their way to Baghdad as payment to the Caliph al-Mu'tamid.[84] In addition to cash payments, it is shown that in-kind tribute had also been affected, as the caliph's horse-producing estates in Egypt were co-opted to provide service for the Ṭūlūnid army instead.[85] While this payment would increase to a far more significant 500,000 dinars per year under his son and successor Khumārawayh (r. 884–896 CE/AH 270–282), it demonstrates a clear shift from the previous early 'Abbāsid model and, once the crisis of the century had reached its peak and the process of recovery had begun, a return towards normalcy. While there has been modern discussion of precisely how autonomous the Ṭūlūnids truly were from the 'Abbāsid centre, this is only tangentially important here: even if Aḥmad b. Ṭūlūn was careful to 'nurture ties to the caliphate',[86] the decrease in revenue earned signals a clear and important shift.

This fracturing of 'Abbāsid authority was not merely limited to the provinces of North Africa, however. In the east and near the heartlands, the establishment of the Ṣaffārid dynasty in Sijistān and the Sāmānid dynasty in Khurāsān only reiterated the declining power of the caliph, and the declining resources available to the caliph's government in Baghdad. Ya'qūb b. al-Layth's near-successful march towards Baghdad in 876 CE/AH 262 further affirmed the turmoil of the era, but the extended rebellion of east African slaves in southern Iraq and Khūzistān under 'Alī b. Muḥammad al-Zanjī between 869 and 883 CE/AH 255 and 270 proved even more damaging. The Zanj revolt not only forced the caliph to focus his attention (and his army and associated resources) against this central threat but also caused considerable damage to the agricultural area south and southeast of the 'Abbāsid heartland, while also starving the 'Abbāsids of the very slave manpower regularly utilized for the upkeep of the lands there.[87]

Kharāj, *Amwāl*, and *Hikma*: Writing the books that were needed

It is against this backdrop of discontent and uncertainty that al-Balādhurī seems certain to have penned both *Futūḥ al-buldān* and *Ansāb al-ashrāf* based on his surviving biographical record. With so much turmoil and change occurring during his lifetime – especially with him, for at least a time, within the inner circle of the ʿAbbāsid central government in Iraq – it is hard to imagine that his writing was uninfluenced by what was occurring around him. The *Ansāb* is a text which seems in many ways to be an evolution of the Arabic historical and biographical traditions, something S. D. Goitein highlighted long ago,[88] and both the *Ansāb* and the *Futūḥ* do have a major common feature: The form of both texts was something that simply was not popularized. Both texts are examples of works that appear to have been created in a very particular time and place, although their intended impacts were likely as different as the form the two texts take. While the *Ansāb* can be seen as a more natural synthesis of the regional or thematic historical works like those of Abū Mikhnaf and al-Madāʾinī or the genealogical/*ṭabaqāt* style of Ibn al-Kalbī and Ibn Saʿd, the *Futūḥ* seems to be a very different kind of synthesis with a unique intention in its creation.

The ninth/third century is the era wherein the earliest surviving Arabic texts came into a written form. These books, however, were certainly not the first compilations of historical information concerning the formative events of Islam, nor were their authors the first to undertake this process. As the state expanded and society became more developed and complex, so, too, did the challenges for the scholars working as a part of both the state and the scholarly community. For although the mid-ninth/third century was one categorized by central turmoil, it was still a time of great productivity – especially in scholarship. New schools of law and theology, the first written compilation and codification of *ḥadīth* collections, and the commitment to writing of the proud ancestral past, all defined this century. So, too, do we find the creation of the texts of *kharāj* and *amwāl* – namely those of Abū Yūsuf, Yaḥyā b. Ādam, Abū ʿUbayd, and Ibn Zanjawayh (d. between 861 and 866 CE/AH 247 and 251) in a very similar period of time to that of the *Futūḥ*. As we shall see in the following chapters, there is even more commonality between these texts than their interest in matters of taxation and legal ownership of lands and goods at first betrays.

With these texts all being compiled and/or written within decades of each other at the most, and in some cases, within only a few years of one another, we can convincingly speculate that this seeming explosion of interest in these matters during this time period was very likely linked to the ongoing affairs of the state. They were all likely written for different reasons and at different times: some at the request of a patron, others, perhaps, as a service to the profession. Undoubtedly, it seems that there was a requirement that needed to be filled and, in many ways, al-Balādhurī's creation of *Futūḥ al-buldān* was the culmination of a need felt by the administrative class within the central government who were struggling to keep the state financially afloat amid the turmoil. We can imagine that these administrators working on behalf of the state – jurists, secretaries, and other bureaucrats – needed various forms of evidence to convince those outside the court that the state was not just still in control, but was also authoritative in its demands. They needed to convince those in the provinces who were increasingly gaining greater autonomy and legitimacy for themselves that the ʿAbbāsids were still in control and deserving of not just deference, but loyalty – fiscal and otherwise. For al-Balādhurī, a secretary at the court and well trained in the history of the region, the legal precedent which governed Muslim society, and the legacy of states which came before, the answer was to bring this knowledge together in a form which could assist his peers: an administrator's handbook.

Its purpose goes even further beyond this practical function, however. In bringing together these traditions and crafting them into a work which was relevant for administrators, he was also preserving the memory of a unified caliphate; of a time before the upheaval and disintegration. For those administrators who continued in the employ of the ʿAbbāsid central government, the *Futūḥ* also served as a collection of the most successful processes which had served caliphal rule for some two hundred years prior. It could serve a role as a *lieu de mémoire* where there was, as Pierre Nora wrote, 'a turning point where consciousness of a break with the past is bound up with the sense that memory has been torn – but torn in such a way as to pose the problem of the embodiment of memory in certain sites where a sense of historical continuity persists'.[89] In this way, the *Futūḥ* served also as a firm testament of the strong foundations of the Islamic state in a time of historical rupture, and this will be explored further as we continue through the analysis of al-Balādhurī's book.

Notes

1 ʿAbd al-Ḥamīd b. Yaḥyā al-Kātib, '*Risāla ilā al-kuttāb*', in *ʿAbd al-Ḥamīd ibn Yaḥyā al-Kātib wa-mā tabaqqā min rasāʾilihi wa-rasāʾil Sālim Abī al-ʿAlāʾ*, ed. Iḥsān ʿAbbās (Amman: Dār al-Shurūq, 1988), 285.

2 Chase F. Robinson, 'The Study of Islamic Historiography: A Progress Report', *Journal of the Royal Asiatic Society of Great Britain and Ireland*, Vol. 7, No. 2 (1997), 199.

3 *Semecarpus Anacardium*, not the nondescript 'cashew nut' that Bayard Dodge rendered it as in his translation of Ibn al-Nadīm's *Fihrist*.

4 Ibn al-Nadīm, *Fihrist*, 125.

5 Mona Semalty, Ajay Semalty, Ashutosh Badola, Geeta Pant Joshi and M. S. M. Rawat, '*Semecarpus anacardium* Linn: A Review', *Pharmacognosy Reviews*, Vol. 4, No. 7 (2010), 88–94.

6 C. H. Becker and Franz Rosenthal, 'al-Balādhurī', *EI*[2]. It should be noted, in discussing al-Balādhurī's entry in the second edition of the *Encyclopaedia of Islam*, that the majority of the entry remains nearly identical to that originally written by Becker in the first edition. Rosenthal updated its dated language, but made few additions. It is a further reminder of just how much time has passed since al-Balādhurī's biography has been fully scrutinized and evaluated.

7 Gerrit Bos, '*Balādhur* (Marking Nut): A Popular Medieval Drug for Strengthening Memory', *Bulletin of the School of Oriental and African Studies*, Vol. 59, No. 2 (1996), 229–36.

8 Al-Jahshiyārī, *Kitāb al-Wuzarā' wa-l-kuttāb*, eds. Muṣṭafā Saqqā, Ibrāhīm Ibyārī and 'Abd al-Ḥafīẓ Shalabī (Cairo: Muṣṭafā al-Bābī al-Ḥalabī wa-Awlāduhu, 1938), 256.

9 Yāqūt, *Irshād al-arīb ilā ma'rifat al-adīb*, ed. D. S. Margoliouth (London: Luzac, 1923–1931), Vol. 2, 127.

10 This Ibn al-Nadīm has been incorrectly linked to the author of the *Fihrist*, but even Yāqūt himself differentiates between Yaḥyā and the actual author of the work, Muḥammad b. Isḥāq al-Nadīm. M. J. de Goeje was one to suggest that the author of the *Fihrist* was one of al-Balādhurī's students, but Ṣalāḥ al-Dīn al-Munajjid has clearly disproved this. Yāqūt, *Irshād*, 127; Ṣalāḥ al-Dīn al-Munajjid, 'Introduction', in al-Balādhurī, *Futūḥ al-buldān*, ed. al-Munajjid, 14.

11 Ibn 'Asākir, *Ta'rīkh madīnat Dimashq*, eds. 'Umar al-'Amrawī and 'Alī Shirī (Beirut: Dār al-Fikr, 1995-2001), Vol. 6, 74; Yāqūt, *Irshād*, Vol. 2, 127; al-Dhahabī, *Siyar a'lām al-nubalā'*, ed. Shu'ayb Arnā'ūṭ and Ḥusayn Asad (Beirut: Mu'assasat al-Risāla, 1981–1988), Vol. 13, 162. An in-depth discussion of some of his teachers and other informants for the *Futūḥ* can be found in Chapter 3 below.

12 Ibn 'Asākir, *Dimashq*, 109.

13 *Māta fī ayyām al-Mu'tamid 'alā Allāh fī awākhirihā*. While the line doesn't explicitly read that al-Balādhurī died at the end of the reign of al-Mu'tamid, the plural *awākhir* and the attached pronoun *hā* seems to refer back to the *ayyām* (days, reign) of the caliph. Yāqūt, *Irshād*, Vol. 2, 127.

14 Riḍā Riḍāzādih Langarudī, 'al-Balādhurī', in *Historians of the Islamic World: Selected Entries from Encyclopaedia of the World of Islam*, eds. Gholamali Haddad

Adel, Mohammad Jafar Elmi and Hassan Taromi-Rad (London: EWI Press, 2013), 2.

15 See, for instance, Hasan al-Naboodah, 'al-Balādhurī', in *Encyclopedia of the Medieval Chronicle* (Leiden: Brill, 2010), Vol. 1, 139–40.

16 See, for instance, Andrew Marsham, *Rituals of Islamic Monarchy: Accession and Succession in the First Muslim Empire* (Edinburgh: Edinburgh University Press, 2009), 161–7; Ehsan Yarshater, 'The Iranian Renaissance and the Rise of the National Language and Literature', in *History of Humanity*, Vol. 4, *From the Seventh to the Sixteenth Century*, eds. M. A. al-Bakhit, L. Bazin and S. M. Cissoko (London: Routledge/UNESCO, 2000), 724–33 and Maaike van Berkel, 'The Bureacracy', in *Crisis and Continuity at the Abbasid Court: Formal and Informal Politics in the Caliphate of al-Muqtadir (295-320/908-32)*, eds. Maaike van Berkel, Nadia Maria El Cheikh, Hugh Kennedy and Letizia Osti (Leiden: Brill, 2013), 87–109.

17 As quoted in Yāqūt, *Irshād*, Vol. 2, 127.

18 Anwar G. Chejne, 'The Boon-Companion in Early 'Abbāsid Times', *Journal of the American Oriental Society*, Vol. 85, No. 3 (1965), 327–35.

19 Niẓām al-Mulk, *The Book of Government or Rules for Kings*, trans. Hubert Darke (London: Routledge, 1960), 89–90.

20 Each of al-Balādhurī's geographically organized chapters of the *Futūḥ* tends to begin with the conquest accounts of a particular region, and these accounts tend to be the only ones that include the more narrative material of the text over the more explicitly judicial/administrative material. The *Ansāb*, however, while also being a substantially longer text, provides a more fitting forum for the demonstration of al-Balādhurī's skill in historical storytelling. For more on this aspect of the *Ansāb*, see Isaac Hasson, '*Ansāb al-Ašrāf* d'al-Balāḏurī est-il un Livre de Ta'rīḫ ou D'Adab?' in *Israel Oriental Studies 19: Compilation and Creation in* Adab *and* Luġa, eds. Albert Arazi, Joseph Sadan and David J. Wasserstein (Winona Lake: Eisenbrauns, 1999), 479–93 and Stefan Leder, 'Features of the Novel in Early Historiography: The Downfall of Xālid al-Qasrī', *Oriens*, Vol. 32 (1990), 72–96.

21 This is largely inferred from the lack of information on al-Balādhurī's life after the reign of al-Mutawakkil. There are no notices that he continued in any official capacity at the court before his death.

22 *wa-jālasa al-Mutawakkil*. Ibn 'Asākir, *Dimashq*, Vol. 2, 109.

23 Yāqūt, *Irshād*, Vol. 2, 128–9.

24 A secretary from a prestigious family of viziers in the Buyid period. Little is known of Ibn Ḥājib, and the surviving information on his life derives from Ibn al-Nadīm and Yāqūt. According to Ibn al-Nadīm, he was the author of an anthology of courtiers, which included secretaries, men of letters, poets, and viziers. Ibn al-Nadīm notes that Ibn al-Ḥājib's list was the continuation of 'the book of Muḥammad b. Dāwud,' likely his *Kitāb al-Waraqa*. On Ibn Ḥājib, see J. C. Vadet,

'Ibn Ḥāḏjib, ʿAlī b. ʿAbd al-ʿAzīz b. Ibrāhīm b. al- Nuʿmān, called Ibn Ḥādḏjib al-Nuʿmān', *EI*[2].

25 Ibn al-Nadīm, *Fihrist*, 190–1. Additionally, Ibn 'Asākir describes him with the epithet 'the secretary' (*al-kātib*). Ibn 'Asākir, *Dimashq*, 109.

26 Ibn Khaldūn, *al-Muqaddima*, trans. Franz Rosenthal as *The Muqaddimah: An Introduction to History* (Princeton: Princeton University Press, 1958), 202.

27 On the 'administrative' categories and the interests of authors at the court on these issues, see Paul L. Heck, *The Construction of Knowledge in Islamic Civilization: Qudāma b. Ja'far and his* Kitāb al-Kharāj wa-ṣinā'at al-kitāba (Leiden: Brill, 2002), 26–93.

28 Namely, that of Ibn Qutayba and Qudāma b. Ja'far. This will be more fully discussed in Chapter 5.

29 Heck, *Construction of Knowledge*, 7.

30 'Abd al-Ḥamīd's reputation as a secretary of some renown was clearly known during al-Balādhurī's lifetime, and he even appears mentioned in *Futūḥ*, 274 (H 368).

31 'Abd al-Ḥamīd b. Yaḥyā al-Kātib, '*Risāla ilā al-kuttāb*', 283.

32 The *'Ahd* appears to have been translated a number of times in a number of forms through Persian (Pahlavi) into Arabic and, in fact, the version al-Balādhurī is said to have created was translated through verse. The work focused on four separate social stratas: the military, the priestly class, the scholarly class (including the secretaries), and the agrarian/merchant classes. See Louise Marlow, *Hierarchy and Egalitarianism in Islamic Thought* (Cambridge: Cambridge University Press, 1997), 73–4.

33 Al-Jāḥiẓ, 'Portrait of a Secretary', in *The Life and Works of Jāḥiẓ*, trans. Charles Pellat and D. M. Hawke (London: Routledge, 1969), 274.

34 Ibn al-Nadīm, *Fihrist*, 126.

35 Langarudī, 'al-Balādhurī', 3. Ibn Kathīr, *al-Bidāya wa-l-nihāya fi-l-ta'rīkh* (Cairo: Maṭba'at al-Sa'āda, 1932), Vol. 2, 65.

36 *Futūḥ*, 528–9 (M 205). This passage is also translated and discussed in Matthew S. Gordon, *The Breaking of a Thousand Swords: A History of the Turkish Military of Samarra (AH 200-275/815-889 C. E.)* (Albany: State University of New York Press, 2001), 31.

37 On the identity and role of the *abnā' al-dawla* in this process, see John P. Turner, 'The *abnā' al-dawla*: The Definition and Legitimation of Identity in Response to the Fourth *Fitna*', *Journal of the American Oriental Society*, Vol. 124, No. 1 (2004), 1–22; Patricia Crone, 'The 'Abbāsid Abnā' and Sasanid Cavalrymen', *Journal of the Royal Asiatic Society*, Vol. 8 (1998), 1–19.

38 On the issues of succession surrounding the fourth *fitna*, see Marsham, *Rituals of Islamic Monarchy*, 259–68. There are questions over the realities of the succession situation between al-Amīn and al-Ma'mūn, which are detailed in the 'Meccan documents' that arose from the pilgrimage of 802 CE/AH 186. Namely, the primary

issue is over just how much autonomy al-Ma'mūn was given in his position as governor of the East. For more on this, see Tayeb El-Hibri, 'Harūn al-Rashīd and the Mecca Protocol of 802: A Plan for Division or Succession?' *International Journal of Middle East Studies*, Vol. 24, No. 3 (1992), 461–80.

39 Michael Cooperson, 'Al-Amīn, Muhammad', *EI*[3].

40 David Ayalon, 'The Military Reforms of Caliph al-Mu'taṣim', in *Islam and the Abode of War: Military Slaves and Islamic Adversaries* (Aldershot: Ashgate Variorum, 1994), 8.

41 'Had the *abnā'* won, the *dawla* would of course have been vindicated, and the *abnā'* could have prided themselves on having saved it as well as having brought it about in the first place … [it] might have been followed by a straightforward Iraqi domination of Khurasan, but in all likelihood Iraq and Khurasan would soon have parted ways.' Crone, *Slaves on Horses*, 76.

42 At this point, it seems useful to present the differences between this Khurāsānī success and the previous role they played in the very beginning during the 'Abbasid revolution. At least a portion of those Khurāsānīs who rallied under the flag of the 'Abbāsids and Abū Muslim to overthrow the Umayyad dynasty were of Arab or mixed-Arab stock: The members of the Syrian-Umayyad armies who had conquered Khurāsān had settled in Marw and the surrounding region and intermarried with the local population and adopted their customs. Identification as Khurāsānī, chiefly a tie to the culture and traditions that already existed in this portion of Persia prior to the arrival of Muslim armies, was the most important identifier. Al-Ma'mūn and al-Mu'taṣim's armies were quite different, coming from the frontier of Khurāsān and beyond its boundaries and including the Bukharis, Khawarizimis, and, more generally, labeled as 'Turks' (*atrāk*). It is, in fact, difficult to categorize the exact ethnic makeup of this army formed by al-Ma'mūn, which is normally labeled in the sources simply as 'Turks' (*atrāk*) regardless of the fact that a number of the units making up al-Ma'mūn's early army seem to have been mixed. On these points, see Amikam Elad, 'The Armies of al-Ma'mūn in Khurāsān (193-202/809 – 817-18): Recruitment of its Contingents and their Commanders and their Social-Ethnic Composition', *Oriens*, Vol. 38 (2010), 35–76; Amikam Elad, 'Al-Ma'mūn's Military Units and their Commanders up to the End of the Siege of Baghdad (195/810-198/813)', in *'Abbāsid Studies*, Vol. 4, *Occasional Papers of the School of 'Abbāsid Studies,* ed. Monique Bernards (Exeter: Gibb Memorial Trust, 2013), 245–84; Ayalon, 'Military Reforms', 5. On the 'Abbasid revolution more generally, see Saleh Said Agha, *The Revolution Which Toppled the Umayyads: Neither Arab nor 'Abbāsid* (Leiden: Brill, 2003).

43 Crone, *Slaves on Horses,* 75–6.

44 Slaves from the region appear to have been common before they were brought in wholesale as a major portion of the army. See Christopher I. Beckwith, 'Aspects of the Early History of the Central Asian Guard Corps in Islam', in *The Turks in the*

Early Islamic World, ed. C. E. Bosworth (Aldershot: Ashgate Variorum, 2007), esp. 282.

45 Al-Tabari, *The History of al-Tabari*, Vol. 32, *The Reunification of the 'Abbasid Caliphate*, trans. C. E. Bosworth (Albany, NY: State University of New York Press, 1987), 78–83 (3: 1024–9).

46 Ayalon, 'Military Reforms', 22. Gordon, *Swords*, 29.

47 'In each district [of Khurasan] he passed through, al-Ma'mūn remained in order to better its condition and see to the needs of its inhabitants … matters in Khurasan had been quiet, its kings had all sworn loyalty … [al-Ma'mūn] conducted himself commendably and won the support of the kings of the provinces.' Al-Ya'qūbī, *Kitāb al-ta'rīkh*, ed. M. Th. Houtsma as *Ibn-Wādhih qui Dicitur al-Ja'qubi Historiae* (Leiden: E. J. Brill, 1883), Vol. 2, 550.

48 Gordon, *Swords*, 47–60.

49 While the title itself might suggest this refers to Berber regiments from North Africa, modern studies have suggested that the *Maghāriba* were likely 'drawn from three sources: nomadic Arab tribes from Egypt, Berbers from North Africa, and possibly East Africans.' The only clear, early reference to their identity comes from al-Mas'ūdī, who places their origin in the Ḥawf region of Egypt. See Gordon, *Swords*, 37–8; al-Mas'ūdī, *Murūj al-dhahab wa-ma'ādin al-jawhar*, ed. and trans. Charles Barbier de Meynard and Charles Pellat as *Les Prairies D'Or* (Paris: Société Asiatique, 1962–1997), Vol. 7, 118.

50 Étienne de La Vaissière, *Samarcande et Samarra: Élites d'Asie Centrale dans l'Empire Abbaside* (Leuven: Peeters Publishers, 2007), esp. 166–7.

51 Calder, *Early Muslim Jurisprudence*, 144–52.

52 Calder's argument (three of his six prominent justifications) rests primarily with the ideological similarities present in *Kitāb al-kharāj* being those that were far more common in the mid-to-late ninth/third century, which makes Calder's suggestion far from a certainty on its own. Since Calder's death, Gregor Schoeler and others have discussed at length the existence of books prior to their formalized commitment to writing by subsequent generations of students of a scholar. Schoeler has shown that a text could be attributed to an earlier author based on that author's earlier compilation of materials even if it was committed to writing only by a later generation of students. The generational gap between Abū Yūsuf and al-Khaṣṣāf is too great for the latter to have been the former's student, requiring at least an additional generation of scholars between the two. The most problematic aspect of Calder's argument is the opening exhortation of praise to the ruler, during which the author notes that the caliph requested he compose a book on the various taxes and issues of finance. While this has often been assumed to be a reference to the caliph during much of Abū Yūsuf's career, Hārūn al-Rashīd, at no point does the text of the exhortation actually name him, instead opting for the general caliphal

title 'Commander of the Believers' (*Amīr al-Mu'minīn*). See Calder, *Early Muslim Jurisprudence*, 144–7; Schoeler, *The Oral and the Written in Early Islam*, 33–7; Sebastian Günther, 'Due Results in the Theory of Source-Criticism in Medieval Arabic Literature', *al-Abhath*, Vol. 42 (1994), 10–11.

53 Calder, *Early Muslim Jurisprudence*, 150–1.

54 It should be mentioned that Waines had only limited access to the significant corpus of Arabic papyrological data, which has greatly furthered understanding of the Islamic tax system and the administration of the Islamic state. While this material is very much regionally limited – primarily to Egypt – Waines was forced to develop his suggestions on the economic crisis of the ninth/third century from an administrative model almost exclusively formed from narrative sources. With this said, however, his work remains an import contribution to the understanding of the crucial economic events surrounding the 'Abbāsid Caliphate in this period. David Waines, 'The Third Century Internal Crisis of the Abbasids', *Journal of the Economic and Social History of the Orient*, Vol. 20, No. 3 (1977), 282–306.

55 Michele Campopiano, 'State, Land Tax, and Agriculture in Iraq from the Arab Conquest to the Crisis of the Abbasid Caliphate (Seventh-Tenth Centuries)', *Studia Islamica*, Vol. 3 (2012), 5–50.

56 See Robert McCormick Adams, *Heartland of Cities: Surveys of Ancient Settlement and Land Use on the Central Floodplain of the Euphrates* (Chicago: Chicago University Press, 1981); Curtis E. Larsen, 'The Mesopotamian Delta region: A Reconsideration of Lees and Falcon', *Journal of the American Oriental Society*, Vol. 95, No. 1 (1975), 43–57; and Robert McCormick Adams, *Land Behind Baghdad: A History of Settlement on the Diyala Plains* (Chicago: University of Chicago Press, 1965).

57 Campopiano, 'State, Land Tax, and Agriculture', 39.

58 This process differed between the two periods, and depended on the location of the land that was given. Lands along the frontier or in certain urban locations were often given to soldiers as payment during the Umayyad period, often to promote the settlement of Muslims in these areas. These soldiers became owners of these lands in perpetuity, and the lands were heritable. This changed in the early 'Abbāsid period, as lands which Hugh Kennedy calls 'agricultural *qaṭā'i'*' could be granted to the elites of 'Abbāsid society as a form of payment, but the lands were not intended to be permanently owned and could not be sold or inherited. Hugh Kennedy, *The Armies of the Caliphs: Military and Society in the Early Islamic State* (London: Routledge, 2001), 81–5.

59 Aḥmad b. Muḥammad al-Ṭā'ī, *The Historical Remains of Hilâl al-Sâbi: First Part of His* Kitab al-Wuzara, ed. H. F. Amedroz (Leiden: E. J. Brill, 1904), 71, based on the account of Abū al-Ḥasan b. al-Furāt (d. 924 CE/AH 312); Campopiano, 'State, Land Tax, and Agriculture', 40.

60 Campopiano, 'State, Land Tax, and Agriculture', 42. The 'limited resource they could speculate on' is specifically referring to the merchants and their interest in grain during this period.

61 Gordon, *Swords*, 118–29.

62 This should not be confused, however, with suggesting these jurists believed any Muslim had a right to take a portion of the proceeds from these lands for himself whenever he wished. Rather, the money would be used by the state for the benefit of the entirety of the Muslim community as it was, along with *khums* and *ṣadaqa*, 'the wealth (*al-amwāl*) which is administered on behalf of the people (*li-l-ra'iyya*).' Abū 'Ubayd al-Qāsim b. Sallām, *Kitāb al-amwāl*, ed. Muḥammad Ḥāmid Fiqī (Cairo: Maktabat al-Tijāriyya al-Kubrā, 1934), 26.

63 In the case of Abū Yūsuf and Abū 'Ubayd, it is the first section immediately following their introduction discussing (and extolling) the ruler. In the case of the *Futūḥ* not beginning with this matter, al-Balādhurī's text is the only one of these not organized thematically, and so this is foreseeable.

64 Abū Yūsuf, *Kitāb al-Kharāj* (Būlāq: al-Maṭba'a al-Mīriyya, 1884), 20; Yaḥyā b. Ādam, *Kitāb al-Kharāj*, ed. Th. W. Juynboll (Leiden: Brill, 1896), 27–9. In the account of Yaḥyā b. Ādam and Abū 'Ubayd, both citing the same authority, it was 'Alī b. Abī Ṭālib – not yet caliph himself – who is said to have changed 'Umar's mind and advised him that it should be 'a common source for all Muslims.'

65 For more on this, see Albrecht Noth, 'On the Relationship in the Caliphate Between Central Power and the Provinces: The '*Sulh*' - "*Anwa*' Traditions for Egypt and Iraq', in *The Expansion of the Islamic State*, ed. Fred M. Donner (Aldershot: Ashgate, 2008), 178–88.

66 Literally, 'for the first of them and for the last of them'. Abū 'Ubayd, *al-Amwāl*, 59.

67 Hugh Kennedy, 'The Decline and Fall of the First Muslim Empire', *Der Islam*, Vol. 81, No. 1 (2004), 1–29.

68 This group, about which little is known aside from their 'distinct military character,' is discussed in Amikam Elad, 'The Armies of al-Ma'mūn in Khurāsān', 45–9. That the term may have developed from the Central Asian *chākars* is discussed in Peter B. Golden, 'Khazar Turkic Ghulāms in Caliphal Service', *Journal Asiatique*, Vol. 292 (2004), 279–309 and expanded on by de La Vaissière.

69 Al-Ṭabarī, *The History of al-Ṭabarī*, Vol. 35, *The Crisis of the 'Abbāsid Caliphate*, trans. George Saliba (Albany: State University of New York Press, 1985), 143 (3: 1685).

70 The early Arabic tradition would have us believe that this was not the process from the outset, however. The Caliph 'Umar b. al-Khaṭṭāb is said to have established the *'aṭā'* system of pensions for those who served, or had family members who served, in the armies of Islam in the early period. By the beginning of the eighth century, however, this is said to have changed to be the salary of

a current soldier rather than an award for service in perpetuity. See Kennedy, *Armies of the Caliphs*, 59, 76–8.

71 Kennedy, 'Decline and Fall', 15–16.

72 On the death of al-Mutawakkil, this period of turmoil, and the issues of succession surrounding the caliphate, see Marsham, *Rituals of Islamic Monarchy*, esp. 280–93.

73 See, for instance, the evidence that suggests al-Mutawakkil may have considered moving the 'Abbāsid capital away from Sāmarrā' and to the old Umayyad capital of Damascus. Paul M. Cobb, 'Al-Mutawakkil's Damascus: A New 'Abbāsid Capital?' *Journal of Near Eastern Studies*, Vol. 58, No. 4 (1999), 241–57.

74 Al-Balawī, *Sīrat Aḥmad b. Ṭūlūn*, ed. Muḥammad Kurd 'Alī (Damascus: al-Maktabat al-'Arabiyya fī Dimashq, 1939), 32–3.

75 *Futūḥ*, 276 (H 370).

76 Kennedy, 'Decline and Fall', 8.

77 For more details on these, see Kosei Morimoto, *The Fiscal Administration of Egypt in the Early Islamic Period* (Kyoto: Dohasha, 1981), 145–72 and Yaacov Lev, 'Coptic Rebellions and the Islamization of Medieval Egypt (8th-10th century): Medieval and Modern Perceptions', *Jerusalem Studies in Arabic and Islam*, Vol. 39 (2012), 303–44.

78 While both he and al-Balādhurī are remembered as serving in posts during al-Mutawakkil's reign, al-Balādhurī contended with his son, Wahb b. Sulaymān. So much so, in fact, that amid the limited biographical material Ibn al-Nadīm transmits about al-Balādhurī, he has preserved a portion of a fart joke al-Balādhurī wittily launched at Wahb, as al-Balādhurī is noted as a regular writer of satire. Ibn al-Nadīm, *Fihrist*, 126.

79 Himself explicitly noted as present when al-Balādhurī is reported to have made the fart joke mentioned in n. 78 above.

80 The lack of specificity is a reminder that this is an anecdote in which the actual years and associated numbers did not matter; what mattered was that Sulaymān was better than the majority of his peers, and that Mūsā's ruse was effective in demonstrating this. Important to note, too, is that Mūsā did not need to concoct these deficiencies from Egypt as part of his ruse, but merely bring attention to them in comparison with Sulaymān's tenure.

81 Al-Tanūkhī, *Kitāb al-Faraj ba'd al-shidda*, ed. 'Abbūd al-Shāljī (Beirut: Dār Ṣādir, 1978), Vol. 1, 215. I am grateful to Julia Bray for her insight in bringing both this text and passage to my attention.

82 Ibn al-Mudabbir, who had been appointed during the reign of al-Mutawakkil, was not able to be easily removed by Aḥmad b. Ṭūlūn. The two battled for influence over each other, and Aḥmad b. Ṭūlūn eventually emerged triumphant.

83 This information comes on the authority of Ibn al-Dayya, in Ibn Sa'īd al-Andalusī, *Al-Mughrib fī ḥulā al-Maghrib*, ed. Shawqī Ḍayf (Cairo: Dār al-Ma'ārif, 1953–1955), Vol. 2, 132.

84 Ernest William Randa, 'The Tulunid Dynasty in Egypt: Loyalty and State Formation During the Dissolution of the 'Abbasid Caliphate' (PhD diss., University of Utah, 1990), 253–66.

85 Ibid., 243. It should be noted that these lands were not completely confiscated from the caliph – merely the product of the estates.

86 Matthew S. Gordon, 'Aḥmad b. Ṭūlūn', *EI*[3].

87 On the revolt of the Zanj, see Alexandre Popovic, *The Revolt of African Slaves in Iraq in the 3rd/9th Century*, trans. Leon King (Princeton: Markus Wiener Publishers, 1999).

88 S. D. Goitein, 'The Place of Balādhurī's *Ansāb al-ashrāf* in Arabic Historiography', in *Atti del XIX Congresso Internazionale degli Orientalisti* (Rome: Tipografia del Senato del Doit G. Bardi, 1938), 603–4.

89 Pierre Nora, 'Between Memory and History: *Les Lieux de Mémoire*', *Representations Special Issue: Memory and Counter-Memory*, Vol. 26 (1989), 7–24.

3

The sources of *Futūḥ al-buldān*

In 1984, Khalil Athamina published an article for *Jerusalem Studies in Arabic and Islam* that discussed the sources of information used by al-Balādhurī in his genealogical history, *Ansāb al-ashrāf*.[1] Athamina had begun working on a critical edition of a portion of the *Ansāb* from the complete manuscript held in Istanbul, and so was an ideal commentator for the topic.[2] He briefly considered the historical tradition of the ninth/third century to which the text and the author belonged, but the bulk of his interest lay in al-Balādhurī's method and content of the material he had available and any associated biases. He suggested that how al-Balādhurī and other authors chose to introduce their accounts suggested a great deal about the sources for this information, namely, whether al-Balādhurī had actually made contact with the source in question, was relying on a pre-existing written source, or was transmitting information that was already in wide circulation.[3]

Athamina not only discussed the method of transmission used by the author for his accounts in the work, but also considered the assertion by some modern scholars that al-Balādhurī is among the most trustworthy and impartial of all early Islamic historians.[4] This view, which has been held by a number of scholars including M. J. de Goeje and 'Abd al-Aziz Duri, asserts that al-Balādhurī's treatment of material presents not only a fairer use of the original source material than many of his peers, but also a fairer depiction of the early Islamic period more generally.[5] 'It is impossible to see in Balādhurī's exposition any partisan tendency. … Balādhurī, if one may so express oneself, was a partisan of one class only: his own class of authors who wish to be interesting and who therefore cannot resist a sensation and even a touch of scandal,' wrote S. D. Goitein, on the matter.[6] But for texts written in the style of the works of al-Balādhurī, having such a focus on evaluating and compiling previously existing traditions into a new work, the informants and sources of the author must be reasonably scrutinized to maintain such a lofty position.

Athamina's work was largely limited to the sources that al-Balādhurī used in his *Ansāb*, however, largely glossing over the other, smaller work by the author, *Futūḥ al-buldān*. This is understandable considering the great size and scope of al-Balādhurī's genealogical effort, which is among the most important sources of early Islamic history and politics. His *Futūḥ* also concentrates on the earliest century of Islam and the Umayyad period in particular, but proves to be a substantially different work on many levels. Its style and organization around geographic regions and the conquests notwithstanding, the *Futūḥ* contains considerable differences in the types of information it is concerned with. Al-Balādhurī's work on the conquests uses that setting largely as a means to contextualize landmark legal precedents, as well as to enshrine the details of how territories came to enter the Islamic world and the agreements made on behalf of the Muslims with the indigenous populations throughout this process. Thus, the *Futūḥ* is a work deeply concerned with the administration of empire, and especially with issues of taxation and the classification of lands. Owing to these significant differences between the *Ansāb* and the *Futūḥ*, it is unsurprising to discover that the sources relied upon by the author for these two works vary considerably, and thus the work of Athamina – while useful for an analysis of one of the works – does not prove definitive for the other.

While there is a definite overlap in the sources relied upon by al-Balādhurī across both works, the differences far outweigh the similarities. The famed historian al-Madā'inī (d. 843 CE/AH 228), for instance, is profoundly relied upon in both works, as is the author of the extant *Kitāb al-ṭabaqāt al-kabīr*, Muḥammad b. Sa'd (d. 845 CE/AH 230). But while Athamina draws attention to al-Balādhurī's considerable reliance on the reports of Hishām b. 'Ammār (d. 859 CE/AH 245) within the *Ansāb*, he is responsible for less than fifteen traditions within the *Futūḥ*. Conversely, the most commonly relied upon transmitter within the *Futūḥ*, a certain al-Ḥusayn b. 'Alī b. al-Aswad, provides less than a dozen traditions for the author's massive genealogical collection. Thus, while the sources al-Balādhurī relied upon often find a presence in both of his surviving works, how and how often they are used differ markedly.

This chapter will consider the use of transmitted material by al-Balādhurī in the *Futūḥ*. Rather than serving as a complete discussion of all of the sources of information and materials al-Balādhurī had at his disposal in writing the *Futūḥ*, this chapter intends to serve as an analysis of the author's citation style and his use of materials from some of his most common authorities, including famed transmitters al-Wāqidī (d. 822–823 CE/AH 207), Hishām b. al-Kalbī (d. ca. 819–821 CE/AH 204–206), al-Madā'ini, and Muḥammad b. Sa'd. The majority of attention, however, will focus on al-Balādhurī's use of introductory phrases and the style of his chains of transmission as an indicator of how the author was learning his information: whether through a written source, or the more traditional oral/aural recitation of the *majlis*. While many of al-Balādhurī's cited informants would likely have had direct contact with the author in a formal or informal teaching setting, he appears to consciously differentiate sources he accessed in a more indirect manner through the variation of his introductory phrases. Thus, the *Futūḥ* is a text which seems to take advantage of a huge number of sources on offer for a Muslim scholar of the 'Abbāsid period, and provides further insight into just how older material was selected and attributed in the creation of texts in the ninth century. The chapter closes with a more thorough discussion of two of his most understudied and yet important informants, al-Ḥusayn b. 'Alī b. al-Aswad al-'Ijlī and Abū 'Ubayd al-Qāsim b. Sallām, while providing further comment on the varying ways he likely accessed their traditions.

Introductory words and the collective *Isnād*

A source-critical analysis of an early Islamic text such as *Futūḥ al-buldān* inevitably begins with an analysis of chains of transmission, or *asānīd* (sing. *isnād*). These chains of transmission provide the audience of the work with a form of 'roadmap' of how the information came to the compiler, and conventionally take the form of 'Person A informed me, on the authority of B, on the authority of C, who witnessed when D did or said something worthy of remembering.' These chains of transmission are part of the very fabric of early Islamic administrative and judicial writing, setting out the authorities upon which an author claims legitimacy for the account in question.[7] The so-called 'atomistic' transmission of these accounts often leads to brief and concise pieces of information that include some form of introduction, normally a multilayered *isnād*, thereafter organized, emplotted, and at times linked together by the compiler of the work.[8] The source-critical method of analysis of *asānīd* was pioneered by Fuat Sezgin and, separately, Manfred Fleischhammer, both of whom worked to document a variety of accounts and their *asānīd* in a single work, investigating those informants who appeared in these chains.[9] In a different method of analysis, Joseph Schacht and, later, G. H. A. Juynboll looked to analyse singular accounts and their purported chain of transmission across many different works.[10] Both methods hoped to shed greater light on the nature of source transmission and construction, and have provided substantial insight for other modern scholars. It is to these studies that the present work has numerous methodological similarities. An analysis of the use of terminology and the employment of *asānīd* by al-Balādhurī can provide many useful ideas on how *Futūḥ al-buldān* was constructed. One must understand, however, that it is a study of only one particular author's use of this terminology and organization. It will not necessarily correspond in an identical fashion with other scholars of the early Arabic tradition, although it is hoped that it will be an additional contribution to how other authors may have differentiated their own use of sources, perhaps allowing comparisons across texts to be made.

Depending on the type of work and the style of the compiler in question, these brief accounts are only introduced by a single word rather than a thorough chain of transmission. A great number of the traditions cited by al-Balādhurī in the *Futūḥ* open with a simple 'they said' (*qālū*), rather than with a standard *isnād* listing the authorities upon which the tradition could be verified as authentic. Athamina suggested that the use of *qālū* in lieu of a proper *isnād* may suggest the amalgamation of multiple, previously separate, traditions into a singular account (*khabar*).[11] In this way, multiple traditions could be joined together to create a singular and unbroken narrative. The authors at the centre of his article, al-Balādhurī and al-Ṭabarī, were not the first to use the techniques of the 'collective *isnād*,' or *ikhtiṣār* (abbreviation, summary), but, rather, were adopting a technique seemingly born in the early eighth century.[12] This practice of combining traditions was reportedly employed by many famed early Muslim scholars, and the Prophetic biographer Ibn Isḥāq (d. ca. 767 CE/AH 150) enshrines an example from al-Zuhrī (d. 742 CE/AH 124) which illustrates this practice well: 'Each of them had transmitted some fragments of this story, some were more conscientious than others, and I have combined together all of what they had transmitted to me.'[13] Athamina's suggestion is convincingly reinforced by a greater consideration of the style and organization of the *Futūḥ*, which in many ways presents a more appropriate testing sample. This is owing to its narrative organization instead of the genealogically organized *Ansāb*, which by its very nature as a work focused on families, tribes, and individuals presents a very different arrangement.

Al-Ṭabarī employs the collective *isnād* with a far lower frequency than his predecessor al-Balādhurī. This is perhaps in line with an approach to his material by a judicial scholar like al-Ṭabarī involved with the science of *ḥadīth* as it had developed in his time. It was these scholars of *ḥadīth*, the *muḥaddithūn*, who pushed towards a preference for thorough, complete, and reliable chains of transmission for their materials.[14] This was viewed as a necessary step for works concerned with judicial precedent in particular, lest their material be cast off as unreliable and untrustworthy. One such early Islamic historian to earn the ire of these *ḥadīth* scholars was al-Wāqidī (d. 822–823 CE/AH 207) – one of al-Balādhurī's most important sources – who was later attacked by the famed jurist Aḥmad b. Ḥanbal (d. 855 CE/AH 241) specifically for his employment of the collective *isnād*.[15] This judicial technique was unlikely to have been completely foreign to al-Balādhurī, but his steady reliance on both the collective *isnād* and his regular use of these chains of transmission with missing links suggest that some of the purposes of his writings (and his intended audience) were less concerned with the minutiae of authenticity than the *muḥaddithūn*. In some instances, he includes a placeholder within an *isnād* for the missing individual(s). This placeholder is found at the ending of an *isnād* and is usually something similar to 'in his chain of transmission' (*fī isnādihi*).[16] At times al-Balādhurī might describe the originators of traditions simply as learned elders of a certain place (*…ʿan shaykh min Ḥimyar qāla…* or *…ʿan qawm min ʿulamāʾihim*, for instance),[17] while occasionally, he provides a more unique break in the chain, such as '…from other people al-Wāqidī names and whose *ḥadīth* are intertwined'.[18]

These shorter or 'stunted' *asānīd* suggest that al-Balādhurī was not to be found among the ranks of the *muḥaddithūn*, but do not suggest he was careless in his treatment of material, either.[19] Rather, they suggest the development of a branch of scholarly writing in the eighth- and ninth-century Islamic world that was still evolving, attempting to marry together the intense authoritative concerns of those dealing in *ḥadīth* and the judicial and administrative traditions, while having one foot firmly in the camp of the narrative historical tradition the likes of which survives in the work of al-Yaʿqūbī (d. ca. early 900s CE/290s AH) and Ibn Aʿtham al-Kūfī (*fl.* late 800s CE/mid-200s AH). It is this historical tradition that was mostly unconcerned with demonstrating the authenticity of material at the beginning of each account, choosing instead to favour a more coherent and uninterrupted narrative.[20] But al-Balādhurī was also a successor of a tradition which had clear interests in legislative matters, and had the jurist Abū Yūsuf among its ranks. Abū Yūsuf's *Kitāb al-Kharāj* informs us that it was written at the behest of the caliph, and greatly concerns itself with materials such as the classification of land and issues of taxation in a way not dissimilar to the *Futūḥ*. It also very frequently fails to provide the authority from which the information originated, or chooses instead to provide *asānīd* even more stunted than those of al-Balādhurī. For him, choosing to include only three traditionists or less as the authorities for his sources is the rule, not the exception.[21] Abū Yūsuf is said to have provided his thoughts on his own methodology apropos the methodology of the *muḥaddithūn* regarding the citation of authorities as such: 'Three categories of scholars are not immune from three evils: those who study astrology are not safe from heresy; those who study alchemy are not safe from poverty; and those who seek to explain the oddities in *ḥadīth* traditions are not safe from falsehood.'[22] Michael Cooperson has emphasized the developments undertaken in *ḥadīth* scholarship in the eighth and ninth centuries, particularly the formalization of *ḥadīth* criteria that left it separate and distinct from the more narrative historical disciplines.[23] Along with this came an increased focus on demonstrating the authenticity of materials cited and utilized in certain types of works, in particular those associated with Islamic legal issues such as *ḥadīth*.[24] Al-Balādhurī's style and use of *asānīd* within the *Futūḥ* suggests a work firmly at the crossroads of the mixed methodologies of narrative sources and legal material.

In light of these differences, it is interesting to note the numerous times when al-Balādhurī does choose to utilize the collective *isnād* within the *Futūḥ*. His use of *qālū* is found in every chapter of the text, and it is difficult to identify precisely when he chooses to employ it. His use is inconsistent: the information included in traditions following this type varies, as do the informants who provide preceding and succeeding traditions. When one begins to fully analyse the makeup of the text, however, there is one type of use of *qālū* that becomes striking: al-Balādhurī tends to rely on it largely when providing the formal narrative of the conquests themselves, a form of place-setting for the administrative and legal material that he thereafter emplots in each geographically organized chapter. The layout of the *Futūḥ* around geographic locations presents a rather cyclical organization, and each individual chapter tends to begin chronologically at the earliest point relevant to that location. For most regions, this is the conquest of that territory by Muslim forces. These first accounts in each chapter tend to offer information such as the movement of armies, the presence of Companions, and how long sieges were sustained, but rarely provide in-depth discussion of judicial or legal matters. Despite the title of al-Balādhurī's *Futūḥ*, it is this material that the author seems to view as preliminary to the work as a whole, and it is this type of material that he often chooses to introduce with the collective *isnād*. In this way, *qālū* can be seen to introduce the setting and environment in which important actions were taken by the Prophet, his Companions, and the subsequent caliphs that would become precedent-setting administrative and legal justifications for Muslim scholars of the ninth/third century.

Numerous examples can be quoted where al-Balādhurī introduces the setting and provides details of the conquest with the collective *isnād* before augmenting this tradition by including a second, more specific account with a fuller chain of transmission. One such example occurs in the chapter on the conquest of western and south-western Persia. The Companion Abū Mūsā al-Ashʿarī's attacks and movements against the enemy in the region are detailed with the simple use of *qālū*, with some non-specific information on the capitulation agreements stating that 'the people [of al-Dīnawar] agreed to pay the poll tax (*jizya*) and land tax (*kharāj*), and they asked for safety for their lives, possessions, and children. Abū Mūsā agreed to that, and he designated his governor over the city.' After these traditions, however, al-Balādhurī provides a lengthy and detailed account attributed to ʿAbbās b. Hishām al-Kalbī discussing the political and administrative background of a certain governor of the region, Kathīr b. Shihāb.[25]

In contrast to this use of the collective *isnād* by al-Balādhurī is his use of fuller *asānīd* in the text. As suggested above, it is the author's inclusion of this material that seems to serve a purpose more in line with judicial texts like Abū Yūsuf's *Kitāb al-Kharāj* that had come before it. And yet, the works are far from being the same, with the clearest difference being al-Balādhurī's more regular use of *asānīd*. As a general rule, al-Balādhurī appears to provide fuller *asānīd* for traditions which would have been of direct legal significance, namely, those *akhbār* which concerned precedent and which were not communicated to him via a written medium (as will be discussed below).

Aside from clear stylistic differences, however, al-Balādhurī's background and training differs from that of other authors of early books on taxation. Most importantly, al-Balādhurī himself is not remembered in any of the surviving biographical resources as a jurist. The scant biographical details on his life do not record his ever having held a judicial post (serving as a *qāḍī*) in any region. Rather, he is described as a man of letters, a poet, and a writer, and the limited biographical information discussed in Chapter 2 on him strongly advocates for a role in the administrative class as a secretary (*kātib*). Previous generations of his family are similarly styled as members of the bureaucracy.[26] Despite this, we find that many of his primary sources of information were precisely these members of the judicial elite, and the secretaries of the court were often expected to have well-rounded educations, which allowed them to know at least a little bit about a great many matters.[27] In reality, and as will be discussed at the end of this chapter, two of al-Balādhurī's primary sources of information were jurists who held judgeships during the early ʿAbbāsid period and also authored two important legal manuals: Yaḥyā b. Ādam, the author of an extant *Kitāb al-Kharāj* (*The Book of Taxation*), and Abū ʿUbayd, the author of an extant *Kitāb al-Amwāl* (*The Book of Revenue*).

Al-Balādhurī's interests clearly include administrative matters dear to the secretarial class to which he belonged, too: For instance, the *Futūḥ* is often cited for its two important stories on the change of the administrative language of the early Islamic state from Greek and Persian to Arabic,[28] and his interest in record keeping is clear through the numerous settlement agreements and land grants enshrined within.[29] But in contrast to his use of the collective *isnād* for the vast majority of the narratives of conquest in the work, it is this marriage of judicial and administrative material that is precisely when al-Balādhurī most often chooses to include complete chains of transmission, demonstrating that it was this material, perhaps, which required such verification in order to be useful to the audience of his text.

Al-Balādhurī's use of *Qāla* as an introductory phrase in the *Futūḥ*

On al-Balādhurī's use of the introductory phrase 'he said' (*qāla*), Athamina suggested that the use of the term '[draws] attention to the fact al-Balādhurī was not confined to a certain kind of source, but had a very wide collection at his disposal, which he exploited selectively. A comparison between the *Ansāb* and other sources confirms this conclusion.'[30] His assertion is an important one, and one that is worthy of further exploration within the *Futūḥ*. While *qāla* is not the most common introductory phrase employed by the author, it appears quite regularly, introducing almost 200 individual accounts of the 1115 that make up the *Futūḥ*.[31] Rather than beginning a standard chain of transmission, however, al-Balādhurī's use of *qāla* would suggest times when he was relying on accounts from sources he did not directly hear himself.[32] More specifically, these are accounts that were likely available in a written form, although whether this was in the form of lecture notes a teacher would have used when lecturing to students (so-called *aides-mémoire*), dictations those students made in those sessions and shared, or more formalized books written for public consumption, is difficult to ascertain.[33] The ninth-/third-century *milieu* to which al-Balādhurī belonged still included an ambivalence or scepticism towards written text, which remained strong well into the next century. These feelings among some scholars of the period were particularly strong, although this did not prevent others from committing their works to writing.[34]

A strong case can be made for al-Balādhurī's use of written resources when three particular criteria are aligned within the *Futūḥ*: his use of a different introductory word (*qāla*) when providing the authority for these accounts; the lack of any additional links in the *asānīd* aside from the main source (the primary guarantor from whom the information is drawn), or a student (informant) and the guarantor;[35] and, finally, the nature of the informant cited in the *isnād* being unlikely or unable to have met al-Balādhurī or to have spent much time interacting with him, dependent on their age. As will be shown, all three of these conditions coincide in the *Futūḥ* fairly regularly.

The first criterion which suggests al-Balādhurī was indicating his use of written sources is fairly clear-cut. Al-Balādhurī uses the ambiguous phrase 'he said' (*qāla*) many times and in a number of forms within the *Futūḥ*. This includes the obvious occurrences where he is providing rarer instances of speech or dialogue, when he is providing a note from a specific transmitter within a larger account,[36] in most instances where he cites poetry,[37] and finally, several times when the immediate source itself is left intentionally obscure, providing instead introductions such as 'some narrators have said' or 'some have said'.[38] Whenever al-Balādhurī chooses to provide a chain of transmission with more than two or three authorities, however, he almost never elects to introduce them with *qāla*,[39] choosing, instead, 'he informed us' (*ḥaddathanā*) or 'he informed me' (*ḥaddathanī*), or far more rarely, 'he related to us' (*akhbaranā*), 'he related to me' (*akhbaranī*), or 'he gave an account' (*rawā*).[40] *Ḥaddathanā* and *ḥaddathanī* are the most commonly used introductory phrases the author employs in both the *Futūḥ* and the *Ansāb*, and they almost always precede a full chain of transmission. While used frequently, *qāla*, on the other hand, tends to introduce stunted *asānīd* or an account which only provides al-Balādhurī's ultimate informant and no other transmission information.

The second criterion which appears to signify when al-Balādhurī was not hearing information directly from another teacher is his use of a limited chain of transmission. In these instances, al-Balādhurī chose to cite only his informant (such as *qāla Muḥammad b. Saʿd*) or an informant and only one other guarantor in the *isnād* (such as *qāla Muḥammad b. Saʿd ʿani al-Wāqidī*). This use is consistent throughout the *Futūḥ* with the exception of the final thematic chapters of the work, what Francis Murgotten has called appendices, where this use becomes somewhat unsystematic. Almost every time the informants listed are introduced with *qāla* in the tradition, there are never more than two other authorities mentioned; but much more commonly, they are the sole named source.[41] While al-Balādhurī's use of stunted *asānīd* that do not include every generational link in the chain between the author and the originator of the tradition has already been discussed, he largely opts to include more than three authorities along the way in these instances. The vast majority of times where he chooses to list only one or, occasionally, two authorities for certain accounts are when the chain of transmission is introduced by *qāla*, and where the informant listed as his source was someone he may never have met or, perhaps, had limited interaction with.

The third and final of these criteria are the individuals involved in these accounts which are introduced by *qāla* and have incomplete chains of transmission. Quite tellingly, it is unlikely or, perhaps, impossible that al-Balādhurī would have met and studied under many of these scholars listed below,[42] as they were all likely deceased either before al-Balādhurī was born or before he would have been competent to be their student. While details of al-Balādhurī's life are limited, one important piece of information is provided by Yāqūt and repeated in later biographical sources: that he died at the end of the reign of the 'Abbāsid Caliph al-Mu'tamid (r. 870–892 CE/AH 256–279), putting the date of his death in circa 892 CE/AH 279, although no source provides his age at death. We are also informed that he would have been mature enough to be a boon companion (*nadīm*) of the Caliph al-Mutawakkil (r. 847–861 CE/AH 232–247) sometime during his reign.[43] In considering transmitters where all three of these criteria align and who also provide at least three individual traditions for al-Balādhurī, we find the following:

1. Abū Mikhnaf (d. 774 CE/AH 157)
2. Hishām b. al-Kalbī (d. ca. 819–821 CE/AH 204–206)
3. al-Wāqidī (d. 822–823 CE/AH 207)
4. Abū 'Ubayda (Ma'mar b. al-Muthannā) (d. ca. 822–828 CE/AH 207–213)
5. al-Walīd b. Hishām b. al-Qahdhamī (d. 837 CE/AH 222)
6. al-Madā'inī ('Ali b. Muḥammad, Abū al-Ḥasan) (d. 843 CE/AH 228)
7. Abū Mas'ūd al-Kūfī ('Uqba b. Khālid b. 'Uqba al-Sakūnī) (d. 803–804 CE/AH 188)

Of these first four authorities, only minimal introduction is necessary. They are remembered for being some of the most prolific transmitters of material in the first two centuries of Islamic history. All of them have an enormous number of works attributed to them as authors, although whether any of these books took a final written form in the lifetime of al-Balādhurī is difficult to establish.[44]

Biographical entries on Abū Mikhnaf ascribe to him composition of some forty works[45] – especially focused on Iraq – and Athamina has briefly posited that al-Balādhurī's use of his material may suggest access to a lost work on the conquest of the eastern frontier, *Kitāb futūḥ Khurāsān*.[46] Hishām b. al-Kalbī is also remembered as a prolific author of more than 150 works, a significant number of which are genealogical in nature, but who also wrote several geographic works including a large and small *Kitāb al-Buldān*.[47] While only one work of al-Wāqidī's has survived to the present,[48] he is remembered for authoring a number of texts, largely on the early Islamic conquests, and a genealogical work (*ṭabaqāt*) that was preserved and expanded by his student, Muḥammad b. Sa'd. He is quoted by a huge number of later historians despite being a rather divisive figure in early Islamic scholarship, and is heavily relied on by al-Balādhurī, too, for some fifty accounts throughout the *Futūḥ*. Of Abū 'Ubayda, more than one hundred works are said to have been authored by him, covering Qur'ānic exegesis, philology, lexicography, poetry, and many other topics. For our purposes, to suggest that some of this abundance of works may have been accessible to al-Balādhurī in the creation of the *Futūḥ* does not seem at all unreasonable.

Considering all of their dates of death and our limited biographical knowledge of al-Balādhurī, one wonders whether he would have been able to receive traditions in a formal educational session directly from these informants. Abū Mikhnaf and Abū Mas'ūd al-Kūfī would certainly have died before al-Balādhurī would have been of a competent age to be their student, even if we ascribe to him an exceptionally long lifetime. At best, he would have been very young to have studied directly under Hishām b. al-Kalbī or al-Wāqidī before either scholar died, and we might express similar scepticism over any potential interaction with Abū 'Ubayda with the uncertainty surrounding his date of death.[49]

What is arguably most important is that none of these first four major scholars are listed as teachers of al-Balādhurī's from whom he heard traditions (*sami'a*) in any of the surviving biographical material despite their many appearances in both the *Futūḥ* and the *Ansāb*. And yet, all seven of these listed authors are collectively relied upon in the *Futūḥ* for approximately 150 individual traditions, making them informants of considerable import in the makeup of the work. It therefore seems likely that our author would have accessed many of their accounts in a different – likely written – form, choosing to differentiate how he received this material from the teachers he had direct contact with by the use of *qāla* over *ḥaddathanā*, *ḥaddathanī*, or any other introductory phrase. Owing again to the manner in which al-Balādhurī cites his material in the

Futūḥ, it seems unlikely that he had these traditions recited to him by any of the students of these four authors, either. If he did, it seems probable that he would have named the student intermediary as his direct guarantor for these main authorities, something he does not seem to take issue with elsewhere in the text.[50] In fact, for two of the above transmitters, he discernibly differentiates when he is citing material he learned from a student intermediary as opposed to these indirect means.

These two cases are those between al-Wāqidī and his student, the so-called 'Scribe of al-Wāqidī,' Muḥammad b. Saʿd,[51] and between Hishām b. al-Kalbī and his son, ʿAbbās. Both of these students are found among al-Balādhurī's most-cited informants in the *Futūḥ*, transmitting more than 100 accounts with them as the named informant. In the material cited by both students, Ibn Saʿd and Hishām overwhelmingly serve as the main authority for the traditions al-Balādhurī includes, and these accounts are almost exclusively introduced through the use of 'he informed me' (*ḥaddathanī*). This is in far greater accordance with how al-Balādhurī cites his 'standard' informants – those who appear in the *Futūḥ*, were alive firmly into his lifetime, and many of whom are cited in the biographical material as his teachers.[52] There is a clear variance in the manner al-Balādhurī quotes the teachers of these students. To use al-Wāqidī as a more specific example, while he is regularly cited by name as al-Balādhurī's direct informant (*qāla al-Wāqidī*), his material also regularly appears as having come to al-Balādhurī through the intermediary of Ibn Saʿd (*ḥaddathanī Muḥammad b. Saʿd ʿani al-Wāqidī*). Al-Wāqidī is almost never cited directly with an introductory phrase other than *qāla*, as can be seen here, where the listed page numbers refer to individual traditions (Table 3.1).

Table 3.1 Appearances of al-Wāqidī as informant

	al-Wāqidī			
Introductory Phrase	***ḥaddathanī***	***ḥaddathanā***	***rawā***	***qāla***
Page Numbers[a]	None	None	129	6; 18; 44; 46; 51; 52; 55; 67; 68; 74; 82; 91; 111; 132; 140; 146; 146; 155; 181; 209; 211; 218; 222; 226; 236; 269; 269; 270; 272; 273; 278; 296; 305; 313; 317; 318; 323; 380; 408; 439; 464; 465; 546; 552; 552; 577; 582

[a]All page numbers are from al-Munajjid's Arabic edition.

In terms of content, there is no identifiable consistency between the types of traditions that were communicated in this manner. Rather, the major difference in these types of traditions is almost certainly how al-Balādhurī accessed the material, with instances of the direct invocation of al-Wāqidī as his informant an indicator of access to a form of written source which does not survive. To prove how stark this differentiation is with al-Balādhurī's normal citation style, we can contrast it with accounts which have Ibn Saʿd appear as his informant (Table 3.2).

It strongly suggests that he accessed this material in a form other than learning from students such as Muḥammad b. Saʿd and ʿAbbās b. Hishām, and this material seems likely to have been accessed in a written form.

In the case of Abū Mikhnaf, his name appears twelve times as an informant in the *Futūḥ*, a much smaller but still significant sample size to consider. Eight of these citations are introduced by *qāla* or a variant, two are introduced by *rawā*, and two appearances are introduced as *thakara Abū Mikhnaf* (Abū Mikhnaf has mentioned). Separately, he also appears cited as the primary guarantor of accounts provided by Hishām b. al-Kalbī many more times. There can be no uncertainty surrounding any potential interaction between al-Balādhurī and Abū Mikhnaf, as the two could never have met before Abū Mikhnaf died. Abū Mikhnaf is never introduced in the *Futūḥ* with al-Balādhurī's normal introductory phrases of *ḥaddathanā*/*ḥaddathanī* (Table 3.3).

Table 3.2 Appearances of Ibn Saʿd as informant

	Muḥammad b. Saʿd				
Introductory Phrase	***ḥaddathanī***	***ḥaddathanā***	***qāla***	***rawā***	***None***
Page Numbers[a]	15; 22; 50; 52; 52; 71; 140; 166; 167; 167; 168; 182; 183; 192; 195; 200; 200; 207; 207; 208; 218; 221; 225; 235; 255; 256; 261; 262; 264; 264; 267; 268; 268; 271; 279; 280; 280; 322; 338; 370; 383; 384; 429; 472; 553; 571; 572; 573; 573; 574; 574; 575; 576; 576; 577; 578; 580; 581	552	201; 204; 577	239	549; 549; 550; 553; 553; 573

[a]All page numbers are from al-Munajjid's Arabic edition.

Table 3.3 Appearances of Abū Mikhnaf as informant

			Abū Mikhnaf		
Introductory Phrase	***ḥaddathanī***	***ḥaddathanā***	***qāla***	***rawā***	***thakara***
Page Numbers[a]	None	None	99; 299; 310; 401; 419; 464; 487; 488	130; 297	128; 308

[a]All page numbers are from al-Munajjid's Arabic edition.

Two of the informants listed above, al-Madā'inī and al-Qahdhamī, seem likely to have met al-Balādhurī at least briefly, but both fit the other criteria and deserve further comment. Much is known about al-Madā'inī, who is among the most important informants in all of the early Islamic period, and someone to whom Ibn al-Nadīm attributes more than one hundred works. He is the one, we can say with certainty, who met al-Balādhurī, as he died later than all of the others, had lived in Baghdad for much of his later career, and most importantly, was mentioned as one of al-Balādhurī's teachers by the biographical sources.[53] This suggestion is again supported by al-Balādhurī's use of introductory phrases: not only does he regularly introduce traditions by al-Madā'inī by using *qāla*, but he also recurrently introduces his traditions by utilizing *ḥaddathanī* (Table 3.4).

He and Abū Mas'ūd are the only sources al-Balādhurī cites regularly in this manner. An explanation for this can be found in both al-Balādhurī's potential experience in studying under al-Madā'inī, citing the material learned directly from his teacher (*ḥaddathanī*) separately from materials he had access to in a written form (*qāla*). It is said that al-Madā'inī did not actually commit any of his copious books to writing (as unlikely as that seems),[54] but while al-Balādhurī may never have used a book written by al-Madā'inī as a source for the *Futūḥ*, it does not rule out his using lecture notes left behind by his teacher, or notes that were taken by his fellow students at lectures al-Balādhurī may not have attended.[55]

As for al-Qaḥdhamī, he took his name from his grandfather, a non-Arab freedman who became a secretary to the Iraqi governor Yūsuf b. 'Umar al-Thaqafī (r. 738–744 CE/AH 120–126). He came to be responsible for the tax office and later the financial register in Baṣra, with access to records and information which would have made him a valued informant for a historian. His reports within the *Futūḥ* were the focus of a recent and convincing study by Wadad al-Qadi, discussing al-Balādhurī's section on Baṣra. All twenty traditions where

Table 3.4 Appearances of al-Madā'inī as informant

al-Madā'inī					
Introductory Phrase	***ḥaddathanī***	***ḥaddathanā***	***qāla***	***akhbaranī***	***None***
Page Numbers[a]	9; 10; 66; 93; 340; 344; 368; 382; 397; 401; 401; 401; 413; 420; 420; 434; 437; 471; 473; 537; 569; 569; 569	None	10; 55; 151; 284; 303; 414; 422; 439; 440; 445; 448; 451; 452; 460; 460; 502; 574	13	257

[a]All page numbers are from al-Munajjid's Arabic edition.

he is clearly named as informant are found in this section. Al-Qadi suggests that al-Balādhurī's use of language in these accounts (specifically names which appear in a form more familiar to Middle Persian rather than Arabic) and al-Qaḥdhamī's reliance on his well-placed grandfather as his main authority suggest that he had access to at least some of the records of the register that he provided al-Balādhurī with.[56] In three of these accounts by al-Qaḥdhamī, his access to written materials is made explicit: first, he introduces that his grandfather was responsible for the *dīwān jund al-'Arab* (the register of the army of the Arabs) before saying that 'I examined (*naẓartu*) the troops of Baṣra,' implying their records in the *dīwān*.[57] Written materials are again referenced when al-Qaḥdhamī transmits 'I found a letter in our possession,' where he then proceeds to provide a letter from the Caliph 'Umar, ending it with the name of a scribe, Mu'ayqīb b. Abī Fāṭima, a fact unusual for the *Futūḥ*.[58] Later in this section, access to the *dīwān* is again referenced in a discussion of the ownership of land known as Muhallabān.[59] All of the traditions included in the *Futūḥ* on the authority of al-Qaḥdhamī are introduced by *qāla*, owing perhaps to his providing al-Balādhurī with these archival materials as the source of his information, rather than oral accounts provided to him and memorized in the more traditional fashion. In this way, al-Balādhurī was noting his use of these written materials provided to him by an individual who 1) was not a well-known scholar himself and 2) was providing him written materials which were from outside the official registers.

In keeping with his *nisba*, the seventh and final informant, Abū Mas'ūd, provides the *Futūḥ* with material concerning the city of Kūfa, and Iraq more generally. Abū Mas'ūd was definitively deceased before the lifetime of al-Balādhurī, but both he and his son, Khālid b. 'Uqba b. Khālid, are recorded as having extended stays in Baghdad.[60] Precisely how al-Balādhurī would have received and transmitted information from Abū Mas'ūd is uncertain, but since he spent time in the 'Abbāsid capital, he may have left accessible materials behind. Both he and al-Qaḥdhamī play very similar roles in providing sources for the founding and development of their linked cities. Of the seven informants listed above, aside from Abū Mikhnaf,[61] Abū Mas'ūd provides the smallest amount of traditions for the *Futūḥ*, and only four are introduced with *qāla* and no further chain of transmission. This makes him the only outlier among these transmitters in that he transmits a number of traditions using *ḥaddathanī* and *qāla* despite his small sample size. All of the appearances of *qāla Abū Mas'ūd* appear in al-Balādhurī's chapter on the founding of Kūfa (Table 3.5).

In the four bolded instances in the table above, a stunted *isnād* is used to introduce the information, each one saying only *ḥaddathanī Abū Mas'ūd wa-ghayrahu qāla*. While his use of Abū Mas'ūd's traditions is at odds with the rest of the data shown above, it does not lessen the stark contrast in citation style found elsewhere, although the unique mix of styles found here may be demonstrating another not-yet-understood means of engagement with historical material on behalf of al-Balādhurī.

Further reinforcing al-Balādhurī's use of *qāla* as a distinct authorial choice in the *Futūḥ* is his similar use of the term in the *Ansāb al-ashrāf*. This is particularly the case when it pertains to the first four transmitters – al-Wāqidī, Abū Mikhnaf, Abū 'Ubayda, and Hishām b. al-Kalbī. All four are consistently introduced with *qāla* and without a complete *isnād*, mimicking the style present in the *Futūḥ*. As the *Ansāb* is a work of far more substantial length, it provides a much greater sample size for evaluation of al-Balādhurī's technique. His extended use of *qāla* within these sources continues to compete with his sustained use of introductory phrases such as *ḥaddathanī* for informants he almost certainly met in person. It strengthens the suggestion that al-Balādhurī had gained the knowledge of these informants in a method other than direct study with them, with the most probable explanation being access to some written form.

Table 3.5 Appearances of Abū Mas'ud as informant

	Abū Mas'ūd al-Kūfī		
Introductory Phrase	***ḥaddathanī***	***ḥaddathanā***	***qāla***
Page Numbers[a]	80; 298; 304; 325; 336; 343; **350**; **351**; 352; 353; 359; **360**; 375; **472**	None	345; 345; 346; 351;

[a]All page numbers are from al-Munajjid's Arabic edition.

A most important informant: Al-Ḥusayn b. ʿAlī b. al-Aswad al-ʿIjlī

To continue with the specific analysis of informants which appear in *Futūḥ al-buldān*, we turn away from the style of citation used by al-Balādhurī to the targeted consideration of two of the most important sources of information the author used in the compilation of his text. The first of these is al-Ḥusayn b. ʿAlī b. al-Aswad al-ʿIjlī. Of all the informants utilized by al-Balādhurī in *Futūḥ al-buldān*, none appear more oft-cited than al-Husayn, although biographical details on him are scant. It seems that his status as a transmitter of material was fairly unremarkable within the medieval period, as information on him does not appear in most of the biographical works on transmitters through to the time of al-Dhahabī (d. 1348 CE/AH 748), an exception being within the work of al-Mizzī (d. 1341 CE/AH 742). Even here, however, biographical details are almost non-existent, the only detail of great importance for our purpose being that he lived in Baghdad, where he may have come into contact with al-Balādhurī.[62] Nonetheless, he has played a vital role for posterity through his use by al-Balādhurī in his extant works. While al-Ḥusayn is only named as an informant scarcely a dozen times in the *Ansāb*, he provides more than eighty individual traditions of varying length in the far shorter *Futūḥ*.

The information relied on by al-Balādhurī from al-Ḥusayn is primarily concerned with the ownership of land and the details of its taxation. He provides al-Balādhurī with many precise instances of taxation on certain cities and regions, in both coin and in kind; for instance, ʿal-Mughīra b. Shuʿba wrote while he was governor of *al-sawād*: "We find here products other than wheat and barley," mentioning Indian peas (*al-māsh*), grapes, clover (*al-raṭba*), and sesame, on which he assessed [a tax of] eight dirhams. He excluded palm trees.'[63] The vast majority of traditions transmitted by al-Ḥusayn are of this type. A number of other traditions provide details on who was given land by the Prophet and the early caliphs for private ownership,[64] land that remained in the hands of the indigenous population and was subjected to taxation,[65] and land that was taken over by the early Islamic state for the benefit of the greater community.[66] The bulk of his traditions are concerned with the central Islamic lands of the Arabian Peninsula (especially the Ḥijāz, Yemen, and Bahrain) and Mesopotamia,[67] but not exclusively so: he provides, for instance, a single tradition in each of al-Balādhurī's chapters on Sijistān and Khurāsān.

Al-Ḥusayn relied on two primary transmitters for the information he passed on to al-Balādhurī. The first of these, Wakīʿ b. al-Jarrāḥ (d. 812 CE/AH 197), was a well-known *ḥadīth* transmitter, and a teacher relied upon by other informants of al-Balādhurī.[68] He provides a mix of material throughout the *Futūḥ*, which includes four repetitive traditions in the chapter on Kūfa praising its population in a variety of terms, all on the authority of 'Umar.[69] Most importantly, though, are the materials he provided al-Ḥusayn on the establishment of the *dīwān* by the early caliphs, and how much money early Muslims – and the wives of the Prophet in particular – received due to their status on the register. All of the information transmitted on the *dīwān* by al-Ḥusayn is provided on the authority of Wakīʿ, meaning that while he is only relied upon for the transmission of twenty-one traditions in the *Futūḥ*, those he provides have a significant impact on providing modern scholars with information on the early Islamic state.

The overwhelming majority of traditions provided to al-Balādhurī in the *Futūḥ* by al-Ḥusayn come on the authority of Yaḥyā b. Ādam b. Sulaymān (d. 818 CE/AH 203). Yaḥyā had worked for a significant portion of his life in Kūfa and, by all accounts, was considered a reliable transmitter, well respected in his age: one of his traditions is present in the *Ṣaḥīh* of Muslim, and upon his death, he is said to have received the funeral rites from the father-in-law of the 'Abbāsid Caliph al-Ma'mūn (r. 813–833 CE/AH 198–218).[70] He is remembered for having composed five books, only one of which survives, a book entitled *Kitāb al-Kharāj* (*The Book of Taxation*), which contains a number of traditions which al-Husayn also provided to al-Balādhurī in the *Futūḥ*.[71] While a deeply insightful work in its own right, the survival of *Kitāb al-Kharāj* is greatly beneficial for the study of how al-Balādhurī used material available to him in the construction of his own administrative book.

Several traditions communicated by Yaḥyā in his own work find verbatim or near-verbatim repetition in the *Futūḥ*. Among these are two briefer traditions concerning the terms made by the commander Khālid b. al-Walīd on behalf of Abū Bakr with the inhabitants of the Mesopotamian towns of al-Ḥīra and 'Ayn al-Tamr.[72] The versions within the *Futūḥ* are word-for-word duplicates of those that appear in *Kitāb al-Kharāj*, and this identical reproduction occurs elsewhere in al-Balādhurī's work, although small variations in words are sometimes found.[73] The chains of transmission in these accounts are also identical from Yaḥyā down to the earliest or original authority. Elsewhere, however, several traditions are copied between both sources, but al-Balādhurī's version in the *Futūḥ* includes minor variations. Two such traditions in the form of letters feature the terms with Najrān and the tribes of the Yemen, and include similar exposition, the first being addressed to 'Amr b. Ḥazm and the second to the kings of Ḥimyar. This second letter details the Muslims' expectations from the Ḥimyarites in exchange for peace. It includes what can be considered standard expectations of conversion for Arab tribes living in the Arabian Peninsula in the conquest period – namely belief in the one God and his Prophet, regular prayer, and the giving of alms (*zakāt*). But owing to Yaḥyā's interests in matters of taxation, the letter also details the levels of taxation charged by the Muslims: that the Ḥimyarites should pay *ṣadaqa*, be charged *'ushr* on land naturally irrigated, and half-*'ushr* on land irrigated by bucket.[74] Both this letter and the letter addressed to 'Amr contain near identical details across sources, and have identical chains of transmission. In terms of the content of the letters, there are some differences – certain cases of words differ slightly, and there is the occasional omission of a word on the part of al-Balādhurī (differences noted in bold):

> To go on – **and he mentioned from it** – God has guided you by his own guidance, if you make peace and obey God and his messenger, you observe **the prayers**, and give **the alms tax (*zakāt*) (Y: given)** from the spoils of war, the fifth belonging to God as well as the share of the prophet and his confidants; and give the *ṣadaqa* that God prescribed to the believers – which is one tenth if the land is watered by spring or watered by rain, and **accordingly,** which is half of one tenth if watered with the bucket.[75]

al-Balādhurī's Version	Yaḥyā b. Ādam's Version
أما بعد فإن الله قد هداكم بهدايته أن أصلحتم	أما بعد **فذكر منه** فإن الله قد هداكم بهدايته أن أصلحتم
وأطعتم الله ورسوله	وأطعتم الله ورسوله
وأقمتم الصلاة وآتيتم الزكاة من المغانم	وأقمتم **الصلوة** وآتيتم **الزكوة وأعطيتم** من المغانم
خمس الله وسهم النبىّ وصفيّه وما كتب الله على	خمس الله وسهم النبىّ وصفيّه وما كتب الله على
المؤمنين من الصدقة من العقار عشر ما سقت العين	المؤمنين من الصدقة من العقار عشر ما سقت العين
وسقت السماء وما سقى بالغرب نصف العشر	وسقت السماء **وعلى** وما سقى بالغرب نصف العشر

A number of traditions shared by both sources purport to contain the correspondence between the Prophet and the early caliphs on the one hand, and the conquered peoples on the other. Elsewhere, al-Balādhurī duplicates a letter Yaḥyā provides between the Caliph 'Umar and the conqueror of Sasanian Persia, Sa'd b. Abī Waqqāṣ, upon the completion of the latter's conquest of Iraq. The letter is not concerned with the conquest of the territory itself, but with the division of the spoils of war (*ghanīma*) among those Muslims victorious in battle. It addresses the status of the fertile Mesopotamian alluvial plain, a region typically referred to as *al-sawād*. Yaḥyā – and al-Balādhurī's – interest in the region is easy to understand. As the most profitable region in all of the conquered territories, the exact status of the land as communal had deep implications. It ensured and protected considerable income for the state, which relied on the taxation and produce of collectively owned lands such as the *sawād* as its primary form of income during the ninth century.[76]

Not all of the traditions found in the *Futūḥ* and transmitted by al-Ḥusayn on the authority of Yaḥyā can be found in *Kitāb al-Kharāj*, however. These accounts, which are not found in the text, vary both in the regions they cover and in their content. In a tradition following the conquest of Egypt, al-Zubayr b. al-ʿAwwām urges the commander ʿAmr b. al-ʿĀṣ to divide the booty among the victorious Muslims. ʿAmr tells him he must wait until he has heard from the Caliph ʿUmar about how the booty should be treated, and ʿUmar orders that the land be left in the hands of the Egyptians so that generations of Muslims may benefit from it.[77] Another is an account with a short *isnād* that lists Yaḥyā as the originator and details the tax required of the inhabitants of al-Ḥīra. At the end of it, Yaḥyā plainly states that he has read the taxation agreement made for the town (*kataba [Khālid] lahum bi-dhālika kitāban qad qaraʾtuhu*).[78]

All of this provides opportunity for some tentative suggestions on how al-Balādhurī was compiling his own book. While it has been demonstrated that some traditions appearing in both the *Futūḥ* and *Kitāb al-Kharāj* are completely identical, that numerous traditions bear even smaller differences suggest that al-Balādhurī was not using a finalized written form of Yaḥyā's work for his own writings.[79] This isn't to decry the quality of al-Ḥusayn/Yaḥyā's contribution to the *Futūḥ*, for as James Robson has written: 'A change of wording is of no great importance when the meaning [of the tradition] is not altered.'[80] But it does suggest that transmission was not simply a matter of scribes duplicating verbatim a previously existing book. Added to this is the difficulty of rectifying how some traditions transmitted by al-Ḥusayn on the authority of Yaḥyā could appear in the *Futūḥ* but not in *Kitāb al-Kharāj*. While Yaḥyā is reported to have compiled more than this one surviving book, none of his other listed works suggest more than a passing interest in the administrative materials al-Balādhurī includes.[81]

Among the most telling issues is an account provided by both authors again briefly discussing the treaty for al-Ḥīra, where they both mention that a saddle (*raḥl*) was included in the settlement agreement, as one of the conquerors did not already have one. Both chains of transmission are identical.[82] But interestingly, Yaḥyā writes that the terms agreed upon were 1,000 dirhams and the saddle, whereas al-Balādhurī describes the payment only as 'such and such and a saddle' (*ʿalā kadhā wa-kadhā wa-raḥl*), omitting the specifics of the money.[83] This difference is critical: Why would al-Balādhurī gloss over this in a work where he provides so many intricate details of payment, where he has already previously included details of the conquest agreement of al-Ḥīra, and where he has elsewhere demonstrated that he does not mind including conflicting reports on different authorities? While it is plausible that al-Balādhurī didn't include the 1000 dirhams' payment because it clashed with or otherwise contradicted what he (or an unnamed patron) wanted the record to contain, this seems very unlikely. After all, if that were the case, al-Balādhurī would have had no reason to include this particular account in the *Futūḥ* at all. It seems far more likely that he – or al-Ḥusayn – simply forgot the specifics of this particular agreement and, because neither was working with an available written source to check it against, they chose, instead, to gloss over it. It is also possible that a later and separate compiler of *Kitāb al-Kharāj* may simply have remembered (or altered) a detail of the tradition to include the specific number.

While Yaḥyā would have been long dead by the time al-Balādhurī was likely preparing the *Futūḥ*, *Kitāb al-Kharāj* did not have to exist in a written form by the time of his death. Rather, it seems likely that one of his students (or even one of his students' students) was the first to actually commit to writing the copious number of traditions attributed to Yaḥyā.[84] A. Ben Shemesh wrote that he believed Yaḥyā must have committed the book to writing himself, for 'how could Yaḥyā, a scholar who wrote several other books, have transmitted orally more than 600 traditions, without writing them down prior to reading them to his students?'[85] Since he has written that, however, many subsequent scholars have made convincing cases for this type of transmission. While Yaḥyā did not have to put into writing a complete form of *Kitāb al-Kharāj,* this did not preclude his utilizing lecture notes for his sessions with students, nor his students' taking their own notes to assist with memorization if the teacher allowed it.[86] And more importantly, Ben Shemesh ignored the surviving manuscript tradition of *Kitāb al-Kharāj* in favour of his own scepticism of oral/aural learning, a tradition which suggests that the work was likely compiled in the lifetime of Ismā'īl b. Muḥammad b. Ismā'īl b. Ṣāliḥ b. 'Abd al-Raḥmān al-Ṣaffār (d. 952 CE/AH 341), a scholar two generations removed from Yaḥyā.[87] Throughout the entire surviving manuscript of the text, al-Ṣaffār is referenced (usually simply as 'Ismā'īl") as the informant for the scribe or compiler in the overwhelming majority of *asānīd*, and appears, along with his own informant, al-Ḥasan b. 'Alī b. 'Affān al-'Āmirī al-Kūfī (usually simply 'al-Ḥasan") in the reading certificates (*samā'āt*) within the manuscript.[88] All of this suggests that in the lifetime of al-Balādhurī, *Kitāb al-Kharāj* did not yet exist in a formalized written form. It may have existed in the form of notes taken by Yaḥyā himself or in notes taken by his students such as al-Ḥusayn, but it seems unlikely to have existed in a final form, and is far more likely to have been what Sebastian Günther suggests should be referred to as a 'literary composition.' In this way, al-Balādhurī's use of the material found in *Kitāb al-Kharāj* suggests that it existed in a more organized form than simple lecture notes, 'characterized by a relatively well thought out concept in the presentation of the material,' but with all other indicators – namely differences in wording, al-Balādhurī's *asānīd* use, and the surviving *Kitāb al-Kharāj* manuscript itself – suggesting that it wasn't brought into a final written form until the lifetime of a later student.[89]

Perhaps most importantly for the case of al-Balādhurī, reliance on an oral or only partially written transmission of Yaḥyā's material over a formalized written one is the presence of al-Ḥusayn himself. If al-Balādhurī had available to him a written copy of *Kitāb al-Kharāj*, he would have had no reason to bother citing an intermediary such as al-Ḥusayn within his own work. Furthermore, as I have stated above, al-Balādhurī does seemingly utilize written materials in other places within the *Futūḥ*, particularly when citing directly from transmitters who were largely deceased before his conscious lifetime. While al-Balādhurī seems to cite that written material through the use of the introductory word *qāla*, despite the substantial number of traditions al-Ḥusayn provides, not a single one of the traditions of al-Ḥusayn is introduced this way, despite their considerable number (Table 3.6).

All of this leads to the position that al-Ḥusayn, as one of the students of Yaḥyā, provided the *Futūḥ* with the traditions of his teacher through direct contact with al-Balādhurī and at a time when *Kitāb al-Kharāj* had not been formally written down.

Table 3.6 Appearances of al-Ḥusayn as informant

	al-Ḥusayn b. 'Alī al-Aswad		
Introductory Phrase	***ḥaddathanī***	***ḥaddathanā***	***qāla***
Page Numbers	10; 10; 12; 12; 12; 12; 13; 14; 14; 14; 24; 25; 32; 76; 77; 79; 84; 84; 85; 86; 89; 97; 97; 97; 97; 179; 179; 204; 217; 256; 298; 300; 300; 301; 303; 325; 326; 326; 327; 329; 335; 336; 430; 486; 505	19; 21; 21; 21; 22; 27; 29; 29; 29; 32; 33; 34; 34; 51; 69; 82; 88; 88; 90; 327; 327; 330; 331; 332; 334; 353; 353; 354; 354; 556; 556; 556; 556; 557; 558; 558; 571	None

Abū 'Ubayd al-Qāsim b. Sallām and *Kitāb al-Amwāl*

Another of al-Balādhurī's most important informants for the *Futūḥ* is al-Qāsim b. Sallām b. 'Abd Allāh al-Khurāsānī, widely known as Abū 'Ubayd, who was born sometime between 770 and 774 CE/AH 154 and 157 in Herāt. Abū 'Ubayd spent his time as a student of Arabic grammar, *ḥadīth*, and Islamic jurisprudence (*fiqh*) in the centres of learning of his time, where his list of teachers and students suggests extended stays in Baṣra and Kūfa. He was appointed as the *Qaḍī* of Tarsus in the year 807–808 CE/AH 192, but eventually came to live in Baghdad by the late 820s. He is said to have left the 'Abbāsid capital in 834 CE/AH 219 to perform the Ḥajj, and came to stay in Mecca, where he died in 838 CE/AH 224.[90]

Abū 'Ubayd is himself said to have been the author of some twenty titles, among his most famous being philological works focused on *gharīb*, or rare words in books, namely the *Gharīb al-Muṣannaf*, *Gharīb al-Qur'ān*, and *Gharīb al-Hadīth*.[91] Only some of these twenty titles survive to the present, and only one of his works of *fiqh*, *Kitāb al-Amwāl* (*The Book of Revenue*). Its survival is invaluable for the purpose of better understanding not only al-Balādhurī's sources in writing the *Futūḥ*, but the reasons why he chose to write his text at all. A comparison between *Kitāb al-Amwāl* and the *Futūḥ* suggests that while al-Balādhurī may have had access to a written form of the text, he likely would have met the ageing Abū 'Ubayd and learned from him directly.

As suggested by the name of the text, the information provided in *Kitāb al-Amwāl* is largely related to the issues surrounding wealth and possession in the early Islamic period. This includes questions of inheritance, taxation on the produce of land (*kharāj*), the poll tax (*jizya*), and perhaps most importantly for our purposes, the status and ownership of lands brought under Muslim control throughout the conquest period. Al-Balādhurī looks favourably upon a substantial number of traditions from Abū 'Ubayd concerning the issues of whether territories conquered by the Muslims were conquered without treaty (*'anwatan*) or by means of some form of peace treaty (*ṣulḥan*). Abū 'Ubayd provides the *Futūḥ* with select conquest accounts of certain regions, but these accounts seem overwhelmingly focused on recording the surrender arrangements (or lack thereof) made between the Muslims and the conquered territories rather than the narrative of conquest itself. The author's interest in Abū 'Ubayd's material is made clear in several instances where he chooses to considerably abridge reports found in *Kitāb al-Amwāl* to excise details that do not directly relate to taxation, or details that could not be classified as interesting for administrative purposes. In some instances, this removal is more subtle: in an abridged account involving an agreement between ʿAmr b. al-ʿĀṣ and the supposed Byzantine Egyptian governor al-Muqawqis, al-Balādhurī chooses to shorten the tradition while deleting mentions of the battle over Alexandria, and a brief letter of the Byzantine emperor Heraclius to the Caliph ʿUmar. This occurs without notice.[92] In another instance, however, this abridgement of materials is overt: in discussing an account involving the Battle of Nihāwand and an elaborate story of the booty gained providing an endowment for certain tribes, al-Balādhurī chooses to remove completely Abū ʿUbayd's narrative of the battle and subsequent capitulation of the city, writing simply, 'Then he [the source's originator] recounted the battle' (*thumma dhakara al-waqʿa*).[93]

Abū ʿUbayd also spends a significant amount of time within his own work utilizing the conquest of certain locations as precedent-setting decisions, in particular, the Prophet's treatment of the oasis of Khaybar in western Arabia, and the conquest of the incredibly fertile region of *al-sawād*. These two locations are juxtaposed by Abū ʿUbayd as separate models for how these lands were to be divided and treated. Khaybar, he writes, was conquered by the Prophet himself, who 'declared it as spoils of war, divided it into five parts, and distributed it' among the Muslims.[94] In the case of the *sawād*, however, the Caliph ʿUmar chose to designate the lands as *fay*', lands whose produce were to remain in the hands of the state in order to benefit the greater Muslim community into posterity.[95] While Abū ʿUbayd chose to explicitly differentiate between these two types of lands appropriated by the conquerors, al-Balādhurī passes over making a direct connection between these two precedents in favour of the quite separate geographic nature of his work.

The similarities between al-Balādhurī's use of the financial and administrative material from al-Ḥusayn/Yaḥyā and Abū ʿUbayd is foreseeable considering the overall focus of the author's work. Yet there is a discernable difference in precisely the details al-Balādhurī selects from each text. He relies on al-Ḥusayn's materials largely to provide specifics on the exact levels of taxation regions agreed to, often detailing the surrender agreements. Abū ʿUbayd's material, however, is far more interested in the classification of these agreements and the land itself. The reasons why *Kitāb al-Amwāl* and, by extension, the *Futūḥ* choose to devote so much space to the details of their capture is clear: how these lands were captured and subsequently designated were important for later bureaucrats to understand. This ensured not only that they be taxed appropriately but that it also covered issues of which lands in certain territories could be bought, sold, gifted, or inherited as private property, and which remained under the control of the central authority. Furthermore, the focus of the early chapters of *Kitāb al-Amwāl* on the authority and responsibility of the ruler suggest the importance of established precedent in the collection of revenue in the ninth-century 'Abbāsid state.

Of the six traditions transmitted by al-Balādhurī originating from Abū 'Ubayd and involving Khaybar and *al-sawād*,[96] none of them are direct quotations from *Kitāb al-Amwāl*.[97] In numerous instances in the *Futūḥ*, al-Balādhurī copies traditions and their chains of transmission in a similar form to what survives in the text of Abū 'Ubayd; generally, the overall content of the accounts remain the same. But unlike the traditions found in the work of Yaḥyā b. Ādam and compiled by al-Balādhurī, more often than not, there are very distinct differences between the form of these accounts in *Kitāb al-Amwāl* and the *Futūḥ*. This includes not only individual word choice, but the organization of complete sentences and even, sporadically, differences in the *asānīd* of these accounts. Examples of these traditions that include identical details but different wording include traditions involving the status of Egypt as having been conquered without covenant (*'aqd*, or *'ahd*),[98] the legality of taking slaves from black tribes in Nubia,[99] and some minor details on the Battle of Bāniqiyyā.[100] In some instances, content remains the same, but along with this different sentence structure comes a completely different *isnād*. In a tradition discussing land grants in al-Yamāma, al-Balādhurī provides a fuller *isnād* that reads Abū 'Ubayd ← al-Ḥarith b. Marra al-Ḥanafī ← Hishām b. Ismā'īl, while the version in *Kitāb al-Amwāl* reads simply 'Sirāj transmitted…' (*wa-l-ma'thūr 'an Sirāj…*).[101] An account discussing the conquest of al-Sūs by Abū Mūsā al-Ash'arī and the execution of the city's leader by the Muslims clearly demonstrates the grammatical and syntactical differences which can occur between the two works:

Al-Balādhurī's Version:

> And it was his eye that was struck at al-Sūs. He said: We besieged its city at the command of Abū Mūsā, and we met fierce resistance. Then, the *dihqān* made terms, agreeing to open the city to him on the condition that he would be provided safe-conduct for himself and one hundred of his household. And thus, he made a covenant with Abū Mūsā, who said to him: 'Separate them.' While he was doing this, Abū Mūsā said to his followers: 'I hope that God will get the better of him.' And so when he had separated the one hundred, God's enemy remained, and Abū Mūsā ordered that he be executed. He cried out, 'Hold on! I can give you great wealth!' But he refused and beheaded him.

Abū 'Ubayd's Version:

> And it was his eye that was struck at al-Sūs. He said: We besieged its city and met fierce resistance, and the army was under the command of Abū Mūsā al-Ash'arī.

And so the *dihqān* made terms, agreeing to open the city to him on the condition that he would be provided safe-conduct for himself and one hundred of his household. And thus, he made a covenant with Abū Mūsā and with whoever was with him. Abū Mūsā said to him: 'Separate them.' While he was doing this, Abū Mūsā said to his followers: 'I hope that God will lead him astray.' And so when he had separated the one hundred, God's enemy remained, and Abū Mūsā ordered it [that he be executed]. He spoke and cried out and offered great wealth, but Abū Mūsā refused and beheaded him.[102]

al-Balādhurī's Version	*Abū 'Ubayd's Version*
وكانت عينه أصيبت بالسوس	وكانت عينه أصيبت بالسوس
قال: حاصرنا مدينتها أميرنا أبو موسى فلقينا جهداً	قال: حاصرنا مدينتها **فلقينا جهداً وأمير الجيش أبو موسى**
ثم صالحه دهقانها على أن يفتح له المدينة ويؤمن	**الأشعرى** فصالحه دهقانها على أن يفتح له المدينة ويؤمن
له منة من أهله ففعل	له مائة من أهله ففعل
فأخذ عهد أبي موسى	فأخذ عهد أبي موسى **الأشعرى ومن معه**
فقال **له**: اعزلهم فجعل يعزلهم	فقال أبو موسى: اعزلهم فجعل يعزلهم
أبو موسى يقول لأصحابه: انى لأرجو أن يغلبه الله	**وجعل** أبو موسى يقول لأصحابه: إنى لأرجو أن **يخدعه** الله
على نفسه	**عن** نفسه
فعزل المنة وبقى عدو الله فأمر به أبو موسى **أن يقتل**	فعزل المائة وبقى عدو الله فأمر به أبو موسى
فنادى رويدك أعطيك مالاً كثيراً	**قال**: فنادى و**بذل** مالاً كثيراً
فأبى وضرب عنقه	فأبى **عليه** وضرب عنقه

The significant differences in sentence structure in so many traditions could be explained by the authorial hand of al-Balādhurī at work, but it seems far more likely to be caused by the 'forking' of the original tradition by Abū 'Ubayd's students prior to *Kitāb al-Amwāl* being formally committed to writing.[103] Al-Balādhurī has demonstrated elsewhere that he would copy exactly some of his source material; his use of Yaḥyā's traditions display this. Goitein previously wrote that al-Balādhurī seems to communicate his traditions with far less editing than his peers, although these assertions are difficult to fully support due to the lack of availability of most of the sources in an original form, and the variations here also contradict aspects of his position.[104] While there are instances where the material found in Yaḥyā's *Kitāb al-Kharāj* differs from the *Futūḥ*, they happen far less often and with even fewer differences than what is seen with Abū 'Ubayd's traditions.

But what exactly can be said about al-Balādhurī's use of Abū 'Ubayd as an informant in the *Futūḥ*? It seems likely that the two would have met personally rather than al-Balādhurī simply relying on the materials his elder had committed to writing. If contact did occur between the two, it seems most likely to have been during the early-mid-830s CE. While we cannot speak to the age of al-Balādhurī in the 830s CE, he would likely have been quite young while the *shaykh* Abū 'Ubayd remained in Baghdad before finally departing the city on his pilgrimage. Additionally, Ibn 'Asākir records that al-Balādhurī heard (*samiʿa*) *ḥadīth* from Abū 'Ubayd,[105] and al-Dhahabī also lists al-Balādhurī among the students who heard directly from Abū 'Ubayd and related traditions from him (*ḥaddatha ʿanhu*).[106] That al-Balādhurī includes material ascribed to Abū 'Ubayd that differs not in the information provided, but in form, style, and in its cited authorities suggests access to the man himself as his direct source. Andreas Görke has also highlighted these subtle differences in the chains of transmission, where, for instance, al-Balādhurī provides an additional link in the chain excluded by the author in the work attributed to him. In one of these instances, al-Balādhurī transmits information on the legality of a Berber tribe selling their women and children into slavery as payment of the *jizya*. Al-Balādhurī's tradition includes the following *isnād*: Abū 'Ubayd ← 'Abd Allāh b. Ṣāliḥ ← al-Layth b. Saʿd ← Yazīd b. Abī Ḥabīb, but the surviving *Kitāb al-Amwāl* does not know Yazīd as the originator of this information.[107] Görke, too, suggests the likelihood that the two would have met in Baghdad, largely owing to al-Balādhurī's style of attributing Abū 'Ubayd's material with the introductory words *ḥaddathanā* ("he informed us") and *ḥaddathanī* ("he informed me"), which he uses seemingly interchangeably (Table 3.7).[108]

Standing on its own, this suggestion is far less secure, but the internal analysis of the *Futūḥ* would seem to confirm Görke's position. There is also the far more telling lack of the introductory word *qāla*, which, as has been mentioned, al-Balādhurī seems to rely upon significantly when consulting sources which

Table 3.7 Appearances of Abū 'Ubayd as informant

	Abū 'Ubayd al-Qāsim b. Sallām		
Introductory Phrase	***ḥaddathanī***	***ḥaddathanā***	***qāla***
Page Numbers[a]	88; 123; 147; 147; 147; 148; 165; 192; 251; 255; 255; 256; 309; 329; 334; 466; 481; 563	8; 13; 13; 18; 20; 24; 28; 29; 31; 36; 41; 49; 86; 96; 101; 111; 112; 254; 255; 265; 281; 281; 300; 330; 373; 469; 555; 557; 557; 558; 558; 559; 559; 560; 561; 561; 561; 562; 563; 564; 564; 565	502; 558

[a]All page numbers are from al-Munajjid's Arabic edition.

were likely accessed by him in a written form. Finally, if we accept the idea that Abū 'Ubayd's work already existed in a written form from which al-Balādhurī learned his information,[109] we would not expect to find the differences in the cited *asānīd* between the two works that exist, nor the significant differences in the style and sentence structure which occur had he been relying on this written form as the basis for his information.[110]

Conclusions

Athamina's original assertion that al-Balādhurī had at his disposal a variety of different sources – both oral and written – in the creation of his works seems confirmed by the source-critical analysis of *Futūḥ al-buldān*. The *Futūḥ* firmly demonstrates the author's reliance not just on the narrative historical tradition of previous generations, but on the scholarly judicial tradition likely born from the eighth/second century and continually developed into his own. He is, however, seemingly innovative in his organization of material and his marriage of the conquest tradition with the interests and needs of the administrative and judicial classes of his time. For while the scant biographical information on al-Balādhurī does not suggest he ever held a judicial post such as *qāḍī*, his teachers and sources utilized reveal a clear interest in the legislative realm of early Islamic society. That material from two jurists, Yaḥyā b. Ādam and Abū 'Ubayd, feature so prominently as sources in the *Futūḥ* is demonstration of his interest in the law. Both men held the position of *qāḍī* in different territories, making them repositories of immense judicial information in the ninth/third century, and their own surviving works corroborate their immense knowledge of legal matters throughout the Islamic world. This all compounds to provide insight on the compilation of knowledge in the ninth/third century, and the place of *Futūḥ al-buldān* as a crucial juncture in this development.

That traditions provided by these two jurists appear in the overwhelming majority of chapters throughout the *Futūḥ* hint at al-Balādhurī's dependence on certain transmitters to provide thematic information not limited to a particular region. We see that the judicial and administrative sources included in the work are largely universal; they are not delineated by geographic exclusivity. In this way, major transmitters like al-Ḥusayn and Abū 'Ubayd could provide vital information on taxation and the classification of lands due to their general expertise on these matters, while not being limited to their reports being clustered in certain regions only. This directly contradicts Duri, who suggested that al-Balādhurī relied on transmitters from certain locales to provide his information, while otherwise leaning on a Medinan school of history.[111] In addition to these two informants, transmitters such as al-Madā'inī, Muḥammad b. Sa'd, and Bakr b. al-Haytham find their traditions used across regions, too, due to their knowledge of specific details of land ownership and the construction and destruction of buildings.

Al-Balādhurī's seemingly intentional decision to demonstrate how he acquired the traditions which make up his text is the final point worth greater elaboration. That al-Balādhurī could not have met at least some of the informants he cites in the *Futūḥ* is irrefutable, as several of those he relied upon were undeniably deceased before his lifetime. In other instances, there was likely little overlap in the lifetime of the informant and al-Balādhurī, and no mention in the biographical record of al-Balādhurī having studied with them directly. In most cases, the author does not explicitly state his reliance on written sources in the creation of the text. But his use of unique introductory words, namely *qāla*, and suggestively shortened chains of transmission served to make clear to his intended audience that certain materials had come to him in a form other than the more traditional oral/aural means of the *majlis*. Precisely how formalized these written materials were in al-Balādhurī's lifetime is difficult to establish. The scepticism towards writing by some portions of the Muslim intelligentsia, however, may mean that these were in the form of *aides-mémoire* or lecture notes taken by students in a session with the teacher that found their way to al-Balādhurī. But that he had access to works by authors such as al-Wāqidī and Abū Mikhnaf in some written form seems undeniable, and the author himself seems to communicate this distinction through his manner of citation.

Notes

1 Khalil Athamina, 'The Sources of al-Balādhurī's *Ansāb al-Ashrāf*, *Jerusalem Studies in Arabic and Islam*, Vol. 5 (1984), 237–62.

2 Kennedy and el Sakkout, 'Book Review: The *Ansāb al-Ashrāf*, Vol. 6B', 410–13.

3 Athamina's discussion was focused on al-Balādhurī's text specifically, but was building on the pioneering work found in Sezgin, *Geschichte*, Vol. 1, 237–56.

4 Athamina, 'Sources', 246–8.

5 de Goeje, 'Praefatio'; 'Abd al-Aziz Duri, *The Rise of Historical Writing Among the Arabs*, ed. and trans. Lawrence I. Conrad (Princeton: Princeton University Press, 1983), 61–2; 'Abd al-Aziz Duri, 'The Iraq School of History to the Ninth Century –

A Sketch', in *Historians of the Middle East,* eds. Bernard Lewis and P. M. Holt (London: Oxford University Press, 1962), 49, 52–3.

6 Goitein, 'The Place of Balādhurī's', 606.

7 On the importance of chains of transmission and their use within the early Islamic legal tradition (with particular reference to *ḥadīth* literature and their use by historians), see Jonathan A. C. Brown, *Hadith: Muhammad's Legacy in the Medieval and Modern World* (Oxford: Oneworld, 2009), esp. 6–8, 41–5; and Tarif Khalidi, *Arabic Historical Thought in the Classical Period* (Cambridge: Cambridge University Press, 1994), esp. 17–30.

8 Here, I use Patricia Crone's oft-quoted description of the brief accounts (*khabar*) that are each introduced by an *isnād*. See Crone, *Slaves on Horses*, 3–17.

9 Sezgin, *Geschichte*, Vol. 1, 29–84; Manfred Fleischhammer, 'Quellenuntersuchungen zum *Kitāb al-Aghānī*' (PhD diss., University of Halle/Saale, 1965).

10 Schacht, *The Origins of Muhammadan Jurisprudence*; G. H. A. Juynboll, *Muslim Tradition: Studies in Chronology, Provenance, and Authorship of Early Ḥadīth* (Cambridge: Cambridge University Press, 1983).

11 Khalil Athamina, 'The Historical Work of al-Ṭabarī and al-Balādhurī: The Author's Attitude Towards the Sources', in *Al-Ṭabarī* ed. Kennedy, 149.

12 H. A. R. Gibb, *Studies on the Civilization of Islam*, ed. Stanford J. Shaw and William R. Polk (Princeton: Princeton University Press, 1962), 111–13; Chase F. Robinson, *Islamic Historiography* (Cambridge: Cambridge University Press, 2003), 97–8; Duri, *Rise of Historical Writing*, 29.

13 Ibn Hishām, *Sīrat al-nabī*, ed. M. M. 'Abd al-Ḥamīd (Cairo: Maktabat Muḥammad 'Alī Ṣubayḥ, 1963), Vol. 3, 764; translation by Athamina, 'al-Ṭabarī and al-Balādhurī', 152. Similarly, al-Balādhurī includes a remarkably similar statement of his own at the beginning of his section on the conquest of Armenia, writing: 'Muḥammad b. Ismā'īl informed me, on the authority of Sākanā [of] Bardha'a and others on the authority of Abū Barā' 'Anbasa b. Baḥr al-Armanī. Muḥammad b. Bishr al-Qalī [also] informed me on the authority of his teachers (*ashyākh*), Barmak b. 'Abd Allāh al-Dabīlī, Muḥammad b. al-Khayyas al-Khilāṭī among others, on the authority of learned people concerning the affairs of Armenia. I have gathered together their traditions, and I repeat some of them [here]. They said (*qālū*):...' *Futūḥ*, 231 (H 305).

14 On the distinction between the *muḥaddithūn* and the *akhbāriyyūn* and their attitudes towards material, see Ella Landau-Tasseron, 'Sayf ibn 'Umar in Medieval and Modern Scholarship', *Der Islam*, Vol. 67, No. 1 (1990), 1–26, esp. 6–12.

15 Khaṭīb al-Baghdādī, *Ta'rīkh Baghdād*, ed. Aḥmad b. al-Ṣiddīq (Cairo: Maktabat al-Khānjī, 1931), Vol. 3, 15–16; Ibn Ḥanbal's dislike of al-Wāqidī's use of the collective *isnād* is explored in Michael Lecker, 'Wāqidī's Account on the Status

of the Jews of Medina: A Study of a Combined Report', *Journal of Near Eastern Studies,* Vol. 54, No. 1 (1995), 15–32, esp. 20–3.

16 See, for instance, a number of times al-Balādhurī does this with traditions learned from Muḥammad b. Sa'd on the authority of al-Wāqidī: *ḥaddathanī Muḥammad b. Sa'd 'an al-Wāqidī fī isnādihī....* *Futūḥ*, 167, 168, 183, 221, 429 (H 216, 217, 238, 289-290; M 66).

17 *Futūḥ,* 280, 13 (H 379-380, 28).

18 *Futūḥ,* 550 (M 242).

19 The medieval Arabic term *munqaṭi'* (cut up) is sometimes used to describe types of *ḥadīth* that are missing links in their chains of transmission.

20 I say 'mostly', as such sources occasionally make reference to an individual who provided information for an account, or whose information they are choosing to contradict. *Asānīd* are an unimportant part of these works, and are almost completely absent. They do, however, often include a superficial nod to the fact that the authors did not witness the events described themselves, but, rather, had the accounts come down to them in some other form. This is done through the regular use of either *qāla* or *qālū* at the beginning of some sections.

21 This is seen throughout the entirety of the work. When only a singular authority is given as a source, he has often chosen to cite the originator of the tradition only. As an example of this, see Abū Yūsuf, *Kitāb al-Kharāj*, 24, 43, 59, 124. More often, however, he chooses to limit his *isnād* by providing a gloss, such as 'some of our learned elders informed me...' instead of a more complete chain of transmission. As examples, see Abū Yūsuf, *Kitāb al-Kharāj*, 13, 14, 35, 65, 67, 74, 126.

22 Ibn Qutayba, *'Uyūn al-akhbār* (Cairo: Dār al-Kutub al-Miṣriyya, 1925–1930), 141; A. Ben Shemesh, *Taxation in Islam*, Vol. 3, *Abū Yūsuf's Kitāb al-Kharāj* (Leiden: E. J. Brill, 1969), 1–3.

23 Michael Cooperson, *Classical Arabic Biography: The Heirs of the Prophets in the Age of al-Ma'mūn* (Cambridge: Cambridge University Press, 2000), 1–23, esp. 4–5.

24 In addition to Cooperson's work cited above, this issue is discussed at length in Khalidi, *Arabic Historical Thought*, 39–48.

25 *Futūḥ,* 373–9 (H 478-480).

26 Specifically, his grandfather Jābir was a secretary for the 'master (*ṣāḥib*) of Egypt'. Ibn al-Nadīm, *Fihrist*, 125.

27 Al-Balādhurī's contemporary Ibn Qutayba (d. 889 CE/286 AH) is another excellent model of this, although he is not known to have written a book primarily concerning financial matters.

28 *Futūḥ,* 230, 368–9 (H 301, 465-466).

29 See, for instance, the discussion of estates and buildings in Baṣra and Kūfa, and the destruction of fortresses in greater Syria. *Futūḥ,* 189–203, 346–54, 425–58 (H 251-64, 442-448; M 67-101).

30 Athamina, 'Sources', 240.

31 Here, for the sake of simplicity and for the benefit of the reader, I am using the numbering of traditions provided by al-Munajjid in his Arabic edition.

32 This was, in fact, something noted by S. D. Goitein in his introduction to the volume he edited of the *Ansāb al-Ashrāf.* Goitein did not, however, explore this position fully, nor did he understand the full extent of al-Balādhurī's use of this written material. See S. D. Goitein, 'Introduction', in *Ansāb al-Ashrāf,* Vol. 5, ed. S. D. Goitein (Jerusalem: Hebrew University Press, 1936), 14–17. Similarly, Athamina elsewhere provided a similarly brief commentary on al-Balādhurī's use of *qāla* in the *Ansāb* in Athamina, 'al-Ṭabarī and al-Balādhurī', 145–6 and in Athamina, 'Introduction,' 15–16.

33 For a thorough discussion of these practices and their differences, see Schoeler, *The Oral and the Written in Early Islam*, especially 28–44; and Schoeler, *The Genesis of Literature in Islam.* Duri has tentatively suggested that al-Balādhurī's use of *qāla* might imply a written source, although he provides no evidence for this point and quickly moves on from it. Duri, *Rise of Historical Writing,* 63.

34 For more on this, see Shawkat M. Toorawa, *Ibn Abī Ṭāhir Ṭayfūr and Arabic Writerly Culture: A Ninth-Century Bookman in Baghdad* (London: Routledge, 2005), 11–31.

35 Here and throughout this work, I will largely conform to the terminology suggested in Sebastian Günther, 'Assessing the Sources of Classical Arabic Compilations: The Issue of Categories and Methodologies', *British Journal of Middle Eastern Studies,* Vol. 32, No. 1 (2005), 75–98. The term guarantor refers to 'any (senior) person in the process of transmission on whom another (junior) individual relies for information is termed a "guarantor" ("Gewährsmann")', while the informant is an individual from whom al-Balādhurī learned his information directly.

36 For instance, within an account discussing a garden in al-Ṭā'if where Yaḥyā b. Ādam is the main authority, Yaḥyā is subsequently cited (*qāla Yaḥyā…*) within the account providing additional information regarding what crops *ṣadaqa* was to be taken on, while another tradition of Abū Ḥanīfa (*qāla Abū Ḥanīfa…*) is provided to contradict Yaḥyā. *Futūḥ,* 69 (H 89).

37 See, for instance, *Futūḥ,* 132, 143, 215, 305, 403–4 (H 170, 184-185, 283, 399-400; M 24).

38 Ibid., 121; 134.

39 While rare, there are a dozen or so instances where al-Balādhurī inexplicably begins a longer *isnād* with *qāla,* with almost all of these appearing in the final

chapters of the work, what Murgotten called appendices. See, for instance, a lone tradition of Abū Ḥafṣ al-Dimashqī on *Futūḥ,* 139 (H 179); and a tradition of Ibn Sa'd on *Futūḥ,* 577 (M 268).

40 On the importance of this terminology within the Islamic legal tradition, see Brown, *Hadith*, 90–2.

41 See, for instance, *Futūḥ,* 306 (H 400).

42 As will be discussed, two of the seven figures below are almost certain to have had significantly overlapping lifespans with al-Balādhurī. They are included here because the rest of the criteria are met, and because al-Balādhurī's unique use of their material in these instances deserves further explanation.

43 Yāqūt, *Irshād*, Vol. 2, 127.

44 Referring to a work as a 'book' does not necessarily mean the same as what a modern audience would traditionally think of: namely, a work set out in a final, written form. For more on this point and the use of the term 'book' in the early Arabic historical tradition, see Günther, 'Due Results', 10–12 and Schoeler, *The Oral and the Written in Early Islam*, 33–6.

45 Ibn al-Nadīm, *Fihrist*, 201–2; Yāqūt, *Irshād*, Vol. 6, 220–2.

46 'Moreover, a number of traditions cited in al-Balādhurī's *Futūḥ,* concerning the Arab conquests of parts of the eastern province, should be seen as evidence of another monograph on the subject of the Muslim conquests, entitled *Kitāb Futūḥ Khurāsān*, as it appears in the list of al-Najāshī'. Khalil Athamina, 'Abū Mikhnaf', *EI*[3].

47 Ibn al-Nadīm, *Fihrist*, 206–13.

48 This work, *Kitāb al-Maghāzī* (*The Book of the Prophetic Expeditions*), is one of several surviving works attributed to al-Wāqidī, but the only one without dubious citation. Among the most famous works attributed to al-Wāqidī is the *Kitāb Futūḥ al-Shām* (*The Book of the Conquest of Syria*), which has been firmly argued by western scholars for the bulk of the last century to be a much later compilation.

49 Reinhard Weipert, 'Abū 'Ubayda', *EI*[3].

50 The primary example of al-Balādhurī's willingness to cite an intermediary student comes with the case of al-Ḥusayn b. 'Alī al-Aswad, which will be discussed at length below.

51 On the relationship between al-Wāqidī and Ibn Sa'd, see Khalidi, *Arabic Historical Thought*, 44–8.

52 This list includes Hishām b. 'Ammār, Abū Ḥafṣ al-Dimashqī, Muḥammad b. Muṣaffā, Muḥammad b. 'Abd al-Raḥmān b. Sahm, Aḥmad b. Mard al-Anṭākī, 'Affān b. Muslim, 'Abd al-A'lā b. Ḥammād, 'Alī b. al-Madīnī, 'Abd Allāh b. Ṣāliḥ al-'Ijlī, Muṣ'ab al-Zubayrī, Abū 'Ubayd, 'Uthmān b. Abī Shayba, al-Madā'inī, and Muḥammad b. Sa'd. Yāqūt, *Irshād*, Vol. 2, 127.

53 Yāqūt, *Irshād*, Vol. 2, 127.

54 Schoeler, *The Oral and the Written in Early Islam*, 35; Ilkka Lindstedt, 'The Transmission of al-Madā'inī's Material: Historiographical Studies' (PhD diss., University of Helsinki, 2013), 33–5.

55 On al-Madā'inī, see Ilkka Lindstedt, 'The Transmission of al-Madā'inī's Material' and Ilkka Lindstedt, 'The Transmission of al-Madā'inī's Historical Material to al-Balādhurī and al-Ṭabarī: A Comparison and Analysis of Two *Khabars*', in *Studia Orientalia*, Vol. 114, *Travelling Through Time: Essays in Honor of Kaj Öhrnberg*, eds. Sylvia Akar, Jaako Hämeen-Anttila and Inka Nokso-Koivisto (Helsinki: Finnish Oriental Society, 2013), 41–59. Where we disagree, however, is on Lindstedt's suggestion ('al-Balādhurī and al-Ṭabarī', 52) that al-Balādhurī may have been using unnamed oral intermediaries for al-Madā'inī's material in the text. While this is possible, I believe it is less likely because of – as I mention below – al-Balādhurī's willingness to cite an intermediary elsewhere, notably in the case of the material he uses from al-Ḥusayn b. 'Alī b. al-Aswad.

56 Wadad al-Qadi, 'The Names of Estates in State Registers Before and After the Arabization of the "Dīwāns"', in *Umayyad Legacies: Medieval Memories from Syria to Spain*, ed. Antoine Borrut and Paul M. Cobb (Leiden: Brill, 2010), 255–80.

57 *Futūḥ*, 429 (M 65-66). This reading is supported by al-Qadi, 'Arabization of the "Dīwāns"', 276.

58 Ibid., 431 (M 67-68).

59 Ibid., 451 (M 93).

60 Al-Dhahabī, *Ta'rīkh al-Islām*, ed. 'Umar al-Tadmurī (Beirut: Dār al-Kitāb al-'Arabī, 1987–1993), Vol. 12, 298.

61 Abū Mikhnaf appears more often in the *Futūḥ* than Abū Mas'ūd when one considers his appearances as a guarantor of a different informant's information, but not as the primary informant himself.

62 Al-Mizzī, *Tahdhīb al-Kamāl fī asmā' al-rijāl*, ed. Bashshār 'Awwād Ma'rūf (Beirut: Mu'assasat al-Risāla, 1980–1992), Vol. 2, 391.

63 *Futūḥ*, 331 (H 427).

64 See, for instance, *Futūḥ*, 12, 13, 21, 22, 29, 32, 88, 300, 334, 430 (H 27, 28, 37, 38, 46-47, 49, 111, 393, 431; M 67).

65 *Futūḥ*, 85, 86 (H 109, 110).

66 *Futūḥ*, 326–30 (H 422-426).

67 Here, I refer to the lands of northern (*al-jazīra*) and southern (*al-sawād*) Mesopotamia.

68 Al-Dhahabī, *Siyar a'lām al-nubalā'*, 140.

69 This includes 'Umar referring to the Kūfans as 'the head of the Arabs' and 'the most distinguished of men.' *Futūḥ*, 353–4 (H 448).

70 Ibn Qutayba, *Kitāb al-Ma'ārif*, ed. Saroite Okacha (Cairo, 1960), 516; A. Ben Shemesh, *Taxation in Islam*, Vol. 1, *Yaḥyā ben Ādam's* Kitāb al-Kharāj (Leiden: E. J. Brill, 1958), 2; Cengiz Kallek, 'Yaḥyā ibn Ādam's *Kitāb al-Kharādj*: Religious

Guidelines for Public Finance', *Journal of the Economic and Social History of the Orient*, Vol. 44, No. 2 (2001), 108–11.

71 Ibn al-Nadīm, *Fihrist*, 67, 78, 82, 549.

72 *Futūḥ*, 303–4 (H 398); Yaḥyā b. Ādam, *Kitāb al-Kharāj*, 35–6.

73 See, for instance, a tradition where the Prophet chose not to allow a salt mine to enter private ownership because he was told that the mine gave salt 'like the water of a well'. *Futūḥ*, 88 (H 111); Yaḥyā b. Ādam, *al-Kharāj*, 76.

74 *Futūḥ*, 85 (H 108-109); Yaḥyā b. Ādam, *al-Kharāj*, 83–4.

75 *Futūḥ*, 85 (H 109); Yaḥyā b. Ādam, *al-Kharāj*, 83–4.

76 Waines, 'The Third Century Internal Crisis of the Abbasids', 282–306; Kennedy, 'The Decline and Fall', 11–15; Michele Campopiano, 'State, Land Tax, and Agriculture in Iraq from the Arab Conquests to the Crisis of the Abbasid Caliphate (Seventh-Tenth Centuries)', *Studia Islamica*, Vol. 107 (2012), 1–37. This is also discussed in greater length in Chapter 2.

77 *Futūḥ*, 256 (H 343).

78 Ibid., 298 (H 391).

79 Similar questions were considered and discussed by Norman Calder when looking at judicial works from the early Islamic period, including *Kitāb al-Kharāj* of Abū Yūsuf. See Calder, *Early Muslim Jurisprudence*, 122–4, 161–97.

80 James Robson, 'The *Isnād* in Muslim Tradition', in *The Ḥadīth*, ed. Mustafa Shah (London: Routledge, 2010), Vol. 2, 19.

81 Aside from *Kitāb al-Kharāj*, Ibn al-Nadīm attributes to him four other works: *Kitāb al-Qirā'āt* (*The Book of Qur'ān Readings*), *Kitāb Mujarrad aḥkām al-Qur'ān* (*The Book of Affirmation of the Judgments of the Qur'ān*), *Kitāb al-Farā'iḍ* (*The Book of Inheritance*) and another titled *Kitāb al-Zawāl* (*The Book of Cessation*, or perhaps, *The Book of Noontime Prayer*). Ibn al-Nadīm, *Fihrist*, 78, 82, 549.

82 Yaḥyā b. Ādam ← al-Ḥasan b. Ṣāliḥ ← al-Aswad b. al-Qays ← The father of al-Aswad b. al-Qays.

83 *Futūḥ*, 300 (H393); Yaḥyā b. Ādam, *al-Kharāj*, 36.

84 For a similar discussion on the work of Abū Yūsuf, see Calder, *Early Muslim Jurisprudence*, 144–52.

85 Ben Shemesh, *Taxation in Islam* Vol. 1, 9.

86 For more on this, see Günther, 'Due Results', 10–11; Schoeler, *The Oral and the Written in Early Islam*, 33–7.

87 This was also the position of Th. W. Juynboll, *Le Livre de L'impôt Foncier de Yahyā ibn Ādam* (Leiden: Brill, 1896), v–ix.

88 Ben Shemesh, *Taxation in Islam* Vol. 1, 8, 167–72; see also G. Vajda, 'Quelques Certificats de Lecture dans les Manuscrits Arabes de la Bibliothèque Nationale de Paris: La Transmission du *Kitāb al-Ḫarāğ* de Yaḥyā b. Ādam', *Arabica*, Vol. 1, No. 3 (1954), 337–42.

89 'On the one hand, these writings give us the impression of being quite plainly more than simple <<lecture-notes>>, as they are known and mentioned in medieval sources with a title, and since they deal with a special literary subject and seem to have been brought by the <<authors>> themselves into a literary form that is characterized by a relatively well thought out concept in the presentation of the material. On the other hand, there are clear signs that the works of this type have not yet developed into <<real books>>, but were first brought into a final written form by a student of the author in question'. Günther, 'Due Results', 11–12.

90 Al-Dhahabī, *Siyar a'lām al-nubalā'*, Vol. 10, 491–2; Reinhard Weipert, 'Abū 'Ubayd al-Qāsim b. Sallām', *EI*^{3}.

91 Ibn al-Nadīm, *Fihrist*, 156–7.

92 *Futūḥ*, 256–7 (H 343-344); Abū 'Ubayd al-Qāsim b. Sallām, *Kitāb al-Amwāl*, 142.

93 In the original, Abū 'Ubayd includes a heroic depiction of the battle and the topos of the 'fallen commanders', where the Caliph 'Umar details who is to be in charge of the battle should the commander be killed, and who should be in charge should the second commander fall, and so on. *Futūḥ*, 373–4 (H 474-475); Abū 'Ubayd, *al-Amwāl*, 652–4. On the topos of the fallen commanders, see Albrecht Noth and Lawrence I. Conrad, *The Early Arabic Historical Tradition: A Source-Critical Study* (Princeton: The Darwin Press, 1994), 120–1.

94 Abū 'Ubayd, *al-Amwāl*, 60.

95 On the classification of *fay'* in the early Islamic period, see Andrew Marsham, 'Fay'', *EI*^{3}.

96 Al-Balādhurī quotes Abū Ubayd on the sealing of the necks of *dhimmī* and the collection of tax from them at al-Khāniqīn. While this specific tradition doesn't appear in *Kitāb al-Amwāl*, more general traditions of neck-sealing are mentioned. Similarly, al-Balādhurī transmits accounts from Abū 'Ubayd of the Prophet capturing Khaybar and dividing its produce into fifths in a similar manner to those found in the *Kitāb*, but the traditions are not overly similar in detail, nor do they include the same *asānīd*. On neck-sealing, see *Futūḥ*, 334 (H 430); Abū 'Ubayd, *al-Amwāl*, 52; and Chase F. Robinson, 'Neck-Sealing in Early Islam', *Journal of the Economic and Social History of the Orient*, Vol. 48, No. 3 (2005), 401–41. On Khaybar, see *Futūḥ*, 31 (H 48); Abū 'Ubayd, *al-Amwāl*, 55–6, 60.

97 Andreas Görke has mentioned this, writing: 'Bis auf eine ließen sich zu allen diesen Traditionen Parallelen im *Kitāb al-Amwāl* finden'. Görke, *Das* Kitāb al-Amwāl, 92.

98 A number of his traditions on the conquest of Egypt, for instance, and its status as having been conquered '*anwātan* are repeated near verbatim from *Kitāb al-Amwāl*, including a speech reportedly given by 'Amr b. al-'Āṣ that all of the people of Egypt except Anṭābulus could be subjected to whatever he saw fit because of their lack

of a covenant. Others, however, include slightly modified wording and sentence structure. *Futūḥ*, 254, 255, 255, 256 (H 342, 343-344); Abū 'Ubayd, *al-Amwāl*, 140, 142, 144.

99 Again, certain words differ. *Futūḥ*, 281 (H 380); Abū 'Ubayd, *al-Amwāl*, 146.

100 This tradition not only includes different wording, but is likewise abridged. Al-Balādhurī chooses to remove details surrounding who also participated in the battles of Mihrān and al-Qādisiyya. *Futūḥ*, 309; Abū 'Ubayd, *al-Amwāl*, 83.

101 *Futūḥ*, 111 (H 141); Abū 'Ubayd, *al-Amwāl*, 280–1.

102 *Futūḥ*, 477 (M 115); Abū 'Ubayd, *al-Amwāl*, 132–3.

103 Similarly, there is considerable overlap between the *Futūḥ* and *Kitāb al-Amwāl* of Ibn Zanjawayh (d. ca. 865 CE/251 AH), but it would not appear that al-Balādhurī received this overlapping information from his contemporary. Rather, the two were both students of Abū 'Ubayd's, and transmitted material on his authority, and the analysis of these overlapping traditions demonstrates this. Ibn Zanjawayh never appears as a named informant in the *Futūḥ*.

104 'A comparison with the parallel sources will prove that Balādhurī in large portions of his book [the *Ansāb*] reproduces the complete version given by his predecessors; sometimes he preserves a longer and more authoritative copy than any other writer. Even when he abridges, his version at times includes passages that are nearer to the original than Ṭabarī's for instance'. Goitein, 'Place of Balādhurī's', 605–6.

105 Ibn 'Asākir, *Dimashq*, Vol. 6, 74.

106 Al-Dhahabī, *Siyar a'lām al-nubalā'*, Vol. 10, 492.

107 Görke, *Das* Kitāb al-Amwāl, 93–4; *Futūḥ* 265 (H 353-354); Abū 'Ubayd, *al-Amwāl*, 146. Similarly, Ibn 'Abd al-Ḥakam's *Futūḥ Miṣr* includes the same tradition on the authority of Abū'Ubayd and is also missing Yazīd as a link in the chain. Ibn 'Abd al-Ḥakam, *Kitāb Futūḥ Miṣr wa-akhbāruhā*, ed. Charles Cutler Torrey (New Haven: Yale University Press, 1922), 170.

108 Görke, *Das* Kitāb al-Amwāl, 91.

109 Information which, unfortunately, the three surviving manuscripts, including the earliest from 1171 CE/567 AH, cannot provide. For a discussion of these manuscripts, see Görke, *Das* Kitāb al-Amwāl, 43.

110 This is not to assume, however, that Görke is wrong in his assertion that *Kitāb al-Amwāl* existed in a written form during the author's lifetime. Rather, my suggestion here is that the evidence for al-Balādhurī learning directly from Abū 'Ubayd himself is convincing, and it seems more likely that the *Futūḥ* contains traditions al-Balādhurī committed to memory and then subsequently transmitted, rather than relying on some written form that was likely not circulating widely in his lifetime.

111 Duri, *Rise of Historical Writing*, 63.

4

The content and themes of the text

> *The* Futūḥ *of Balādhurī face in several directions: the accuracy of the civil servant, the taste of the man of letters quoting verse that seems genuine and contemporaneous, the scholarly concerns of the* faqīh *citing at length the debates of lawyers on issues of land-tax and of war. These leave little room for fantasy or miracle, for the conquests are transfigured into the genesis and development of empire.*[1]

Tarif Khalidi's comments above on al-Balādhurī's *Futūḥ al-buldān* summarize the likely intention of the text's existence: a depository of information on the Islamic state and the development of Islamic rule. Despite the fact that modern historians and litterateurs of early Islam often note the sober nature of the *Futūḥ* in comparison with substantially more attractive literature the Islamic world produced in the early centuries, there is a distinguishable purpose and method behind the form the book takes that is worth exploring entirely. There are identifiable themes al-Balādhurī seems to have had in mind as he brought together the materials which make up the *Futūḥ*. It is to the identification and analysis of the major themes of the text that the present chapter now turns, in an attempt to ascertain how al-Balādhurī 'transfigures' his material into the embodiment of two centuries of imperial administration in the Middle East. While al-Balādhurī may not have had full awareness that he was contributing to already established genres and subgenres of the early Arabic historical tradition in his *Futūḥ al-buldān*, he does appear to have had a clear and coherent vision of the types of information relevant for his imagined audience in the creation of the text.

As with Chapter 2, we must consider fully the backdrop of al-Balādhurī's authorship of the *Futūḥ* apropos of the events of the ninth/third century and the state of Arabic writerly culture at that time. Al-Balādhurī's lifetime was not the genesis of this written Arabic tradition, but it remained in a very early phase characterized by change and experimentation. As Chase Robinson has written of the developments in Arabic historical writing in the ninth/third century:

> It was one thing for a Kufan to embellish some family history by crowing (often at the expense of the Basrans) about his heroic participation in a Kufan conquest, but when a historian collated Kufan conquests with Basran conquests, integrated the resulting collation in a work on the conquests as a whole, and, finally, integrated this putative conquest work into a universal history, the end product is unmistakably imperial in design. Individual history, tribal history, local history, Islamic history – a great deal depends on perspective, and perspective is what our historians were imposing on their narratives.
>
> So the amalgamation of disparate and fragmented accounts in the large, synthetic works of the mid-ninth century represents more than an ingenious solution to a thorny problem of how to organize all the material made increasingly available to historians through the passing of time and the production of knowledge. It marks a massive project of rethinking history, in which contesting visions and versions of the past were integrated (and, to a large extent, harmonized) according to an imperial project.[2]

Robinson's commentary on these developments during this period resonates clearly, and al-Balādhurī's work as an 'imperial project' seems apt given this description. While there remains no evidence that either the *Futūḥ* or *Ansāb al-ashrāf* were works requested or sanctioned by the caliph himself, the previous chapters have worked to demonstrate that the *Futūḥ* seems certain to have been born from those involved in the central administration of the Islamic state. In Robinson's assertion that the ninth century saw the establishment of these 'imperial projects' within Islamic historiography, we find the *Futūḥ* as the embodiment of this imperial narrative. It does not need the behest of a head of state to be described as such; it builds towards an overall goal of cataloguing and organizing the state's successes and property, while serving as the epitome of strong central administration in the late antique and early medieval periods.

This chapter, then, will continue to look at the entirety of al-Balādhurī's *Futūḥ* in order to identify contextual themes, anecdotes, and motifs, which can help us further understand his intentions in the creation of his text. It will be far more inward-looking, but as with Chapter 5, it will continue to compare both the content and style of al-Balādhurī's book with the surviving Arabic works of his contemporaries and near-contemporaries. It will also home in on al-Balādhurī's omissions of material that was almost certainly available to him. In doing so, we will have a better sense of the authorial hand of al-Balādhurī in the stitching of these previously separate traditions that he has chosen to weave together into his singular narrative effort. In its content, the *Futūḥ's* transmission of settlement agreements, information on the produce and resources of the Islamic lands, and the construction of cities and public works projects demonstrates the author's deep focus on the practical affairs of the Islamic state. And yet, despite his focus on this material – much of which can be seen as archival or serving an archival purpose – this chapter will also consider the literary aspects of the text, its approach in depicting a number of important figures of the early Islamic state, and its use of poetry in the communication of its content and themes. All of this contributes to *Futūḥ al-buldān* becoming a 'site of memory' for the earliest Islamic centuries.

Administering conquest: The conquest context and al-Balādhurī's presentation of history

How, though, does al-Balādhurī demonstrate his interest in creating an 'imperial project' to the reader of the text? It is most clearly seen through an identification of the common threads which course through the whole *Futūḥ*, the recurring themes and features of the text that are present from beginning to end. Some of these features are more obvious than others; while al-Balādhurī may not have called his book *Futūḥ al-buldān* himself, any reader will find it apparent that the vast majority of traditions which make up the text date from the period of the greater Islamic conquests of the seventh and eighth centuries. Less immediately obvious, though, is how the information al-Balādhurī chose to include in his book demonstrates his overall focus on the administration of the empire. In a number of cases, it can be almost certainly established that al-Balādhurī had access to a body of traditions which would have greatly aided his creation of a narrative work on the early Islamic conquests; and yet, much of these traditions are passed over, with the author favouring, instead, those which were more fit for his intentions.

Up to this current chapter, the present research has been continually building the argument that al-Balādhurī's *Futūḥ*, while focusing on the traditions and policies which developed during this period, was not created with the primary purpose of serving as a narrative of the Islamic conquest period. The informants and sources involved in this process include figures such as al-Madā'inī (d. 843 CE/AH 228), Abū Mikhnaf (d. 774 CE/AH 157), and al-Wāqidī (d. 822–823 CE/AH 207), who are famed for their transmission of historical *akhbār* detailing the conquests and the Umayyad period, and who created books of this material on their own.[3] On their knowledge, Ibn al-Nadīm (d. 987–988 CE/AH 377) transmits the words of Aḥmad b. al-Ḥārith al-Khazzāz on these three figures, among the most important transmitters of information in the *Futūḥ*:

> The scholars (*al-ʿulamāʾ*) have said that Abū Mikhnaf [excelled] on the subject of (*bi-amr*) Iraq, its historical traditions and its conquest (*akhbāruhā wa-futūḥuhā*) over others; al-Madāʾinī on the subject of Khurāsān, India (*al-hind*), and Persia (*fāris*); and al-Wāqidī on the subject of the Ḥijāz and prophetic biography (*al-sīra*). They shared together in [the knowledge of] the conquest of Syria (*al-shām*).[4]

None of these works on the conquest period of the early caliphate survives with the exception of al-Wāqidī's *Kitāb al-maghazī* (*Book of Prophetic Expeditions*), where there is only minimal thematic overlap between the primary interests of that book (prophetic biography) and al-Balādhurī's *Futūḥ*. Despite this, however, an enormous number of traditions from these authors' works endure in not just al-Balādhurī's surviving works, but also in the works of many early authors of Arabic texts such as Khalīfa b. Khayyāṭ (d. 854 CE/AH 239), Muḥammad b. Saʿd (d. 845 CE/AH 230), ʿUmar b. Shabba (d. 878 CE/AH 262), and al-Ṭabarī (d. 923 CE/AH 310). While their traditions are often discussed for their narrative quality and analysed for the information they provide for a reconstruction of the early Islamic period, the traditions al-Balādhurī employs by these scholars are selected less for their narrative cohesiveness than their value for al-Balādhurī's overall purpose of cataloguing long-lasting administrative decisions. This is precisely because the thematic focus of *Futūḥ al-buldān* is not simply on the general factual developments of the conquest and Umayyad period, but specifically on how the Islamic state was founded and afterwards advanced.

To use the case of al-Madāʾinī as an example, of the 41 traditions attributed to him within the *Futūḥ*, the overwhelming majority directly deal with the affairs of state, such as the construction of public works (the planting of palm trees in al-Ghāba,[5] the creation of a dam and canal near Medina and Baṣra);[6] the classification of lands and personal wealth (tax on the inhabitants of Ṭāʾif,[7] (a letter of the Caliph ʿUmar b. al-Khaṭṭāb (r. 634–644 CE/AH 13–23) rebuking ʿAmr b. al-ʿĀṣ while placing a claim over his wealth and possessions);[8] a discussion on the use of resources (a letter from the Caliph ʿUmar b. ʿAbd al-ʿAzīz (r. 717–720 CE/AH 99–101) regarding the produce of Oman (*ʿUmān*) being used for the needy of Baṣra);[9] and several appearances in the final thematic chapters of the work detailing the traditional use of the seal on official documents and a single tradition on coinage.[10] Additionally, al-Balādhurī provides several lines of poetry transmitted by al-Madāʾinī, one of which is a lengthy account which advises the

Caliph ʿUmar b. al-Khaṭṭāb to be watchful of the accrual of wealth and expenses by his administrators (*ʿummāl*) of al-Ahwāz and elsewhere.[11]

The use of Abū Mikhnaf and al-Wāqidī's traditions will often augment the conquest narrative of al-Balādhurī's text, but are still regularly used not for their descriptive value of the conquests, but for their discussion of matters of state – just as al-Madāʾinī's are employed. On Abū Mikhnaf's 23 traditions,[12] the majority are directly concerned with the details of battles. More of his traditions are concerned with the affairs of battle than any other single transmitter in the text, but as is the case with the *Futūḥ*, there is still little detail of how battles actually progressed.[13] Instead, his traditions focus on who was in command of the armies, when battles occurred, and whether a location resisted the conquest or made a peace agreement. In a number of cases, however, Abū Mikhnaf's traditions provide the names and activities of governors over an array of regions, but especially in the eastern provinces, such as this one:

> ʿUthmān b. Abī al-ʿĀṣ personally crossed the sea to Fārs and landed at Tawwaj, conquered it, built the mosque, made it a home (*dāran*) for the Muslims, and settled the ʿAbd al-Qays and other tribes there. He made incursions from it against Arrajān, which bordered it. Afterwards, he went from Fārs to Oman and al-Baḥrayn, in accordance with a letter of ʿUmar instructing him to do that.[14]

He also provides a tradition detailing the much-discussed issue of the Arab tribe of Banū Taghlib, Christians who chose to remain in their religion while having a special tax dispensation over other non-Muslims owing to their status as Arabs.[15]

In the case of al-Wāqidī, who provides extensive conquest accounts throughout the *Futūḥ*, he also provides a great amount of material in three of the thematic chapters at the end of the book: on the stipends (*ʿaṭāʾ*) established by ʿUmar, on the matter of coinage, and on the near eastern scribal tradition. Of these three transmitters, he is the one who provides the material most used by al-Balādhurī for the narrative reconstruction of the conquests themselves. The biographical information on al-Wāqidī attributes to him several works concerning the conquests – and it has at times been dubiously suggested that a portion of his books have survived.[16] It seems quite likely, based both on the titles provided by Ibn al-Nadīm and on al-Balādhurī's citation style cited in Chapter 3, that material from his *Book of the Conquest of Syria* (*Kitāb Futūḥ al-Shām*), *Book of the Conquest of Iraq* (*Kitāb Futūḥ al-ʿIrāq*), and *Book of the Historical Traditions of Mecca* (*Kitāb Akhbār Makka*) are all found in *Futūḥ al-buldān*. It is a second category of his contributions, however – which seem likely to have been legal/*ḥadīth* texts or epistles – from where the bulk of al-Balādhurī's reused material likely derives. The descriptive titles of these works provided by Ibn al-Nadīm include *The Claims of the Quraysh and the Anṣār to Land Grants* (*Kitāb madāʿī Quraysh wa-l-Anṣār fi-l-qaṭāʾiʿ*), *The Establishment by ʿUmar of the Registers and Classifications of Tribes* (*Waḍʿ ʿUmar al-dawāwīn wa-taṣnīf al-qabāʾil*), and *The Book of Minting Gold Coins and Silver Coins* (*Kitāb ḍarb al-danānīr wa-l-darāhim*).[17] All of these likely would have contained information on the matters found in the thematic final chapters of the *Futūḥ* (where we find a substantial number of traditions of al-Wāqidī), but also are scattered throughout the text's regional chapters.[18]

Of note regarding the *akhbāriyyūn* involved in the transmission of conquest material in the early Arabic tradition is a significant omission from al-Balādhurī's surviving works: that of the prominent *akhbārī* Sayf b. ʿUmar al-Tamīmī (*fl. ca.* late 700s/late 100s). Sayf, often heavily criticized as a traditionist by a considerable number of his near-contemporaries, has had his traditions influentially survive into posterity, in no small part because of the jurist al-Ṭabarī's selection of his material for his own *Taʾrīkh*.[19] For both the *Futūḥ* and the *Ansāb*, however, al-Balādhurī makes almost no explicit use of the copious conquest traditions of Sayf, perhaps the most glaring omission of any known source on the conquests in the entirety of these works. Fortunately, we are also provided important insight into the fact that this omission was almost certainly intentional – either directly or indirectly – because the *Futūḥ* shows an awareness of Sayf as a transmitter of historical material.[20] The *Futūḥ* includes two accounts which mention Sayf: one as a guarantor within a larger chain of transmission, with the informant named as Muḥammad b. ʿUqba b. Mukrim al-Ḍabbī, and the other with only him named.[21]

The omission of Sayf's conquest accounts within the *Futūḥ* is revealing. Even one of the traditions which al-Balādhurī chooses to include illuminates his interests in the creation of the *Futūḥ*, as despite Sayf's reputation in the transmission of *Futūḥ* material, his tradition in al-Balādhurī's section on 'al-Dīnawar, Māsabadhān, and Mihrijānqadhaf' is concerned not with the conquest of al-Jibāl, but only with how a nearby mountain peak earned its name:

> When the Muslims invaded al-Jibāl, they passed by the eastern summit called *Sinn Sumayra*,- Sumayra being a woman of the Ḍabba from the Banū Muʿāwiya b. Kaʿb b. Thaʿlaba b. Saʿd b. Ḍabba, and one of the Emigrants (*al-Muhājirāt*). Sumayra had a tooth [protruding], hence the name of the peak *Sinn Sumayra*.[22]

That Sayf does not feature prominently in the *Futūḥ* is not especially confounding, as his traditions found in al-Ṭabarī's history and the portion of his own work which has survived demonstrate that the stylistic characteristics of the *futūḥ* theme, which will be discussed in Chapter 5 were staples of his *akhbār*. There was only minimal room for tales of valour on the battlefield in a book focused on the affairs of the state, and so Sayf's work could be easily excluded for this reason alone.[23] More concerning, however, is the lack of *any* of Sayf's traditions in the far more elaborate (and altogether lengthier) *Ansāb*. This strongly suggests that al-Balādhurī may have had a negative attitude towards Sayf's material to omit it almost entirely from his writing.

There is a complication, however, in dissecting al-Balādhurī's conquest traditions in the text, namely his use of *ikhtiṣār* (amalgamation, summarization) via the introductory phrase *qālū* discussed in Chapter 3. These traditions tend to begin almost every chapter of the *Futūḥ*, and they provide the context for the entire section. They were likely an amalgamation of a number of previously separate materials which al-Balādhurī had available, and where he felt it unnecessary to cite each piece of information and its informant individually; instead, he favoured a more cohesive narrative structure which provided the details on how a region came to be controlled by the Muslims. Al-Balādhurī had at his disposal an immense amount of material which would have greatly aided the creation of a book which provided a historical overview of the early Islamic period, or which intended to demonstrate the strength of the ruling regime and of the Muslim community as God's chosen as its primary goals. Despite the availability of this material, however, he either chooses to pass over it or largely merge it all at the beginning of each chapter. Did important *akhbārī* such as Sayf have their traditions folded into a narrative as part of this unification process? Possibly, but the surviving form of the text and the alterations made by al-Balādhurī to these traditions makes it impossible to say this with confidence.

What can be ascertained from these processes, however, is that the form the *Futūḥ* came to take was the deliberate choice of its author. He had at his disposal a substantial amount of components from the leading historical transmitters of the early Islamic period – including, but not limited to, the four discussed above – and his selection (and omission) of material from among these sources demonstrates intent and a clear vision. That vision involved the selection of accounts which provided information on the historical and legal practices integral to the founding of the Islamic state. The types of accounts which reveal this clear motivation, however, came not just from a variety of sources, but were also found in a variety of forms. All of them, however, focused on an imperial project relevant for the officials involved in the running of the state.

Conquered status and settlement agreements

Any reader of the *Futūḥ* is immediately struck by the huge number of traditions which, within every chapter, purport to provide the agreements the Muslim conquerors made with subjugated peoples during the conquests. The importance of these agreements to the management of the Islamic world under the ʿAbbāsids appears to have been long-standing, despite the fact that they were almost exclusively made in the first century of Islamic history. These agreements concerned how lands and their proceeds came to be an entitlement of the Islamic state, and their appearance in a wide variety of sources concerning the conquest period strongly indicates their continued relevance or, perhaps, an increased importance as time passed and the encumbrances of earlier generations began to chafe. This is explicitly shown in a statement made in the jurist Abū Yūsuf's (d. 798 CE/AH 182) *Kitāb al-Kharāj,* which includes this important passage concerning a disagreement between the ʿAbbāsid state and the people of Edessa over the issue of taxation and the state's right to proceeds from the provinces:

> By way of proof, learned people argue (*fa-ahl al-ʿilm bi-l-ḥujja yaqūlūna*): our right is in our possession, and those before you held us to it; it is [also] established in your records (*wa-huwa thābit fī dawāwīnikum*). You are now ignorant, as we are now ignorant, of how things were at the beginning (*wa-qad jahiltum wa-jahilnā kayfa kāna awwal al-amr*). How can you see fit to impose on us something for which you can provide no established precedent, and how can you break from this practice, which is verifiable in our records, and according to which we still operate?[24]

Within the *Futūḥ's* discussion on Nubia, we also find further mention of the problems which could arise when the state did not have proper records or evidence of agreements. In this case, too, we have an example where this reportedly occurred concerning an agreement between the Nubians and the ʿAbbāsids dating from the reign of the Caliph al-Mahdī (r. 775–785 CE/AH 158–169):[25]

> [The Nubians] claimed recently that the tribute (*al-baqṭ*) is not due from them every year. The tribute was demanded from them in the caliphate of al-Mahdī, at which time they contended that this tribute was a part of what they took as slaves from their enemies and therefore, if they could not raise enough, they needed to use their own children and offer them.... This could not be found, however, in the registers (*dawāwīn*) of al-Ḥadrah, but it was found in the register in Egypt (*dīwān bi-Miṣr*).[26]

The importance of this conquest history, discussed at length by Norman Calder and later added to by Chase Robinson, is demonstrated not just by these extraordinary accounts, however.[27] The narrative historical works of the Islamic tradition which cover the early Islamic conquests often include comments on the agreements made between the conquered and the conquerors, and whether merely to add to an account's authenticity or as a genuine transmission of a document, they at times claim to include the full agreement itself rather than a simple summarization notice.[28] This is something which seems to have occurred from both the Muslim and non-Muslim sides: The 'rediscovery' of a treaty between the Prophet Muḥammad and the Christians of Najrān in the mid-ninth/third century by a Christian monk in the *Chronicle of Seert* providing protections for their community attests to this.[29] While it is common to find mentions of settlement terms in Arabic texts describing the conquest period, al-Balādhurī is steadfast in his cataloguing of them in the *Futūḥ*. The designation of a region's status as captured either *ṣulḥan* (by treaty) or *'anwatan* (without treaty) is one of the chief foci of almost every section of his book.[30] Other early Arabic works which cover the Islamic conquests will include such occasional notices of how a location came under the control of the burgeoning caliphate, but none of these early sources approaches the level of attention to this information as al-Balādhurī's *Futūḥ*. This is reinforced by the early computer-mediated data collection of D. R. Hill, who compiled the following data on conquest classification through the caliphate of 'Uthmān (r. 644–656 CE/AH 23–35) from a number of early sources (Table 4.1).

Table 4.1 Hill's Data on conquest reports[a]

	Source	*Ṣulḥ/'Anwa Reports*
1.	al-Balādhurī – *Futūḥ*	244
2.	al-Ṭabarī	124
3.	al-Ya'qūbī	48
4.	Ibn 'Abd al-Ḥakam	32
5.	Abū Yūsuf	29
6.	Abū 'Ubayd	29
7.	al-Dīnawarī	15
8.	Others	23

[a]D. R. Hill, *The Termination of Hostilities in the Early Arab Conquests, A.D. 634-656* (London: Luzac & Company, 1971), esp. 168–70.

Hill's compilation of these traditions – while both limited and dated – remains a useful sampling of traditions concerning the conquest of territory during the first two decades following the Prophet Muḥammad's death.[31] Of the 544 traditions compiled by Hill, some 45 per cent originated from al-Balādhurī's *Futūḥ*. Despite the massive disparity in size between al-Balādhurī's text and the next most common source of these traditions, al-Ṭabarī's *Taʾrīkh*, the *Futūḥ* includes almost twice as many accounts classifying the conquest of regions in this period. The results here speak volumes about the *Futūḥ's* clear thematic concentration on the aggregation of this material. Other early Arabic texts include similar traditions and information as al-Balādhurī, but none contains the same ratio of these conquest classifications to the overall amount of traditions within the work.

Before moving on to further discussion of some of the content of these alleged agreements contained throughout the *Futūḥ*, it is worth expressing a certain amount of caution over their acceptance as accurate historical information. The reader of these documents is rarely presented with convincing and comprehensive information on the collection and receipt of goods or taxes levied, nor anything but generic statements about what was part of an agreement in a region. Moreover, the formulaic or anachronistic nature of a large subset of these agreements is problematic,[32] although this does not mean that they are all fabrications; far more likely, it hints at a lengthy and unseen process of emendation that they underwent along the way to codification in the surviving texts.[33] It seems much more likely that their consistent appearance in the *Futūḥ* served as general information for those who were engaging with them. Their inclusion was more about documenting the productivity and produce of a region and the types of in-kind payment which could be expected or requested, rather than as historical receipt of past payment. In this way, it further demonstrates the disconnect between our Arabic narrative sources like the *Futūḥ*, which represent a centralized and insulated view of the early Islamic period, and the equally limited local reality of the outlying provinces that the available papyrological evidence provides.

The exploitation of land and resources

A fundamental reality of life in the medieval period was the dichotomy between those living in the urban centres and those who lived rurally. The distinction between the urban and rural populace was clearly delineated not just in the different types of settlements these communities chose to inhabit, but in the reality that one group were the primary producers of society and the other the primary consumers.[34] This does not mean, of course, that city dwellers did not produce any commodities of their own; far from it, in fact, and a number of studies in the fields of Islamic art and architecture have demonstrated a great deal of commonality in craftsmanship and, ergo, skilled labour, across vast regions of the Islamic world when it came to luxury goods.[35] When it came to the most fundamental forms of resource production, however – grains, livestock, and other foodstuffs; precious metals; plants used in the creation of textiles – all of these essential resources needed to be provided by the country for the consumption and use, primarily, of the inhabitants of the city.

It is to the claim and privilege of these staples outside regional centres that we find the clear attention of al-Balādhurī throughout the *Futūḥ*, and in direct contrast to what is found in other works which cover the conquest period. While other texts covering this era occasionally include minor details on the terms agreed upon between the conquerors and the conquered, we find more in the *Futūḥ*. Regular statements are found in al-Balādhurī's text concerning the actual resources of a region which were included as part of tax payments in these settlement agreements. The reader is never provided exhaustive lists of the produce of a region or detailed commentaries on these resources, agreements, and their ensuing economic implications, and yet the author includes these traditions throughout the texts. The most common resources mentioned as part of these agreements are those of wheat (usually indicated merely by the measure required, such as the *jarīb*, but including other explicit foodstuffs such as barley, sugar cane, and grapes),[36] oil and vinegar,[37] honey,[38] cattle,[39] vineyards themselves,[40] gold and silver,[41] and textiles.[42]

This emphasis on the productivity of the rural lands and their long-standing agreements with the central government are occasionally reiterated in different types of traditions in the text. They are not exclusively limited to agreements made during the seventh-century conquest period, either. In the chapter on Palestine, the reader is provided insight into the problems of the rural populace's abandonment of their lands. These people are then urged to return by the government through the provision of tax incentives. Traditions such as these only further demonstrate the challenges the rural, resource-producing populace faced in the early ʿAbbāsid period, and the importance placed on ensuring these vital lands were not left fallow. Several modern scholars have argued that the tax burdens on farmers in the early ʿAbbāsid period and the high costs of the upkeep of land led many to abandon their roles[43] – very likely for cities – but the challenges facing this portion of society were numerous. Here, al-Balādhurī shows the Caliph Hārūn al-Rashīd (r. 786–809 CE/AH 170–193) attempting to combat the loss of cultivable lands by assigning an agent to return them to productivity:

> Certain estates (*ḍiyāʿ*) were abandoned in the caliphate of al-Rashīd and deserted by their occupants, and al-Rashīd sent Harthama b. Aʿyan to return them to cultivation. Harthama asked some of their old tenants and farmers to return to [their lands], with the understanding that he would lessen their *kharāj* (the land tax) and would treat them more leniently. Some returned, and those were awarded 'reductions' (*aṣḥāb al-takhāfīf*). Others came after that, and their old lands were restored to them. They were awarded 'restorations' (*aṣḥāb al-rudūd*).[44]

Such a tradition reveals a great deal about the situation. First, the fact that it reports that the farmers 'went back' (*al-rujūʿ ilayhā, fa-rajaʿū*) to their lands would suggest that it was the same generation who had abandoned these lands that were later coaxed back by Hārūn's suggested tax incentives. Those involved in this may well be the Samaritans, as in another chapter al-Balādhurī discusses how lands in Palestine were brought out of cultivation due to a plague that affected entire households, eventually leading Hārūn al-Rashīd to intervene and, in so doing, converting these lands from private property into property of the state:

> There was in Palestine in the beginning of the caliphate of al-Rashīd a violent plague (*ṭāʿūn*) which could destroy an entire household. Their land was destroyed and rendered unusable. The *sulṭān*[45] put [the land] in charge of those who would cultivate it (*ʿamarahā*), and attracted the farmers back to it. They became government-owned estates (*ḍiyāʿ al-khilāfa*), and the Samaritans lived on them.[46]

Second, the tradition recalls the differentiation of reward provided to those who trusted Harthama (and, by association, the caliph) from the outset in contrast to those who chose to return later (and, perhaps, who waited to see the success the state had achieved in returning these lands to cultivation). This also appears to be an occasion where the reader is given a clear appearance of al-Balādhurī's own research practice in the *Futūḥ*, as the introduction of this tradition suggests that it is not a mere historical tradition passed down to him by one of his teachers, but, rather, a summary of what he found in an archive of Palestine: 'In Palestine, there is a special place containing records from the caliphs, separate from the tax [records] of the common people.' (*wa-bi-filasṭīn farūz bi-sijillāt min al-khulafā' mufrada min kharāj al-'āmma*).[47]

Building projects and cities

In apposition to al-Balādhurī's reminders of the responsibility of the resource-producing periphery to the centre of the realm are al-Balādhurī's lengthy discussions of the important urban centres of the early Islamic world themselves. The Iraqi cities of Baṣra and Kūfa are the clearest demonstration of this interest in urban development, as al-Balādhurī spends considerable time discussing the founding of these two cities, their layout, building projects, irrigation improvements, distribution of land, and prominent families. Far more attention is spent on the layout and expansion of these two cities than any other within the *Futūḥ*, although his interest in building and irrigation projects are noticeable throughout the text. Additionally, al-Balādhurī includes a discussion of the founding and construction of both the primary 'Abbāsid capital of Baghdad and the mid-ninth-century capital to the north at Sāmarrā'. He discusses the roles both places served as caliphal residences in addition to detailing what might be considered more minute information: why certain sections of the city came to be known by particular names, for instance, and which leading men of the 'Abbāsid period were given possession (or the benefits) of certain plots within the city.[48]

In al-Balādhurī's discussions of both Baṣra and Kūfa, the information provided on both cities is surprisingly thorough and informative. Wadad al-Qadi highlighted the extensive amount of information included in the chapters of the *Futūḥ* on these cities, and has convincingly argued for al-Balādhurī's use of the records of the *dīwān* in detailing the history of Baṣra, as already discussed at various times in the present research.[49] Her discussion and arguments surrounding the landed estate of Baṣra can quite easily be applied to the *Futūḥ*'s less lengthy but still substantial section on Baṣra's great cultural and political rival Kūfa, but an important question remains. Which was the actual impetus for the form his sections on these cities takes: al-Balādhurī's access to copious and detailed records on both locations, or his interest in including such detailed information which caused him to seek out relevant materials?

Such a question is exceedingly difficult to answer, but I would suggest that his reason was far more likely the latter. These two sections are far from the only chapters where al-Balādhurī demonstrates – whether directly or indirectly – access to actual state records in the collation of his traditions. While his chapters on both Baṣra and Kūfa are more thorough than any other discussion of the cities of the Islamic world barring Mecca, the types of material we find in these sections often interest the author in almost every other chapter of the work, just to a far lesser extent. Whereas al-Balādhurī includes several pages of accounts on the founding and development of the mosque of Kūfa,[50] we often find at least one tradition describing aspects of the mosque in other less prominent cities in ʿAbbāsid times, such as Ḥims, an unnamed location in Ifrīqiyya, al-Rayy, and Ardabīl.[51] Similarly, while there are lengthy discussions of the irrigation projects in Baṣra,[52] there are still smaller accounts of these developments in urban settlements like Medina and Ramla.[53] Extensive details about the building projects which took place in the seventh-ninth/first-third centuries in both Baṣra and Kūfa are detailed, but likewise, explanations of building projects in smaller urban centres are found, as is widespread information on the fortifications of frontier settlements along the border with the Byzantines in Syria and Anatolia and the foundation of fortifications throughout Persia. The foundation of building projects and other public works are a major thematic focus of al-Balādhurī's in the *Futūḥ*, and prove again to be revealing of how al-Balādhurī intended the *Futūḥ* to be utilized.

In discussing the foundation, expansion, and maintenance of the great early Islamic cities of Iraq, Hugh Kennedy established the importance of al-Balādhurī's information for our historical and economic knowledge of these two cities, but of Baṣra in particular. He has written at length about the matters of landholding in the early Islamic period, and has analysed the public works projects of these cities, especially noting 'the obligation of the government to provide drinking-water' to cities, while also noting that one particular account included by al-Balādhurī links 'the great Caliph ʿUmar himself...[to] the provision of water as part of the function of government'.[54] Despite this, however, Kennedy regularly notes the roles of people 'rich enough to invest substantial funds in making the land productive,' specifically, in bringing dead land (*mawāt*) back into cultivation, with the large investment resulting in the privatization of that land through the expansion of the legal framework of *qaṭīʿa* (pl. *qaṭāʾiʿ*).[55] In considering these important early legal and financial matters, however, Kennedy finds the bulk of his most convincing evidence on these cities in the *Futūḥ*. It is not, however, just the *Futūḥ's* section on Baṣra which includes these many accounts on the construction of public works projects such as canals and other forms of irrigation, nor the thorough details of land ownership history. This is an important and perceptible theme that characterizes the *Futūḥ* and the author's overall interest, as al-Balādhurī is the only author who discusses these combinations of points at any length. Even the early books of *kharāj* and *amwāl* – so often the source for the majority of al-Balādhurī's legal opinions on land ownership rights, and the material primarily used by Kennedy to augment his discussion of Baṣra – are not the originators of al-Balādhurī's information on which lands were given as *qaṭā'i'* and the people involved in this process. I strongly support Kennedy's opinion that this material is likely representative of early Islamic realities, but the fact that al-Balādhurī is committed to describing these events not just in Baṣra but throughout his discussions of the cities of the Islamic world further establishes an overall theme of this particular text: the cataloguing of land developments, and the Islamic state's integral role in their expansion and maintenance.

Al-Balādhurī includes so much material on the construction projects of urban settlements, and the produce, of rural regions not merely as a demonstration of the achievement of certain caliphs or the strength of the Islamic state, however. Asserting the legitimacy of the caliphate and its impact on the positive productivity of the entire *dār al-Islām* would very likely have been a part of this process of historical cataloguing, but it does not alone account for the great amount of time al-Balādhurī spends on the physical institutions and manifestations of power found in the *Futūḥ*. These traditions serve as a means of assessing the rights of the state and individual groups to the benefits of these urban centres and rural resources, as the ultimate means of asserting historical control over not just local identity and memory, but of the goods necessary for the continued success of these communities and the Islamic world as a whole. For court bureaucrats attempting to further the 'Abbāsid caliph's claim to power, legitimacy, and the continued subordination of the regions of the Islamic world outside of central Iraq, the *Futūḥ* provided a clearly bound reference to allow these administrators to demonstrate that they were not, in fact, 'ignorant of how things were at the beginning.' The practical application for many of the traditions on urban and rural land ownership in the *Futūḥ* should also not be overlooked, as precisely when and how individuals (or the state) came into possession of lands or public works could be imagined to have an effect on the benefits that the state could expect to gain from the resources contained within. The *Futūḥ*, in containing such a large number of traditions that directly spoke to the assignments of these locations and their benefits as *qaṭī'a*, served the concrete purpose of ensuring that the administrators of the court handling the state's finances were aware of what could and could not be expected of regions, as well as how tax law could and could not be applied.

Attitudes towards the Umayyads, the 'Abbāsids, and the caliphal office

> The task of ferreting out a compiler's political or religious agenda thus becomes a matter of first importance, but it is usually a difficult task because the compilers seldom offer an explicit declaration of their own viewpoint. Moreover, a compiler's agenda is seldom readily apparent, because such works, by virtue of the very fact that they are compilations of older reports of diverse kinds, almost never speak with one voice. The existence in a compilation of reports representing contending points of view…obscures the intentions and agenda of the compiler himself, and may delude us into thinking that, in fact he does not have any agenda or that his agenda can safely be ignored.[56]

It has long been an assumption since the days of Julius Wellhausen that the Umayyads are, overall, depicted quite negatively in the 'Abbāsid-era historical tradition.[57] This idea has finally begun to be criticized, as many have recently highlighted that this position has needed to be nuanced or, in some cases, completely corrected.[58] The success of the 'Abbāsid Revolution crushed the power of the Umayyad family and scrubbed much of their physical manifestation from the Islamic world, but the success of the Revolution ushered in not just a new ruling family, but a great number of changes within the greater Muslim *umma*. These changes included greater opportunities for non-Arab converts to the religion as well as a greater development of the *'ulamā'*, the class of religious scholars who would come to define the Islamic sciences in the classical period. Despite the successes of the new ruling family, however, the legacy of the Umayyads clearly lived on in historical memory. Nowhere else is the important role of Islam's first dynasty in the shaping of the Islamic state more clear as in the work of al-Balādhurī.

The historiography surrounding the first *fitna*, or Islamic civil war, is intricately linked to the memory of the Umayyads.[59] Erling Petersen, in his study on the attitudes and 'tendencies' of authors towards the issues surrounding the first *fitna*, spoke positively overall of al-Balādhurī's impartial handling of traditions surrounding what is among the most volatile issues in all of the early Islamic tradition.[60] For his study, however, a focus on the first *fitna* led him to consider al-Balādhurī's attitudes towards the Umayyads through a near exclusive concentration on *Ansāb al-ashrāf*, as the civil war has almost no presence within the *Futūḥ* for Petersen to have evaluated. Petersen was prescient in many of his comments on the *Futūḥ*,[61] but he spent little time evaluating the attitude of the *Futūḥ* towards the Umayyads. Similarly, Khalil Athamina examined the sources of the *Ansāb* – more specifically, the traditions of al-Madā'inī and al-Haytham b. 'Adī – and he came to a similar conclusion as Petersen that al-Balādhurī does not seem to display a partisan tendency, but he, too, focused exclusively on the *Ansāb*.[62] Because of this, we must look at a number of different indicators in an attempt to evaluate al-Balādhurī's attitude towards Islam's first dynasty, while additionally contributing to these earlier suggestions on the author's overall attitude towards them in the *Ansāb*.

Karl Wurtzel conducted a more detailed survey of attitudes towards the Umayyads, 'Alīds, 'Abbāsids, and Khārijites in his discussion of another early Arabic historical source, the *Ta'rīkh* of Khalīfa b. Khayyāṭ. Through a comparison of Khalīfa's accounts with other early historical works including those of al-Ṭabarī and al-Balādhurī's *Ansāb al-ashrāf*, Wurtzel would not be drawn to attach to Khalīfa a pro-Umayyad stance. This was largely owed to Khalīfa's brevity – a brevity which is, in many ways, not dissimilar to the style of al-Balādhurī's own *Futūḥ*. Wurtzel noted that while Khalīfa is presented with a number of opportunities to include denigrating remarks towards Islam's first dynasty, individual depravity on behalf of some Umayyad caliphs, or their overall lack of a claim to rule as strong as the reigning 'Abbāsids, these opportunities are passed over with almost no note. Wurtzel then refuses to rule out 'the possibility…that at least some of the anti-Umayyad comments and stories as they appear in the works of aṭ-Ṭabarī and others, were later additions to, and embellishments of, older, less hostile traditions'.[63]

One of the indicators Wurtzel used in his discussion of Khalīfa's attitude towards the Umayyads was to note the author's naming practices surrounding a Companion of the Prophet Muḥammad and early Islamic administrator, Ziyād b. Abī Sufyān.[64] Allegedly, the son of the infamous Umayyad Abū Sufyān and a slave woman, Ziyād is referred to in a great number of texts by the name Ziyād b. Abīhi (Ziyād, the son of his father) because of his status as a bastard. While this may have been a name by which many referred to him for the bulk of his early life before being recognized (*istilḥāq*) by the Umayyad Caliph Mu'āwiya as his brother in 665 CE/AH 44,[65] he came to be known as the son of Abū Sufyān. The name 'son of his father' appeared to be used derogatively by a number of later authors for an early Umayyad administrator who proved to be extremely divisive – not unlike his half-brother. He served at various times as the governor of both Baṣra and Kūfa, and the Islamic tradition remembers him in a variety of conflicting fashions, both as a tremendous administrator and orator and as a depraved, conniving, and brutal overlord.[66] Al-Balādhurī, as with Khalīfa's *Ta'rīkh*, only refers to him by his affiliated name, 'the son of Abū

Sufyān,' and, overall, provides a seemingly fair impression of his governorship, providing mostly impartial accounts of his tenure. This includes al-Balādhurī's transmission of an anecdote about Ziyād's ensuring the canonical ritual in the mosques of Kūfa and Baṣra,[67] a glimpse at his vanity in the naming of a canal dug in Baṣra,[68] and the attribution to him of the first financial register using an official seal (*dīwān zimām wa-khātim*).[69]

Al-Balādhurī's attitude towards the Umayyads can be seen as seemingly neutral, despite the fact that it might seem almost paradoxical for a scholar at the court of the Umayyads' vanquishers to be such. In fact, if we consider attributions of their lasting achievements in policy as indicators of success, his depiction of the dynasty overall is quite positive. This is despite the attitude of the 'Abbāsids that the Umayyads never held any real right to rule through the legitimizing factors that became more clearly defined in the 'Abbāsid period: excellence (*manqaba*, pl. *manāqib*), virtue (*faḍīla*, pl. *faḍā'il*), and/or precedence (*sābiqa*, pl. *sawābiq*).[70] Within the *Futūḥ*, however, al-Balādhurī makes no statements on the legitimacy of the Umayyads right to rule and discusses none of these issues, primarily because it was not within the scope of his interests in creating the text. Instead, however, al-Balādhurī seems to recognize the general primacy of place of the office of the caliph – especially relevant for those working within the bureaucratic apparatus – regardless of who occupied it. While there have been numerous modern studies looking at the office of the caliph and how that position's power, legitimacy, and authority changed between the Umayyad and early 'Abbāsid period, the position always remained intimately tied to administrative authority. While the *vizier* grew increasingly more prominent as the chief central administrator of the caliphate, even among the tumultuous decades of the mid-ninth-/third century, he continued to answer to the 'Abbāsid caliph. In turn, since the early decades of Islamic rule, the caliph maintained oversight in the matter of the appointment of officials within the central bureau as well as executives in the outlying provinces.

A great number of early caliphs, even those who receive a mixed reception or largely negative reception in early Arabic historical memory such as al-Walīd b. Yazīd (r. 743–744 CE/AH 125–126), Mu'āwiya b. Abī Sufyān, and 'Uthmān b. 'Affān, are provided very little character development within the confines of the *Futūḥ*. Any indicators of al-Balādhurī's personal feelings towards them are far subtler than ever constituting outright condemnation in the book. Al-Walīd is notorious for tales of his hedonism in many Arabic sources, including in a huge number of traditions al-Balādhurī selected for his *Ansāb al-ashrāf*. There is no mention, however, of his negative personality traits in the seven instances his name is invoked in the *Futūḥ*.[71] Whereas it has already been strongly argued that al-Balādhurī held a negative attitude towards al-Walīd in his overall characterization of the Umayyad caliphate in the *Ansāb*,[72] we see absolutely no presence of this characterization or these feelings in the *Futūḥ*, and he would have been among the easiest targets of anti-Umayyad ire should the author have intended to make those feelings known.

Muʿāwiya, on the other hand, is among the more interesting Umayyad depictions in the text. If we view the important and/or lasting policy developments attributed to Muʿāwiya as an indicator of the author's positive feeling towards the caliph, then al-Balādhurī must have felt very positively indeed about Muʿāwiya's contributions. And yet, the reader finds an opportunity seized upon by the author to leave Muʿāwiya appearing in a much less flattering light, as this brief tradition in the chapter on the scribes of Muḥammad at the end of the *Futūḥ* divulges:

> When it was the year of the conquest (*ʿām al-fatḥ*),[73] Muʿāwiya converted to Islam, and he also acted as a scribe for Muḥammad. One day [Muḥammad] summoned him while he was eating, and he delayed coming. The Prophet said 'God, may his belly never be satisfied!' Muʿāwiya would say 'The prayer of the Prophet of God has been fulfilled!' He used to eat around seven meals a day.[74]

The tradition seems intent to portray Muʿāwiya in a negative light, as it has the future caliph establishing the limited commitment he had towards God's messenger and, in a more abstract way, Muʿāwiya's desire for the goodness of this world over the promise of Paradise. This particular tradition would seem to further support the impressions of Tayeb El-Hibri: that a sizeable portion of ʿAbbāsid-era traditions on the Umayyad rulers take on a 'moralizing undercurrent,' especially those surrounding Muʿāwiya.[75]

This tradition, however, is even more revealing of al-Balādhurī's attitudes towards the caliphal office and of a unified caliphate more generally. The report occurs, of course, long before the Umayyad Muʿāwiya would assume the title of caliph following the murder of ʿAlī b. Abī Ṭālib. This is, in fact, the only tradition in the entirety of the *Futūḥ* that discusses the earlier years of Muʿāwiya's life, and it is consequently the only tradition in the book which depicts Muʿāwiya so decidedly negatively. The Caliph Muʿāwiya is never so clearly derided, and despite his presence in an enormous number of traditions throughout the *Futūḥ*, there is no other clear attempt at a negative characterization of him although undesirable characterizations of other figures do occasionally occur.

One more example along these lines occurs with the Caliph 'Uthmān, another particularly problematic character in the early Islamic historical tradition. While eventually coming to be classified by the Sunnīs as one of the four 'rightly guided' (*rāshidūn*) caliphs – the first four caliphs after Muḥammad's death – 'Uthmān is remembered for a variety of prominent stories that portray him both positively and negatively. His early support – especially financial – of the Prophet and his apparent role in the codification of the Qur'ān are always spoken of in positive terms, but there are equally a huge number of accounts regarding his nepotism and avarice and his (acrimonious) murder at the hands of rebels unhappy with his supposedly unjust policies. In the middle of all of this is the reality that 'Uthmān was genealogically the first Umayyad Caliph even though he is not considered the founder of the dynasty, and he is remembered for, in essence, 'six good years' followed by 'six bad years' of rule.[76] 'An evaluation of 'Uthmān's rule, policies, and behavior,' writes Tayeb El-Hibri, 'must be mindful of the spectrum of representations applied to him'.[77]

Unlike al-Walīd, 'Uthmān appears in a far more appreciable subset of traditions in the *Futūḥ*, and so there is a much greater opportunity for a characterization of him and his reign to appear. Despite the negative depictions of 'Uthmān's character that exist elsewhere, the reader of the *Futūḥ* finds little of this. Nonetheless, that is not to say that events which occurred during his reign are not often portrayed negatively. An excellent example of this occurs in al-Balādhurī's discussion of the buildings in the city of Baṣra, which includes a tale of how 'Uthmān's freedman Ḥumrān b. Abān came to settle in the city. 'Uthmān, after training Ḥumrān and taking him as a scribe, sent him to the governor of the Ḥijāz, al-Walīd b. 'Uqba, to investigate 'something…which [al-Walīd] had been accused of.' Ḥumrān, we are informed, accepted bribes from al-Walīd (*irtashā minhu*), and this resulted in 'Uthmān's banishing his freedman from his presence. Choosing to live in Baṣra, Ḥumrān reportedly asked 'Uthmān for a large piece of land for his new home, to which 'Uthmān – believing this to be excessive – refused, telling his agent to 'give him a house like any of your houses'.[78]

Here, again, we find that al-Balādhurī appears reticent to provide an overly negative characterization of anyone holding the caliphal office – even if the person holding it was an Umayyad. Notwithstanding this, however, al-Balādhurī finds more cunning ways to accomplish this without ever bringing the head of state's position directly into disrepute: He tends to accomplish this by negatively depicting the agents surrounding the caliph who worked on his behalf. In the above account, 'Uthmān appears both wise and cautious of the excesses of those around him, and yet two important agents of his caliphate are indicted as corrupt: Ḥumrān, the freedman whom ʿUthmān himself, we are informed, identified, purchased, and trained; and al-Walīd b. ʿUqba, the governor of one of the most important regions of the Islamic world and himself a member of the Umayyad clan. The blame, therefore, is deflected away from the caliphal office itself and onto its administrators, leaving the reader of the *Futūḥ* to see the flaws in a caliph's reign not in the depiction of the caliphs themselves, but in their retinue and their executives. The office itself is presented as almost sacrosanct, even if al-Balādhurī may have had some unstated personal disagreements over the legitimacy of one caliph over another. In this manner, we find support for Petersen's comment that 'a salient feature in Balādhurī's physiognomy is seen to be that he recognizes the legality of the Umayyad caliphate and its effective rule; he thus naturally avoids any hiatus in the continuity of the caliphate from the early caliphs to the Abbasids'.[79] In reality, however, a more thorough thematic project seems to be undertaken by al-Balādhurī: he was working not just to project a respect and power towards the caliphal office, but also to depict the earliest centuries of Islam as a period of unity that could remind and inspire the readers of the ʿAbbāsid period facing the collapse of caliphal authority.

In this way, asking questions about the author's attitude towards a particular dynasty or caliph does not strike at the heart of a major thematic intention of al-Balādhurī. It ignores the role the *Futūḥ* likely played as a *lieu de mémoire* for an imagined unified caliphate where the caliphal office was powerful and respected. It is for this reason that we find caliphs like those mentioned above depicted without the conflict that their questionable legacies would normally engender, especially within other sources. It is also why we see almost no mention of any of the civil wars which had rocked the Islamic world four times already by the time of al-Balādhurī's lifetime.[80] His great exposition of the first two civil wars in the *Ansāb* exhibits that he was well informed concerning these events, but they showed the Islamic world in tumultuous eras of disunity and struggle, and so they are omitted almost completely from the *Futūḥ*. The events of the *rāshidūn*, Umayyad, and early ʿAbbāsid periods were undergoing a process of canonization in the middle ʿAbbāsid period, and could be harkened back to as models during a period of historical rupture. Creating a similar, unifying thematic program in geographies has also been identified by André Miquel and Zayde Antrim, but a similar idea has not previously been put forward about the *Futūḥ*.[81]

Additionally, Petersen argued overall that al-Balādhurī was concerned with 'the Arab kingdom' and 'Arab self-assertion,' – almost certainly influenced by Wellhausen – but one wonders just how clear this assertion is within the *Futūḥ*.[82]

While it seems correct to suggest the idea of an uninterrupted caliphate as a salient motif of the *Futūḥ*, the idea that Arabness was of vital import to the author is not anywhere near as striking in the text. Writing a genealogically focused and organized text like the *Ansāb* is not in itself a demonstration of al-Balādhurī's belief in Arab superiority, although it is a form of recognition that many aspects of Arabian culture had by the ninth/third century become indelibly tied to Islam and the society's elites. One might think, however, that the centrality of Arabia supports Petersen's suggestion. The *Futūḥ* begins with a discussion of the Prophet's city of Medina and the lifetime of the Prophet and, after winding through the entirety of the Islamic world in its geographically organized chapters, comes in the end to its final section on 'The Matter of Writing.' That chapter itself deals almost exclusively with the scribes of the Prophet Muḥammad in Mecca and Medina and their characteristics. The Islamic state and Islamic culture's genesis and development through to al-Balādhurī's lifetime is hence depicted full-circle, with both its beginning and end to be found in the Prophet's lifetime and in his homelands of western Arabia. But this was an Islamic motivation – Arabia was the home of the Prophet – rather than because Arabia was the home of the Arabs. Hence, we see no discussion within the *Futūḥ* of pre-Islamic Arab tribes and of Arab origins, and it seems that Petersen's suggestion of a focus on an 'Arab kingdom' in al-Balādhurī's *Futūḥ* is misguided.

Administrators on horses: Commanders, governors, and executive bureaucrats

While it is true that there is little character elaboration of the various *Rāshidūn*, Umayyad, and 'Abbāsid caliphs in the *Futūḥ*, this does not mean that there is not any exploration of the figures found in al-Balādhurī's book. He primarily reserves his glimpses of greater characterization for the executives involved in both the conquests and the establishment of early Islamic policies in the conquered territories, and offers much more characterization of these figures than he does of caliphs. The executives at the centre of this presentation are the commanders, governors, and, in some cases, judges of the seventh-century Islamic realm. Remembered first for their remarkable achievements in the conquest of vast and varied territories, often these same figures were subsequently tasked with the actual governance of these locations thereafter.[83]

A great amount of research has been conducted over the last several decades on the Muslims' maintenance of the low-level administrative bureaucracy left over by the Byzantines and Sasanians and the new state's continued use of their services.[84] From the perspective of later historians, however, lower-level administrative officials such as tax collectors and local scribes rarely garnered the attention of their prestigious superiors, who are often recalled as embodying all three of the above roles within a single personage by al-Balādhurī and later Muslim authors. In particular, anecdotal traditions surrounding these figures are often found to fit certain models: overarching thematic models that match the author's intentions for the text, and for the articulation of the supremacy of Islam's early leaders as the founders of the early Islamic state. Al-Balādhurī presents the reader with a consistent theme of the importance of these administrative figures in the entire process of Islamic state formation, from the point of entry of a region into the *dār al-Islām* (its conquest) through to its subsequent administration in later decades and centuries. In fact, a thematic focus on the reigns of important early Islamic rulers is one of the clear commonalities between the *Futūḥ* and *Ansāb al-ashrāf*, with the life and careers of the Umayyads Mu'āwiya and 'Abd al-Malik being among the lengthiest entries in the text, while Petersen has already noted that the last thorough biography of the work is dedicated to the infamous Umayyad governor of Iraq, al-Ḥajjāj b. Yūsuf (d. 713–714 CE/AH 95).[85]

As commanders, these individuals were responsible for leading men into battle during the conquest period, assigning sub-commanders to the different sections of the army, and liaising with the caliph regarding troop movements and when and where to engage the enemy. While this latter caliphal involvement suggests an authoritative central hand dictating much of the events of the conquests, commanders remained invested with one particularly important power by al-Balādhurī and several other historians. They had the authority to negotiate capitulation terms and succeeding levels of taxation for the conquered peoples, while the caliph would simply approve those terms after an agreement had already been made. In one instance, al-Balādhurī even makes clear that the sub-commanders of an army could also make binding terms on behalf of the caliph and his supreme commander.[86] Here, al-Balādhurī reports that the famed Arab general Khālid b. al-Walīd had been replaced as commander of the conquest forces in Syria by Abū 'Ubayda b. al-Jarrāḥ prior to the conquest of Damascus. During the siege of the city and with a portion of the army under Abū 'Ubayda about to forcefully capture the city,

> the bishop hurried to Khālid [b. al-Walīd] and made peace terms with him, and so he opened the eastern gate for him. Khālid entered, and the bishop was

> with him, unfolding his agreement that Khālid had written for him. Some of the Muslims said 'By God! Khālid is not the commander, so how could his terms be binding?' Abū 'Ubayda said 'Even the lowest of the Muslims can make binding terms on their behalf.' He approved his agreement, and he signed it.[87]

Similarly, during the conquest of Caesarea in Palestine, al-Balādhurī includes another tradition where Mu'āwiya makes his own terms with a Jewish man named Yūsuf, who shows him a way into the city. While this took place during the Caliphate of 'Umar, there is no mention of the caliph's eventual ratification of this agreement, as often appears elsewhere.[88]

A distinct characteristic of early Arabic works which focus on the Islamic conquests is the presentation of the endeavour as a highly organized and singular affair. The central authority – represented by the caliph himself – is often portrayed as having a very heavy hand in the planning and development of the Islamic conquests.[89] The caliph is presented as ordering the direction of the conquests – starting with the capture of the Arabian Peninsula, moving onwards to Mesopotamia, then to Syria, Palestine, Egypt, the Jazīra, and so on. The narrative sources rarely present the idea that the conquests flowed naturally, where one commander's victory in the field would lead him to immediately press his enemies for greater gains. The caliph's intervention is often seen as necessary in order for the conquests to progress.[90] Unsurprisingly, there is never a hint that these early Arab-Muslim armies could be disorganized, out of touch with the central authority, or motivated by the opportunity for material gain in the directions their aggression took them.

The way in which these authors of early Arabic texts kept the central authority engaged with the ongoing conquests and governance of frontier territories was through regular letter writing. Albrecht Noth, Lawrence Conrad, and, more recently, Nicola Clarke have demonstrated how a *topos* of letter writing allowed the caliph and other governors near-constant communication with commanders in the field in order to approve any decisions made. As Noth/Conrad highlight, often this letter writing defies logic, with the distance involved between the Caliph and his commanders sometimes requiring several days of travel just for the delivery of a dispatch *one way*.[91] When we consider these letters as a literary form helping to develop the narrative, they make more sense. However, they also suggest a Muslim 'capital city' in Medina in full control of all aspects of the conquests and early Muslim governance. They imagine, almost certainly anachronistically, a Muslim central government that was born, and fully formed, from the lifetime of the Prophet.

The texts of *futūḥ* often do a poor job of representing the grand scale involved in the conquest of such a vast amount of territory, despite the fact that they are quick to celebrate how God's favour is the only thing that could have made such success possible.[92] They also give a very poor impression of the time involved in the entire conquest process, often suggesting a truncated timeline and the immense speed of the conquests.[93] There is not any attention traditionally paid to the idea of simultaneous conquest: of the conquests of different territories by different armies under different commanders at the same time. The closest 'bridging' accounts that tend to present the reader with the idea that there were multiple ongoing frontlines of conflict during the Islamic conquests is the story of Khālid b. al-Walīd's desert journey between the fronts of Mesopotamia and Syria.[94] Even here, however, the narrative seems to take a pause, showing that while the conflict in Mesopotamia was begun almost immediately after Arabia was subjugated, it was Syria where the conquests properly gained their first successes.

With all of this said, however, al-Balādhurī's narrative promotes the role and overall decision-making capacity of commanders and governors instead of the central authority, and this is where this theme diverges somewhat from the one present in the *Ansāb*.[95] As previously discussed, among the primary themes of al-Balādhurī's text is the importance of contractual obligations between both the conquered and the conquerors in the seventh century. Along with the author's clear intention of enshrining these agreements for posterity, however, we see a distinctive variance in the importance of the caliph in this process towards that of commanders and governors. As opposed to other early Arabic texts, the creator of the agreement and the contract's ultimate guarantor is very often the commander or governor himself. In other Arabic histories, the caliphs are far more often invoked, particularly as a means to 'certify' seemingly important agreements, events, or decisions made by the commanders in the field. The most famous example of this is perhaps the surrender of the city of Jerusalem to the Muslims, wherein the inhabitants of the city insisted that the Caliph 'Umar be present at the agreement of terms.[96] This was a confirmation that, having been 'formally' approved by the caliph, these occurrences had received the highest level of authority and verification. In the *Futūḥ*, the surrender of Jerusalem and its clear caliphal involvement is the exception, not the rule.[97] The vast majority of the agreements detailed by al-Balādhurī in the *Futūḥ* do not include direct caliphal intervention, but, rather, are left to the good judgement of his appointed agents in the field.

The difference between al-Balādhurī's accounts of these conquest events is especially stark when specific examples are observed between the *Futūḥ* and the text to which it is most often compared: al-Ṭabarī's *Ta'rīkh.* See here the traditions of al-Balādhurī and al-Ṭabarī regarding the conquest and governance of northern Iraq and Azerbaijan by 'Utba b. Farqad al-Sulamī:

> 'Umar b. al-Khaṭṭāb appointed 'Utba b. Farqad al-Sulamī [as governor] over Mosul in the year 20 (640–641 CE). The people of Nineveh fought with him, but he captured their eastern fort by force and crossed the Tigris. The people of the other fort made peace with him agreeing to the payment of tax (*jizya*), with safe passage provided for whoever wanted to depart with those emigrating. He found monasteries in Mosul, and made peace with them in exchange for the payment of tax (*jizya*). Then he conquered al-Marj and its villages, as well as the land of Bāhudhrā, Ḥibtūn, al-Hunnāna, al-Ma'alla, Dāmīr, and all of the strongholds of the Kurds.[98]

Contrast this depiction of al-Balādhurī with similar accounts by al-Ṭabarī of 'Utba's conquests:

> All the area [of Azerbaijan] fell to them except what was fortified. Isfandiyādh [remained] in (Bukayr's) custody, having taken the regions near him, while 'Utba b. Farqad had taken those near him. Bukayr said to Simāk, when the latter came to him, joking with him: 'What am I to do with you and 'Utba…? If I obey my instinct, I shall advance and leave you two behind as deputies. But you can remain with me if you so wish, or you can join 'Utba if you so wish. I give you a free hand, as I see no alternative but to leave you both and go after something more unpleasant than this!' So (Bukayr) sought permission of 'Umar to be excused, and he wrote back to him permitting him to advance on al-Bāb and ordering him to appoint a deputy over his province [of Azerbaijan]. So he appointed 'Utba…'Umar united the whole of Azerbaijan under 'Utba b. Farqad.
>
> …Battle was joined and 'Utba defeated [Bahrām], who fled. When the news reached Isfandiyādh…he said 'Now the peace is complete and war has been brought to an end.' So [Bukayr] made peace with Isfandiyādh, and all [the people of Azerbaijan] agreed to this. The country returned to a state of peace. Bukayr and 'Utba wrote to inform 'Umar of this and sent the fifth of what booty God had granted them.[99]

Aside from the obvious differences in length between the two sources (al-Balādhurī's text is considerably more compact than the massive history of al-Ṭabarī), there are very clear differences in the authors' thematic approach to the development of the conquests and early governorship. While 'Umar is invoked in al-Balādhurī's work for the original appointment of 'Utba, this is his only mention; he does not provide orders for 'Utba or direct his conquests in the region, nor is he consulted for guidance. Following the agreement between 'Utba and the people of Azerbaijan, al-Ṭabarī even cites problems that 'Umar would be forced to insightfully handle:

> Now 'Umar used to require his governors every year to perform the pilgrimage, thereby restraining them from any act of tyranny and preventing them from [doing any such thing].[100]

In al-Ṭabarī, the piety of 'Umar's governors is even overseen by the Caliph, and there is near-constant promotion of the foresight of the ruler and his strong personal command. All of this is either absent in al-Balādhurī's *Futūḥ* or is, at the least, noticeably dulled.

There must be a recognition of a theme concerning the promotion of gubernatorial importance in al-Balādhurī's text beyond what is seen in many other early Arabic sources. The reason for this may again be found in the audience that al-Balādhurī imagined would be engaging with his completed *Futūḥ*. The *Futūḥ* delivers no clues that it was ever prepared for a ruler, nor that it was even to be read and debated within the caliph's inner circle. If it was written with 'Abbāsid administrators in mind, however, its emphasis not just on administrative detail but on early administrators themselves makes a great deal more sense: aside from merely detailing those policies and attributing them to an instigator, we occasionally see glimpses of the exempla of the ideal officials both at the court and in the provinces.

Literary features of the *Futūḥ*

> The truth, if God wills, is that the first person to enjoy evening stories (*samr bi-l-layl*) was Alexander the Great, who had a group to make him laugh and tell him stories which he did not seek for amusement, but to safeguard and preserve them. Thus also the kings who came after him.[101]

While al-Balādhurī's *Futūḥ* is not well remembered for its literary style or narrative anecdotes, a sizeable amount of the surviving early Arabic historical tradition is made up of narrative *akhbār* that have a dimension as a form of *asmār* (sing. *samr*), 'stories apt of being told at evening conversations'.[102] Their value as a medium of entertainment is apparent, as they promote stories of heroic figures, wise rulers, cunning ruses, and clever uses of language. Stefan

Leder has discussed at length the features of 'fictional narration' which are sometimes present within early Arabic historiography and, in particular, of how the entertaining aspects of storytelling become wrapped in a more serious purpose summed up by Ibn al-Nadīm's quote above: edification and inspiration. Imaginative, fictional storytelling for its own entertainment value was something often scorned;[103] elements of this storytelling adopted to entertain so that the audience could attain some educational benefit through them, however, was among the cornerstones of *adab*, or *belles-lettres*.[104]

There is a far smaller proportion of al-Balādhurī's accounts which share these aspects than the historical works of his contemporaries (or near-contemporaries), such as Ibn Qutayba (d. 889 CE/AH 286), al-Ya'qūbī, Ibn A'tham al-Kūfī, Ibn 'Abd al-Ḥakam, and al-Ṭabarī. Of al-Balādhurī's two surviving works, *Ansāb al-ashrāf* has a far higher proportion of materials which can be more clearly identified as sharing common features of *adab*. This characteristic of the text has already been highlighted by Isaac Hasson,[105] but this analysis has not previously been extended to the *Futūḥ*. Within the *Futūḥ*, the reader is occasionally given insight into what al-Balādhurī viewed as characteristics important for good administrators to have that are very much in line with works of *adab*. This is accomplished through accounts of the actions of seventh-century Muslims involved in the process of expansion of the Islamic state. This material can only really be referred to as a 'lesser theme' within the *Futūḥ* and, I would argue, would not fully classify his text within the so-called genre of *adab*. Works of *adab* are often characterized by a variety of features, and some researchers – such as Hilary Kilpatrick – have argued against classifying them as a genre in their own right: 'Modern scholars have often described *adab* itself as a genre, but the term 'genre' does not normally correspond to the reality of *adab*. Rather, *adab* can be seen as an *approach* to writing'.[106]

This 'approach' to writing includes a variety of literary techniques and forms that predated the coming of Islam, from both Arabia and its surroundings, such as poetry, anecdotes, battle narratives, and 'mirrors for princes,' and by no means precludes the inclusion of factual material.[107] In fact, many specialists of Arabic literature have begun to underline the characteristics of *adab* in early Islamic texts that are not usually considered works of high literature, which has only emphasized, in many ways, the role of the author's training and audience in the production of a work.[108] Especially accentuated by the recent research of James Montgomery, the previously imagined dichotomy between these works – one treated as some form of non-fiction prose and the other as artistic literature – is being further eroded. Imagined differences between the two, with one written for the 'cramped, self-fulfilling and bureaucratic … the other, gentlemanly, cultured, and inquisitive' are impossible to maintain especially when, as Montgomery highlights, the authors of the latter works were very often found in the same professions as the former.[109] So it is with al-Balādhurī, described as an *adīb* himself and with an audience in mind of these administrators already familiar with aspects of *adab*, I think it unsurprising that we find the occasional anecdote and flavouring of the *adīb* within the pages of the *Futūḥ*.

Among works of *adab* popular in the eighth and ninth centuries were the so-called 'mirrors for princes,' guidebooks on manners, etiquette, and general good governance written to educate rulers and the nobility on the characteristics and decisions which made moral leaders. The *Futūḥ* is quite far from a text which could easily be compared to other works of this type, though, and it almost certainly did not have the highest members of Muslim society – the caliph and his family – as its intended audience. With that said, however, as a text which was likely intended to be used by administrators and other bureaucrats as a guidebook, it is perhaps unsurprising that al-Balādhurī chooses to include the occasional account which describes the traits associated with those chosen for governorships and other important administrative positions during the exemplary period of the seventh century and beyond. In particular, the Muslims involved in the conquest of territories and their subsequent administration during the seventh century were being shaped into exempla by the time of the ninth century. They were the individuals who had heard Muḥammad's message, were convinced to join the young and challenged Muslim community, and as the sources depict, were often the individuals who were provided with divine favour on the battlefield. Thus, the Arabic narrative sources present an idealized depiction of these early commanders and governors, and al-Balādhurī provides the reader with an opportunity to see which of these qualities were to be found in good – and bad – agents of the state. Such characterizations of these figures are among the only anecdotal accounts to be found in the text, and we will now see examples of such anecdotes.

Kathīr b. Shihāb was a governor of portions of western and central Persia at various points during the caliphates of Muʿāwiya and his son, Yazīd. In the *Futūḥ*, al-Balādhurī provides a brief description of how Kathīr originally came to be chosen for a governorship by Ziyād b. Abī Sufyān, the governor of Baṣra and Kūfa:

> Ziyād was traveling one day, when the belt of his robe became loose. Kathīr b. Shihāb brought out a needle and thread that was stuck into his cap, and with

> them he mended the belt. Ziyād said to him: 'You are prudent (*ḥāzim*), and one such as you should never be without a post.' He appointed him over a portion of al-Jabal.[110]

Kathīr and his preparedness are further elaborated in another section of the text, which also provides further insight into the characteristics that led him to his governorship:

> He [Kathīr] was handsome and prudent (*ḥāzim*), but crippled. It was said: 'he is the only cripple who is not a burden on his family.' Whenever he rode [his horse], his legs were as steady as two ploughs. Whenever he conducted a raid, all who were with him took a shield, chest armor, a helmet, five needles, linen thread, an awl, scissors, and a nosebag. He was miserly (*bakhīl*). He had a dish in front of him, and if a man came to him he would say: 'Off with you! Did you expect to have food from us?'[111]

Kathīr's preparedness, then, is seen as being an important characteristic for a governor to have. His miserly nature, though, is not seen as enough of a character flaw to see him removed from consideration as a governor – and his career in several different locations in Persia attests to this. Despite this, however, Kathīr is used as a peculiar model by al-Balādhurī in the text, as he is not universally depicted positively; just before this, we are told on the authority of al-'Abbās b. Hishām al-Kalbī that Kathīr was an 'Uthmānī who 'spoke evil' of the Caliph Alī b. Abī Ṭālib, and while assigned governorships by Mu'āwiya, was imprisoned and flogged.[112]

Elsewhere, in discussing the governorship of Bahrain, there is scriptural precedent invoked by the Caliph 'Umar concerning a potential appointment for Abū Hurayra (d. ca. 678–680 CE/AH 57–59):

> Finally 'Umar asked 'Would you become governor, Abū Hurayra?' I replied 'No.' 'Umar said 'Why not? Men greater than you were appointed governor, such as Joseph. '[Joseph] said: Appoint me over the granaries of the land."' I replied 'Joseph was a prophet and the son of a prophet, and I am [only] Abū Hurayra son of Umayma. I am fearful of three things and two things.' 'Umar said 'And why did you not say five?' I said 'I fear that you will strike my back and defame my honour and take my possessions. And I hate to speak without forbearance (*ḥilm*) and to rule without knowledge.'[113]

In the Qur'ānic story, Joseph had the gift of prophecy but was shunned by jealous siblings before eventually being sold to a family in Egypt. When he reached maturity, God gave him 'judgment and knowledge' (*ḥukm wa-'ilm*).[114] Foreseeing seven years of plentiful harvests followed by seven years of drought, Joseph convinces the King of Egypt to install him over the granaries. While wisdom and knowledge are explicitly cited as gifts from God to Joseph in addition to his foresight, one could again identify prudence as being central to his new position over the storehouses. In doing so, he ensures that the people of Egypt are able to survive the seven years of poor harvests by preparing their reserves accordingly. More importantly, though, Abū Hurayra is explicit as to the reasons why he would not be a good choice for a governorship: that he lacks forbearance (*ḥilm*), a trait often associated with the good governance of the Umayyad Caliph Muʿāwiya, and the wisdom which was explicitly given by God to Joseph. In another instance, the religious devotion of a North African governor, ʿUqba b. Nāfiʿ al-Fihrī (d. 683 CE/AH 63) is made plain as he removes deadly animals including snakes and scorpions from the surroundings of Qayrawān by praying: ʻIbn Nāfiʿ was a righteous man whose prayer was answered. He prayed to his Lord, who drove all of them [the animals] out, until the beasts had to carry their children as fugitives from [the land]'.[115]

Elsewhere, Ḥabīb b. Maslama al-Fihrī's (*fl.* mid-600s CE/AH mid-first century) exploits in the conquest of Armenia are lauded, leading the Caliph ʿUthmān to strongly consider appointing him as the governor of the region. He decides against the idea, however, 'for his capability in whatever he undertook to do (*li-ghanā'ihi fīmā kāna yanhaḍu lahu min dhālika*)',[116] opting instead to shift Ḥabīb to raiding borderlands between Syria and the Jazīra against the Byzantine Empire. It was this trait which apparently made Ḥabīb more useful as a front line commander than as an administrator of already-conquered territory.

But why would al-Balādhurī choose to include traditions like this in the *Futūḥ* at all? In some ways, the reason for this might be simple: They provide brief, lighthearted breaks in a text which can, at times, be fairly dry. As Isabel Toral-Niehoff has written, 'Historiography…is influenced by the *adab* approach, with its tendency to mix historical accounts with entertaining anecdotes using literary embellishment'.[117] Aside from the inclusion of the sporadic lines of verse – which we will come to shortly – the prose of the *Futūḥ* is simple and straightforward, very much uncharacteristic of the well-known works of *adab*, which often take the opportunity to display the linguistic ability of their authors.[118] Above all, however, it seems that these occasional anecdotes – so many of which speak directly to the qualities of these executives and other administrators and *not* to the exemplar caliphs – were intended to lighten the overall tone of the work for those reading it. Those readers would likely have been handling many of the same tasks of these earlier officials, but now at the ʿAbbāsid court of Baghdad. Nonetheless, these details speak directly to later bureaucrats, who could have confirmation and support for their attitudes and approaches to official work, while also imagining themselves as the heirs of these figures and their institutions.

An argument that the *Futūḥ* itself was a text created with the primary goal of edifying its audience in a similar fashion to the great works of *adab* born from the ninth and tenth centuries does not have nearly enough evidence to be sustained. To return to Kilpatrick's comments on *adab* not being classified as a genre of literary writing itself, but as a set of recurring themes and features, the use of anecdote in the *Futūḥ* is very much part of this tradition, but would not convincingly classify the text as an exemplar of this style. These occasional flourishes, however, in the form of these character sketches would likely have served as a form of positive reinforcement for the administrative readers of the *Futūḥ*. They would have functioned as a clear and constant indicator that the great heroes of the Islamic foundational period were, aside from being the most pious and the most righteous of God's people, establishing the practices that they then followed; they became tasked with the same administrative responsibilities of running a state that the readers themselves were engaged with daily.

Poetry, the *Futūḥ*, and the early Arabic historical tradition

In looking at the aspects of *adab* within the *Futūḥ*, we now turn to an interesting feature of the text which has been largely overlooked by historians hoping to learn more about the realities of the early Islamic period: a sizeable amount of poetry which is disseminated amid the historical *akhbār*. Especially as I have advocated that the *Futūḥ* was likely intended for an audience of secretaries and administrators, it is worth addressing how the inclusion of verse in the book provides further information on al-Balādhurī's compilation process, and perhaps also on the envisioned audience itself.

Al-Balādhurī's writings are hardly the only Arabic historical sources which are found sprinkled with Arabic poetry. On the combination of historical prose and verse, Peter Webb has written:

> The first generation of Arabic compilers of historical traditions crafted their narratives by collecting both anecdotal stories (*akhbār*) and short poems (*ashʿār*), which together formed the raw material of the early community's historical consciousness…But despite poetry's scarcity in later Arabic historiography, during the first two and a half centuries of Islam there are strong indications that poetry had an enhanced status and impacted early interpretations of history in ways deserving fresh analysis.[119]

A number of modern scholars of classical Arabic literature have worked to address the inclusion and use of poetry in historical texts, including A. F. L. Beeston and Lawrence Conrad,[120] Wolfhart Heinrichs,[121] Peter Heath, Geert Jan van Gelder, and Suleiman Mourad,[122] but the historiographical issues surrounding it are multifaceted. Early written compilers of *akhbār* recognized poetry as an important vehicle for the communication of information and concepts, but was it intrinsically linked to the oral/aural transmission of material, which defined the pre-Islamic period and the first two centuries of Islamic history? Did the performance of this material play a role in its inclusion amid the prose?[123] And can anything be said of how intricately linked the prose and verse were in these early sources?

It is an interesting question whether the prose tradition and the poetry were originally intricately bound together in the *Futūḥ*, or whether the poetry – originating from elsewhere – was the original historical artifact upon which a prose account was constructed.[124] In considering the poems included in the *Futūḥ*, they would propose a mix of the two. In the text, al-Balādhurī uses poetry in several different forms, with an example of each:

1) Battle odes and details

   [Al-Muhājir] went away with his sword and fought until he was martyred. And the people of Manādhir took his head and set it up on their stronghold between two battlements. It was said about him:

   > *'And in Manādhir, when they gathered for war,*
   > *al-Muhājir went in fulfilment of an oath, with camels;*
   > *And his house, the house of the banū al-Dayyān, we know*
   > *Among the family of Madhḥij as the pearl of great price'.*[125]

2) Praise verses

   Al-Mukhtār b. Ka'b al-Ju'fī says of Qutayba [b. Muslim]:

   > *'He subdued the Sughd with the tribes until,*
   > *He left the Sogdians sitting in nakedness'.*[126]

3) Details about physical geography or landmarks

   Ibn Jumāna al-Bāhilī has said, referring to Salmān [b. Rabī'a] and Qutayba b. Muslim:

   > *'We have two tombs – one at Balanjar,*
   > *And another at Ṣīn Istān (China) – and what a tomb that is!*
   > *The one who lies in China has conquered it all,*
   > *And the merits of the other cause abundant rain to fall'.*[127]

4) The speech of caliphs or other officials
   During [the Prophet's] illness, Abū Bakr often repeated:

   'One in the morning may lie amidst his family,
   and death may be nearer to him than the strap of his sandal'.[128]

5) Derogatory verses
   It was he who heard a Jew in the caliphate of 'Umar recite the verse [about al-Ash'ath b. Qays, the future governor of Azerbaijan]:

   'Oh Ash'ath! Islam has diverted his attention from me,
   All good night, I have been alone with his wife'.[129]

Much of this type of material is matter of course. These were popular touchstones and forms for poetry which had thrived even in the pre-Islamic period.[130]

Beatrice Gruendler has written about the link between fiscal matters and poetry within historical *akhbār*, but many of her examples emphasize the relief of burden on poets or reward for their skill, whether requested or otherwise.[131] Gruendler emphasizes that 'verse and taxes' can often go hand in hand in this ninth-/third-century material, and that they can often serve an important role for scene-setting and performance in particular.[132] None of these types of poems appear in the *Futūḥ*, however, which seems a strange fact in itself for a work that is both so heavily interested in fiscal issues and containing so much poetry otherwise. For one, the poets themselves have very little presence in the *Futūḥ* other than with the brief interjection of statements such as 'thus the poet said…' (*qāla al-shā'ir…*),[133] while in Gruendler's abundance of examples, they are front and centre in this process. The poet in the *Futūḥ* is never more than peripheral when named at all, and the included poetry seems intended to bring flavour to the text and to bolster the accounts included within. While a view towards performance and oral recitation may have been a defining characteristic of a great deal of poetry from the period, none of this type of poetry is found in the *Futūḥ*. It does have, however, a key role in legitimizing the surrounding traditions and the narrative as a whole. In each of the five types and five examples above, the poetry is well settled among the rest of the traditions, and all of it fits well the primary themes of the *Futūḥ* that have been discussed here. There is praise for early Muslims participating in the conquest and the incredible feats of Muslim armies; descriptions of public works and landmarks that defined the regions al-Balādhurī discusses; and in the case of derogatory verses, commentary on, or rejoinders against, depravity or inefficiency among administrators.

As Webb has written, poetry and the transmission of historical material were intricately linked in the early Islamic period, even if this would change in later centuries.[134] Modern historians have also tended to shun this material as being almost ahistorical and, in some cases, not part of original transmission but perhaps a later addition. The presence of poetry throughout al-Balādhurī's text is as much a technique for bolstering the acceptability of his work as it was a sign of the methods of historical transmission that defined the early Arabic tradition before it was eventually abandoned by the field.[135] This is especially the case if we imagine that the author was writing this work to be read by other secretaries – the people who were already well educated themselves in the arts, and likely with a solid grasp of bureaucratic and grammatical works as well as poetry. Although al-Balādhurī does not place the spotlight on the poets themselves in his work, the presence of their material and how tightly interwoven it is throughout the overwhelming majority of the *Futūḥ*'s chapters emphasizes not just al-Balādhurī's interest in this material, but his skill with it. The very fact that we modern readers must probe the material and ponder the questions of whether the verse was inserted separately or part of the original whole is telling in itself.

Despite the fact that al-Balādhurī is observed in the biographical record as a poet well before he is noted as a secretary,[136] none of the poetry he transmits within the *Futūḥ* appears to be original. This is not surprising, however, as the *Futūḥ* has no pretensions of serving as a collection (*dīwān*, a record) of his poetry, nor is any of it said to have been written by him. But being a poet was not merely about originality, and imitation played a very major role in the process of being a Muslim poet; the classical Arabic poet required an in-depth understanding of 'the interplay between imitation and creation'.[137] Building a repertoire of poetry of previous masters was a vital part of this, and it is these imprints that allowed a poet to build from a past foundation. But the inclusion of poetry within historical *akhbār* was not something which required being a professional poet; it was, in the early 'Abbāsid period, still intrinsically linked to working with historical components, and the inclusion of such an ample amount of poetry by a jurist like al-Ṭabarī in his *History* testifies to this.

While the *Futūḥ* is hardly a *dīwān* of Arabic poetry, this does not take away from the reality that it and *Ansāb al-ashrāf* are repositories of early Arabic poetry of significant literary value. While this fact was noted by S. D. Goitein for the *Ansāb*,[138] the smaller collection of poetry contained within the *Futūḥ* is also of great value. In both texts, the verses included by al-Balādhurī tend to be limited to only a few lines of verse at a time, and in the *Futūḥ*, the occasions where we find an extended instance of poetry that goes beyond six lines of Arabic are exceedingly rare.[139] The vast majority of poetry appears in two to four lines. This is in contrast to the *Ta'rīkh* of al-Ṭabarī, for instance, where long excerpts of poetry are found throughout.

Conclusions

Creating an 'imperial project,' to return to Robinson's phrase, characterized the ninth-/third-century Arabic tradition. It had as much to do with the systemization and collation of a variety of traditions as it did with the authors who were creating the first Arabic written texts. Their selection and shaping of previously circulating information was crucial for the creation of a historical orthodoxy in early Islam; not everything which came to the author was preserved unexpurgated, nor was everything which came to the author agreeable with his agenda. The selection of materials was heavily defined by factors – conscious and subconscious – that exerted influence over the authors of these early texts. Those factors came in a variety of forms, which ranged from the power and sway of a patron to a desire to present one's own tribe or region as superior to others, and al-Balādhurī was undeniably an actor in this process. Above all, however, he was influenced by the environment in which and for which he was writing his book. Guided by a predisposition which led him to select materials of interest to those at the centre of the Islamic world, he crafted a text which spoke to educated bureaucrats not just about the realities and traditions of their roles in the state, but with a vocabulary of style and symbols that many were likely intimately familiar.

The content of the *Futūḥ* was evidently selected by its author on thematic grounds, and this has hitherto only been passively recognized. While many such as Khalidi and Kennedy have identified some of these thematic features of the text, modern scholars have continued to pass over the issues of authorial intent and envisioned reception that are intricately linked to the identification of these themes. Al-Balādhurī's selection and organization of material and what he chose to omit (which, in the case of someone like Sayf b. 'Umar, was almost certainly available to him), exhibits a desire to select material which was of direct relevance to the establishment of the Islamic state, its institutions, and its possessions. There could be little reason to construct a text with a thematic interest in these topics for any other reason, especially at the exclusion of traditions that would have provided a more interesting and/or cohesive narrative – and, in fact, these traditions are found in other Arabic texts attributed to many of the same transmitters he relied upon. That he includes such a thorough collection of accounts related to settlement agreements, land ownership, public works projects, and practical details about the administrative apparatus itself – at a significantly higher ratio than his contemporaries and near-contemporaries – only further confirms this.

When the *Futūḥ* does overlap with other Arabic literature, it likewise betrays further insight into the background of the author and, perhaps, the audience he had in mind in compiling the text. While the *Futūḥ's* narrative flourishes are few and far between, they clearly make up a lesser theme of the text, especially when the modern reader considers al-Balādhurī's characterization of administrators and his employment of poetry throughout the book. While his use of poetry astride the prose is not unique, it *is* when considering the rest of the material he chooses to focus his attention on in the rest of the text. It is a further aspect which characterizes an *adīb* who appears not just to have been transmitting historical poetry from previous compilers like al-Madā'inī, but from other, lesser-known sources as well, while also linking that poetry to the traditions of conquest and governance.

Then, there is the role these traditions and included anecdotes played in cataloguing not just the practical aspects of caliphal governance, but the historic strength of the caliphate at its foundation and in its earliest days. In this aspect of the *Futūḥ*, the idea of Robinson's 'imperial project' perhaps fits best of all when we see it as a site of collective memory of import specific to the administrators. To quote Geoffrey Cubitt:

> Social formations cannot subsist unless people within them have a certain capacity to remember things that have happened previously. Again, what is being said here is not something grand, about the need for societies to have a kind of 'collective memory' of their past as a community, but – in the first instance at least – something more prosaic: people cannot secure, or even envisage, the benefits of social exchange and social co-operation, and therefore cannot be brought to engage in these things in more than a very occasional and momentary way, unless they can place some faith in their own and in other people's ability to recall previous experience and agreements previously entered on. Social operations depend on a capacity for deferred action: the functioning of society at any given moment depends, firstly, on people allowing their present

> conduct to be guided by an awareness of what they and others have said or done previously, and secondly, on their being willing to act now in ways which will make sense only on the assumption that this action will be remembered and taken account of in framing later courses of action.[140]

The *Futūḥ* served a vital role for the secretaries in confirming their role as part of an epistemic community. It presented them with images of the past that recalled the success of the Islamic state previously: what had worked, how it worked, and why it could work again. The middle of the ninth/third century was a time of challenge for the state and its institutions, but the strength and successes of their predecessors were also reminders of why the state maintained authority amid disorder.

Notes

1 Khalidi, *Arabic Historical Thought*, 68.

2 Robinson, *Islamic Historiography*, 40–1.

3 As discussed in chapter 3, however, whether these works were ever committed to writing as complete, coherent, and written books is another matter entirely.

4 Ibn al-Nadīm, *Fihrist*, 102.

5 *Futūḥ*, 9 (H 24).

6 *Futūḥ*, 10, 437 (H 25-26, M 77).

7 *Futūḥ*, 66 (H 86).

8 *Futūḥ*, 257 (H 344-345).

9 *Futūḥ*, 93 (H 188-199).

10 *Futūḥ*, 569, 574 (M 259-260, 265).

11 *Futūḥ*, 473 (M 122-123). On the transmission of the poetry from al-Madā'inī in the early Arabic historical tradition, see A. F. L. Beeston and Lawrence I. Conrad, 'On Some Umayyad Poetry in the *History* of al-Ṭabarī', *Journal of the Royal Asiatic Society*, Vol. 3, No. 2 (1993), 191–206.

12 In contrast to Figure 3.3, which appears in Chapter 3, this number also includes traditions where Abū Mikhnaf appears as a guarantor within a larger chain of transmission as well as those traditions where he is named as the informant.

13 Khalil Athamina has recently written in the *Encyclopaedia of Islam* of Abū Mikhnaf: 'His version of the conquest of Iraq is the one al-Balādhurī preferred to those of al-Wāqidī and al-Madā'inī', but this opinion is overstated. Abū Mikhnaf's details surrounding the *battles* of the Muslim armies in Iraq are favoured in many instances, but these traditions make up only a small portion of those that appear in al-Balādhurī's chapters on the region, and a substantial number of al-Wāqidī

and al-Madā'inī's traditions on the region are also found in these chapters. Khalil Athamina, 'Abū Mikhnaf', *EI*[3]. Separately, the lack of detailed battle accounts is a problem of conquest literature more generally, and is discussed in Albrecht Noth, 'Iṣfahān-Nihāwand: Eine quellenkritische Studie zur frühislamischen Historiographie', *Zeitschrift der Deutschen Morgenländischen Gesellschaft*, Vol. 118 (1968), 274–96.

14 *Futūḥ*, 476 (M 127-128), but see also *Futūḥ*, 99–100, 401, 412 (H 124-125, M 21, 40-41). On the conquest of Fārs and the sources that discuss these events, see Martin Hinds, 'The First Arab Conquests in Fārs', *Iran*, Vol. 22 (1984), 39–53. Hinds spends much of his time discussing the details of *who* was involved in the conquest and subsequent governance of the region precisely because of the availability of this information in the sources.

15 *Futūḥ*, 216–17 (H 284-285). The status of the Banū Taghlib and their refusal to pay the normal tax required of non-Muslims, the *jizya*, instead being charged twice the *ṣadaqa* tax levied on Muslims, has been much discussed by modern scholars. See, for instance, Michael Lecker, 'Tribes in Pre- and Early Islamic Arabia', in *People, Tribes, and Society in Arabic Around the Time of Muḥammad* (Aldershot: Ashgate, 2005), 34–47; Antoine Fattal, *Le statut legal des non-musulmans en pays d'Islam* (Beirut: Impr. Catholique, 1958); and A. S. Tritton, *The Caliphs and Their Non-Muslim Subjects: A Critical Study of the Covenant of 'Umar* (London: Oxford University Press, 1930), 89–100.

16 On the problematic nature of al-Wāqidī's surviving *oeuvre*, see Rudi Paret, 'The Legendary *Futūḥ* Literature', in *The Expansion of the Early Islamic State*, ed. Fred M. Donner (Aldershot: Ashgate, 2008), 164–6; and Rosenthal, *Muslim Historiography*, 186–93.

17 Ibn al-Nadīm, *Fihrist*, 107.

18 There is an additional remark born from this above evidence: These famed *akhbāriyyūn* remembered so clearly in both the later medieval and modern scholarly traditions for their accounts of the early Islamic conquests obviously had within their repertoire information concerning the formation of the early Islamic administrative apparatus. It is also interesting to note that despite the very positive reception al-Balādhurī receives from his medieval successors, al-Wāqidī did not fare so well: He is heavily criticized for his *ḥadīth* transmission while his *akhbār* material was considered acceptable. And yet, in looking closely at the titles of his non-extant works and the overlapping material al-Balādhurī chooses to adopt from him within the *Futūḥ*, a large number of these traditions seem not to have taken the form of narrative *akhbār*, but of the legal *ḥadīth* for which he was attacked.

19 Sayf, despite his importance in transmitting so much of the surviving narrative traditions concerning early Islamic history, has had surprisingly little focused research conducted on him. For a discussion of his reputation and study in the

modern period, see Landau-Tasseron, 'Sayf ibn 'Umar in Medieval and Modern Scholarship', 1–26.

20 Here, I refer to the fact that the omissions of Sayf's material may well have been completely (or, at the least, strongly) influenced by al-Balādhurī's informants themselves, who may have chosen to share only a small portion of Sayf's material with him. This does, however, seem less likely, as it would seem unusual for al-Balādhurī's informants to decide that at least *some* of Sayf's material was trustworthy enough to pass on through generations of students while also seemingly telling our author that the rest of his conquest material was simply unacceptable. It seems far more likely that al-Balādhurī made the conscious decision to exclude Sayf's traditions.

21 The second of these traditions, where only Sayf is named, concerns a battle at al-Buwayb, where a commander of the Persian ruler Yazdigird named Mihrān was killed. The entire tradition itself is exceedingly brief, completely unlike the material of Sayf's that appears in al-Ṭabarī's *Ta'rīkh*. The tradition can be found in *Futūḥ*, 311 (H 406). This tradition was previously identified by Boaz Shoshan, who also hypothesizes on some of the reasons why al-Balādhurī does not use much material from Sayf. For more on this, see Boaz Shoshan, *The Arabic Historical Tradition and the Early Islamic Conquests: Folklore, Tribal Lore, Holy War* (New York: Routledge, 2016), 11–12.

22 *Futūḥ*, 377 (H 479).

23 Shoshan also suggests, however, in reference to al-Balādhurī's reporting on the Battle of al-Qādisiyya, that 'the resemblance to Sayf is obvious' even if he is not mentioned by name as the originator of the compiled traditions. I find this suggestion, however, more problematic, as while some of the details between Sayf's accounts of the battle in al-Ṭabarī and those of al-Balādhurī are the same, much of the language used is entirely different (the importance of this linguistic variation will be discussed at length in Chapter 6), and important parts of the account (such as the role of the westerly wind) are entirely omitted. See Shoshan, *Arabic Historical Tradition*, 11. On the historiography surrounding the Battle of al-Qādisiyya more generally, see D. Gershon Lewental, 'Qādisiyyah, Then and Now: A Case Study of History and Memory, Religion, and Nationalism in Middle Eastern Discourse' (PhD diss., Brandeis University, 2011).

24 Abū Yūsuf, *Kitāb al-Kharāj*, trans. Chase F. Robinson, *Empires and Elites After the Muslim Conquest: The Transformation of Northern Mesopotamia* (Cambridge: Cambridge University Press, 2000), 3.

25 For a critical discussion of the relations between the Muslims and the Nubians and the importance of pacts between the two, see Martin Hinds and Hamdi Sakkout, 'A Letter From the Governor of Egypt to the King of Nubia and Muqurra Concerning Egyptian-Nubian Relations in 141/758', in *Studia Arabica et Islamica: Festschrift*

for Ihsan 'Abbas on His Sixtieth Birthday, ed. Wadad al-Qadi (Beirut: American University of Beirut, 1981), 209–30.

26 *Futūḥ*, 281 (H 381). It is worth noting, however, that the agreement the 'Abbāsids had with the Nubians appears to have been non-standard, and the people of the region were treated more as tributaries rather than as protected (*dhimma*) peoples. On the issues surrounding this purported treaty, see Milka Levy-Rubin, *Non-Muslims in the Early Islamic Empire: From Surrender to Coexistence* (Cambridge: Cambridge University Press, 2011), 55–6.

27 See Calder, *Early Muslim Jurisprudence*, 137–41; Robinson, *Empires and Elites*, 1–32, esp. 1–5.

28 On the problematic nature and unverifiability of many of these documents and their analysis as literary forms in the Islamic tradition, see Noth and Conrad, *The Early Arabic Historical Tradition*, 62–76.

29 For a discussion of this tradition, the *Chronicle of Seert* more generally, and the suggestion that this 'letter' is a later reworking of the past, see Philip Wood, *The Chronicle of Seert: Christian Historical Imagination in Late Antique Iraq* (Oxford: Oxford University Press, 2013), 244–7.

30 On these classifications, see Noth, 'On the Relationship in the Caliphate Between Central Power and the Provinces', 178–88.

31 It should be especially noted that Hill provides only limited analysis of these traditions and of the texts he relies upon for their compilation. Despite this, however, as a database of traditions, his research retains a great amount of usefulness, as does his attention to the Arabic phrases *ṣulḥan, 'anwatan, jizya, kharāj,* and *dhimma.*

32 Noth and Conrad, *Arabic Historical Tradition*, 64–76.

33 On the status and general reliability of these settlement agreements found in the early Islamic tradition, see Milka Levy-Rubin, *Non-Muslims in the Early Islamic Empire*, 8–57 and Milka Levy-Rubin, '*Shurūṭ 'Umar* and Its Alternatives: The Legal Debate on the Status of the *Dhimmīs*', *Jerusalem Studies in Arabic and Islam*, Vol. 30 (2005), 170–206.

34 While the challenges of social history in the medieval period are numerous and well documented, there is a useful contribution to economic history in the medieval Islamic period focusing on issues such as the division of labour and occupational structures, although it does focus primarily on the matters of urban centres. See Maya Shatzmiller, *Labour in the Medieval Islamic World* (Leiden: Brill, 1994).

35 See, for instance, Richard Ettinghausen's general comments on the material culture of the medieval Islamic world in 'The Impact of Muslim Decorative Arts and Painting on the Arts of Europe', in *The Legacy of Islam*, ed. Joseph Schacht and C. E. Bosworth (Oxford: Clarendon Press, 1974), 275; regarding Islamic architecture

and, in particular, painting techniques, see David T. Rice, *Islamic Art* (London: Thames and Hudson, 1965), 82–6; and on the metalwork industry of the Islamic world, see James W. Allan, 'The Nishapur Metalwork: Cultural Interaction in Early Islamic Iran', in *Content and Context of Visual Arts in the Islamic World*, ed. Priscilla P. Soucek (University Park: Pennsylvania State University Press, 1988), 1–12.

36 *Futūḥ*, 174, 175, 179–80, 190–1, 205, 211, 251–2, 253–4, 329–3 (H 227, 228, 234, 249, 271, 278, 338, 341, 426-429).

37 *Futūḥ*, 179–80, 190–1, 205, 211, 251–2, 253–4 (H 234, 249, 271, 278, 338, 341).

38 *Futūḥ*, 205, 251–2, 253–4 (H 271, 338, 341).

39 *Futūḥ*, 217 (H 286).

40 *Futūḥ*, 239 (H 317).

41 *Futūḥ*, 218, 267–8 (H 286, 357).

42 *Futūḥ*, 301, 332–3 (H 395, 429).

43 See, for instance, Hugh Kennedy, 'The Feeding of the Five Hundred Thousand: Cities and Agriculture in Early Islamic Mesopotamia', *Iraq*, Vol. 73 (2011), 177–99; Campopiano, 'State, Land Tax, and Agriculture', 5–50; and Albrecht Noth, 'Some Remarks on the Nationalization of Conquered Lands at the Time of the Umayyads', in *Land Tenure and Social Transformation in the Middle East*, ed. Tarif Khalidi (Beirut: American University of Beirut, 1984), 223–8.

44 *Futūḥ*, 171 (H 221). Here, I am relying on Hitti's translation of the terms '*al-takhāfīf' and 'al-rudūd'*, but neither term is defined by al-Balādhurī or by Hitti.

45 This may refer to Hārūn al-Rashīd, but this is not explicit. The term *sulṭān* is non-specific, and in early Arabic sources, the term is usually used to refer just to the government – 'the authority'.

46 *Futūḥ*, 187 (H 244-245). As al-Balādhurī does not directly link these traditions together himself, however, it would be careless to speak definitively that the lands discussed in the first tradition are the same ones referenced in the second.

47 *Futūḥ*, 171 (H 221).

48 *Futūḥ*, 361–7 (H 457-464).

49 Wadad al-Qadi, 'The Names of Estates in State Registers Before and After the Arabization of the "Dīwāns"', 255–80.

50 *Futūḥ*, 340–1 (H 436-439).

51 *Futūḥ*, 155, 269, 391, 406 (H 201, 359; M 6, 24). Based on where al-Balādhurī emplots the tradition of the mosque in Ifrīqiyya, it may be referring more specifically to the mosque of Kairouan (Qayrawān).

52 *Futūḥ*, 434–58 (M 77-101).

53 *Futūḥ*, 14–15, 170 (H 29, 220-221).

54 Kennedy, 'Five Hundred Thousand', 183.

55 Hugh Kennedy, 'Landholding and Law in the Early Islamic State', in *Diverging Paths? The Shapes of Power and Institutions in Medieval Christendom and Islam*,

eds. John Hudson and Ana Rodríguez (Leiden: Brill, 2014), 159–81 and Kennedy, 'Five Hundred Thousand', 182.

56 Fred M. Donner, "Uthmān and the *Rāshidūn* Caliphs in Ibn 'Asākir's *Ta'rīkh madīnat Dimashq*: A Study in Strategies of Compilation', in *Ibn 'Asākir and Early Islamic History*, ed. James E. Lindsay (Princeton: The Darwin Press, 2001), 46–7.

57 Julius Wellhausen, *Die religiös-politischen Oppositionsparteien im alten Islam* (Berlin: Weidmannsche Buchhandlung, 1901); English edition translated by Robin Ostle and Sofie Walzer as *The Religio-Political Factions in Early Islam* (Amsterdam: North-Holland Publishing Co., 1975); and *Das Arabische Reich und sein Sturz* (Berlin: De Gruyter, 1902); English edition translated by Margaret Graham Weir as *The Arab Kingdom and Its Fall* (Calcutta: University of Calcutta, 1927).

58 See especially Tayeb El-Hibri, 'The Redemption of Umayyad Memory by the 'Abbāsids', *Journal of Near Eastern Studies*, Vol. 61, No. 4 (2002), 241–65, Borrut, *Entre mémoire et pouvoir*, and many of the chapters dedicated to precisely this issue in *Umayyad Legacies*, eds. Borrut and Cobb.

59 The first *fitna* was the Islamic civil war fought between the fourth Caliph 'Alī (656-661 CE/AH 23-35) and the eventual founder of the Umayyad dynasty, Mu'āwiya b. Abī Sufyān (r. 661-680 CE/AH 41-46), largely for vengeance over the murder of the latter's kinsman.

60 Petersen, *'Alī and Mu'āwiya*, 136–48.

61 This includes the suggestion that the text could not have been completed prior to the end of the 860s and comments on al-Balādhurī's use of both oral and written sources in the creation of his works, although he does not understand, as I have previously argued, how al-Balādhurī's introductory phrases are marking these differences. See Petersen, *'Alī and Mu'āwiya*, 137–8.

62 Athamina, 'Sources', 237–62.

63 Wurtzel, 'Introduction', in *Khalifa ibn Khayyat's History on the Umayyad Dynasty*, 29.

64 Ibid., 27.

65 Although he certainly would not have referred to himself by such a pejorative term. On the biography of Ziyād and his adoption by Mu'āwiya as his brother, see Isaac Hasson, 'Ziyād b. Abīhi', *EI*[2] and Isaac Hasson, 'L'affiliation (*di'wa*) de Ziyād b. Abīhi', *Jerusalem Studies in Arabic and Islam*, Vol. 29 (2004), 413–25.

66 On his positive characteristics, see the (very dated) article of K. A. Fariq, 'A Remarkable Early Muslim Governor Zayīd b. Abīh', *Islamic Quarterly*, Vol. 26, No. 4 (1952), 1–31.

67 This tradition is repeated twice in the text and linked to the construction and changes of the great mosques in both cities, once in the chapter on Kūfa and the other in the chapter on Baṣra. *Futūḥ*, 339–40, 427 (H 436-437, M 63).

68 *Futūḥ*, 439–40 (M 80).

69 *Futūḥ*, 569 (M 259-260).

70 On these issues regarding the right to rule in the early Islamic period, see Asma Afsaruddin, *Excellence and Precedence in Medieval Islamic Discourse on Legitimate Leadership* (Leiden: Brill, 2002).

71 Almost all of these mentions of al-Walīd are incidental, with the exception of his role in punishing the frontier territory of Cyprus. In these instances, al-Walīd 1) is mentioned as the Caliph when the governor of Iraq, Yūsuf b. ʻUmar, reverts the level of required tax over the exiled people of Najrān to a lesser earlier level (80 - H 104); 2) expels the people of Cyprus from their island because of an accusation of collusion with the enemy, which the reader is told was unpopular (183 - H 238); 3) is mentioned in a letter of a jurist for his (disliked) role in expelling the people of Cyprus (185 - H 241); 4) is mentioned as the Caliph when an old Roman fort was destroyed by the Byzantines in the frontier territories between the Umayyads and the Byzantines (228 - H 298); 5) is mentioned as having just died when Marwān b. Muḥammad was campaigning in the Caucasus (246 - H 328); 6) is mentioned when a revolt by ʻAbd al-Raḥmān b. Ḥabīb al-Fihrī in North Africa occurred at the beginning of his reign, causing him to send no governor there (274 - H 367-368); and 7) is mentioned as a successor of Yazīd b. ʻAbd al-Malik when discussing affairs in the border region of Khurāsān (525 - M 199).

72 Steven C. Judd, 'Narratives and Character Development: Al-Ṭabarī and al-Balādhurī on Late Umayyad History', in *Ideas, Images, and Methods of Portrayal: Insights Into Classical Arabic Literature and Islam*, ed. Sebastian Günther (Leiden: Brill, 2005), 209–26.

73 Referring to the capture of Mecca by the Muslims in the year 629-630 CE/8 AH.

74 *Futūḥ*, 582 (M 273).

75 El-Hibri, 'Redemption of Umayyad Memory', 242, 252–6.

76 M. A. Shaban, *Islamic History, A New Interpretation*, Vol. 1, *AD 600-750 (AH 132)* (Cambridge: Cambridge University Press, 1971), 63.

77 Tayeb El-Hibri, *Parable and Politics in Early Islamic History: The Rashidun Caliphs* (New York: Columbia University Press, 2010), 148.

78 *Futūḥ*, 432 (M 69-70).

79 Petersen, *ʻAlī and Muʻāwiya*, 148.

80 Almost all mentions of the civil wars in the *Futūḥ* are only ever incidental, and usually relate to dating when another event happened. See, for instance, several times where 'the days of Ibn al-Zubayr' or 'the *fitna* of Ibn al-Zubayr' are mentioned (62, 168, 221, 270 - H 82, 219-220, 289, 360). The one time where it is more relevant is when discussing why ʻAbd al-Malik made tributary terms with the Byzantine Emperor because of his preoccupation with the second *fitna* (189 - H 247). The only other times Ibn al-Zubayr is mentioned in the text relate to the damage of the Kaʻba during al-Ḥajjāj's siege of Mecca's mosque and its reconstruction afterwards (54-55 - H 74-76), and to his role as a conqueror of

North Africa before the second *fitna* (250, 267, H 337, 356). There is never any mention of the Abbāsid Revolution, nor of the fourth *fitna* between al-Amīn and al-Ma'mūn.

81 See André Miquel, *Le géographie humaine du monde musulman jusqu'au milieu du 11e siècle: Les travaux et les jours* (Paris: Éditions de l'École des hautes études en sciences sociales, 1967–1987) and Zayde Antrim, *Routes & Realms: The Power of Place in the Early Islamic World* (Oxford: Oxford University Press, 2012).

82 See, for instance, Petersen, *'Alī and Mu'āwiya*, 137, 148.

83 It should be said that their titles in these roles often offer little explanation for their actual roles: the Arabic term *amīr* is used to refer to a military commander regardless of his position in the chain of command; the term *wālī* can often be used to describe a governor (although al-Balādhurī uses this term fairly infrequently), and the generic Arabic term *'āmil* (literally, 'official' or 'agent') is used to refer to a variety of administrative positions in the new state including, but not limited to, the governorship.

84 See, for instance, the discussion of this issue in Sijpesteijn, *Shaping a Muslim State*, 64–81.

85 Petersen, *'Alī and Mu'āwiya*, 137.

86 This was previously noted by Noth/Conrad, who wrote that 'documents are, as a rule, issued in the name of the Muslim general in command at the time in question. The caliph is mentioned only rarely'. Such a direct example as the one below, however, is exceptionally rare. Noth and Conrad, *Arabic Historical Tradition*, 64.

87 *Futūḥ*, 145 (H 188).

88 *Futūḥ*, 167–8 (H 217-218).

89 This is not only limited to the caliph in a faraway capital city, but is also seen with particularly famous major governors such as al-Ḥajjāj b. Yūsuf. On al-Ḥajjāj's constant oversight of the conquests in Khurāsān and his control of the general Qutayba b. Muslim, see Nicola Clarke, *The Muslim Conquest of Iberia: Medieval Arabic Narratives* (London: Routledge, 2012), 118–33.

90 An excellent example of this is found in *Futūḥ al-shām* of al-Azdī, where the conquest of Syria is put to a halt as the Muslim commanders learn of the amassing Byzantine army at Antioch. Unsure of what to do, we are told they write several letters to the Caliph Abū Bakr asking him for advice and assistance, and they do nothing until they receive his orders. Al-Azdī, *Futūḥ al-shām*, ed. William Nassau Lees as *The Fotooh al-Sha'm: Being an Account of the Moslim Conquests in Syria* (Calcutta: Baptist Mission Press, 1854), 24–39.

91 Noth and Conrad, *Arabic Historical Tradition*, 76–87; Clarke, *Muslim Conquest of Iberia*, 126–31.

92 On the legitimizing factors of the *futūḥ* literature for the Muslims' right to rule, see Donner, *Narratives of Islamic Origins*, 177–8.
93 This issue of the 'breakneck speed' of the Islamic conquests and the reality that it was a much more drawn-out process than the Arabic sources suggest has recently been addressed in Robert G. Hoyland, *In God's Path: The Arab Conquests and the Creation of an Islamic Empire* (Oxford: Oxford University Press, 2015), esp. 1–6.
94 On the artistic and literary nature of Khālid's desert march and its purpose within the narrative of the conquests, see Ryan J. Lynch, 'Linking Information, Creating a Legend: The Desert March of Khālid b. al-Walīd', *Lights: The MESSA Journal of the University of Chicago*, Vol. 2, No. 2 (2013), 28–41.
95 As noted above, the *Ansāb* focuses a considerable amount of attention on the reigns of Mu'āwiya and 'Abd al-Malik, and especially their roles and actions as caliphs. While there is still a great amount of attention paid to outstanding and well-known governors in the *Ansāb*, the caliphs are the figures who stand out front and centre among the many notables of the early Islamic period, as opposed to his focus in the *Futūḥ*.
96 *Futūḥ*, 164 (H 214-214).
97 It should be noted that the case of Jerusalem itself was unusual – a defeated people insisting that the ruler of their conqueror personally attend the surrender of the city. The legend that surrounds the meeting between the Patriarch of Jerusalem and the Caliph 'Umar became an important touchstone for dialogue between Christians and Muslims. On this, see Daniel J. Sahas, 'The Face to Face Encounter Between Patriarch Sophronius of Jerusalem and the Caliph 'Umar ibn al-Khaṭṭāb: Friends or Foes?' in *The Encounter of Eastern Christianity with Early Islam*, eds. Emmanouela Grypeou, Mark Swanson and David Thomas (Leiden: Brill, 2005), 33–44.
98 *Futūḥ*, 407 (M 31-32).
99 Al-Ṭabarī, *The History of al-Ṭabarī*, Vol. 14, *The Conquest of Iran*, trans. G. Rex Smith (Albany: State University of New York Press, 1994), 32–3 (2: 2661).
100 Ibid., 34 (2: 2662).
101 Ibn al-Nadīm, *Fihrist*, 363; from the translation of Bayard Dodge in *The Fihrist of Ibn al-Nadīm: A Tenth Century Survey of Muslim Culture* (New York: Columbia University Press, 1970), Vol. 2, 714.
102 On this, see Stefan Leder, 'Conventions of Fictional Narration in Learned Literature', in *Story-Telling in the Framework of Non-Fictional Arabic Literature*, ed. Stefan Leder (Wiesbaden: Harrassowitz Verlag, 1998), 40.
103 As Robert Hoyland has written, 'Such fanciful tales told for amusement (*khurāfāt* or *asmār*) were disdained by most scholars, who saw merit only in a "true," historical report, termed *ḥadīth* or *khabar*'. Robert G. Hoyland, 'History, Fiction, and Authorship in the First Centuries of Islam', in *Writing and Representation in Medieval Islam*, ed. Julia Bray (London: Routledge, 2006), 17.

104 Leder, 'Conventions of Fictional Narration', 34–60.
105 Hasson, 'Ansāb al-Ašrāf d'al-Balāḏurī est-il un Livre de Ta'rīḫ ou d'Adab?', 479–93.
106 Hilary Kilpatrick, '*Adab*', in *Encyclopedia of Arabic Literature*, eds. Julie Scott Meisami and Paul Starkey (London: Routledge, 1998), 56.
107 Ibid.
108 See especially James E. Montgomery, 'Serendipity, Resistance, and Multivalency: Ibn Khurradādhbih and his *Kitāb al-Masālik wa-l-mamālik*', in *On Fiction and* Adab *in Medieval Arabic Literature*, ed. Philip F. Kennedy (Wiesbaden: Harrassowitz Verlag, 2005), 177–230; James E. Montgomery, 'Ibn Rusta's Lack of "Eloquence," the *Rūs*, and Samanid Cosmography', *Edebiyāt*, Vol. 12 (2001), 73–93; Julia Bray, 'ʿAbbasid Myth and the Human Act: Ibn ʿAbd Rabbih and Others', in *On Fiction and* Adab *in Medieval Arabic Literature*, ed. Kennedy, 1–54; and Stefan Leder and Hilary Kilpatrick, 'Classical Arabic Prose Literature: A Researchers' Sketch Map', *Journal of Arabic Literature*, Vol. 23 (1992), 2–26.
109 Montgomery, 'Serendipity', 181–2.
110 *Futūḥ*, 379 (H 480).
111 *Futūḥ*, 390–1 (M 5).
112 *Futūḥ*, 378–9 (H 479-480).
113 *Futūḥ*, 100–1 (H 126). (Q 12:55).
114 Q 12:22.
115 *Futūḥ*, 269 (H 358-359).
116 *Futūḥ*, 241 (H 320).
117 Isabel Toral-Niehoff, 'History in *Adab* Context: 'The Book on Caliphal Histories' by Ibn 'Abd Rabbih (246/860-328/940)', *Journal of Abbasid Studies*, Vol. 2 (2015), 63.
118 See, concerning the *Kitāb al-aghānī*, Hilary Kilpatrick, *Making the Great Book of Songs: Compilation and the Author's Craft in Abū l-Faraj al-Iṣbahānī's* Kitāb al-aghānī (London: Routledge, 2003), esp. 89–99.
119 Peter Webb, 'Poetry and the Early Islamic Historical Tradition: Poetry and Narrative of the Battle of Ṣiffīn', in *Warfare and Poetry in the Middle East*, ed. Hugh Kennedy (London: I.B. Tauris, 2013), 119–20.
120 Beeston and Conrad, 'Umayyad Poetry'.
121 Wolfhart Heinrichs, 'Prosimentrical Genres in Classical Arabic Literature', in *Prosimetrum: Cross Cultural Perspectives on Narrative in Prose and Verse*, eds. Joseph Harris and Karl Reichl (Cambridge: D. S. Brewer, 1997), 249–75.
122 Peter Heath, 'Some Functions of Poetry in Premodern Historical and Pseudo-Historical Texts: Comparing *Ayyām al-'Arab*, al-Ṭabarī's *History*, and *Sirāt 'Antar*'; Geert Jan van Gelder, 'Poetry in Historiography: The Case of *al-Fakhrī* by Ibn Ṭiqṭaqā'; and Suleiman A. Mourad, 'Poetry, History, and the Early Arab-Islamic Conquests of *al-Shām* (Greater Syria)', all three of which are found in *Poetry and History: The Value of Poetry in Reconstructing Arab History*, eds. Ramzi Baalbaki,

Saleh Said Agha and Tarif Khalidi (Beirut: American University of Beirut Press, 2011).

123 See, for instance, Samer M. Ali, *Arabic Literary Salons in the Islamic Middle Ages: Poetry, Public Performance and the Presentation of the Past* (Notre Dame: University of Notre Dame Press, 2010).

124 On the matter of external verse serving as the basis for a prose narrative construction, see the suggestion of Suleiman Mourad and the desert march of Khālid b. al-Walīd, which is based on evidence from the *Futūḥ*. Mourad, 'Poetry', 179-80.

125 *Futūḥ*, 465 (M 113). The translation of this and the majority of the poetry here are by Hitti and Murgotten, with only brief emendation of my own.

126 *Futūḥ*, 518–19 (M 189).

127 *Futūḥ*, 241 (H 320).

128 *Futūḥ*, 11 (H 26).

129 *Futūḥ*, 403 (M 24).

130 Webb, 'Poetry and the Early Islamic Historical Tradition', 131–2.

131 Beatrice Gruendler, 'Verse and Taxes: The Function of Poetry in Selected Literary *Akhbār* of the Third/Ninth Century', in *On Fiction and* Adab *in Medieval Arabic Literature*, ed. Kennedy, 85–124.

132 Gruendler, 'Verse and Taxes', 89–90; Leder, 'Conventions of Fictional Narration', 36–9.

133 As an example, see *Futūḥ*, 235 (H 311).

134 Webb, 'Poetry and the Early Islamic Historical Tradition', 121–3.

135 Ibid., 123–4.

136 Ibn al-Nadīm, *Fihrist*, 125; repeated in Yāqūt, *Irshād*, Vol. 2, 127–8.

137 Abdelfattah Kilito, *The Author and His Doubles: Essays on Classical Arabic Culture*, trans. Michael Cooperson (Syracuse: Syracuse University Press, 2001), esp. 9–23.

138 Goitein, 'Introduction', 20.

139 Examples in the *Futūḥ* of these rare extended instances of verse include praise of the sword Samsāma, details of combat at the Battle of Qādisiyya, and an injunction to the Caliph ʿUmar b. al-Khaṭṭāb to be wary of the corruption of his agents and governors (*ʿāmil*) in the provinces. Worth noting regarding the poetry detailing the Battle of Qādisiyya, the extended verses in this section also include several smaller verses from different poets brought together to detail these events. In his translation of this section, Hitti has inexplicably chosen not to note that the final pages of this section are entirely verse. *Futūḥ*, 143, 319–21, 473 (H 185, 414-416, M 122-123).

140 Geoffrey Cubitt, *History and Memory* (Manchester: Manchester University Press, 2007), 119.

5

The matter of genre and the classification of *Futūḥ al-buldān*

> *I have noticed that historians follow different purposes. Some restrict themselves to the commemoration* (dhikr) *of the beginning [of Creation]. Others restrict themselves to the recollection of kings and caliphs.* Ḥadīth *scholars prefer the recollection of [religious] scholars. Ascetics* (zuhhād) *love the recollection of pious men. Litterateurs* (arbāb al-adab) *are inclined toward experts in the Arabic language and lore, as well as poets. It is known that everything is worth studying, and rejected [historical information] still remains desirable.*[1]

The above quotation, attributed to Ibn al-Jawzī (d. 1201 CE/AH 597) in the work of al-Sakhāwī (d. 1497 CE/AH 902), is primarily aimed at listing the value various types of historical information can have within different genres, even if authors and critics of other genres may reject that material as unfit for the purpose. At the same time, however, it demonstrates that by the later medieval period, authors of Arabic historical works were aware of the contours of literary categories and how, at the least, their selection of content for inclusion in works helped to define the boundaries of those pre-existing categories. The recognition of their contributions to these established categories is found through their very collection of acceptable information fit to share with their reader; this comment is, at its core, about authorial intention and genre through the choice of that suitable content.

As Justin Lake has written in reference to the medieval west, 'The question of why medieval historians wrote, and what they were hoping to accomplish, cannot be divorced from the subject of genre, since the form that a historical work took is an obvious and important clue to the intentions of the author.'[2] To know more about al-Balādhurī and his *Futūḥ al-buldān*, we must understand not just the *milieu* in which he was writing, but the landscape to which he was contributing. Both the form and content of a text are key considerations when discussing the genre of a literary work. However, the matter of al-Balādhurī's intended versus actual audience – a key issue at the centre of this entire study – should also be considered as a major factor in a text's classification. Importantly, all of these characteristics of a work are entwined, and therefore influence a modern assessment of how a medieval text and wider literary genres should be defined.

The field of early Arabic historiography and early Islamic tradition continues to lag behind scholarship on the medieval west when it comes to genre theory, and there are still only few studies concerning the classification and issues of genre. This is despite the regular reliance on narrative texts and comparisons between those works identified as similar. Regarding medieval western texts and their authorship, there have been substantial offerings on their form and classification,[3] and individual studies on the genres of romance,[4] lyric,[5] pilgrimage plays,[6] and even more abstract types such as children's literature.[7] Many of these studies have fruitfully married the techniques of historical analysis to those of literary criticism in an attempt to more fully address authorial intention within a variety of works.

Studies of this type within the early Arabic historical tradition have been rarer, although the last two decades have seen a marked shift towards improvement in the field of Arabic historiography.[8] Tarif Khalidi filled some of this dearth among modern secondary literature through the classification of early Islamic historical writing under 'four dominant epistemic canopies or modes', those of *ḥadīth* (traditions, essentially history), *adab* (belles-lettres),[9] *ḥikma* (wisdom literature), and *siyāsa* (governance literature). Each, he suggests, defined different periods of classical Islamic historical thought, with the recognition that we find regular overlap between them.[10] Chase Robinson's *Islamic Historiography* took this in a different direction, by suggesting the division of early historiography into three cardinal types: biography, prosopography, and chronography.[11] Robinson, too, stresses the flexibility of these identifications, however, and their analysis provides a useful starting point for focus and expansion in future scholarship.

Building upon Robinson's work, this chapter will work to identify and discuss the genres of early Arabic historical writing crossed by *Futūḥ al-buldān*. It will work from the broad genre of texts classified as 'histories' as those texts which have consciously and purposely brought together accounts and traditions of the past deemed important in a variety of forms – whether narrative or otherwise – that have the primary goal of informing the reader of what occurred in the past. Owing to the contradictory nature of many accounts in early Islamic history – where one author will include several different traditions of the same purported event – this definition makes no assumptions as to the authenticity of the entirety of the work. As authorship itself in the early Arabic tradition is fraught with challenges, this discussion of genre will largely focus on the texts and their traditions as a complete compiled entity, rather than working to define and classify the individual traditions contained within.

Where this research will go beyond Khalidi and Robinson, however, is in the classification of a number of additional genres and subgenres and the characteristics that give them their own distinct identity. With this said, however, there is a problem with the definition of terminology for the various discussed genres and subgenres within early Islamic history. The present study will lean heavily on the work by Paul Heck on the Muslim author and secretary (*kātib*) Qudāma b. Jaʿfar (d. 948 CE/AH 337).[12] Heck's methodological approach to Qudāma's text is a holistic one, as he identifies and discusses not just the background of Qudāma and his influences on the creation of his text, but definitions of genre and terminology within the sphere of Islamic secretarial works. Through a similar analysis and discussion of *Futūḥ al-buldān*, it is hoped that greater attention can be brought to these issues by way of a classification and discussion of the overlapping genres of this particular work.

As such, the discussion in this chapter will focus on three particular modern subgenre classifications within Arabic historical writing and how they overlap with *Futūḥ al-buldān*: that of conquest literature; judicial and legal texts; and administrative geographies. While providing introductory information on the content and style of these subgenres, it will challenge the simple classification of the *Futūḥ* as a piece of conquest literature or as a mere history. It will demonstrate that the modern classification of the *Futūḥ* within a single genre of Arabic writing is problematic, a fact which has actually plagued scholars since the medieval period surrounding the naming of the text itself. Finally, through the comparison of the *Futūḥ* with other contemporary and near-contemporary early Arabic works, it will establish that none of these early Arabic texts or genre classifications provide an ideal analogue for al-Balādhurī's text alone, suggesting that the work was likely created at a unique time and place. In bringing together diverse material in a different style, it will be argued that this – combined with the sources used to construct the text and the content and form of the accounts with which it is made – strongly advocates for a target audience of secretaries and administrators as the work's intended readership.

What's in a name? Medieval classifications of *Futūḥ al-buldān*

Precisely how early we can imagine Muslim authors thinking about their roles as contributors to the greater matter of genre is problematic in itself. The evidence for al-Balādhurī's own awareness of his contributions to pre-existing genres of historical writing in writing the *Futūḥ* is almost non-existent, and his immediate successors further demonstrate their own confusion over how best to describe his book. There has been an ambiguity – among both later medieval authors and the modern scholars who have since used the text – about how to classify the *Futūḥ*, and this has not been aided by confusion over the book's title and its lack of a stated intention upon its conception.[13] Several times in the much larger *Ansāb*, al-Balādhurī makes reference to his previous writing in the book we now seemingly know as *Futūḥ al-buldān* by calling it only 'the book of lands,' *Kitāb al-Buldān*.[14] Ibn al-Nadīm (d. ca. 995–998 CE/AH 385–388), to whom we owe our earliest surviving biographical reference to al-Balādhurī, seems to refer to it only as 'the small book of lands' (*kitāb al-buldān al-ṣaghīr*), separating it, likely erroneously,[15] from a second text, 'the large book of the lands', which Ibn al-Nadīm says the author did not finish.[16] The two *kitābā al-buldān* make up half of the four works that he attributes to al-Balādhurī.[17] At the outset of *Futūḥ al-buldān*, the reader is provided only two lines describing the construction of the work, the first of which reads: 'Aḥmad b. Yaḥyā b. Jābir [al-Balādhurī] says: I have been informed by men learned in traditions (*ḥadīth*), prophetic biography (*sīra*), and the conquest of lands (*Futūḥ al-buldān*).' There is no further elaboration by the author describing the text as a book on the conquests above all else. Al-Mas'ūdī (d. 956 CE/AH 345), in his introductory chapter of the *Murūj al-dhahab*, refers to 'the book of history (*kitāb al-ta'rīkh*) by Aḥmad b. Yaḥyā al-Balādhurī', going on to detail some of its contents before saying that 'we do not know of [anything] greater than it on the subject of the conquest of lands (*Futūḥ al-buldān*)'.[18] Problematically, Yāqūt (d. 1229 CE/AH 626) later provides a list of al-Balādhurī's works on the authority of Ibn al-Nadīm, and yet confusingly lists a fifth book called simply 'the book of the conquests' (*kitāb al-futūḥ*) totally separately from his naming of the two books called *al-Buldān*.[19] Al-Mas'ūdī could not have relied on Ibn al-Nadīm's work as the source of his information,[20] and his comments on the content of the book and the superiority of al-Balādhurī's text reveal al-Mas'ūdī's familiarity with, and understanding of, the text. This is something that Ibn al-Nadīm's explanation does not provide. Furthermore, it seems that al-Maʿsūdī's description of a text as '*Futūḥ al-buldān*' is the title that eventually came to be applied to it, although it was not universally cited as a work of *futūḥ* by all medieval scholars between the careers of Ibn al-Nadīm and al-Sakhāwī. Even by the fifteenth century when al-Sakhāwī was writing, he chose to classify al-Balādhurī's *Futūḥ* in a section on 'the most numerous' (*wa-hiya kathīra jiddan*) geographical works, along with the *Muʿjam al-buldān* (*Dictionary of Lands*) of Yāqūt and *Kitāb al-Masālik wa-l-mamālik* (*The Book of Roads and Kingdoms*) of Abū ʿUbayd al-Bakrī (d. 1094 CE/AH 487).[21]

Several important pieces of information are communicated to the modern scholar through this mixed and at times contradictory information, not least of which is the formative nature of Arabic historical writing in the earliest centuries. It shows the varied and unusual nature of al-Balādhurī's *Futūḥ al-buldān*, which shares characteristics with multiple different genres of Arabic writing as they would come to be classified. There are many questions that can be asked about how much we can expect from historical genres which were still being developed and which other medieval scholars also differed in describing. But perhaps one of the most important questions which must be asked is just what al-Balādhurī believed he was doing in the creation of *Futūḥ al-buldān*. Did he see himself as writing a history? A compilation of the conquests? A legal text? A secretarial work? A work of literature? A handbook? It is difficult for modern scholars to consider these questions on our own. Among the most crucial pieces of evidence that survive to help answer the genre question is an analysis of the works he himself relied on in the creation of his own text.[22] Furthermore, authors were still experimenting not just with the form of these texts, but with their included and excluded content as well. We must also express uncertainty over whether these authors of early Arabic texts believed themselves to be engaging with and contributing to a wider genre of historical writing, or if utility was of paramount importance. There must be caution expressed over whether the later assignment of genres to ninth-century Arabic texts – even in the later medieval period – was not anachronistic, as the evidence demonstrating that early Muslim authors were aware of their contribution to a defined field is limited.[23]

Abdelfattah Kilito, in his discussion of authorship and genre in classical Arabic literature and culture, described the near impossible nature of attempting to identify a text's author based purely on style. The genre of a classical Arabic text, he argued, was another matter entirely, and he suggests that this can easily be ascertained through a comparison of one work with others containing similar features:

> Instead, each genre possesses its own 'composition', a set of recurrent features common to a number of works. Given these features, the reader can easily determine the genre to which a given text belongs and move from that text to the consideration of related texts. … Authorship is a flimsy notion, whereas genre is a highly specific and determined category, so much so that authors were perhaps nothing but products of their genres.[24]

While authorship in the early Islamic period may well be the 'flimsy notion' Kilito suggested, his comments on genre in the same period are far less convincing. His description might work better for the later Islamic period, as al-Sakhāwī's quotation of Ibn al-Jawzī revealed, but the earliest Islamic centuries remained an experimental period in the creation of Arabic texts where the boundaries of 'highly specific and determined categories' were yet to be established. Even the medieval authors who were attempting to describe and catalogue al-Balādhurī's output differ in their categorization and descriptions of the *Futūḥ*, so how well defined could these genres of writing have been in these periods? Comparing the *Futūḥ* to similar surviving Arabic works of the ninth/third and tenth/fourth centuries provides us an opportunity to test Kilito's assertion that genre is something easily determined in the early Islamic period, while also providing answers for how exactly al-Balādhurī's text should be classified and utilized going forward.

Futūḥ al-buldān as conquest literature

Of particular interest for our purposes is a discussion of the classification of the so-called '*futūḥ*' literature, or the conquest theme more generally. While this type of text has been classified by a considerable number of modern scholars as an important form and theme of the Arabic historical tradition, there has been far less committed to writing regarding these texts as a distinct genre in their own right. Albrecht Noth and Lawrence Conrad, for instance, discussed the *futūḥ* as an important primary theme of the early Arabic tradition, and one which consisted of a number of subthemes – but not as a genre itself.[25] The form of these texts can vary, as they can present a particularly narrow geographical focus, or can take a broader view of the entire Islamic world – as al-Balādhurī's text does. The *futūḥ* section may capture only a portion of the attention of a larger work – like those of al-Ṭabarī (d. 923 CE/AH 310) and Qudāma b. Jaʿfar – and considering it a theme there may be most appropriate. But it can also be the entire subject of a work, such as al-Azdī's (*fl.* late 700s CE/AH mid-100s)[26] *Futūḥ al-Shām* (*The Conquest of Syria*).[27]

We must, therefore, be cautious when attributing a text to a 'genre of *futūḥ*' without thinking more critically about precisely what this means and, indeed, the greater problems this type of classification causes when approaching these texts. If we consider texts belonging to the *futūḥ* genre simply as those books which provide narrative accounts of the period of the Islamic conquests, then we must consider a significant proportion of surviving early Arabic texts to also belong to this genre. This, understandably, seems unwise. It seems almost a requirement of these early texts to provide some form of outline of the conquest period in order to be recognized as any form of serious historical scholarship. But whether the *futūḥ* sections should be considered a text's primary classification over its other content is a rather different issue.

Noth and Conrad categorize the *futūḥ* theme as contextualizing the traditions which discuss 'the first decades of Islamic history after the death of Muḥammad', and most notably 'the first large-scale conquest of the Muslims outside the Arabian Peninsula – in Syria/Palestine, Iraq/Iran, and Egypt/North Africa'.[28] This is problematic. The issue here is obvious for those using historical works such as Ibn Aʿtham al-Kūfī's (*fl.* late 800s CE/AH mid-200s) *Kitāb al-futūḥ* (*The Book of the Conquests*), which goes far beyond these early decades of Islamic history and does not conclude until the reign of the ʿAbbāsid Caliph al-Muʿtaṣim (r. 833–842 CE/AH 218–227).[29] Is a text like this simply mistitled? Or does the problem with its label go deeper, with the attribution of the *futūḥ* theme by modern scholars to only the earliest Islamic conquests and the reigns of the first four caliphs, and not to the conquests of more peripheral regions such as al-Andalus or India, or the continued and sustained raiding of the frontiers with the Byzantine Empire and Turkic groups in Central Asia?

The *futūḥ* genre should not be categorized only by titles which are restricted to this particular time period, but rather, to texts which provide a substantial focus on the recollection of Muslim conflict and the expansion of *dār al-Islām* against external forces. External conflict is specified, as the texts variously labelled as *futūḥ* choose to handle internal strife differently. When it comes to conflict within the Muslim community, Noth and Conrad rightly identify a separate – yet often linked – theme of *fitna* (civil war) within historical texts.[30] It is a separate consideration and a conscious decision the author needed to make to include this theme. The surviving portion of *Kitāb al-Ridda wa-l-futūḥ*

(*The Book of the Apostasy and the Conquests*) of Sayf b. ʻUmar (*fl.* late 700s/AH mid-100s) makes clear this marriage of interests between *futūḥ* and *fitna*,[31] for instance, and the first two civil wars feature prominently in the *futūḥ* sections of al-Ṭabarī, al-Yaʻqūbī (*fl.* late 800s CE/AH mid-200s), Ibn Aʻtham, and many others. Yet, both conflicts have almost no presence at all in *Futūḥ al-buldān*. The closest reference to the events comes in the form of dating, when, in the case of the second *fitna*, al-Balādhurī cites several events having occurred during 'the *fitna* of Ibn al-Zubayr'.[32] It was not simply that al-Balādhurī did not have outstanding knowledge of these two formative events within Islam, as both are thoroughly covered at various times in his *Ansāb al-ashrāf*. It was a conscious decision by the author to exclude them from the scope of *Futūḥ al-buldān*.

As Robinson described, some conquest works like that of Ibn Aʻtham were 'conquest monographs where romantic heroism is as prominent as a careful chronology is absent'.[33] If we consider grand or romanticized accounts of Muslim battles (whether formulaic or otherwise) during the conquest period as a defining feature of *futūḥ* texts, there is a different problem entirely when considering al-Balādhurī's work as a part of this genre. Namely, al-Balādhurī's book noticeably excludes a great number of these types of accounts. Famed battles such as Fiḥl (Pella, 635 CE/AH 13), al-Yarmūk (636 CE/AH 15), and al-Qādisiyya (ca. 636–637 CE/AH 15) are all present in the text, and yet only al-Qādisiyya earns any literary ornamentation.[34] These accounts are ostensibly stripped of the literary artifice present in other works (both earlier than and contemporaneous with al-Balādhurī's), which include far more elaborate material recounting these events. Al-Balādhurī's accounts do not include numerous tales of individual combat, the elaborate and motivating speeches by Muslim commanders to their armies, or descriptions of the setup of the armies in battle which categorize these sections in other early Arabic works on the conquests.[35] Instead, details on battles themselves rarely exceed more than a few lines of exposition in Arabic. Al-Balādhurī chose to focus, instead, on the effects of Muslim victory on a particular region, while often providing lists of martyrs of each of these famed excursions.[36] His brief traditions surrounding the Battle of Fiḥl, for instance, dedicate less than half of their attention to the battle itself, writing only as follows:

> The battle of Fiḥl, part of the Jordan, was fought two nights before the end of Dhū al-Qaʻda and five months after the accession of ʻUmar b. al-Khaṭṭāb as caliph (24 January 635 CE). … This battle occurred because [the Byzantine Emperor] Heraclius, when he came to Antioch, summoned for war the Romans and the people of the Jazīra, putting them under the command of a man whom

> he trusted. They met the Muslims at Fiḥl, part of the Jordan, and they fought an intense battle. It ended, by God's assistance, in the victory of the Muslims, and the Byzantine patrician, along with about 10,000 men, was killed. The remainder scattered throughout the cities of Syria, some of them joining Heraclius.[37]

This is all that is included on the battle itself. The remainder of al-Balādhurī's attention in this small subsection of the *Futūḥ* is dedicated to a discussion of Khālid b. al-Walīd's relief of command over the Muslim conquest armies in Syria, the appointment of Abū 'Ubayda b. al-Jarrāḥ as his replacement, and the observation that the region surrendered peacefully.[38] In contrast, al-Ṭabarī and Ibn A'tham include far longer sections on the Battle of Fiḥl and the conquest of its environs, including statements on the makeup of the army;[39] on the Byzantine attempts to hinder the Muslim army by breaking a dam and causing the dirt to turn to mud;[40] on the problems the Byzantine army faced with fighting the Muslims at night;[41] on Qays b. Hubayra al-Murādī's ferociousness, which resulted in the breaking of his spear in battle;[42] and on motivational speeches by Abū 'Ubayda and Khālid.[43]

If the *futūḥ* genre is to be identified merely as texts which have their main focus on the period of the expansion of the Islamic world, then al-Balādhurī's text must undoubtedly be a part of this classification. This definition, with a limited scope in content and setting, however, seems the wrong way to classify a conquest genre. Certain characteristics which were once described by Rudi Paret as the 'legendary *futūḥ* literature' must, I would suggest, come to the fore as the defining style and devices of the genre, even if a major goal of Paret's work was to disparage the quality – historical or otherwise – of these texts.[44] His discussion of the presence of rhetorical devices in these texts is useful for defining the genre, however, such as the emphasis on the unlikely success of the Muslims because of the odds against them, interactions between the Muslims and their enemy amid the conflict, discussions of theological positions, evidence of God's favour and role in Muslim successes, and details of combat and prowess in battle. Paret also highlights that the authors of some of these texts, such as pseudo-Wāqidī and his *Futūḥ al-Shām*, are explicit in their intent to inspire and edify the audience:

> There is one instance in which the author [pseudo-Wāqidī] express himself concerning the intention and aims of his work. After emphasizing the truthfulness of his account, he continues: 'It was my intention to present clearly the excellent qualities of the Companions of God's Messenger and their endeavour in the Holy War (*jihādahum*), in order to teach a lesson to (*ḥattā uraghghima*) the apostates who reject custom and law.'[45]

This is a position Fred Donner has since usefully expanded upon as one of three purposes of the historical theme of *futūḥ*.[46] These texts of *futūḥ*, then, should be classified as those works which focus on the accounts and deeds of Muslims against external forces while attempting to expand the borders of Islam, with the express intention of educating and/or entertaining the target audience. These are all features that these texts often labelled as *futūḥ* have in common. The comparison of these characteristics with *Futūḥ al-buldān*, however, brings the issue of classifying al-Balādhurī's text this way to the fore. Indeed, if it is these features of these texts that earn them classification as works of *futūḥ*, we must largely exclude *Futūḥ al-buldān*. It clearly lacks the rhetorical devices and style these other texts share; its classification as *futūḥ* does not comfortably fit. There are commonalities between it and these *futūḥ* texts, certainly, but the differences are far more abundant. It quickly becomes apparent that the conquests are the context for al-Balādhurī's interests and the information he intends to transmit, but not the primary interest itself.

Futūḥ al-buldān as a legal text

Other important studies of Islamic historical works have benefitted from having insight into the author's background, training, and purpose directly from the source. Information is provided on the training of the author, his *milieu*, his purpose and intentions in the creation of the work and, sometimes through panegyric, clear insight into patronage and associated biases. Scholarly work on Qudāma b. Jaʿfar, al-Masʿūdī,[47] and al-Bayhaqī[48] have all benefitted from analyses of this information when considering the background and creation of a work. When it comes to al-Balādhurī, as has been discussed, we are provided no such insight; his surviving works provide neither any form of formal introduction nor explicit discussion of his purpose or techniques in writing. There are minimal biographical materials provided by Ibn al-Nadīm and Ibn ʿAsākir and later compiled by Yāqūt that give us only the most basic of information: that he died at the end of the reign of the ʿAbbāsid Caliph al-Muʿtamid (r. 870–892 CE/AH 256–279), putting his date of death at circa 892 CE/AH 279, and that he was a boon companion (*nadīm*) of the Caliph al-Mutawakkil (r. 847–861 CE/AH 232–247) sometime during his reign.[49] A brief description of him is also provided, describing him as a man of letters, a poet, and a writer, suggesting a role in the administrative class as a secretary (*kātib*) that is explicitly confirmed by Ibn al-Nadīm.[50] At no point is there information about al-Balādhurī's having trained as a jurist or having held a judgeship.

Despite this, however, an analysis of both the content and the sources of information which make up the bulk of *Futūḥ al-buldān* suggests that jurists played a significant role in providing the materials al-Balādhurī felt were most relevant for the purposes of his book.[51] In addition to the great *akhbārīs* al-Wāqidī, Muḥammad b. Sa'd, Ibn al-Kalbī, and al-Madā'inī, among the most important informants of al-Balādhurī was the jurist Abū 'Ubayd al-Qāsim b. Sallām (d. 838 CE/AH 224). Beyond Abū 'Ubayd, by far the most regularly invoked transmitter within the *Futūḥ* is al-Ḥusayn b. 'Alī b. al-Aswad al-'Ijlī (*fl.* mid-800s CE/AH early 200s). Al-Ḥusayn is remembered only as a fairly unremarkable transmitter of material in the ninth century, save for his role as the intermediary in the transmission of information to al-Balādhurī from his teacher, the jurist Yaḥyā b. Ādam b. Sulaymān (d. 818 CE/AH 203).

The reason this is of particular relevance for the classification of al-Balādhurī's text is the author's considerable reliance on common material from the surviving works of Yaḥyā b. Ādam, *Kitāb al-Kharāj* (*The Book of Taxation*), and Abū 'Ubayd's *Kitāb al-Amwāl* (*The Book of Revenue*).[52] The two texts are among the fundamental judicial texts from the early Islamic period concerning the law surrounding taxation and personal possession. Both deal with issues of land ownership, land tenure, land classification, taxation (of a person and on produce), and more. All of these issues are also of keen interest to the *Futūḥ*, and capture the text's attention in almost every chapter. This type of content is usual for what can be classified as *kharāj/amwāl*, which could be classified as a subgenre of legal writing. In this subgenre, the formation and style of the texts are distinctive: The traditions themselves tend to be brief *akhbār* (reports, sing. *khabar*) grouped together thematically without any (or at the most, very little) connecting exposition; there is a clear emphasis on authenticity and verifiability of the material through the explicit use of chains of transmission (*asānīd*, sing. *isnād*). In their content, the material is entirely focused on legal positions and proofs.

While there is an extensive amount of overlap between the *Futūḥ* and these other two texts, there are clear differences in organization and in certain aspects of content: Both Yaḥyā and Abū 'Ubayd's texts almost completely forego the narrative context of the landmark judicial rulings from the conquest period. *Kitāb al-Kharāj* and *Kitāb al-Amwāl* take the majority of their legal justification from this period, but the information concerning the 'when and hows' of the conquest are almost completely excluded. The texts themselves are also organized along legal themes or issues, such as 'the opinions regarding the slaves of the conquerors from among the prisoners of war and women (*al-sabāyā*)',[53] and 'the precedent (*sunna*) regarding the alms tax (*ṣadaqa*) on the produce of land'.[54]

In al-Balādhurī's text, however, these judicial opinions which were originally compiled and discussed by Yaḥyā and Abū 'Ubayd are provided with their historical conquest context. Al-Balādhurī typically provides information on the arrival of Muslim armies into each region he discusses, how the conquest of that region occurred, and finally, the important information on whether a particular region was conquered *ṣulḥan* (by treaty) or *'anwatan* (without treaty). This differentiation was of enormous importance, as it had long-standing implications for the level of tax which could be expected (and collected) by the state from a particular region, as well as what could be done with the variety of profitable lands within the dominion of the caliph.[55] Al-Balādhurī's text is also interested in not just the same legal issues that the other two jurists focus on in their own works, but often goes beyond the earliest prophetic or caliphal precedents to provide information on how the state may have altered, developed, or applied the law in succeeding periods.

As an example, let us look at the differences in the approach to covering the Prophet's possession of the *fay'* lands of Khaybar and Fadak.[56] The *fay'* lands were those which were considered to be collectively owned by the greater Muslim community, the proceeds of which went to cover the expense of the state – especially the expenses of the military. As such, in the 'Abbāsid period, the stewards of these lands were normally the caliph and his administration itself. In Yaḥyā b. Ādam's section on these territories, he provides little detail on how these lands came into the possession of the Prophet, writing, 'The possessions of the Banū Naḍīr were from what God gave to the Prophet, and were not rushed upon by horse nor by camel.'[57] He offers additional material on it, namely how the above tradition relates to the revelation of Qur'ān 59:2-7, before providing a tradition on the authority of al-Zuhrī that both Yaḥyā and al-Balādhurī use:

> A portion of the people of Khaybar fortified themselves and asked the Prophet to spare their lives and let them go out, and he agreed. The people of Fadak heard of this and agreed [terms] similar to that. Thus, it came to the Prophet exclusively, as it was not rushed upon by horse nor camel.[58]

Before this, al-Balādhurī alone more fully provides the context of the Prophet's ownership of the lands that is completely absent in Yaḥyā's work:

> As the Prophet departed from Khaybar, he sent Muḥayyiṣa b. Mas'ūd al-Anṣārī to the people of Fadak to [have them] submit. Their chief was one of them

> named Yūshaʿ b. Nūn, the Jew. They made terms with the Prophet, agreeing to give up one-half of the land with its soil. The Prophet accepted. Thus, one-half was assigned wholly to the Prophet because the Muslims 'did not rush against it with horse or camel …'. The inhabitants of Fadak remained in it until ʿUmar b. al-Khaṭṭāb became caliph and expelled the Jews of the Ḥijāz. At that time, he sent Abū al-Haytham Mālik b. al-Tayyihān, Sahl b. Abī Ḥaythama al-Anṣārī, and Zayd b. Thābit al-Anṣārī, who estimated justly the value of one-half of its soil. This value ʿUmar paid to the Jews and expelled them to Syria.[59]

Worth noting here is not just the additional chronological development al-Balādhurī provides after the death of the Prophet, but the added information – namely, the details concerning which Companions of the Prophet served as both conquerors and state officials in deciding its classification. Following this explanation, al-Balādhurī invokes many of the traditions of Yaḥyā's *Kitāb al-Kharāj*. He then continues to discuss legal issues not covered by Yaḥyā, including the inheritance of these lands by the Prophet's family, ending this section with the ʿAbbāsid caliphs al-Maʾmūn (r. 813–833 CE/AH 198–218) and al-Mutawakkil's intervention in the ownership issues regarding this land.[60]

The significant reliance by al-Balādhurī on the compilations and traditions of jurists is undeniable when these works are compared, as is his interest in legal precedent more generally. The narrative quality of portions of the *Futūḥ* means that the form of his text has considerable differences from that of other surviving books on taxation and possession, however. Yet, the striking similarities in content and interests between these works of *kharāj*/*amwāl* and *Futūḥ al-buldān* do not just demonstrate that al-Balādhurī engaged with these types of legal texts; they require that we consider the *Futūḥ* as overlapping with this subgenre of legal writing to a far more significant degree than modern scholarship has up until this point.

Futūḥ al-buldān as administrative geography

The commonalities between al-Balādhurī's *Futūḥ* and the field of geographical writing as a whole may not immediately seem the most obvious, and yet the medieval descriptions of al-Balādhurī's work reveal that the text shares far more common features with this genre than have been hitherto recognized. These commonalities clearly permeate the entirety of al-Balādhurī's work, and are first found in the very foundation of the text's construction – in how the author chooses to organize the work. The text does not follow a chronological structure (such as, for instance, the *Ta'rīkh* of Khalīfa b. Khayyāṭ (d. 854 CE/AH 239) or the *Ta'rīkh* of al-Ṭabarī), nor is it organized by regnal years (as in the *Ta'rīkh* of al-Ya'qūbī). Instead, it opts for a geographical organization based on regions – the same way that one of his teachers, Muḥammad b. Sa'd, chose to structure his *Ṭabaqāt*. For the majority of sections within the text, the narrative begins with the earliest part of a region's history that was relevant for al-Balādhurī's audience. In most cases, this is the arrival of the Muslim conquest armies into a region and its subsequent capture.[61]

When considering the seeming uniqueness of al-Balādhurī's chosen organization for the *Futūḥ*, one is immediately struck by the strangeness of this configuration. If the author intended the work to be read simply as a history of the conquests, his chosen order seems illogical. The *Futūḥ*'s timeline tends to begin in the conquest period while moving forward in time through events of the Umayyad and 'Abbāsid eras. The chronology essentially 'resets' at the beginning of each region, beginning anew and continually repeating the cycle, which is jarring for any reader intending to consume a straightforward, chronological narrative of past events. This makes little sense for someone interested only in understanding the author's account of how the conquests occurred and developed. Nor does al-Balādhurī choose to organize his work thematically around a particular issue, as many of the legal texts discussed above do, and where the *Futūḥ* has a substantial amount of common ground. Instead, the *Futūḥ*'s organization immediately invokes the idea of a geographical text and it was, I suggest, a conscious decision of the author to organize the text in this way. It would have made the material easiest to follow and obtain for an audience reading a reference handbook.

Heck's work on Qudāma b. Ja'far – which has a similar organization – provided a definition and classification of the genre of 'administrative geography', which can better illuminate the purpose and classification of the *Futūḥ*. This definition lends itself to a comparison between al-Balādhurī's text and other works Heck has classified as being of this type, namely those of al-Balādhurī's contemporary, the secretary al-Ya'qūbī, and of al-Iṣṭakhrī (*fl.* 900s CE/AH 300s) and Ibn Khurradādhbih (*fl.* late 800s CE/AH mid-200s). Heck defined the subgenre of administrative geography as the type of geographical works that 'note the importance of state interest, especially fiscal and military ones', observing that these types of works developed through 'the exigencies of managing an empire considered to be Islamic and thus the abode of a community which understood itself as destined to inherit the legacy of both prophets and kings'.[62] In addition, Heck recognized that the focus of these texts remains firmly on the domain of

Islam (*mamlakat al-islām*), and rarely strays from a discussion of those territories held within it. The travel accounts and tales of wonders (*ʿajāʾib*) outside the realm of Islam often associated with geographies are usually absent, as are tales aggrandizing certain regions (*faḍāʾil*) that are common in local histories.[63] The geographies themselves that make up this subgenre may differ in the minutiae of state interests they choose to focus on, but they all share these common features. It is geography in service of the state, and as such, the texts are shaped by the needs of the state and its bureau. Heck's definition of administrative geography is an important one and deserves emphasis: it is not simply commonalities in the content or form of these texts that define this subgenre, but the likely intentions of the author in the creation of the work.

Heck identifies al-Yaʿqūbī's *Kitāb al-Buldān* (*The Book of Lands*) as belonging firmly within the scope of administrative geography, and it is a categorization which certainly fits.[64] The comparisons between al-Yaʿqūbī's and al-Balādhurī's texts may not immediately seem apparent because of their more obvious variations: both are organized by regions with a focus on the chief cities of a particular region, but al-Yaʿqūbī's text has its organization influenced by the explicit consideration of administrative districts (*ajnād*). Furthermore, where al-Balādhurī opens his regional discussion with traditions detailing their conquest, al-Yaʿqūbī often begins his with a discussion of roads and the physical location of cities – discussions which are almost completely absent from the former. Yet, their overall thematic emphases include a substantial amount of overlap, and this may be due to their likely intention to serve different branches of the bureaucracy. Both texts have a considerable focus on issues important to the state such as the establishment of regional taxes, the classification of lands, lists of governors and other officials, information on buildings, and so on.

The comparisons demonstrate their similarities and differences more clearly when the treatment of a particular region, such as Sijistān, is compared between the two texts. Al-Balādhurī and al-Yaʿqūbī open their sections on the region in the style typical of the rest of their work, with a discussion of the conquests and physical locations, respectively. Al-Yaʿqūbī then moves on to a subsection titled 'The Governors of Sijistān', which is largely a list of officials and those whom they served under. Many of these officials and their roles are also mentioned by al-Balādhurī, who is clearly interested in preserving these figures for posterity, too. In some cases, simple listings are almost identical, as is the case with a short listing of the governors between the Caliph Muʿāwiya (r. 661–680 CE/AH 41–60) and the second *fitna*.[65] While a list provided by the two authors of these early

Islamic governors of the region would be identical, these figures are given a historical context or additional information by al-Balādhurī, rather than simply having their names listed. While al-Yaʿqūbī merely notes a change of governor by Muʿāwiya by writing ʻal-Rabīʿ b. Ziyād al-Ḥārithī was also [governor] on behalf (*min qibal*) of Ziyād [b. Abī Sufyān], and ʻUbayd Allāh b. Abī Bakra was also [governor] on behalf of Ziyād in the days of Muʿāwiya',[66] the *Futūḥ* notes:

> Then Ziyād b. Abī Sufyān removed al-Rabīʿ b. Ziyād al-Ḥārithī, and he appointed ʻUbayd Allāh b. Abī Bakra over Sijistān. He [continued] raiding, and when he reached Razān, Ratbīl sent to him asking for a peace agreement for his country and the land of Kābul in return for 1,200,000 dirhams. When he consented, Ratbīl asked him if he would remit 200,000 and he agreed. Peace [was agreed] conditional upon the payment of 1,000,000 dirhams.[67]

Both authors viewed the inclusion of the names of these agents as important, but they appear to have had different purposes in doing so.[68] It might be suggested that the regular inclusion and naming of these governors and officials was useful not just for posterity but also for verifying archival material that court bureaucrats were provided with. In this way, the commonality between these administrative geographies and al-Balādhurī's *Futūḥ* may again be seen, and a suggested audience of administrators – perhaps, more specifically, those members of the secretariat – would have been well served in being able to access and reference this information as part of their duties. Through the *Futūḥ,* they were provided with the information not just on who had authority over a particular region during a period but also on the important decisions made during an executive's tenure that would have lasting ramifications.

Elsewhere, in a discussion of al-Iṣṭakhrī's geographical work *Kitāb al-Masālik wa-l-mamālik* (*The Book of Roads and Kingdoms*), Heck suggested that the author ʻdid not travel far and wide for his geographical material', but instead, a significant proportion of his material was taken from the state archives, a point the author even admits in his own work.[69] Similarly, and with a different geographical work sharing the same name – Ibn Khurradādhbih's *Kitāb al-Masālik wa-l-mamālik* – we find a comparable situation when considering the origins of the text's sources. Travis Zadeh, in exploring the codicology and transmission history of Ibn Khurradādhbih's book, wrote that ʻwe should think of Ibn Khurradādhbih not as initiating the tradition of Arabic administrative geography, but rather as a courtier and ʻAbbāsid official who built upon a pre-existing corpus of material that had long circulated amongst the secretariat'.[70] In following both Heck and Zadeh's analyses, comments, and line of enquiry, there are many similarities to be drawn with al-Balādhurī's compilation of the *Futūḥ* and the established geographical works like those of al-Iṣṭakhrī and Ibn Khurradādhbih.

Al-Iṣṭakhrī's chapter on Fārs is one of the longest in the entire text, and 'replete with administrative material' including information on the land tax, names and roles of state officials, building works, and administrative divisions.[71] Within the *Futūḥ*, very comparable examples are found throughout the text, but most notably in the author's sections on Baṣra and Kūfa. Here, he similarly discusses not just the founding of these prominent cities, but demonstrates access to official records likely from the state register (*dīwān*) as a primary source of knowledge about the region.[72] As was discussed in Chapter 3, al-Balādhurī's access to administrative records in the creation of the *Futūḥ* is not just hinted at throughout the work, but is even made explicit on a number of occasions. The inclusion of a substantial amount of administrative material obtained from the *dīwān* by al-Iṣṭakhrī and others is a clear trait within the subgenre of administrative geography that al-Balādhurī's *Futūḥ* shares with these works.

In discussing these geographies, there are further examples of shared content across al-Balādhurī's *Futūḥ* and two more of the earliest classified works within this genre, the *Masālik* of Ibn Khurradādhbih and *Kitāb al-Buldān* of Ibn al-Faqīh al-Hamadhānī (*fl.* late 800s CE/AH late 200s). The dating of the former text has proven a troublesome question still without a definitive answer, but it seems likely to date from the end of the ninth century.[73] The latter text has been more firmly attributed to the early tenth century, ca. 903 CE/AH 290.[74] Both geographies, however, share a number of traditions in common with the *Futūḥ*, demonstrating that more than just al-Balādhurī's organization and methods of compilation found commonality within this subgenre.

A good example of this is provided by the reuse of a number of accounts concerning the defence of the Caucasian borderland and the establishment of Sasanian fortifications in the area. The cornerstone of the pre-Islamic traditions which define the opening of al-Balādhurī's section on Armenia is a tale of the Sasanian *Shāhanshāh* Khusrau Anūshirwān's (r. 531–579 CE) interactions with an unnamed 'King of the Turks' (*malik al-turk,* in one separate instance referred to by the title *khāqān*) at a place called al-Barshaliyya, and an outward attempt to create peace between the two parties.[75] The Turks, the *Futūḥ* informs us, had been harassing the Sasanians' northern borders, forcing them to develop a new series of frontier defences to prevent continued incursions in the region, but the Persians desired greater security. Through a series of ruses and a false attempt at friendship – including a marriage proposal – Khusrau is finally able to suggest that the two groups should be separated by the construction of a permanent wall for their mutual benefit: 'No one will enter to [your land] from us and to us from [your land], except whomever you want and we want.'[76]

A cursory search of other early Arabic texts immediately provides the impression that this tradition on Khusrau's meeting and the construction of the wall was fairly widespread, particularly within geographical works. In looking slightly deeper, however, it would seem that the transmission of this particular account takes a more linear trajectory than might immediately be recognized. In addition to being found in al-Balādhurī's *Futūḥ*, the tradition can also be found in Ibn Khurradādhbih's *Masālik*, Ibn al-Faqīh's *Kitāb al-Buldān*, and Yāqūt al-Ḥamawī's (d. 1229 CE/AH 626) *Mu'jam al-buldān* (*The Dictionary of Lands*). In each case, the similarities between the stories are clear, although each includes slight variations. The majority of the details in the stories remain the same, although whether the story is found simply in a regional discussion of Azerbaijan or the Caucasus more generally is another matter.

Ibn Khurradādhbih's version of the tradition appears in his seventh chapter, on 'the frontiers (*thughūr*) of Islam, its people, and the races of men (*al-ajyāl*) which surround it'.[77] The account in *Futūḥ al-buldān* is unspecific in detailing the group of Turks that Khusrau interacted with that resulted in the creation of the wall in Arrān, but Ibn Khurradādhbih is, instead, more specific. While including a near identical account of Khusrau's deceptive marriage proposal, the fires to the camps, and the suggestion and successful construction of the wall 'of rock and lead' (*bi-l-ṣakhr wa-l-raṣāṣ*), Ibn Khurradādhbih's version specifies that it was the Khazars whom Khusrau deceived. Furthermore, while the traditions in the *Futūḥ* and the *Masālik* are tremendously similar in the form they take and the content they include, the Arabic syntax varies regularly, although the vocabulary largely stays the same.

There are several propositions for why this differentiation might have occurred: Ibn Khurradādhbih, likely compiling his *Masālik wa-l-mamālik* firmly after al-Balādhurī's *Futūḥ* was completed, was relying on an unspecified, separate, and more informative source than al-Balādhurī was; or, perhaps Ibn Khurradādhbih or one of his informants was more interested in reflecting the reality of his own lifetime, where the group which now occupied Arrān and the surrounding region of the Caucasus were the Khazars. He then chose to assume that this was how it had always been. This would not be completely out of place, as al-Balādhurī's *Futūḥ* is far more interested in the past history of regions and the development of policy therein, while the *Masālik* is far more concerned with the realities of the Islamic world contemporaneous with its writing. It seems highly likely that the two authors were, at the least, relying on a common source. The accounts are far too similar and with much too limited variation to not be directly connected. Prior to this account of the meeting between Khusrau and the Turkic king, Ibn Khurradādhbih even includes an almost identical version of the traditions naming the settlements in the region Khusrau founded that is also included in al-Balādhurī's *Futūḥ* – and in the same order.[78] The close similarity between al-Balādhurī's and Ibn Khurradādhbih's accounts – both in vocabulary and in the details contained within –would strongly suggest a common source or, perhaps, the *Masālik's* direct reliance on the *Futūḥ* as the uncredited basis of the story.

The remaining texts which quote the wall tradition seem to rely on either al-Balādhurī or Ibn Khurradādhbih as their source for the account, but the source of this account is unspecified. There are only minor variations to the tradition, and neither ever states whether the *Futūḥ* or Ibn Khurradādhbih's *Masālik* was actually the source of the accounts. Within Ibn al-Faqīh's version, we are given slightly more information than found in al-Balādhurī and Ibn Khurradādhbih. He agrees with Ibn Khurradādhbih's perspective that the Turks in question were the Khazars, but frames the entire event as explicitly occurring just outside Bāb al-Abwāb. Citing a certain Abū al-'Abbās al-Ṭūsī, the 'Abbāsid Caliph al-Manṣūr is purported to have asked if anyone 'knew how Anūshirwān built the wall which is called "the gate" (*al-bāb*)', before providing a similar version of the account.[79] The version of the account found in Ibn al-Faqīh's text, including the dialogue between al-Manṣūr and his courtiers, is reproduced completely verbatim by Yāqūt, and is attributed to him directly as 'Abū Bakr Aḥmad b. Muḥammad al-Hamadhānī'.[80] This is unsurprising, as Ibn al-Faqīh's *Kitāb al-Buldān* has already been demonstrated to be a major informant for Yāqūt's own work.[81]

It can be identified that al-Balādhurī's *Futūḥ* shares more characteristics with geographical texts than simply its form. The similarities of this wall tradition between the *Futūḥ* and these three other geographical works demonstrate that there are substantive similarities to be seen between texts already classified within this genre and al-Balādhurī's own work, which seems likely to have been the antecedent of a tradition which was subsequently carried through three of the touchstone geographical works of the classical Islamic period. There is a considerable amount of content overlap and perhaps, in some cases, overlap in the very sources relied upon for their information, all of which suggests the great commonality between the *Futūḥ* and other texts of the subgenre of administrative geography.

Origins of a profession: *Futūḥ al-buldān's* 'appendices'

A clear structural shift from the majority of the *Futūḥ* comes in al-Balādhurī's final chapters of his text, which Francis Murgotten has problematically referred to as the 'appendices'. My quarrel with referring to these chapters as appendices is that such a title suggests that they either did not belong as a part of the original whole or were added to it at a later date. These sections do not appear as an afterthought, but rather, very much engage with al-Balādhurī's intended audience at large, and they include the same sources and much of the same style as the rest of the *Futūḥ* despite their thematic organization. This section of the work breaks from an easier comparison to the above genres, but its content shares characteristics with manuals and letters of the secretariat aimed at others within the profession, such as that of Ibrāhīm al-Shaybānī (d. 911 CE/AH 298), namely his *al-Risāla al-ʿadhrā'* (*The Virgin Epistle*), along with al-Balādhurī's contemporary Ibn Qutayba (d. 889 CE/AH 286), and his extant *Kitāb al-Maʿārif* (*The Book of Knowledge*).

Al-Shaybānī's high level of Arabic in the *Risāla* demonstrates that it was both an exercise in skill from a writer at the top of his craft and a manual of style aimed at improving his peers. His interest in the administrator's craft and his explicit mention of his intended recipient – the ʿAbbāsid executive Ibn al-Mudabbir (d. 892–893 CE/AH 279) – is useful for comparisons with the *Futūḥ's* thematic chapters.[82] Similarly, Ibn Qutayba – who may well have been found within the same courtly circles frequented by al-Balādhurī under al-Mutawakkil – is known for his important literary contributions and *adab* works, including his manual *al-Maʿārif* and the philological compendium *Adab al-Kātib* (*The Literature of the Secretary*), the latter of which shares a great deal in common with al-Shaybānī's epistle. Julia Bray has previously highlighted the 'unevenness' of *al-Maʿārif's* execution while suggesting that it is a 'handbook of socially useful general knowledge and history written for an emerging new class of reader, the self educated'.[83] One can only wonder, however, if this audience could not easily and reasonably overlap with the less senior members of the administrative bureau, who used *al-Maʿārif* as a form of training manual of the sorts of general knowledge that all secretaries of the Islamic world should possess.

This administrative literature has a surprising amount of intersection with al-Balādhurī's final sections, and comparisons between these and similar writings only emphasize the parallels. These final chapters within the *Futūḥ* provide some of the clearest insight into precisely which audience al-Balādhurī expected to be engaging with the completed *Futūḥ,* as the very selection of these topics for the final chapters of the work betrays an overt interest in the administrative craft. The similarities in content targeting this potential audience and the audience detailed by Qudāma, al-Shaybānī, and Ibn Qutayba further strengthens the connections between these writings.

The five sections of the *Futūḥ* which make up these thematic chapters are:

1) Concerning the Legal Opinions (*aḥkām*) of the Land Tax
2) Recollection of the [Establishment of the] Stipends (*'aṭā'*) in the Caliphate of 'Umar b. al-Khaṭṭāb
3) The Matter of the Seal
4) The Matter of Coinage
5) The Matter of Writing

The most noticeable shift is away from the text's geographical organization to a purely thematic organization, with direct parallels to the books of taxation discussed above. In al-Balādhurī's thematic chapters as well as the works on taxation of Abū Yūsuf and Yaḥyā b. Ādam, for instance, the organization of the section follows an order of precedence which is usually chronological, with addenda to these positions occurring when necessary, often expressing the development of a particular issue or position.[84] Additionally, al-Balādhurī provides varying (and at times conflicting) traditions on a particular issue, but unlike the thematic chapters of Abū 'Ubayd, he chooses not to explicitly identify which traditions he believed to be more authentic than others.[85]

These chapters share the thematic grouping espoused by the books of taxation, while also having three of the five above chapters directly related to fiscal matters. The structural similarity between the *Futūḥ* and these other books does not go beyond the first thematic subdivision, however. A large number of the traditions of Yaḥyā and Abū 'Ubayd find duplication in these sections of the *Futūḥ,* but with definite separation and, at times, a completely new grouping. The *Futūḥ,* for instance, contains duplicate traditions of Abū 'Ubayd's *Kitāb al-Amwāl* concerning the stipends of the various 'Mothers of the Believers' – the wives of the Prophet – and other important Companions.[86] Similarly, both authors also include traditions on whether Qur'ān readers should be awarded stipends simply for having memorized the holy book.[87] While these issues are grouped together in al-Balādhurī's sections on the establishment of the *'atā'* stipendiary register and the levels at which certain individuals or groups were paid, they are separated into completely different sections in Abū 'Ubayd's *Kitāb al-Amwāl.*[88]

Additionally, while al-Balādhurī's chapter on coinage could certainly be considered linked to the issues of taxation and the establishment of the early Islamic monetary system, these traditions have almost no presence in the highly juristic books of taxation.[89] This can be anticipated: the *Futūḥ's* section on coinage is highly technical and absorbed with the physical aspects of currency and the minting process, including weights of coins and other various measures, as well as the identification and treatment of counterfeit currency. Historical traditions of great modern importance are also present, including mention of the changes to coinage during the Umayyad period and the Iraqi governor al-Ḥajjāj b. Yūsuf's (d.713–714 CE/AH 95) apparently vital role in the development of currency during his reign.[90] These traditions are incidental, however, to the section's dry, technical focus.

Al-Balādhurī ends the *Futūḥ* with his section on writing itself, discussing at length the early scribes of the Prophet Muḥammad and the writing practices of the early Muslim Arabs. This section's interest to the secretarial class, whose own profession was intricately linked to their ability to write and their mastery of language, is evident. The content of all five chapters, however, is inherently focused on an audience of this class, the secretaries, and the technical nature of the content within only emphasizes this. The historical aspects of these chapters are focused, first and foremost, on the precedents established among the early Muslim community, examples which were intended to serve as models for how later Muslims should be conducting themselves. The final portion of the *Futūḥ* also shows the reader, however, the very origins of a profession. There is the explicit transmission of the genesis of the secretarial class found in the fifth chapter, which discusses not just the perceived beginnings of Arabic writing, but the first scribes selected by Muḥammad himself and their background.[91] The origins of the secretarial class are seen, however, in the entirety of the *Futūḥ's* final sections, as the content contained within directly concerns the work of these administrators: the importance of tax and how it should be levied; the establishment and maintenance of the stipendiary registers; the use of seals on official documents from the time of the Byzantines and Sasanians through to the early Islamic period, and how those who forge the seal should be punished; the development of the Islamic state's official currency, the standard weights and measures, and how to identify counterfeits and punish the counterfeiters; and, finally, a discussion of the first of the Muslims purportedly capable of writing and their positive and negative characteristics.

In Heck's discussion of 'language and administration' in the typology of early Arabic writing, he classifies three categories of secretarial writing that share common features with the work of Qudāma: the grammatical category, the bureaucratic category, and the linguistic category. In opening his discussion on the bureaucratic category, Heck wrote:

> The bureaucratic category of administrative literature, while assuming standards of language and grammar, does not, in contrast to the grammatical category, draw as intensely upon the tradition of language, grammar and stylistics. Rather, the goal here is more precise: to illuminate bureaucratic custom and procedure, especially technical language specific to the craft of bureaucratic writing, i.e. terminology related to the tools and the steps required for composing a document or letter.[92]

While the bulk of al-Balādhurī's *Futūḥ* accomplishes very little of this, the unique thematic ending of the work is another matter entirely. The common feature between all five sections is precisely the 'illuminat[ion of] bureaucratic custom and procedure', even if the technical nature of writing itself is not the topic of these chapters, as it is in al-Shaybānī's epistle. All five topics are fixated not just on the craft of writing itself, but with the sorts of practical issues of direct concern to the bureau within the ninth-century 'Abbāsid court. Qudāma's work, as with al-Balādhurī's *Futūḥ*, shares a similarity with these categories as with a number of other historical genres, but the focus always remains on the types of material that would find tangible use within the administrative secretariat. These similarities, I would suggest, are very much intentional. They speak directly to the subject of the audience al-Balādhurī was anticipating would engage with the completed *Futūḥ*.

A unique time and place: The audience of *Futūḥ al-buldān*

In the article on al-Balādhurī in the *Encyclopeadia of Islam*, C. H. Becker and Franz Rosenthal concluded:

> al-Balādhurī's style aims at conciseness at the expense, at times, of the artistic effect. We seldom meet with fairly long stories, though they do occur. In the *Futūḥ*, al-Balādhurī continued the old method of dividing up the historical narrative and presenting it in separate articles.[93]

Becker and Rosenthal's summaries of the author and his work largely served as the standard for the second half of the twentieth century through to the present day, despite considerable concerns with their analysis. At the core of the above comment remains a fundamental flaw of analysis by the two Islamicists concerning al-Balādhurī's work: They assume al-Balādhurī was writing with the intention of creating a standard 'history', something that was simply intended to entertain and inform all who read it.

Their observation of the conciseness of al-Balādhurī's *Futūḥ* is well noted, although that comment does not extend well to his *Ansāb al-ashrāf*.[94] While there is not a clear explanation of what 'artistic effect' of the work is lacking, the following sentence goes a long way towards defining this. When describing 'artistic effect', they are describing the complete lack of rhetorical exposition, the literary crafting that was to be found in many other Arabic historical works. There are none of the types of 'exciting' accounts of battles, speeches, and other forms of exposition which have generally categorized the *futūḥ* genre as discussed above. As a narrative of history, something which was intended to be read and enjoyed, Becker and Rosenthal's comments make sense. But was the text's entertainment value to its readers ever really a primary concern of al-Balādhurī in its construction? As a secondary theme, perhaps, but if the author viewed his principal role in the creation of the *Futūḥ* to be that of storyteller or edifier, he would never have created a work in anything like the form it currently survives.

While Becker and Rosenthal identified the peculiarity of al-Balādhurī's oeuvre, they made no attempt to try and explain precisely why the text takes a form so unlike any of the other surviving early Arabic historical works. As this discussion has demonstrated, the *Futūḥ* overlaps heavily with a wide variety of different historical genres, and yet, it does not fit neatly within any one of them. Similarities abound, but the differences in both form and content cannot be simply passed over. Why, then, does al-Balādhurī's *Futūḥ* seemingly stand uniquely on its own, and how best should the text be classified? The answer, it appears, is found within this analysis of form and content, and the target audience that we might speculate al-Balādhurī was aiming at: the secretariat.

The content of the *Futūḥ* itself is the chief evidence for this fact, as even aside from the thematic portion, every chapter of the text is engrossed with the types of information that would be of direct interest to the secretaries. In its discussion of the conquests, we find almost no examples of dialogue between commanders, as we do in al-Azdī's *Futūḥ al-Shām*,[95] nor the emphasis on narrativity seen in Ibn Aʿtham's *Kitāb al-Futūḥ*; we do find, however, an ever-present interest in whether a location was conquered *ṣulḥan* or *ʿanwatan*. The interest here is in the legal status of lands, people, and resources, and not in the conquest narratives themselves. In its geographical organization and descriptions of the development of lands and their demographics, we find mentions of past governors and the types of people that lived therein, and yet we find no lengthy discussions of the customs of the local populations, nor of routes and roads which link together different regions, as are found in al-Ya'qūbī's *Kitāb al-Buldān* and Ibn Khurradādhbih's *Masālik*. The interest here is in the construction of sites and their subsequent development, and the roots of administrative policies in a specific location, rather than in the tales and descriptions of a traveller. In its prodigious transmission of legal traditions, handed down by jurists, we find all of this material intimately linked to the *locations* those traditions were concerned with, rather than their overall thematic focus, as are seen in *kutub al-kharāj*. This organization lends itself to a reader searching for the history, law, and traditions related to a particular area, whereas *kutub al-kharāj* are compilations and discussions of all the relevant legal precedents on a particular issue. In each case, while their content and interests overlap, their purposes remain clearly different.

The reason for this, I would suggest, lay in how al-Balādhurī intended the *Futūḥ* to be utilized by his unspecified audience. Scrutinizing the makeup of the traditions within the text clearly demonstrates that the book contains a huge number of traditions of direct relevance to the administrators of the Islamic polity – exactly the members of the state secretarial profession to which al-Balādhurī also belonged.[96] The *Futūḥ* comprises a much stronger overall narrative than the majority of texts within the legal and geographical genres, but that narrative is contained within the individual chapters and does not, by and large, span the entirety of the work as it does in other genres. The narrative is self-contained within each region and, even when the text seems to be speaking of a similar issue or a similar precedent to something discussed elsewhere in the book, it is seldom self-referential.[97] The focus remains on a particular location in question and not on an overall theme or precedent.

There is still much work to be done on the issues of audience and reading practices of early 'Abbāsid-era Muslims, and the lack of direct evidence we have for the readership of the *Futūḥ* is problematic.[98] The text's form and organization, however, would strongly suggest that the work was created with the intention of serving as a reference handbook[99] – more specifically, an administrator's handbook, with its primary perceived audience being al-Balādhurī's colleagues in the ninth-century 'Abbāsid court. These secretaries, tasked with the work of budgeting for the expenses of the central 'Abbāsid state, collecting taxes sent by the provinces, and resolving the disputes which developed therein, could rely on al-Balādhurī's handbook as a catalogue of the legal and administrative decisions and developments of the early Islamic period. As discussed in Chapter 2, the period during al-Balādhurī's adult lifetime was characterized by the deterioration of 'Abbāsid central authority and the rise of regional dynasties which only passingly acknowledged their relationship with and obligations to the ʿAbbāsids in Iraq. These territories, which were relied upon to provide the resources necessary for the upkeep of the central Islamic state, began to neglect those commitments. It was left to the secretariat within the ʿAbbāsid court to manage the established budget and expenses.

The most important justification they had for laying claim to the funds and other resources necessary to keep the state afloat from these peripheral regions was the history of those agreements which could be invoked in their favour.[100] Al-Balādhurī's *Futūḥ* was created to serve as a catalogue of those agreements, providing not just the agreements themselves, but the context for their agreement and descriptions of the region and its resources. It was categorized by those regions in question so that the reader could see all of the relevant traditions for that locality. It included not just the long-agreed-upon terms which the state expected to be honoured, but also the relevant context for those terms – the history which brought a region into the caliphate, as well as the figures who were remembered as important in that process. It included the legal precedent which had been established (and, at times, applied elsewhere) due to an event in a particular area. It also included, for the benefit of the reader, the legal and administrative developments which had occurred since the location was first conquered by the Muslims. It was intended to be – within a single, easily digestible form – the home of the ʿAbbāsid state's legal and administrative justification for its demands for contributions from the provinces. When a province did not provide its expected payments, we can imagine that these original agreements could be cited and the legal precedent demonstrated in order to assert the central treasury's right to resources.

Conclusions

Reflecting on Kilito's original comment that genre in Arabic works was something well defined and easy to identify, the analysis of *Futūḥ al-buldān* demonstrates that this statement must clearly be nuanced. The ninth/third century nurtured the young written Arabic historical and literary tradition, and it was also a period of vibrant experimentation and great production – even if much of it does not survive.[101] In many ways, it can be anticipated that in a period where various forms of information, edification, and entertainment were only first being committed to a written form, certain elements and features did not survive the test of time. The growth of writerly communities and the audiences around these texts would lead them to iterate and, subsequently, innovate. While the ninth century was a defining period in the advancement of the Arabic written tradition, it was only the first part of a long and ever-evolving process. Even texts that were created in this period and share a great similarity with one another exhibit differences. As Kilito relates language, historical material, and their commentaries to coin, we must recognize that the above comparisons of the *Futūḥ* demonstrate that genre is a less rigid die than might have previously been suggested, more than capable of being reshaped and combined with others to create varied forms.

Much of modern scholarship has been quick to identify al-Balādhurī's *Futūḥ* simply as a conquest history, and many have been unquestioningly happy to use it as such. Yet, the comparison between al-Balādhurī's book and other important surviving early Islamic texts demonstrates that it should be classified as something other than 'just' a piece of conquest literature, despite the obvious similarities. This, in turn, should be affecting how we read and use the text. The common features that the *Futūḥ* shares with the legal manuals of *kharāj* and *amwāl*, administrative geographies, and secretarial literature demonstrate that al-Balādhurī's work has a substantial amount of shared fabric. Despite these extensive similarities, however, it remains a unique amalgamation of these genres, and the work that shares the greatest similarity to it is undoubtedly the surviving portion of Qudāma b. Jaʿfar's *Kitāb al-Kharāj,* which, as Heck already demonstrated, shared a great deal of commonality with other Arabic genres as well. It is no coincidence that the present research has relied so firmly on Heck's discussion and analysis of Qudāma's book, not simply for its methodological approach, but also for discussions of genres easily comparable to the *Futūḥ.* While Qudāma's work is significantly longer and far from a perfect counterpart to al-Balādhurī's text, the similarities in its content, style, and audience are unmistakable, and as will be discussed in Chapter 6, Qudāma's direct reliance on al-Balādhurī's work is discernable. Both are works that were created for the administrative bureau, and it is to this genre of administratively focused secretarial literature that the *Futūḥ* most fully belongs.

Despite this, no work within this genre of writing is identical to the *Futūḥ.* Its creation was intended to synthesize and augment the content of works in this multitude of genres and subgenres, likely for the use of courtly administrators for whom the material contained within was essential. All of the information al-Balādhurī chose to include and exclude – issues of legal precedent dating back to the Prophet and first caliphs, land ownership details, levels of taxation, and details of the original conquest settlement agreements – was information necessary for the administration of the 'Abbāsid state. It was essential information collated by a secretary at the court for use by other administrators, as they worked to maintain a grip on the affairs of state during a period of waning 'Abbāsid authority in the ninth century. Al-Balādhurī's *Futūḥ* is unique because it was necessary for it to be such; it was an essential product of its time. It was a form of hybrid historical work that shares characteristics with a number of ninth-century genres, while remaining distinct for the needs of the era he intended to serve.

Notes

1 Abū al-Faraj b. al-Jawzī, quoted by al-Sakhāwī, *al-I'lān bi-t-tawbīkh li-man dhamma al-ta'rīkh,* ed. Franz Rosenthal (Beirut: Dār al-Kutub al-'Illmiyya, 1986), 336–7. Rosenthal notes in his translation of the text that al-Sakhāwī provides a similar quotation attributed to Sibṭ b. al-Jawzī (1256 CE/AH 654), and he is unsure if 'both authors expressed themselves in the same vein', or if one of the attributions is incorrect. Rosenthal, *Muslim Historiography*, 515.

2 Justin Lake, 'Authorial Intention in Medieval Historiography', *History Compass,* Vol. 12, No. 4 (2014), 345.

3 Among the most important in defining medieval genre theory are R. C. van Caenegem, *Guide to the Sources of Medieval History* (Amsterdam: North-Holland Publishing Co., 1978) and Herbert Grundmann, *Geschichtsshreibung im Mittelalter: Gattungen, Epochen, Eigenart* (Göttingen: Vandenhoeck and Ruprecht, 1978).

4 See, for instance, K. S. Whetter, *Understanding Genre and Medieval Romance* (Aldershot: Ashgate, 2008).

5 See, for instance, *Medieval Lyric: Genres in Historical Context*, ed. William D. Paden (Urbana: University of Illinois Press, 2000).

6 See, for instance, F. C. Gardiner, *The Pilgrimage of Desire: A Study of Theme and Genre in Medieval Literature* (Leiden: E. J. Brill, 1971).

7 Gillian Adams, 'Medieval Children's Literature: Its Possibility and Actuality', *Children's Literature*, Vol. 26 (1998), 1–24.

8 Among the notable contributions of literary approaches applied to early Islamic history are the works of Albrecht Noth and Lawrence I. Conrad, which will be discussed below, in addition to the work of El-Hibri, *Parable and Politics* and his earlier *Reinterpreting Islamic Historiography: Hārūn al-Rashīd and the Narrative of the 'Abbāsid Caliphate* (Cambridge: Cambridge University Press, 1999). It should be noted, however, that while there has been a marked improvement in the analysis of Arabic historical works, other Middle Eastern languages, notably Persian,

have had even fewer in-depth studies. On the field of Persian historiography, see Julie Scott Meisami, *Persian Historiography to the End of the Twelfth Century* (Edinburgh: Edinburgh University Press, 1999).

9 It is worth repeating that the category of *adab* is complex, and by no means static through this early period and beyond, and this is discussed more fully in Chapter 4. On the nature of *adab*, however, see Kilpatrick, '*Adab*', 56; and on the very different forms of this category, Hilary Kilpatrick, 'A Genre in Classical Arabic Literature: The *Adab* Encyclopedia', in *Union Européenne des Arabisants et Islamisants 10th Congress Proceedings*, ed. Robert Hillenbrand (Edinburgh: Union Européenne des Arabistants et Islamisants, 1982), 34–43.

10 Khalidi, *Arabic Historical Thought*, esp. xii.

11 Robinson, *Islamic Historiography*, 55–79.

12 Heck, *Construction of Knowledge.*

13 This is not, however, atypical. Titles were often fluid in early medieval literature, and this is especially the case when we consider early Islamic works, which may not have been written texts for several generations after their original 'compiler' died. The creation of modern editions of these medieval texts has undoubtedly been of huge value to the field of historical study as a whole, but they often do not communicate effectively any ambiguity that may exist over titling.

14 This was previously observed by Khalil Athamina in his introduction to his edited volume of *Ansāb al-ashrāf*. Athamina also notes the confusion surrounding the title of the book we now know as the *Ansāb*, likely owing to the fact that al-Balādhurī never finished it. See Athamina, 'Introduction,' 8.

15 This issue is explored in Jørgen Bæk Simonsen, 'Deux versions de *Futūḥ al-Buldān*?', in *Living Waters: Scandinavian Orientalistic Studies,* eds. Egon Keck, Svend Søndergaard and Ellen Wulff (Copenhagen: Museum Tusculanum Press, 1990), 339–45.

16 Ibn al-Nadīm, *Fihrist*, 126.

17 The other two works mentioned are *Kitāb al-Akhbār wa-l-ansāb* (*The Book of Reports and Lineages*), which is likely the work that has come down to us as *Ansāb al-ashrāf*, and a version of *'Ahd Ardashīr* (*The Testament of Ardashīr*) in verse.

18 Al-Masʿūdī, *Murūj al-dhahab wa-maʿādin al-jawhar*, Vol. 1, 13–14.

19 Yāqūt, *Irshād*, Vol. 2, 131.

20 Owing to his date of death being a generation earlier than that of Ibn al-Nadīm.

21 Al-Sakhāwī, *al-Iʿlān bi-t-tawbīkh*, 289–90; Rosenthal, *Muslim Historiography*, 486–7. Al-Sakhāwī's information on al-Balādhurī in this section is borrowed directly from al-Masʿūdī, although the subheading classification and organization remain his own. The point concerning the *Futūḥ* being classified as a geographical work (*taṣānīf al-buldān*) was briefly raised by Isaac Hasson, who also highlighted that the *Encyclopaedia of Islam* entries on geographies fail to make any mention

of al-Balādhurī's work. See Hasson, '*Ansāb al-ašrāf* d'al-Balāḏurī est-il un Livre de Ta'rīḫ ou d'Adab?', 480; S. Maqbul Ahmad, 'Djughrāfiyā', *EI*[2].

22 There are questions over whether some of the sources of al-Balādhurī's information actually existed in a written form by this time, and many of these issues are discussed in Chapter 3.

23 This is not to suggest that modern scholars cannot identify similarities in these early texts and subsequently categorize them within a genre, but we must be aware that the boundaries we establish within modern genre theory may not have emerged fully in the medieval author's lifetime, if they were existent at all.

24 Kilito, *The Author and His Doubles*, 2–3.

25 Noth and Conrad, *The Early Arabic Historical Tradition*, 31–3.

26 There have been concerns expressed over just how early *Futūḥ al-Shām* was created, as well as precisely who the named al-Azdī was. The most convincing discussion of the text and its author, dating the work to some time in the late eighth/mid-second century, is found in Suleiman A. Mourad, 'On Early Historiography: Abū Ismā'īl al-Azdī and His *Futūḥ al-Shām*', *Journal of the American Oriental Society*, Vol. 120, No. 4 (2000), 577–93, and it is also discussed in Marina Pyrovolaki, '*Futūḥ al-Shām* and other *futūḥ* texts: A Study of the Perception of Marginal Conquest Narratives in Arabic in Medieval and Modern Times' (DPhil diss., University of Oxford, 2008).

27 Fred Donner has critiqued Noth and Conrad's suggested evolution of the *Futūḥ* theme, as well as how later works used this *Futūḥ* material 'to establish guidelines relating to matters of land tenure, taxation, and administration', in Donner, *Narratives of Islamic Origins*, 174–82.

28 Noth and Conrad, *Arabic Historical Tradition*, 31.

29 The problematic manuscript and editorial tradition of this text should be noted here, as well as the lack of major publication not just on the text itself, but on the questions of who precisely Ibn A'tham was. There is also a suggestion that the later portion of this text, namely the period from the reign of Hārūn al-Rashīd (r. 786–809 CE/AH 170–193) onwards, may have been a secondary text or a later addition. Among the few significant contributions to these issues is Pyrovolaki, '*Futūḥ al-Shām* and other *Futūḥ* texts'. On the problematic dating of Ibn A'tham and the suggestion that he died at the beginning of the tenth/fourth century, see Ilkka Lindstedt, 'al-Madā'inī's *Kitāb al-Dawla* and the Death of Ibrahim al-Imām', in *Case Studies in Transmission*, eds. Ilkka Lindstedt, Jaakko Hämeen-Anttila, Raija Mattila, and Robert Rollinger (Munster: Ugarit-Verlag, 2014), 103–30, specifically the appendix 'When did Ibn A'tham al-Kūfī live?', 118–23. For the recently published but much older argument by Conrad for an earlier life of Ibn A'tham challenged by Lindstedt, see Lawrence I. Conrad, 'Ibn A'tham and His History', *al-'Uṣūr al-Wusṭā*, Vol. 23 (2015), 87–125.

30 Noth and Conrad, *Arabic Historical Tradition*, 33–5.

31 Despite its title and the wide breadth of material the entire book probably included, the surviving sections are focused on the internal strife of the Muslim *umma* during the reign of the caliphs ʿUthmān (r. 644–656 CE/AH 23–35) and ʿAlī (r. 656–661 CE/AH 35–40) that resulted in the first *fitna*.

32 See, for instance, where al-Balādhurī transmits that 'the Byzantines destroyed ʿAṣqalān and expelled its people in the days of Ibn al-Zubayr'. The only real instance of something which occurred due to a direct link with Ibn al-Zubayr's reign in the Ḥijāz is, expectedly, a discussion of the destruction and reconstruction of the Kaʿba. *Futūḥ*, 54, 169 (H 74-76, 219-220).

33 Robinson, *Islamic Historiography*, 42. Where I must express misgivings about Robinson's comments, however, is in his suggestion that works such as these 'are characterized by storytelling narrative styles that would be elbowed aside (if not entirely eliminated) by what emerged as the normative tradition', an opinion which is likely influenced by the work of Tarif Khalidi. While Robinson is right to suggest that the ninth century was a time of change in the creation of Arabic historical works, his comment suggests that there was a development from the more narrative, 'artistic' histories like those of al-Azdī and Ibn Aʿtham to the 'sober and eirenic traditionalism exemplified by al-Ṭabarī or al-Balādhurī', that one replaced the other. There is not sufficient evidence to demonstrate that this was a development, rather than different authors trained in different ways with different goals in mind in the creation of their works. The more recent suggestions on the life of Ibn Aʿtham, mentioned in n. 29 above, cast further doubt on Robinson's suggestion, as Ibn Aʿtham may well have been writing *after* al-Balādhurī and, at the least, contemporaneous with al-Ṭabarī.

34 For the date of the Battle of al-Qādisiyya, upon which there is a great amount of disagreement in the early Arabic tradition, I have chosen to list the year AH 15 provided by *Futūḥ*, 312 (H 409). Interestingly, of these three major battles, al-Qādisiyya is the only one that receives any reasonable amount of background exposition, including background of the Persian general Rustam and his brief encounter with two Muslims. On the general background to the Battle of al-Qādisiyya, see Donner, *The Early Islamic Conquests*, esp. 175–6, 202–9, 212.

35 This was a characteristic of the *Futūḥ* also noted by Khalidi, *Arabic Historical Thought*, 68.

36 These comments are independently echoed in Shoshan, *The Arabic Historical Tradition and the Early Islamic Conquests*, 11.

37 *Futūḥ*, 137 (H 176-177).

38 'They asked for a treaty of protection (*saʾalū al-amān*) on condition that they pay tax on their heads (*jizya*) and the land tax (*kharāj*).' *Futūḥ*, 137 (H 177).

39 Al-Ṭabarī includes the statement that Khālid b. al-Walīd remained in charge of the vanguard of the army, while also naming ten commanders that Abū ʿUbayda sent to Fiḥl. Al-Ṭabarī, *The History of al-Ṭabarī*, Vol. 11: *The Challenge to the Empires*,

trans. Khalid Yahya Blankinship (Albany: State University of New York Press, 1993), 164 (2: 2150-2151).

40 Ibid., 160, 164 (2: 2145–6, 2151).

41 Ibid., 170–1 (2: 2156–8).

42 Ibn A'tham, *al-Futūḥ*, Vol. 1, 190–1.

43 Ibid.

44 Paret defines the legendary *Futūḥ* literature as 'fiction with a historical background', which 'pretends to have scholarly character. It claims to be historical literature in the narrowest sense of the term'. His low opinion of the quality of these texts is then taken further at the end of the article, where he writes, 'But subject matter and stylistic devices alone are not sufficient for producing a literary work of art. What is needed above all is the genius of an artist, and that was lacking. The Arab world did not produce a Firdausi.' Paret, 'The Legendary *Futūḥ* Literature', 163–75.

45 Paret, 'Legendary *Futūḥ* Literature', 169–70.

46 Donner, *Narratives of Islamic Origin*, 177–82.

47 Shboul, *Al-Mas'ūdī and His World.*

48 Waldman, *Toward a Theory of Historical Narrative.*

49 Yāqūt, *Irshād*, Vol. 2, 127.

50 Ibn al-Nadīm, *Fihrist*, 125.

51 On the substantial number of jurists who make up the named informants for al-Balādhurī's *Futūḥ*, see Chapter 3.

52 As discussed in Chapter 3, however, neither book was likely accessed by al-Balādhurī in a finalized written form. He seems likely to have heard his material directly from Abū 'Ubayd and not from using a written version of *Kitāb al-Amwāl.* With Yaḥyā's material, he heard Yaḥyā's traditions through the intermediary of al-Ḥusayn b. 'Alī b. al-Aswad al-'Ijlī rather than through a written *Kitāb al-Kharāj.*

53 Abū 'Ubayd al-Qāsim b. Sallām, *Kitāb al-Amwāl*, 124.

54 Abū 'Ubayd, *al-Amwāl*, 468–76; Yaḥyā b. Ādam, *Kitāb al-Kharāj*, 78–87.

55 For more on this, see Waines, 'The Third Century Internal Crisis of the Abbasids', 282–306; Kennedy, 'The Decline and Fall', 11–15; and Michele Campopiano, 'State, Land Tax and Agriculture in Iraq from the Arab Conquests to the Crisis of the Abbasid Caliphate (Seventh-Tenth Centuries)', 1–37.

56 On the history and classification of the *fay'* lands, see Andrew Marsham, 'Fay'', *EI*[3].

57 Yaḥyā b. Ādam, *al-Kharāj*, 18.

58 Ibid., 22; *Futūḥ,* 33–4 (H 51).

59 *Futūḥ*, 33 (H 50).

60 The lands of Fadak are remembered by some as having been given by the Prophet Muḥammad to his daughter, Fāṭima, thereby making the lands heritable property of her descendants. Al-Balādhurī includes a great number of traditions on how Fāṭima and her descendants' rights to this land were regularly compromised

and shifted during the Umayyad and ʿAbbāsid period. At the end of the section, he records a lengthy letter from al-Maʾmūn returning the benefits of the land to Fāṭima's descendants, only to then note that al-Mutawakkil reverted the land 'to its condition before al-Maʾmūn', meaning to state control. *Futūḥ*, 34–8 (H 51-56). For a discussion of the issue of the lands of Fadak and the broader issue of whether a Prophet can leave an inheritance, see Harry Munt, 'Caliphal Estates and Properties Around Medina in the Umayyad Period', in *Authority and Control in the Countryside: Continuity and Change in the Mediterranean, 6th-10th Centuries*, eds. Alain Delattre, Marie Legendre and Petra Sijpesteijn (Princeton: The Darwin Press, *forthcoming*) and Moshe Gil, 'The Earliest Waqf Foundations', *Journal of Near Eastern Studies*, Vol. 57, No. 2 (1998), 125–40.

61 In one section – the *Futūḥ's* section on Armenia – the pre-Islamic past provides the starting point for the narrative. This is, however, the only chapter in the entirety of the text where this occurs.

62 Heck, *Construction of Knowledge,* 111–12.

63 On these aspects of Arabic geographies, see Travis Zadeh, *Mapping Frontiers Across Medieval Islam: Geography, Translation, and the ʿAbbāsid Empire* (London: I.B. Tauris, 2011) and S. Maqbul Ahmad, *A History of Arab-Islamic Geography (9th – 16th Century A. D.)* (Amman: Al al-Bayt University, 1995).

64 It is worth highlighting the difference in the likely date of composition between al-Yaʿqūbī and al-Balādhurī's texts. While the two authors were contemporaries and al-Yaʿqūbī's *Kitāb al-Buldān* is considered among the earliest surviving Arabic geographical texts, it seems probable that al-Balādhurī's *Futūḥ* is the earlier of the two, with no information in the text post-dating the reign of the ʿAbbāsid Caliph al-Muʿtazz (r. 866–869 CE/AH 252–255). Meanwhile, Muhammad Qasim Zaman has suggested that al-Yaʿqūbī's text wasn't completed until 891 CE/AH 278 – perhaps around the death of al-Balādhurī – meaning that al-Balādhurī is likely to have been contributing his completed *Futūḥ* to the genre several decades earlier than al-Yaʿqūbī's text came to settle in its surviving form. It is impossible to rule out that al-Yaʿqūbī had formed a version of his text before it was actually committed to writing, however. He may also have been working on the ideas of the text for some time before it was completed. Regardless, the surviving *Kitāb al-Buldān* seems likely to have had the benefit of having al-Balādhurī's *Futūḥ* in a finalized form some time before it was finished. Muhammad Qasim Zaman, 'al-Yaʿḳūbī', *EI*[2].

65 Al-Yaʿqūbī, *Kitāb al-Buldān,* ed. T. J. G. Juynboll (Leiden: E. J. Brill, 1861), 59–60; *Futūḥ*, 490 (M 148).

66 Al-Yaʿqūbī, *al-Buldān*, 59–60.

67 *Futūḥ*, 489–90 (M 148).

68 Al-Yaʿqūbī's reasons for writing and his intended audience are areas of scholarship that are sorely lacking, while also being beyond the scope of this current research.

It is hoped that future analysis of al-Yaʿqūbī's authorship will further expand our understanding of ninth-century ʿAbbāsid historical writing.

69 Heck, *Construction of Knowledge,* 117; al-Iṣṭakhrī, *Kitāb al-Masālik wa-l-mamālik,* ed. Muḥammad Jābir Ḥīnī (Cairo: al-Idāra al-ʿĀmma li-l-Thaqāfa, 1961), 67–8.

70 Travis Zadeh, 'Of Mummies, Poets, and Water Nymphs: Tracing the Codicological Limits of Ibn Khurradādhbih's Geography', in *'Abbasid Studies*, Vol. 4, *Occasional Papers of the School of 'Abbasid Studies,* ed. Monique Bernards (Oxford: Gibb Memorial Trust, 2013), 33.

71 Heck, *Construction of Knowledge,* 117; al-Iṣṭakhrī, *al-Masālik,* 67–96.

72 For a discussion of this, see Wadad al-Qadi, 'The Names of Estates in State Registers Before and After the Arabization of the "Dīwāns"', 255–80, as well as the discussion found in Chapter 3. On al-Balādhurī's access and use of documentary evidence via Abū ʿUbayd concerning Cyprus in the early ʿAbbāsid period, see Ryan J. Lynch, 'Cyprus and Its Legal and Historiographical Significance in Early Islamic History', *Journal of the American Oriental Society*, Vol. 136, No. 3 (2016), 535–50.

73 The most recent suggestions regarding Ibn Khurradādhbih's text come from Travis Zadeh, who has analysed not just the work's content, but the available – and quite distinct – surviving manuscripts of the text. Despite this in-depth and extremely important analysis, Zadeh understandably will not be drawn on dating the text any more precisely than classifying it as a ninth-century work, but his evidence casts significant doubt over M. J. de Goeje's original suggestion that the first version of the text dates from as early as 848–849 CE/AH 234. See Zadeh, 'Of Mummies, Poets, and Water Nymphs', 8–75.

74 Henri Massé, 'Ibn al-Faḳīh', *EI*[2], based on the dating of Aloys Sprenger, *Die Post- und Reiserouten des Orients* (Leipzig: F. A. Brockhaus, 1864), xvii.

75 This al-Barshaliyya's exact location within the eastern Caucasus is poorly specified, and Yāqūt describes only that it was 'a place (*waḍʿ*) of Arrān, mentioned in the account of the King of Persia (*al-Fars*)'. Yāqūt, *Muʿjam al-buldān,* ed. Ferdinand Wüstenfeld as *Jacut's Geographisches Wörterbuch* (Leipzig: F. A. Brockhaus, 1866–1873), Vol. 1, 566.

76 Ibn Khurradādhbih, *Kitāb al-Masālik wa-l-mamālik*, ed. and trans. M. J. de Goeje as *Bibliotheca Geographorum Arabicorum*, Vol. 6 (Leiden: E. J. Brill, 1889), 260; *Futūḥ,* 233 (H 308). While the tradition's authenticity itself is extremely suspect, especially as D. M. Dunlop has previously highlighted an account of the Byzantine Priscus (d. after 472 CE) with great similarity to the beginning of this wall account, the tradition is distinct, and serves a variety of al-Balādhurī's purposes within his chapter. These purposes, and the tradition in question, are discussed more fully in Lynch, Ryan J. "'The Wall of Rock and Lead": ʿAbbāsid Reflections on Sasanian Caucasian Policy in Arrān', in *From Albania to Arran: The East Caucasus between Antiquity and Medieval Islam*, ed. Robert G. Hoyland (Piscataway: Gorgias Press,

2019). On the account of Priscus, see D. M. Dunlop, *The History of the Jewish Khazars* (Princeton: Princeton University Press, 1954), 24.

77 Ibn Khurradādhbih, *al-Masālik*, 252.

78 Ibid., 259; *Futūḥ*, 231–2 (H 306-307).

79 Ibn al-Faqīh, *Kitāb al-Buldān*, ed. Yūsuf al-Hādī (Beirut: ʿĀlam al-Kutub, 1996), 586–7.

80 Yāqūt, *Muʿjam*, Vol. 1, 439.

81 Yāqūt's reliance on Ibn al-Faqīh was already recognized by M. J. de Goeje, who wrote that the latter's text 'was among the main sources of Yāqūt'. See M. J. de Goeje, 'Prefatio', in *Bibliotheca Geographorum Arabicorum*, Vol. 5 (Leiden: E. J. Brill, 1885), viii–xiii; Massé, 'Ibn al-Faḳīh'.

82 Ibrāhīm al-Shaybānī, *al-Risāla al-ʿadhrāʾ*, in *Etude Critique sur la Lettre Vierge d'Ibn al-Mudabber*, ed. Zaki Mubarak (Cairo: Imp. de la Bibliothèque Egyptienne, 1931). While Mubarak's text is the best edition of the text currently available and provides useful comments on the epistle itself, it suffers from an unfortunate yet fundamental misidentification of its author, which both Mubarak and EI^2 author H. L. Gottschalk ('Ibn al-Mudabbir') believed was the ʿAbbāsid official Ibrāhīm b. al-Mudabbir. Rather, Ibn al-Mudabbir was al-Shaybānī's intended recipient. On these points, see Mohamed Mokhtar Labidi, 'al-Shaybānī', EI^2.

83 Julia Bray, 'Lists and Memory: Ibn Qutayba and Muḥammad b. Ḥabīb', in *Culture and Memory in Medieval Islam: Essays in Honour of Wilferd Madelung*, ed. Farhard Daftary and Josef W. Meri (London: I.B. Tauris and the Institute of Ismaili Studies, 2003), 210–31.

84 In early Islamic jurisprudence, the earlier a precedent could be traced and authenticated, the more weight it could carry towards its ruling. Thus, a prophetic statement which had been vetted would take precedence over a ruling from a companion or other caliph. When a ruling on an issue could not be traced back to the Prophet, however, the earliest caliphs would also serve a similar purpose, with none more prominent as the progenitor of law post-Muḥammad than the second caliph, ʿUmar b. al-Khaṭṭāb, who plays this vital role throughout the *Futūḥ*. For more on this, see El-Hibri, *Parable and Politics*, 77–84; Avraham Hakim, "Umar b. al-Ḫaṭṭāb: L'autorité religieuse et morale', *Arabica*, Vol. 55, No. 1 (2008), 1–34.

85 See, for instance, al-Balādhurī's discussion on the stipends which should be awarded to the veterans of the Battle of Badr. *Futūḥ*, 557 (M 249).

86 Abū ʿUbayd, *al-Amwāl*, 224–7; *Futūḥ*, 555–7 (M 247-249).

87 See Abū ʿUbayd, *al-Amwāl*, 261–2; *Futūḥ*, 551, 557 (M 243-244, 249).

88 While Abū ʿUbayd chose to include his positions on Qurʾān reciters in his chapter on the *dīwān*, he included mention of ʿUmar's establishment of the *dīwān* and the identical traditions on these grants to the Prophet's wives and other exceptional individuals in his section on the *fayʾ*.

89 Only a single tradition from Yaḥyā opens al-Balādhurī's section on 'The Matter of Coinage', and this tradition is not present in the author's surviving *Kitāb al-Kharāj*. Despite this, Yaḥyā does include a section on the matter of weights and measures, which serves the purpose of detailing whether tax should be levied on produce above or below certain weights. Yaḥyā b. Ādam, *al-Kharāj*, 96–102.

90 This includes an important notice of al-Ḥajjāj's minting coins bearing the phrases 'In the Name of God', and 'God is one, God is the eternal (*al-ṣamad*)', in the year AH 75 (694–695 CE), which 'displeased the jurists (*fuqahā'*)'. *Futūḥ*, 575 (M 266-267).

91 *Futūḥ*, 579–83 (M 270-274).

92 Heck, *Construction of Knowledge*, 60.

93 C. H. Becker and Franz Rosenthal, 'al-Balādhurī', *EI* and *EI*[2].

94 The lack of a well-edited critical edition of the *Ansāb* and the lack of scholarship on the construction of the text during the authors' lifetimes must be considered when evaluating this comment, however.

95 See, for instance, the discussion between the Muslim commander Khālid b. al-Walīd and the Byzantine Bāhān. They discuss their theological positions and their reasons for fighting, while the reader is provided insight into the difference between a pious Muslim and a corrupt Christian, the latter of whom is more interested in worldly position than everlasting life. Al-Azdī, *Futūḥ al-Shām*, 178–9. This type of dialogue between figures within the early Arabic historical tradition is discussed in Nancy Khalek, '"He Was Tall and Slender, and His Virtues Were Numerous": Byzantine Hagiographical Topoi and the Companions of Muḥammad in al-Azdī's *Futūḥ al-Shām*', in *Writing True Stories: Historians and Hagiographers in the Late Antique and Medieval Near East*, ed. Arietta Papaconstantinou (New York: Brepols Publishers, 2010), 105–23, esp. 114–20.

96 For a discussion of the roles of the *kuttāb* at the court, see R. Sellheim and D. Sourdel, 'Kātib', *EI*[2] and C. E. Bosworth, 'Administrative Literature', in *Religion, Learning, and Science in the 'Abbāsid Period*, eds. M. J. L. Young, J. D. Latham and R. B. Serjeant (Cambridge: Cambridge University Press, 1990), 155–6.

97 Meaning that neither an account within the text nor the author himself ever refer back to a different section of the book. This is primarily born from al-Balādhurī's almost completely removing himself from explicit commentary on the accounts he transmits. Occasionally, within similar regions, you will see a rare exception to this. In one instance, in discussing the conquest of the Egyptian city of Alexandria, an account describes that the city was conquered by 'Amr b. al-'Āṣ forcefully, and that for the people therein, 'he made them protected (*al-dhimma*), like the people of al-Yūna (Fusṭāṭ, modern Cairo)'. The conquest of al-Yūna and the terms made afterwards are described in the preceding chapter, 'The Conquest of Egypt and the Maghrib'. *Futūḥ*, 251–2, 259 (H 338-339, 347).

98 On the issues of reading practices in the post-classical, or 'middle period' of Islamic history, see Konrad Hirschler, *The Written Word in the Medieval Arabic Lands: A Social and Cultural History of Reading Practices* (Edinburgh: Edinburgh University Press, 2012) and 'Reading Certificates (*samāʿāt*) as a Prosopographical Source: Cultural and Social Practices of an Elite Family in Zangid and Ayyubid Damascus', in *Manuscript Notes as Documentary Sources*, eds. Görke and Hirschler, 73–92. Hirschler's study and others like it have benefitted, however, from the availability and analysis of material such as reading certificates (*samāʿāt*) within the manuscript tradition of certain texts, which are not present in the surviving manuscripts of the *Futūḥ*. The surviving evidence concerning which medieval scholars engaged with al-Balādhurī's text and transmitted his materials in successive generations is discussed in Chapter 6 below.

99 It is worth noting that this would be separate from a type of training manual, although there would be many overlapping interests. It seems unlikely that the *Futūḥ* could have served as a primary training manual for court bureaucrats, owing to the fact that it never pauses to define the bulk of its legal terminology, and it seems already to assume some level of knowledge of the practices in question.

100 It is for this reason that we likely see the 'discovery' of such documents over the third/ninth century, including the Prophet's letter to the inhabitants of Najrān, cited in the *Chronicle of Seert*.

101 This topic has been the subject of a number of enlightening recent studies, the most important of which are Toorawa, *Ibn Abī Ṭāhir Ṭayfūr and Arabic Writerly Culture* and Schoeler, *The Oral and the Written in Early Islam*.

6

The medieval reception and reuse of the *Futūḥ*

The present chapter will consider the legacy of *Futūḥ al-buldān* within the medieval period, primarily through a discussion of the textual reuse of material found in al-Balādhurī's text by subsequent authors. Textual reuse is the 'meaningful reiteration of text, usually beyond the simple repetition of common language;'[1] beyond the mere duplication of words, it is the reintroduction and reuse of ideas, concepts, and in this case, historical information between authors. Material can be reshaped and reorganized to achieve different ends. Put simply, 'reuse is to have some text blocks which you can use in repeatedly different contexts',[2] a definition which proves remarkably appropriate for the often-dissociative nature of *akhbār* and *ḥadīth* in the early Islamic tradition, brought together by authors in the creation of these texts and their narratives.

While al-Balādhurī's text has been a popular and commonly used source of information on the early Islamic period during the modern era, this chapter will demonstrate through textual reuse analysis that al-Balādhurī's *Futūḥ* was a respected text that continued to be used throughout the medieval period as well. It will show that the *Futūḥ* was immediately engaged with by other authors within a generation of al-Balādhurī's own lifetime, and remained an important and relevant source of information through, at the least, the thirteenth/seventh century. As with the approach of Chapter 5 and its discussion of the *Futūḥ* as a text that does not neatly fit within modern genre classifications, this textual reuse comparison will demonstrate that the *Futūḥ*'s material found popularity within other texts in diverse genres. The discussion in this chapter will include texts that make evident that they are transmitting information from al-Balādhurī as well as those which do not. It will provide examples of verbatim and near-verbatim textual reuse, while also identifying instances of less obvious abbreviation and recasting of material that seems likely to have derived from the *Futūḥ*. In doing so, it will identify some of the types of material that later authors were ostensibly the most interested in borrowing from the *Futūḥ*, and will include general comments on the form and function of the reuse of material in the classical Arabic historical tradition. While a brief discussion of quotation from the *Ansāb al-ashrāf* was long ago undertaken by S. D. Goitein, there has been almost no thorough analysis of reuse of the *Futūḥ's* accounts up to this point, save the occasional notations of Hitti and Murgotten in their translation of the text.[3]

Textual reuse and the *Futūḥ*: To cite or not to cite?

The enormous size and breadth of the entirety of the classical Arabic tradition means that the task of identifying all examples of textual reuse by later authors of al-Balādhurī's material in the *Futūḥ* is not practical in this current research. With that said, however, advances in the computer-mediated analysis of Arabic texts allows for an easier preliminary identification of verbatim text reuse, at which point a researcher is able to search for brief, precisely repeated phrases which appear in both texts, and then compare the texts more thoroughly in an attempt to identify greater overlap. By verbatim reuse, I mean the identical repetition of extended phrases, paragraphs, and at times entire accounts between texts. By near-verbatim reuse, I refer to a number of minor variations which might occur between accounts, including the inclusion of additional conjunctions such as 'and' (*wa-*) and 'and so' (*fa-*); slight shifts in word order where the vocabulary otherwise stays identical; and occasional variations in the morphology of words – especially verbs and the use of *kāna* and its variants – which might be altered by these factors. In all of these cases, the content of the traditions remains the same despite these minor variations, and in many examples, it may only be a single phrase or sentence within a much larger verbatim tradition that might contain this minor variation.

As a compilation of previously existing accounts and traditions, some of which can demonstrably be shown to appear in other surviving Arabic texts[4] and others which may have existed but no longer survive, a certain amount of caution must be exercised in comparing each line of the *Futūḥ* to other surviving Arabic works. Al-Balādhurī's text may well have been the intermediary for these traditions to pass into later compilations of historical material, or these accounts may have survived in the work of other scholars who served as that intermediary. In some cases, this example of reuse will be almost impossible to identify, especially when we are often not just missing a text by the original compiler of information, but also the texts of the generational intermediar(ies) between that original compiler and the comparison work.[5] At other times, as Ella Landau-Tasseron and Stefan Leder have previously commented, an earlier author or text may be claimed as the originator of certain information by a later author, but that material may have been significantly reworked so as to have lost its original form, or may have been misattributed to an earlier master to claim greater prestige.[6] What I hope to have demonstrated in Chapter 3, however, through the comparisons of the traditions in the surviving *Kitāb al-Kharāj* and *Kitāb al-Amwāl* with those of the *Futūḥ*, is that there often exists a noteworthy amount of variation in texts which may have already existed in some written form even as al-Balādhurī was writing the *Futūḥ* – and which include those same traditions.

In this way, I would like to return to a suggestion already made through that comparison: that a tradition being more similar between two texts does not necessarily indicate that it was compiled without an intermediary, and, conversely, near-verbatim reuse as opposed to verbatim reuse does not necessarily indicate that it was compiled with an intermediary or in an oral form. In much of what is to follow, Gernot Rotter's suggestion that an author who had access to both written sources and oral sources would be much more faithful in using the latter will be further challenged.[7] At the same time, Gregor Schoeler's opinion that literal precision was of less importance than the transmission and application of reliable early sources in later works will find further support in the analysis of *Futūḥ* reuse.[8]

The where and what of *Futūḥ* reuse

The best way to identify direct reuse of material between texts is certainly the most obvious, and is found in the choice of authors to cite or not cite the sources or contacts that they relied on. While this might be accomplished through the provision of a chain of transmission (*isnād*) for that material, this is not always the case: especially when a later source is citing an earlier, still extant written source, there was no need to quote the entire oral/aural chain that information travelled along before first being committed to writing. Naming a source of information is straightforward, and provides an easier means for a researcher to compare the types of quotation and reuse occurring by one author of another's material. This signpost, however, is not often available. Many authors in the early Arabic tradition choose not to name their source at all – whether by citing a book they read or a teacher they learned from directly. What will also be demonstrated below is that just because an author chose to name his source some of the time does not guarantee that all examples of that reuse in a given text were similarly noted, nor that all of the reuse that occurred by even that *one author* was similarly noted.

In some cases, however, the reuse of material found in al-Balādhurī's *Futūḥ* can be more clearly identified. This reuse can come in two forms, the first being where the later compiler of material has chosen to cite al-Balādhurī as an intermediary or the informant of that material which was reused. The other, rarer instance is that the material which originated elsewhere and was compiled by al-Balādhurī also survived in another line of transmission and in a different source. These limited occurrences will not be debated here, as the discussion will focus on texts that definitely borrow from *Futūḥ al-buldān*. Suffice it so say, however, that there is scope to return to this matter in future research. Searching for the overlap of material within the *Futūḥ* that is also found in later texts leads to the identification of varying levels of overlap. The discussion here, however, will primarily be limited to bulk verbatim or near-verbatim reuse of material identified using a computer algorithm based on an *ngram* of 10, referring to a sequence of at least 10 contiguous letters appearing in a comparable sequence.[9]

The following texts include the most extensive amount of overlap with material originally appearing in *Futūḥ al-buldān*. They are listed in Table 6.1 according to how much of the *Futūḥ's* material appears in the named text (starting with the greatest amount of reuse).

The first point worthy of comment is that this is not an exhaustive list of classical books where reuse of the *Futūḥ* occurs.[10] They are, however, representative of the

Table 6.1 Texts compared to *Futūḥ al-buldān* and their authors

Author	Text Name
Qudāma b. Ja'far (d. 948 CE/AH 337)	*Kitāb al-Kharāj wa-ṣinā'at al-kitāba*
Yāqūt al-Ḥamawī (d. 1229 CE/AH 626)	*Mu'jam al-buldān*
Ibn al-'Adīm (d. 1262 CE/AH 660)	*Bughyat al-ṭalab fī ta'rīkh Ḥalab*
Ibn al-Athīr (d. 1233 CE/AH 630)	*al-Kāmil fi-l-ta'rīkh*
Ibn al-Faqīh (*fl.* late 800s CE/AH late 200s)	*Kitāb al-Buldān*
Ibn 'Asākir (d. 1176 CE/AH 571)	*Ta'rīkh madīnat Dimashq*

many forms in which that reuse can occur. Smaller amounts of reuse occur in a number of other texts that merit future comparison and discussion, including *Nihāyat al-arab fī funūn al-adab* (*The Ultimate Ambition in the Arts of Erudition*) of al-Nuwayrī (d. 1333 CE/AH 733) and *al-Sunan al-kubrā* (*The Great Customary Practices*) of al-Bayhaqī (d. 1066 CE/AH 458). Additionally, this sample shows that reused material features in a group of texts that is diverse as regards both time of composition and literary genre. Harkening back to the discussion of Chapter 5, the multivalent nature of the *Futūḥ* and its similarities to a variety of different genres likely meant it was a synthesis of material that had multiple uses and forms. This is only further reinforced when looking at the above list, which includes physical geographies, administrative geographies, local/regional histories, and biographical compendiums. Several of the above texts are not just well known, but are also celebrated for their status as vital depositories of traditions – many now lost – from earlier periods.

Nevertheless, what material is reused, and can we say anything further about this reuse? We will speak more in depth about the text with the largest amount of reuse, Qudāma b. Jaʿfar's *Kitāb al-kharāj*, further below, but the other texts listed here will provide an interesting opportunity not just to identity the reuse of al-Balādhurī's material by later authors, but to speak in greater detail about which types of information they were interested in and the variety of forms this reuse took. Each of the above texts provides unique examples of the various guises textual reuse can take within the classical Arabic tradition. This will hopefully help other researchers working on Arabic and Persian historiography to better identify the sources of information relied on by a particular author or text.

Ibn al-Faqīh's *Kitāb al-Buldān*

We can begin our detailed study of the reception of al-Balādhurī's *Futūḥ* with the surviving abridgement of *Kitāb al-Buldān* (*The Book of Lands*) by Ibn al-Faqīh al-Hamadhānī, a geographical work that is an abridgement of a now-lost larger work. It is characterized by a number of 'digressions concerning *adab*', giving it a more literary flavour than other, later physical geographies.[11] Ibn al-Faqīh's text is the only one to have been compared to al-Balādhurī's *Futūḥ* for reuse up until this point. Yūsuf Hādī, in the opening sections of his edition of *al-Buldān*, discussed the use of material by Ibn al-Faqīh from his predecessors that occurs in the book.[12] In his discussion of *Futūḥ al-buldān*,

Hādī asserts (incorrectly) that al-Balādhurī's name is invoked three times in Ibn al-Faqīh's text (it actually appears twice),[13] and Ibn al-Faqīh attributes large sections of material to al-Balādhurī in both of these instances. What is most surprising about these sections, however, is that this material – related to discussions of Ṭabaristān and Khurāsān respectively – does not appear in either the *Futūḥ* or the *Ansāb*. This is, as far as I am currently aware, the only instance of material attributed to al-Balādhurī that is not found in either of his extant works, and because of this, it is an exceptionally valuable citation. Hādī suggests that this material may originate from the so-called *Greater Book of the Conquest of Lands* (*Kitāb Futūḥ al-buldān al-kabīr*) mentioned by Ibn al-Nadīm as having never been completed. While this is a distinct possibility, I find it exceedingly unusual that no other material attributed to al-Balādhurī outside of the *Futūḥ* and *Ansāb* survives in a later work, and that Ibn al-Faqīh would have been the only medieval Muslim author who was apparently able to make use of its content. While little is known of Ibn al-Faqīh's life, it seems likely that he wrote *Kitāb al-Buldān* in the early tenth century, and Henri Massé has suggested that it was completed ca. 903 CE/AH 290, as no event after this date is revealed in the text.[14] If Massé is correct, it is possible that Ibn al-Faqīh heard the traditions regarding these two regions from a student of al-Balādhurī's or, perhaps, even from al-Balādhurī himself.

This material on Ṭabaristān and Khurāsān does not appear, however, to be the only example where Ibn al-Faqīh makes use of al-Balādhurī's material from the *Futūḥ*. It just happens to be the only portion of the surviving text where he names al-Balādhurī as his source. Hādī himself addressed this issue, by comparing two traditions that appear in the *Futūḥ* to very similar ones found in *al-Buldān*. The first is a tradition which al-Balādhurī attributes to Jaʿfar b. Muḥammad al-Rāzī, which details the ʿAbbāsid Caliph al-Mahdī's founding of the Persian city al-Rayy,[15] and the second is a brief tradition only credited to an unnamed sheikh (*baʿḍ al-mashāyikh*) which mentions how a spring in central Iraq, ʿAyn al-Jamal, earned its name.[16] In both cases, the traditions are muddled and words reordered or changed, enough so that to call their inclusion an example of near-verbatim reuse is an uncomfortable stretch. Yet, their similarity is unmistakable as is the bulk of the vocabulary used, and there can therefore be no doubt that either Ibn al-Faqīh took this material directly from the *Futūḥ* or the two texts shared a common source.

If these were the only instances of similarity between the two texts, the latter might be considered the more plausible of these options. However, this is not the case, and I have already mentioned the repetition of traditions concerning the Sasanian construction of frontier fortifications in the Caucasus in Chapter 5. But it is not simply al-Balādhurī's material which Ibn al-Faqīh indiscriminately borrows from without full attribution; he also does this with the work of al-Jāḥiẓ (whom he cites only three times in the text despite borrowing 'a great deal' from him) and Ibn Rabban al-Ṭabarī, so much so that another medieval geographer, al-Muqaddasī (*fl.* late 900s CE/AH mid-300s), made note of his regular use of the former's material.[17] Ibn al-Faqīh appears to have consciously been altering the versions of material he found in other early Arabic texts without any desire to fully attribute that material to its original source. Why he chose to do this, however, is a much more difficult question to answer, and is deserving of greater attention than can be given here. Whether he was intending to mask his original source of information in an effort to have greater claim to originality, or he (and, more likely, his unnamed audience) simply felt it unnecessary to cite his material more thoroughly is uncertain.

Yāqūt's *Muʿjam al-buldān*

Yāqūt's *Muʿjam al-buldān* (*Dictionary of Countries*) is among the best known compilations of geographical material from the classical period of Islamic history, and is well known for cataloguing a wide variety of information which had previously appeared in earlier sources. We have already noted by way of his *Irshād al-arīb ilā maʿrifat al-adīb* (*Guiding the Intelligent to the Knowledge of Learned Men*) that Yāqūt had a positive opinion of al-Balādhurī. This opinion, nevertheless, is made much more plain when the *Muʿjam* and the *Futūḥ* are compared side by side, as the reuse of material across the two texts is among the largest of any of the above examples. The verbatim reuse of material from the *Futūḥ* spans almost the entirety of the text, beginning with the very first tradition in the very first chapter of al-Balādhurī's book concerning the Prophet Muḥammad's *hijra* to Medina and the mosque at Qubā',[18] and continuing through to his final, non-thematic chapter on the conquests of South Asia (al-Sind).[19] The duplicate material between the texts is substantial, and comes in a variety of forms. Looking at one example from the extreme end of al-Balādhurī's text will demonstrate the type of reuse Yāqūt made of his text, while we will observe examples of a different type of reuse from the *Futūḥ's* section on al-Baḥrayn.[20]

In his section on al-Sind, al-Balādhurī opens the chapter with a discussion of border raids near India under the first several caliphs. This includes details of raiding under the reign of the Caliph ʻUthmān (r. 644–656 CE/AH 23–35), who ordered the governor of Iraq, ʻAbd Allāh b. ʻĀmir b. Kurayz, to send someone to the region on a fact-finding mission. The man sent on this mission, Ḥakī b. Jabala al-ʻAbdī, travelled to the region and then to the caliph to report, where the following dialogue is recorded:

> And so when he returned, [ʻAbd Allāh] dispatched him to ʻUthmān. ʻUthmān asked him about the condition of the country, and he responded: ʻOh Commander of the Believers! I know it, and I have examined it.' ʻUthmān said: ʻDescribe it to me'. ʻThe water is scant, the dates are inferior, and the bandits are bold. There, a small army would be lost, and a large one would starve'.
>
> ʻUthmān asked: ʻAre you a reporter or a versifier?', and Ḥakī replied that it was information. And so, ʻUthmān did not have anyone raid the land.[21]

In the texts, the two accounts appear as follows:

<table>
<tr>
<td>فلما رجع أوفده إِلى عثمان فسأله عن حال البلاد
فقال يا أمير المؤمنين قد عرفتها وتنحرتها
قال فصفها لي

قال ماؤها وشل وثمرها دقل ولصها بطل إن قل
الجيش فيها ضاعوا وإن كثروا جاعوا
فقال له عثمان أخابر أم ساجع
قال بل خابر فلم يغزها أحدا</td>
<td>فلما رجع أوفده إلى عثمان فسأله عن حال البلاد
فقال يا أمير المؤمنين قد عرفتها وخبرتها
فقال صفها لي

فقال ماؤها وشل وثمرها دقل ولصها بطل إن قل
الجيش فيها ضاعوا وإن كثروا جاعوا
فقال عثمان أخابر أم ساجع
فقال بل خابر فلم يغزها أحد في أيامه</td>
</tr>
<tr>
<td>al-Balādhurī's Version</td>
<td>Yāqūt's Version</td>
</tr>
</table>

The two traditions show minor variation, and may well have originated from the same source based solely on their very close similarity revealed through comparison. Looking only at these duplicate passages, the inclusion of al-Ḥakī's rhymed *saj*ʻ regarding the dangers of the region may be well argued as the original narrative vehicle upon which the rest of the account was built, but fortunately, in this case, the reader has a bit more context for the transmission of this material.

Al-Balādhurī's section opens with a discussion of the first raids on al-Sind under the Caliph ʻUmar (r. 634–644 CE/AH 13–23), and this does not appear in Yāqūt's section.[22] This lengthy opening tradition, including this above account and the information on the raids during ʻUmar's reign, appear to come on the authority of al-Balādhurī's informant al-Madāʾinī (here formally named as Alī b. Muḥammad b. ʻAbd Allāh b. Abī Sayf), which Yāqūt makes no mention of.[23]

Instead, however, he speaks plainly: the information he includes on the region came from Aḥmad b. Yaḥyā b. Jābir, referring to al-Balādhurī. All of this is quite useful. First, it demonstrates that Yāqūt was willing to cite when his information came from al-Balādhurī's *Futūḥ* and was not making some veiled attempt at secrecy over how the account came to him. Next, the fact that the author himself discloses that this information came to him from al-Balādhurī reveals a great deal more about the reuse of material across generations. Al-Balādhurī and Yāqūt could never have met, and with so many centuries between their lifetimes, we can be reasonably confident that Yāqūt accessed his material from a written copy of the *Futūḥ*. Despite this, however, we find throughout *Muʿjam al-buldān* that these accounts were not just broken apart and emplotted in different sections that fit his own organization, but that occasional variations in wording and morphology would still occur. Even if it was one author and/or scribe copying the work of a previous author/scribe, these variations still arose whether consciously or otherwise, and so transmitted material did not need to appear in a totally exact form to have been copied directly from another source. Near-verbatim transmission is enough to mark out these traditions as directly reused.

In his section on al-Baḥrayn, we find even more telling forms of the reuse of material from the *Futūḥ*. Some of the reuse of material in this section comes on the authority of the eminent Abū Mikhnaf (d. 774 CE/AH 157), and concerns the appointment of governors over al-Baḥrayn during ʿUmar's caliphate. The tradition itself is an example of near-verbatim reuse, as it includes several words which have their order swapped and one instance where a fairly important word describing Abū Hurayra's role differs. As it reads in the *Futūḥ* (and with variations marked in bold):

> Abū Mikhnaf has said: ʿUmar b. al-Khaṭṭāb, **God's blessings be upon him**, wrote to al-ʿAlāʾ b. al-Ḥaḍramī, who was his governor over al-Baḥrayn, **ordering him to return**. He appointed ʿUthmān b. Abī al-ʿĀṣ **al-Thaqafī** over al-Baḥrayn and Oman. When al-ʿAlāʾ came to Medina he was appointed over Baṣra in place of ʿUtba b. Ghazwān. He died there as soon as he arrived, **and that was in** the year 14 or in the beginning of the year 15. Then, ʿUmar tasked Qudāma b. Maẓʿūn al-Jumaḥī with the levying of taxes in al-Baḥrayn, and he tasked Abū Hurayra with [management] of the **guard and prayers**. ʿUmar later dismissed Qudāma and punished him for drinking wine; he tasked Abū Hurayra with [management] of **prayers and the guard (Y: the levying of taxes along with the guard)**. Later, ʿUmar dismissed Abū Hurayra, and confiscated a portion of his wealth. He then appointed ʿUthmān b. Abī al-ʿĀṣ over **al-Baḥrayn and Oman.**[24]

And the original Arabic of both texts:

وقال أبو مخنف: كتب عمر بن الخطاب رضي الله عنه إلى العلاء بن الحضرمي وهو عامله على البحرين يأمره بالقدوم عليه
وولى عثمان بن أبي العاصي الثقفي البحرين وعمان فلما قدم العلاء المدينة ولاه البصرة مكان عتبة بن غزوان فلم يصل إليها حتى مات وذلك في سنة أربعة عشر أو في أول سنة خمسة عشر

ثم أن عمر ولى قدامة بن مظعون الجمحي جباية البحرين وولى أبا هريرة لأحداث والصلاة ثم عزل قدامة وحده على شرب الخمر وولى أبا هريرة الصلاة والأحداث ثم عزله وقاسمه ماله

ثم ولى عثمان بن أبي العاصي البحرين وعمان

al-Balādhurī's Version

وقال أبو مخنف: كتب عمر بن الخطاب الى العلاء بن الحضرمي يستقدمه

وولى عثمان بن أبي العاصي البحرين مكانه وعمان فلما قدم العلاء المدينة ولاه البصرة مكان عتبة بن غزوان فلم يصل إليها حتى مات ودفن في طريق البصرة في سنة أربعة عشر أو في أول سنة خمسة عشر
ثم ان عمر ولى قدامة ابن مظعون الجمحي جباية البحرين وولى أبا هريرة الصلاة والاحداث ثم عزل قدامة وحده على شرب الخمر وولى أبا هريرة الجباية مع الاحداث ثم عزله وقاسمه ماله
ثم ولى عثمان بن أبي العاصي عمان والبحرين

Yāqūt's Version

For what should have been a set tradition clearly on the authority of a well-known early transmitter, there are definite variations in the text. Most of this is minor (the inclusion of blessings for 'Umar; the order of 'guard and prayers'), but the difference in the later line over what Abū Hurayra was later tasked with (prayers? or the collection of tax?) is more significant. In all probability, Yāqūt was merely amending the tradition as al-Balādhurī had compiled it to remove the repetition of Abū Huyraya's role (he was already in charge of the guard and the conduct of prayer before Qudāma was dismissed), while at the same time making clear that Abū Hurayra assumed responsibility for the role that was vacated by Qudāma's dismissal: the collection of taxes. This serves as yet another important reminder that the traditions of great early Islamic transmitters of *akhbār* like Abū Mikhnaf were more malleable than some readers in the modern period might be comfortable admitting. These early transmitters developed even more impressive reputations as the centuries passed after their death, and their material still remained in circulation in these historical compilations. The benefit of having a written source available when compiling a later collection – namely, the opportunity for unaltered, word-for-word transmission from these great authorities – was obviously not of the utmost significance to every author. Clarity and corrections were of equal importance, just as it has been shown in the scientific tradition.[25]

While it is also possible that Yāqūt received this account from a source other than al-Balādhurī – especially as the tradition appears to continue following the death of the Caliph ʿUmar in Yāqūt's text – this seems dubious based on the traditions which surround it. Just before Abū Mikhnaf's account in Yāqūt's text are two traditions which discuss gubernatorial assignments over al-Baḥrayn and Yemen from the time of the Prophet, including overlapping information on ʿUmar's appointments. Both traditions are introduced without any cited authority, but merely a 'they said' (*qālū*). The traditions are undoubtedly al-Balādhurī's, signalled not just by the fact that they contain only five words of minor variation (blessings are left out following the name of the Caliph Abū Bakr, one instance each of the words 'then' (*thumma*) and 'it was' (*kāna*) are dropped), but the fact that all three traditions appear in precisely the same order in both texts as well. The use of 'they said', already established as al-Balādhurī's indication for his use of abbreviation (*ikhtiṣār*) of other traditions, marks an account as al-Balādhurī's own, and that these two traditions appear here in Yāqūt's work in almost identical form is even more telling.

Despite the fact that such a large portion of his entry on al-Baḥrayn is taken from the *Futūḥ*, Yāqūt makes no attempt in this section of the *Muʿjam* to cite him as the source of his information. This, overall, is surprising; while it was already shown above that Yāqūt was willing to say when information came on the authority of al-Balādhurī, the account about al-Sind above was hardly the exception. Al-Balādhurī is cited by his name Aḥmad b. Yaḥyā b. Jābir a total of 32 times throughout the *Muʿjam*, and another 56 times by the name al-Balādhurī. Yāqūt was more than willing to cite al-Balādhurī in the text, but he chooses not to always do this. We might speculate on the reason for this, but without more information, it is impossible to come up with a convincing suggestion. What all of these points to, however, is not just the regular and sustained deployment of traditions from *Futūḥ al-buldān* by Yāqūt throughout the latter's text, but the plentiful amount of stylistic differentiation of Arabic textual reuse which can occur by just one author within a single text.

Ibn al-ʿAdīm's *Bughyat al-ṭalab fī taʾrīkh Ḥalab*

The great thirteenth/seventh-century historian of Aleppo, Kamāl al-Dīn Ibn al-ʿAdīm, was the son of a prominent Syrian family who held the judgeship of Aleppo for some five generations, including under both Zangid and Ayyūbid emirs. Of the two surviving texts that he wrote, *Bughyat al-ṭalab fī taʾrīkh Ḥalab* (*Everything Desirable About the History of Aleppo*) is the larger, but only partially survives.[26] A primarily genealogical history of individuals and families connected with the Syrian city he knew so well, in the creation of the *Bughyat al-ṭalab,* Ibn al-ʿAdīm used 'oral information, documents, and a great number of manuscript sources which are meticulously cited and for the most part lost'.[27]

'Meticulous' is an apt way to describe Ibn al-ʿAdīm's citations throughout the *Bughyat al-ṭalab*, especially when his technique is compared with the forms of reuse in the majority of the texts discussed here. Unlike many of these other texts, Ibn al-ʿAdīm's overlap with al-Balādhurī's material is contained primarily – although not completely – in three distinct sections of the *Futūḥ*, and he transmits the overwhelming majority of material from these sections. While the *Futūḥ* is not one of the primary sources of information relied upon by the author in the creation of his book, his citations are clear. He not just credits al-Balādhurī regularly as the originator of his quoted material, but also mentions which specific book it came from, referring to the *futūḥ* as 'The Book of Reports of Lands and Their Conquest' (*Kitāb Akhbār al-buldān wa-futūḥihā*) and 'The Book of Lands' (*Kitāb al-Buldān*), and the *Ansāb* as 'The Book of the Lineage of Nobles' (*Kitāb Ansāb al-ashrāf*) and 'The Book of the Entire Lineage of Nobles' (*Kitāb Jumal ansāb al-ashrāf*). Interesting to note, too, is that despite the genealogical nature of the main part of Ibn al-ʿAdīm's text and the occasional presence of a quote from the *Ansāb*, the preponderance of traditions which he uses from al-Balādhurī definitively originate from the *Futūḥ*.

Almost the entirety of Ibn al-ʿAdīm's reuse from al-Balādhurī is verbatim, with the only typical variations occurring when he chooses to leave out an honorific (for instance, the title 'Commander of the Believers' from the ʿAbbāsid Caliph al-Mahdī below). The three primary sections of reuse from the *Futūḥ* come from the sections on 'The Conquest of Qinnasrīn and al-ʿAwāṣim' (*Futūḥ qinnasrīn wa-l-ʿawāṣim*), 'The Matter of the *Jarājima*' (*Amr al-jarājima*), and 'The Conquest of Malatya' (*Futūḥ Malaṭya*).[28] In the case of the first two sections, large chunks of text originally introduced by al-Balādhurī with an informant as well as traditions which he introduced without any chain of transmission ('they said', *qālū*) are repeated verbatim, although Ibn al-ʿAdīm will at times cut off al-Balādhurī's tradition early or inject it part way through before combining it with the tradition of another named informant. Inside a larger tradition at the outset of his section on Qinnasrīn in the *Futūḥ*, we find this tradition about the *Ḥāḍir Qinnasrīn* that Ibn al-ʿAdīm discusses in its own section:

> The *Ḥāḍir Qinnasrīn* has been settled by the tribe of Tanūkh since they first came to Syria and pitched their tents. They later built their homes there.

> Abū 'Ubayda summoned them to convert to Islam, and some of them converted. However, the tribe of Ṣāliḥ b. Ḥulwān b. 'Imrān b. al-Ḥafi b. Quḍā'a remained Christian.
>
> Some of the children of Yazīd b. Ḥunayn al-Ṭā'ī al-Anṭakī informed me, on the authority of their elders (*ashyākhihim*), that a group from among the people of this *Ḥāḍir* converted to Islam in the caliphate of **the Commander of the Believers**[29] al-Mahdī. And so, 'Qinnasrīn' was written on their hands in green (*fa-kutiba 'alā aydīhim bi-l-khuḍra Qinnasrīn*).[30]

The first part of the tradition which appears before this information on the *Ḥāḍir* gives details of the conquest of Qinnasrīn proper, and Ibn al-'Adīm would not have needed this information in his section on the *Ḥayḍir*. Ibn al-'Adīm places these two originally separate traditions after information from Bakhṭ b. Kujka al-'Absī al-Ḥalabī's *Kitāb Sīrat al-mu'taḍid* (*The Book of the Life of al-Mu'taḍid*), then he omits more information from al-Balādhurī that was not pertinent for him before returning to more of the *Futūḥ*'s accounts which concerned the *Ḥayḍir*. In each instance, the use of the *Futūḥ*'s traditions are copied verbatim and are noted to have come from al-Balādhurī. The second partial tradition, on the authority of Yazīd's children and noted as such, actually appears in the *Bughyat al-ṭalab* twice, although in the second instance, it does not mention that it comes from the *Futūḥ*.[31]

In his reuse from al-Balādhurī's section on the 'Conquest of Malatya', however, several pages of Arabic are quoted completely verbatim throughout the entire chapter. This again includes large traditions introduced by *qālū* as well as sizeable accounts on the authority of an earlier transmitter (in this case, Ibn Sa'd and al-Wāqidī). In all of these cases – even when Ibn al-'Adīm introduces accounts in the middle of his transmission from the *Futūḥ* that do not appear in al-Balādhurī's text – the material appears in the identical order as it does in the *Futūḥ*. Outside of these three sections of Ibn al-'Adīm's work, however, there is little reuse of the *Futūḥ's* material which occurs.

Ibn al-Athīr's *al-Kāmil fi-l-ta'rīkh*

'Izz al-Dīn b. al-Athīr is known for being among the most important historians of the Crusades-era Middle East, and his *al-Kāmil fi-l-ta'rīkh* (*The Complete History*) is an impressive history of the Muslim world until the thirteenth century, which has benefitted from a number of modern studies.[32] In addition to lengthy details on the crusading movement from the perspective of the Muslim world, the work is a universal history beginning with creation and stretching across the author's own lifetime. As noted by Franz Rosenthal, *al-Ta'rīkh* is 'distinguished by the well-balanced selection of its vast material, by its clear presentation, and by the author's occasional flashes of historical insight, [but] it is somewhat marred, from the modern point of view, by its failure to indicate its sources and the restrictiveness of its annalistic form'.[33] Despite the text's importance – and likely owing to the form taken by Ibn al-Athīr's recycling – there have only been passing references to textual reuse in *al-Kāmil fi-l-ta'rīkh*,[34] and it seems highly likely that al-Balādhurī's *Futūḥ* is among those sources he employed.

Ibn al-Athīr's reliance on earlier written sources is so difficult to identify precisely because he eschews almost entirely the chain of transmission popular in other sources. Added to this, of course, is the work's considerable size, and the fact that its value as a contemporary or near-contemporary source for the period of the Crusades means that its material on the first Islamic centuries and earlier has had, disappointingly, only limited in-depth analysis.[35] To further complicate the situation, Ibn al-Athīr's use of earlier information seems to rarely, if ever, take the form of verbatim reuse. Concerning material from the *Futūḥ*, Ibn al-Athīr appears to be engaged in a very thorough process of abbreviation and summarization which would be significantly more difficult to identify without computer-mediated analysis, although his reliance on other early historical masters such as al-Ṭabarī (d. 923 CE/AH 310) and al-Mas'ūdī (d. 956 CE/AH 345) takes a slightly different form.[36] It is rare that an extended account is transmitted from the *Futūḥ* in a complete or near-complete form. Ibn al-Athīr often makes use of lines from the *Futūḥ* within a larger tradition not found in al-Balādhurī's text, before quickly moving to provide either his own commentary or material from yet another unnamed source. This type of reuse can be seen here, concerning relations with the people of the south Arabian city of Najrān:

Al-Balādhurī's Version:

> The population of Najrān had reached some 40,000, and jealousy developed among them. They came to 'Umar b. al-Khaṭṭāb, God be pleased with him, and they said: 'Transplant us from the land.' 'Umar had feared for the Muslims because of them, and so he took advantage of the situation and removed them from the land. Later, they regretted this, and they came to 'Umar and said: 'Reinstate us.' 'Umar refused that. When 'Alī b. Abī Ṭālib acceded, they came to

> him and said: 'We implore you, by your writing with your right hand, and with your intercession on our behalf through your Prophet: reinstate us.' 'Alī replied: "Umar was of sound judgment in this matter, and I hate to differ from him'.
>
> Abū Mas'ūd al-Kūfī informed on, on the authority of Muḥammad b. Marwān and al-Haytham b. 'Adī, on the authority of al-Kalbī who said: The master of the Najrānis in Kūfa would send out a messenger to all of those who were in Syria and other districts from the people of Najrān … (*ṣāḥib al-Najrāniyya bi-l-Kūfa kāna yab'ath rasūlahu ilā jamī' man bi-l-Shām wa-l-nawāḥī min ahl Najrān*).[37]

Ibn al-Athīr's Version:

> The population of Najrān had reached some 40,000, and jealousy developed among them. They came to 'Umar b. al-Khaṭṭāb and they said: 'Transplant us from the land.' 'Umar b. al-Khaṭṭāb had feared for the Muslims because of them, and so he took advantage of the situation and removed them from the land. Later, they regretted this. Then, they beseeched him [for assistance], but 'Umar refused that. And so it remained like that through the Caliphate of 'Uthmān. When 'Alī was appointed caliph, they came to him and they said: 'We implore you, by God, by your writing with your right hand.' 'Alī replied: "Umar was of sound judgement in this matter, and I hate to differ from him.' It was 'Uthmān who subtracted from them 200 garbs, and it was the master of the Najrānis in Kūfa who would send out a messenger to all of those who were in Syria and other districts from the people of Najrān (*ṣāḥib al-Najrāniyya bi-l-Kūfa yab'ath ilā man bi-l-Shām wa-l-nawāḥī min ahl Najrān*) to levy the robes from them.[38]

Between the two traditions, there is a great amount of interesting information revealed. The translated section from al-Balādhurī above comes on the authority al-Ḥusayn b. 'Alī b. al-Aswad, the minor transmitter of historical information who is nonetheless one of the primary informants for the *Futūḥ* as already discussed in Chapter 3, and it includes a full *isnād*. Ibn al-Athīr's version includes no details on the origin of his information. That the bulk of this tradition shows evidence of verbatim and near-verbatim textual reuse is also clear, and even the minor variations in the texts which occur – including, for instance, the invocation to God – could be seen as an attempt to make the original tradition slightly clearer. In *al-Kāmil*, al-Ḥusayn's tradition does not stand on its own, but, rather, occurs near the beginning of his chapter on the events of the year ten (631–632 CE), and is enclosed by the discussion – a portion of which is seen at the end of Ibn al-Athīr's version above – regarding the payment of tax in garments by the dispersed people of Najrān. Several traditions before this, the *Futūḥ* purports to record the original agreement made between the Prophet Muḥammad and the people of Najrān which detailed the payment of these robes, and Ibn al-Athīr's text discusses this briefly without including the lengthy treaty itself. The end of Ibn al-Athīr's tradition addressing ʿUthmān's reduction of their payment of robes is also included in the next tradition of al-Balādhurī's within the *Futūḥ* – from his informant Abū Masʿūd al-Kūfī – and Ibn al-Athīr seems to have abbreviated the most important content from al-Balādhurī's account into the two lines of Arabic seen above. Even some of the vocabulary is reused (he sent out to Syria and its districts, the title of the leader of the people of Najrān as 'the master of the Najrānis in Kūfa'), and the extreme similarity of the traditions continues further as both discuss the Najrānis' status under Muʿāwiya and his son Yazīd in an abbreviated form with similar vocabulary again. In each case, there is no mention by Ibn al-Athīr of where his information came from.

Interestingly, the largest example of reuse by Ibn al-Athīr of material found in the *Futūḥ* again concerns al-Sind, where he includes a great number of traditions describing border raiding in the region:

Al-Balādhurī's Version:

> Then ʿAbd Allāh b. ʿĀmir, in the time of Muʿāwiya b. Abī Sufyān, appointed ʿAbd Allāh b. Sawwār al-ʿAbdī over the frontier of al-Hind – although some say Muʿāwiya himself appointed him. He raided al-Qīqān and earned spoils of war. Then, he went to Muʿāwiya and presented him with Qīqānī horses, and he remained with him. Later, he returned to al-Qīqān but the Turks (*al-turk*) had gathered an army and they killed him. The poet says about him:
>
> 'The Son of Sawwār, against his enemies, kindles the fire and kills the hunger.'[39]

ثم ولى عبد الله بن عامر في زمن معاوية بن أبي سفيان عبد الله بن سوار العبدي ويقال ولاه معاوية من قبله ثغر الهند فغزا القيقان فأصاب مغنما ثم وفد إلى معاوية وأهدى إليه خيلا قيقانية وأقام عنده ثم رجع إلى القيقان فاستجاشوا الترك فقتلوه وفيه يقول الشاعر: وابن سوار على عدانه (علاّته) موقد النار وقتال السغب	استعمل عبد الله بن عامر على ثغر الهند عبد الله بن سوارالعبدي ويقال ولاه معاوية من قبله فغزا الْقيقان فأصاب مغنما ووفد على معاوية وأهدى له خيلا قيقانية ورجع فغزا القيقان فاستنجدوا بالترك فقتلوه وفيه يقول الشاعر: وابن سوّارعلى عدانه موقد النار وقتال الشغب
al-Balādhurī's Version	*Ibn al-Athīr's Version*

This repetition of material, however, requires some caution: much of this tradition also occurs in Yāqūt's *Muʿjam* in his entry on Qīqān,[40] and it is possible that Ibn al-Athīr copied this material – which itself appears in an amended form from al-Balādhurī's *Futūḥ* without attribution – from his contemporary, Yāqūt. At first glance, in the available critical editions of the three texts, this might actually appear as the most likely scenario, as the verse quoted in the tradition appears the same in both Ibn al-Athīr and Yāqūt's versions, and yet appears differently in the editions of the *Futūḥ* (noted by italics and parentheses above). This seems, however, to be an error of de Goeje and al-Munajjid's editions of the *Futūḥ*, as the Yale manuscript of al-Balādhurī's work has the same Arabic verse as the other authors.[41] Despite this possibility, however, that the *Futūḥ* would have been available to Ibn al-Athīr at the time of the writing of his *History* is not in doubt, and the other instances of reuse in his text like the traditions of the people of Najrān above leaves no doubt that he was using the accounts of the *Futūḥ*. The heavy abbreviation of many of these traditions, however, as well as their emplotment in the longer, more narrative historical prose of Ibn al-Athīr's text would suggest that there are likely many more classical Islamic sources which informed him. There is much greater opportunity for comparison by those analysing and/or using the early Islamic sections of *al-Kāmil fi-l-taʾrīkh* to apply similar techniques of identification between Ibn al-Athīr's work and that of earlier authors.

Ibn ʿAsākir's *Taʾrīkh madīnat Dimashq*

The use of al-Balādhurī's material in Ibn ʿAsākir's monumental local compendium on Damascus and its hinterlands, *Taʾrīkh madīnat Dimashq* (*The History of the City of Damascus*) is sporadic, but clear. Ibn ʿAsākir's *Taʾrīkh* has already benefitted from several important analyses of his sections on early Islamic history, but with little definitive discussion of the original sources of information.[42] Ibn ʿAsākir chose to cite al-Balādhurī as the source of a wide variety of traditions in his text, while usually naming the primary transmitter with which that tradition had come to al-Balādhurī. Hence, we find cited traditions from al-Madāʾinī[43] and al-ʿAbbās b. Hishām al-Kalbī[44] via al-Balādhurī, but Ibn ʿAsākir's naming of al-Balādhurī as a source of information is different from many of the other authors on the above list who cite him. The reuse comes in one of two forms between the two texts: Ibn ʿAsākir either repeats material from al-Balādhurī completely verbatim, or he includes only a very minor reference to something in al-Balādhurī's texts without any direct reuse. As an example of verbatim reuse, in discussing how an area around Damascus came to earn its name, al-Balādhurī provides a tradition from al-Wāqidī (introduced simply with 'al-Wāqidī said' (*qāla al-Wāqidī*):

> Khālid [b. al-Walīd] headed to *Thaniyyat* which is now known as *Thaniyyat al-ʿUqāb*, in Damascus. He stayed there for an hour, unfurling his banner, which was the black banner that had belonged to the Prophet. And so ever since, it was called *Thaniyyat al-ʿUqāb*, as the Arabs call a banner "*uqāb*." Others say (*wa-qawm yaqūlūn*) it was called *ʿuqāb* because of the bird (*min al-ṭayr*; the Arabic word for vulture is *ʿuqāb*) which descended onto [the banner]. The first explanation, however, is more reliable. I heard some say that there was something like a stone [statue] of a vulture there, but there is no truth to that statement.[45]

This tradition of al-Wāqidī's is very typical of the sort of information al-Balādhurī includes within his *Futūḥ*, as he often chooses to provide information on how locally or strangely named locations came to earn their monikers. What is more unique, however, is how Ibn ʿAsākir usually engages with al-Balādhurī's material and how he chooses to credit the compiler.

Similar information appears in *Taʾrīkh madīnat Dimashq*, in Ibn ʿAsākir's section on the virtues of the areas surrounding Damascus. He makes no mention of al-Wāqidī as the originator of any of this material, and includes only a single overlapping line from the *Futūḥ*: 'Others say it was called *ʿuqāb* because of the bird which descended onto [the banner].' This is the only part of the tradition he chooses to provide, and he also omits the clarification found in the *Futūḥ* that one tradition was more authentic than the other. Ibn ʿAsākir is plain in describing where this information came from, too, saying 'Abū Bakr Aḥmad b. Yaḥyā al-Balādhurī has mentioned this meaning (*hādhā al-maʿnā*)' before then quoting the line.[46] Ibn ʿAsākir may have believed that this part of the tradition was, in fact, not al-Wāqidī speaking, but an interpolation by al-Balādhurī himself, and hence why he chose to cite al-Balādhurī as the only authority for the comment. He may have even had a copy of al-Wāqidī's text to confirm this. Ibn ʿAsākir is remarkably useful for a historiographically minded researcher, in that he states plainly when the accounts of a more famous originator came to him through an intermediary text like al-Balādhurī's. So it is, then, with a tradition mentioned earlier from al-ʿAbbās b. Hishām al-Kalbī and his family regarding Khālid b. al-Walīd's exploits in the capture of Dūmat al-Jandal in the northern Arabian desert, where it is again introduced with 'Aḥmad b. Yaḥyā al-Balādhurī has mentioned...'

> Al-'Abbās b. Hishām al-Kalbī informed me, on the authority of his father, on the authority of his grandfather, who said: The Prophet sent Khālid b. al-Walīd to Ukaydir, and so he brought Ukaydir before the Prophet and he converted to Islam.[47] And so he wrote for him an agreement (*kitāb*). When the Prophet died, Ukaydir stopped paying tax (*al-ṣadaqa*), he violated the covenant (*al-'ahd*), and he left Dūmat al-Jandal for al-Ḥīra. He erected a building there and called it Dūma after Dūmat al-Jandal. Al-Ḥurayth b. 'Abd al-Malik, his brother, converted to Islam, and took possession of the property that had belonged to his brother.[48]

While the bulk of the al-'Abbās' tradition is included verbatim, Ibn 'Asākir chose to omit the final line of the tradition regarding the rights to property which did not fit his own purpose in the *Ta'rīkh Dimashq*, but did fit al-Balādhurī's purpose in the *Futūḥ*.[49] Verbatim reuse of traditions from al-Balādhurī like these occur throughout Ibn 'Asākir's text from both the *Futūḥ* and the *Ansāb*, although al-Balādhurī cannot be considered anything more than a minor source of information for his book. There are no long quotations of al-Balādhurī's texts that appear in the *Ta'rīkh*, nor are there even instances of multiple accounts from either the *Futūḥ* or the *Ansāb* appearing adjacently in a single section of the *Ta'rīkh*.

Much more regularly, on the other hand, Ibn 'Asākir will mention that al-Balādhurī has said something on a particular issue or person he is discussing in his own text, but this material includes none of al-Balādhurī's original context and, almost always, is more a reference than it is an example of material reuse. The content included is typically a brief summarization which appeared in one of al-Balādhurī's works, and is almost exclusively from the *Ansāb*. Ibn 'Asākir's own extensive genealogical section in his *Ta'rīkh* means that his preference for material from the *Ansāb* over the *Futūḥ* is perhaps predictable. As an example of these mere references to al-Balādhurī's text which are made by Ibn 'Asākir, we find a note that 'Aḥmad b. Yaḥyā al-Balādhurī has mentioned that Isḥāq b. Muslim (*fl* mid 700s CE/AH 100s) went on pilgrimage with Abū Ja'far al-Manṣūr (the 'Abbāsid caliph)'.[50] This sentence is not identical to the notice that appears in the *Ansāb*, and nothing else in Ibn 'Asākir's entry on Isḥāq b. Muslim comes from al-Balādhurī. Elsewhere, we find al-Balādhurī's book cited to suggest a different name for an individual or to correct a date of death.

When it comes to modern western expectations of historical writing, Ibn ʿAsākir's use and citation of al-Balādhurī's material is comfortable and easy to digest. He clearly cites al-Balādhurī whenever he borrows information from him, and occasionally even notes whether that information came from the *Futūḥ* or the *Ansāb*. Especially in the case of his material from the *Futūḥ*, he is interested not in al-Balādhurī's own summarizations of traditions – those introduced with phrases like 'they said' (*qālū*) – but primarily in the traditions of earlier transmitters that al-Balādhurī had compiled, especially al-ʿAbbās b. Hishām al-Kalbī and al-Madāʾinī.

Qudāma b. Jaʿfar and *Kitāb al-khāraj's Futūḥ* section

While the methods of the digital humanities are increasingly making the identification of textual reuse more straightforward, there remains an important need for the analysis of this data by scholars of the tradition itself. This is more clearly seen when we compare the *Futūḥ* and the extant sections of Qudāma b. Jaʿfar's *Kitāb al-Kharāj wa-ṣināʿat al-kitāba* (*The Book of Taxation and the Craft of Writing*), which also exhibits a fundamental connection with al-Balādhurī's *Futūḥ*. This connection demonstrates not just the reuse of material, however. The reliance of *Kitāb al-Kharāj* on the *Futūḥ* goes beyond verbatim reuse to the very core of Qudāma's text: that of how he organizes an entire section of his book.

The reliance of Qudāma's text on the *Futūḥ* is not immediately made apparent. While Qudāma's complete book would have been substantially longer than al-Balādhurī's *Futūḥ* had the entirety of the work survived, his surviving Chapter 19, entitled 'On the Conquest of the Regions and Garrison Towns' (*fī Futūḥ al-nawāḥī wa-l-amṣār*), is essentially a work of *futūḥ* detailing the Islamic conquests of the seventh and eighth centuries. Strikingly, Qudāma's organization of the whole of this section appears to completely mimic al-Balādhurī's *Futūḥ al-buldān*. While his subheadings of the conquest of regions may occasionally differ from al-Balādhurī's – as an example, Qudāma titles one section on a portion of Syria as 'The Conquest of Qinnasrīn and al-ʿAwāṣim' (*Futūḥ Qinnasrīn wa-al-ʿAwāṣim*), while al-Balādhurī titles his section as 'The Matter of the District of Qinnasrīn and the Cities which are Called al-ʿAwāsim' (*Amr jund Qinnasrīn wa-al-mudun allatī tudʿā al-ʿAwāṣim*) – all of the sections that Qudāma includes take the identical order as al-Balādhurī's *Futūḥ*, as seen here in a list of the first chapters of each book, starting from the beginning:

Futūḥ al-buldān

1) Medina[51]
2) The Possessions of the Banū Naḍīr (*Amwāl banī al-Naḍīr*)
3) The Possessions of the Banū Qurayẓa
4) Khaybar
5) Fadak (*Fadak*)
6) The Matter of Wādī al-Qurā and Taymā'
7) Mecca
8) Mention of the Wells of Mecca
9) The Matter of Floods in Mecca
10) Al-Ṭā'if (*al-Ṭā'if*)
11) Tabāla and Jurash
12) Tabūk, Ayla, Adhruḥ, Maqnā, and al-Jarbā'
13) Dumat al-Jandal
14) The Peace Agreement of Najrān
15) Yemen
16) Oman

Kitāb al-Kharāj

1) The Conquest of Regions and Cities[52]
2) The Possessions of the Banū Naḍīr, the Jews (*Amwāl banī al-Naḍīr min al-Yahūd*)
3) The Possessions of the Banū Qurayẓa
4) Khaybar
5) The Matter of Fadak (*Amr Fadak*)
6) The Matter of Wādī al-Qurā
7) The Matter of Taymā'
8) Mecca
9) The Matter of al-Ṭā'if (*Amr al-Ṭā'if*)
10) The Matter of Tabāla and Jurash
11) Tabūk, Ayla, Adhruḥ, Maqnā, and al-Jarbā'
12) Dumat al-Jandal
13) The Peace Agreement of Najrān
14) Yemen
15) Oman

Both start with traditions on Medina and the arrival of the Prophet Muḥammad, and both end with 'The Conquest of al-Sind.' While all of the sections Qudāma includes are considerably smaller than what is found in al-Balādhurī's text,[53] the traditions he selects and seems likely to have copied directly from the *Futūḥ* even appear *in the same order* within each subsection, and there is substantial verbatim reuse of material.

Fascinatingly, however, al-Balādhurī is not cited at any point in the entirety of the surviving portion of Qudāma's book, although his reliance on it for the construction of his own work is both obvious and conclusive. This may be purely because Qudāma's text survives in only a partial form, and perhaps the author made clear his indebtedness to the *Futūḥ* and other earlier authors at the outset of his book. It seems unusual that he would not do this at all in the section that al-Balādhurī is so clearly relied upon, however. Alternatively, one wonders if Qudāma does not cite al-Balādhurī as the informant of the information in his *Futūḥ* section precisely because it was obvious where it came from. Qudāma was only a generation or two removed from al-Balādhurī at most, more than long enough for al-Balādhurī's work to have gained a positive reputation and readership while not so long as to have lost its relevance for a secretarial audience – to which Qudāma himself belonged. This suggestion, however, relies on evidence which we must piece together: for one, it requires a recognition that al-Balādhurī's text was popular enough to have had a readership and use which recognized its quality into the tenth/fourth century. This is not too difficult to imagine, especially as we have already established above that texts several centuries later than Qudāma's were still relying on and integrating the accounts of the *Futūḥ* in their own works. But we have no direct surviving indication of who was actually reading the *Futūḥ* outside of this reuse in other texts. Additionally, it requires that the same bureaucratic audience that Qudāma was writing his *Kitāb al-Kharāj* for would also have enough familiarity with al-Balādhurī's text to have known, without reference, that much of the material contained within Qudāma's *Futūḥ* section originated from there. In some cases, this would not have mattered, as Qudāma relies heavily on the accounts of al-Wāqidī which also are included in the *Futūḥ*, but many of which al-Balādhurī may not have made any emendations to, either.

These suggestions all seem compelling, and yet there is another aspect of Qudāma's reuse that is of vital importance for understanding his technique. Al-Dhahabī (d. 1348 CE/AH 748) names among al-Balādhurī's students a certain Jaʿfar b. Qudāma.[54] This Jaʿfar seems very likely to be Jaʿfar b. Qudāma b. Ziyād (*fl.* late 800s/AH mid-300s), Qudāma's father, himself remembered in the *Taʾrīkh Baghdād* (*History of Baghdad*) as a secretary (*kātib*) and man of letters (*adīb*) and the author of administrative works, but of whom little else is known.[55] Problematically, the same source does not list al-Balādhurī among Ja'far's few mentioned teachers, and he has no entry on Qudāma himself.[56] While there has been some confusion over whether Ja'far and Qudāma were one and the same person,[57] and whether *Kitāb al-Kharāj's* author was himself a student of al-Balādhurī,[58] both seem extremely unlikely – especially the latter option, as the available dates for Qudāma and al-Balādhurī seem unlikely to have left little (if any) overlap between their two lifetimes.[59] Whether al-Dhahabī connects al-Balādhurī and Ja'far because of some long-understood knowledge that simply went unmentioned in other biographical sources or because he (or his informants) were aware of the similarities between *Kitāb al-Kharāj* and the *Futūḥ* is a completely different matter.

While there has been recent research within the Arabic medical tradition to convincingly demonstrate that ninth/third- and tenth/fourth-century authors seemed to be intentionally obscuring where they originally found some of their information, the same cannot as easily be assumed of the early Arabic historical tradition.[60] Imitation was considered an essential part of this tradition, especially in the case of legal/*ḥadīth* transmission, but so, too, was verifiability – the inclusion of chains of transmission which authenticated the information attached to it. In the case of *akhbār*, however, imitation seems to have been equally valued but without this scientific focus on verifiability. In the case of the modern scholar working with these texts, our authors are often nothing more than the products of their surviving body of writing, now and again augmented by later biographical comment. For our purposes, whether Ja'far or Qudāma was the author of *Kitāb al-Kharāj* is much less relevant than what can be said about the relationship between the two texts themselves. Al-Balādhurī's *Futūḥ* is indisputably the primary source for not just the bulk of the traditions within *Kitāb al-Kharāj's* surviving conquest section, but this evaluation shows that it is also the definitive inspiration for the organization of that entire section of the surviving book. It is distinctly possible that this is due to Ja'far/Qudāma being a disciple – directly or indirectly – of al-Balādhurī, but it may well be born from the fact that the two texts had enormously similar audiences in mind in their creation. *Kitāb al-Kharāj*, then, recognized the quality and importance of al-Balādhurī's contribution to the secretariat, and took this much further by incorporating additional interests from other texts, namely the practical craft and skills of writing. The audience of the two works seem to be the same and hence, the overlap in content between them; their intentions, however, were different, and show the generational gap between the creation of the two.

Repetition and emendation: The common features of reused material

To discuss the types of information that these later authors were choosing to reuse from the *Futūḥ* first requires a forthright and unassuming comment: the types of information that an author was interested in claiming from the *Futūḥ* had more to do with that author's goals in the creation of his text than anything else. Thus, it is not strange for us to recognize that Ibn al-ʿAdīm's work on Aleppo is absorbed almost solely with the *Futūḥ*'s chapters on Syria, or that Yāqūt's use of al-Balādhurī's material is the most segregated, owing to his need for concise traditions on very precise locations rather than a focus on extended narrative. With Yāqūt's work, the cohesive narrative is sacrificed for this targeted information. In many ways, the analysis of textual reuse between the *Futūḥ* and the *Muʿjam* emphasizes that there was already a medieval recognition of al-Balādhurī's status as a respected master before modern scholars returned to the text for the reconstruction of the late antique and early medieval Middle East.

In general, two sections of the *Futūḥ* have material reused in almost each of the above texts: his section on Qinnasrīn in Syria, and his section on the conquest of South Asia and China (al-Sind and al-Hind). Only small amounts of his Qinnasrīn traditions appear in these texts, with the exception being Ibn al-ʿAdīm's, where the majority of that material is repeated. A large amount of the accounts from his chapter on 'The Conquest of al-Sind', however, are included in the books of Yāqūt, Ibn al-Athīr, and Qudāma b. Jaʿfar. With so much reuse of this material from Islam's easternmost frontiers between just this sample of texts, there is room for greater research emphasis on the historiography of this region in the surviving tradition and the survival of traditions outside the *Futūḥ* on its conquest more generally. There is every likelihood that al-Balādhurī's traditions on this frontier region were so popular precisely because there were few other Arabic texts which detailed Islam's arrival into the region.

With regards to the technical, directly bureaucratic material from the *Futūḥ*'s thematic final chapters, this material was not popularly reused. Only Qudāma and Ibn ʿAsākir include any of these traditions in their own texts, and neither includes very many. Qudāma's book comprises only traditions from al-Balādhurī's chapter on the seal (*al-khātim*), while Ibn ʿAsākir is interested in traditions concerning ʿUmar's establishment of the stipendiary register (*ʿaṭāʾ*). The inclusion of these traditions says a great deal about al-Balādhurī's intention in the creation of the *Futūḥ*, but they seemed to hold little interest for authors far removed from al-Balādhurī's lifetime. This may be simply because this information was superseded by later, superior books more directly focused on the practicality of the professional secretary. Or, perhaps, it emphasizes my suggestion that al-Balādhurī's need to create a text for secretaries at a unique time in the life cycle of the 'Abbāsid state had long since passed, and so, too, had these traditions' relevance for later audiences.

In many ways, the most revelatory information which is born from the analysis of textual reuse from the *Futūḥ* are the matters which are largely passed over by other authors. The *Futūḥ's* thematic emphasis on discussing public works and urban environments more generally has been much appreciated by modern scholars, and his sections on the layout and constructions within cities such as Baṣra, Kūfa, and Medina are among the largest sections of al-Balādhurī's work. Despite this, this material features only minimally amid the reuse between these texts, although al-Balādhurī's explanations of how a location earned a unique name are oft-repeated. Similarly, the regular inclusion of al-Balādhurī's purported settlement agreements between the fledgling Islamic state and conquered territories are also almost completely absent in the reuse found in these later texts. There are examples of a brief line or two of text which mention the payment agreed upon between a location and the conquerors – see, for instance, Ibn al-Athīr's inclusion of a tradition on the payment of two million dirhams and two-thousand slaves by the province of Sijistān in exchange for their surrender.[61] But al-Balādhurī's inclusion of full agreements or the discussions of a land's produce/access to materials are not retransmitted in these later texts. One can only wonder, again, if the reason for this is largely because their time of usefulness had waned. As more and more 'breakaway' dynasties claimed authority over sections of the previously unified empire from the tenth/fourth century onwards, they began making their own decisions concerning land distribution and law. What had occurred in the earliest conquest period may well have lost its legitimizing force in this argument. By the lifetimes of Yāqūt, Ibn 'Asākir, and Ibn al-'Adīm, such information was little more than quaint artefacts of memory with no practical application; their time of usefulness in the early 'Abbāsid period had ended.

But what about the form this reuse takes? From the perspective of a modern scholar, Ibn al-'Adīm's reuse of material from al-Balādhurī is largely conventional and logical, and is only conspicuous due to the fact that so many of the above medieval authors *do not* follow similar processes in their reuse. It would be unfair to expect that all medieval Muslim authors should have attributed and recognized the efforts of their predecessors in the same way across genres and centuries. Nevertheless, interesting results about textual reuse in the Arabic tradition are certainly raised throughout this process of analysis, and agree with Landau-Tasseron's suggestions and findings that at least some of these later authors were free from slavishly copying verbatim the words of earlier masters.[62] But were some authors intentionally trying to mask where their material originated from, in an attempt to attain some greater acclaim for themselves? Was there a 'gold standard' for alteration to a previous tradition, at which point the original transmitter's name could be omitted and authorship of that material claimed anew? Or was there – perhaps with Qudāma's work – an expectation that the audience would already be able to recognize where these traditions came from?

The answer to these questions are likely different for each author in each time period, and further analysis of textual reuse patterns in the early Arabic tradition could help to provide more definitive answers. Even so, some tentative suggestions can be made based on the comparisons between these texts and al-Balādhurī's. Ibn al-ʿAdīm's and Ibn ʿAsākir's reuse of material is clearly signposted and, in the latter's case, includes the fewest examples of extended reuse anyway. Yāqūt's reuse is fairly straightforward despite how thorough it is: he regularly chooses to name al-Balādhurī and his *Futūḥ* as the source of his information, but he will often omit al-Balādhurī's name in favour of an earlier transmitter on whose authority the information had originally come to al-Balādhurī. As an encyclopaedia, this makes a great deal of sense even to a modern reader; he is not attempting to conceal where he gained that information. The close similarity in wording between these traditions, however, and that so much material can otherwise be found in the *Futūḥ* suggests that a great deal of additional material from famed transmitters like Abū Mikhnaf came to Yāqūt from the *Futūḥ*. As for Ibn al-Athīr's *al-Kāmil fi-l-taʾrīkh*, the author may well have felt that his abbreviation, consolidation, and reorganization of traditions gave him a claim to 'ownership' of this material, and thereby he did not feel compelled to cite al-Balādhurī's text (along with many others) as his source.

Identifying the intent of Ibn al-Faqīh and Qudāma in their books is, in many ways, the most challenging in this analysis. With both authors living and working at such an early date, there is every possibility that they may have had access to some of the same sources al-Balādhurī had taken advantage of only a generation or two earlier.[63] Especially in the case of Ibn al-Faqīh's *Kitāb al-Buldān*, which contains some of the most significant variation in traditions that still seem far too similar to al-Balādhurī's to not have some type of connection, there is the greatest case to be made for an author attempting to mask the *Futūḥ* as his original source of information. Despite this, however, these similar traditions reside in a text which is largely unconcerned with the citation of sources. It seems more likely that Ibn al-Faqīh's proximity to al-Balādhurī and/or those who knew him (as demonstrated by the inclusion of this material which does not appear to survive elsewhere) and the early state of the written tradition during his lifetime influenced his decision to use the traditions in the form he did. Similarly, Qudāma's family were recognized from such an early date as being the students of al-Balādhurī, and their audience seems likely to have overlapped. Thus, it also seems obvious that Qudāma's *Futūḥ* section should heavily copy the master al-Balādhurī's previous work. This would have especially been the case to an audience of well-educated secretaries, themselves not long removed from *Futūḥ al-buldān's* writing.

Conclusions

> *It is well known that [al-Balādhurī] is an accepted Sunni (*al-ʿāmma*, literally 'the commoners') authority; that he is far from supporting the Shīʿa; [and that despite this] he is exact in everything he records (*al-ḍabṭ li-mā yarwīhi maʿrūf*).*[64]

The Shīʿī Sharīf al-Murtaḍā (d. 1044–1045 CE/AH 436), in his *Kitāb al-Shāfī*, puts into words what this chapter has hence demonstrated: al-Balādhurī's reputation throughout the medieval period was a very positive one, and the support for his work was found across time periods and genres of writing. We see this not just in biographical reports, but through the consistent reuse of his material within some of the most important geographical and historical texts of the classical Islamic period. It is one thing for a later author to speak of the training and work of a peer with glowing admiration, but quite another to actually rely and copy the material contained in that earlier work in the construction of a new one.

The analysis and comparison of quoted material from the *Futūḥ's* text shows that there is a great amount of variety in both the types of information that is reused and the forms that reuse took. The accounts of the *Futūḥ* have been quoted for hundreds of years, starting, at the least, from the early tenth/third century – almost immediately following the creation of the book. These accounts are found in an assortment of texts including geographies and histories, and the style and form that quotation takes appears to be very dependent on the personal style and goals of the author in question. In short, the impact of al-Balādhurī's *Futūḥ* seems long-lasting, and while his work never reached the universal acclaim achieved by al-Ṭabarī's *Ta'rīkh* – the text it is most often compared with today – there is good reason why al-Balādhurī's positive reputation continues to be extended by modern studies of early Islamic history.

Notes

1 Here, I borrow the definition from a panel discussion on 'Rethinking Text Reuse as Digital Classicists' at the 2014 *Digital Humanities Conference* in Lausanne, Switzerland.

2 Erlend Øverby, 'Problems with Linking, and Reuse of Text', accessed 19 February 2016, https://www.infoloom.com/media/gcaconfs/WEB/granada99/ove.HTM

3 Goitein, 'Introduction', 24–5.

4 See, for instance, Lindstedt, 'The Transmission of al-Madā'inī's Historical Material to al-Balādhurī and al-Ṭabarī', 41–59; Judd, 'Narratives and Character Development', 209–26; and Leder, 'Features of the Novel', 72–96.

5 On the possible use by a later source of an intermediate recension which does not survive, see the work of Harry Munt in reconstructing the historiography of Medina in Harry Munt, 'Writing the History of an Arabian Holy City: Ibn Zabāla and the First Local History of Medina', *Arabica*, Vol. 59 (2012), 1–34, esp. 9–11.

6 Ella Landau-Tasseron, 'On the Reconstruction of Lost Sources', *Al-Qanṭara*, Vol. 25 (2004), 45–91, and Leder, 'Features of the Novel', 72–96.

7 Gernot Rotter, 'Zur Überlieferung einiger historischer Werke Madā'inīs in Ṭabarīs *Annalen*', *Oriens*, Vol. 23–4 (1974), 103–33.

8 Schoeler, *The Oral and the Written in Early Islam*, 28–44.

9 This algorithm disregards the varying morphology of those letters in Arabic (whether the letter appears in its initial, medial, or final form, as well as the various forms of *hamza*). The algorithm is also trained to skip over common phrases such as blessings that are regularly found throughout early Islamic texts (including honorifics and phrases such as 'may God be pleased with him'). This algorithm was developed and applied to a digital corpus of Arabic texts as a part of a digital text 'hackathon' held at Aga Khan University in September 2015. It is being developed by a team led by Sarah Bowen Savant called the *KITAB* Project, which is looking to apply textual reuse methods from other fields and languages of the humanities to Islamic sources. For this particular algorithm, the focus of debt is owed to Maxim

Romanov for its development. While holding immense potential, it still remains in a preliminary stage, and includes a number of limitations. In particular, the analysis of identified reuse remains completely up to the individual skill and interests of the researcher in question, and the algorithm's application to texts will only ever be as good as its available corpus. Thus, the analysis of texts compared and about to be discussed is presently limited to those texts that are already available digitally, and crucially, is currently heavily skewed towards well-known classical Sunnī texts.

10 As mentioned in n. 9 above, this is especially limited to classical Arabic texts that are already available in a digital form and hence can be compared through computer analysis to the *Futūḥ*.

11 Massé, 'Ibn al-Faḳīh'.

12 Ibn al-Faqīh, *al-Buldān*, 15–16.

13 I have not been able to identify where Hādī has found the third reference, as the name 'al-Balādhurī' – the one Hādī himself states – only appears twice in the text. Additionally, I have scoured the text for other names that al-Balādhurī is known by (Aḥmad b. Yaḥyā, Aḥmad b. Yaḥyā b. Jābir, Abū Bakr Aḥmad b. Yaḥyā, and others), but none appear in *Kitāb al-Buldān*.

14 Massé, 'Ibn al-Faḳīh'.

15 *Futūḥ*, 391–2 (M 6-7); Ibn al-Faqīh, *al-Buldān*, 537.

16 *Futūḥ*, 365 (H 462); Ibn al-Faqīh, *al-Buldān*, 226.

17 Massé, 'Ibn al-Faḳīh'. Although this is perhaps due, in part, to the fact that al-Muqaddasī imagined himself as bringing something new and original to the genre, which he states at the outset of his book. In this way, he may have chosen to mention Ibn al-Faqīh's reuse of previous material as a means to distinguish himself from what had come before.

18 *Futūḥ*, 1 (H 15-16); Yāqūt, *Muʿjam*, Vol. 4, 33–4.

19 *Futūḥ*, 530 (M 209-210); Yāqūt, *Muʿjam*, Vol. 4, 613–14.

20 Baḥrayn here refers not to the modern island nation, but to the area of the eastern Arabian Peninsula.

21 *Futūḥ*, 530 (M 209-210); Yāqūt, *Muʿjam*, Vol. 4, 613–14.

22 This is not unusual, however, as the first part of this tradition details an army being sent to Tānah, an area near modern Bombay. Yāqūt, on the other hand, chose to include the above traditions in a more specific section of his *Muʿjam*, linking the tradition to the province of Mukrān and its associated entry.

23 I have chosen to use the word 'appear' here, as this section of the *Futūḥ* opens with several pages of what could be separate traditions only introduced by the phrase '*akhbaranā ʿAlī b. Muḥammad b. ʿAbd Allāh b. Abī Sayf*' at the very beginning. This is not, in fact, unusual for al-Balādhurī's information on far-flung frontier regions, and it may be that the lack of easily available details for these places left him to rely on more limited sources for his information.

24 *Futūḥ*, 99–100 (H 124-125); Yāqūt, *Mu'jam*, Vol. 1, 509.

25 On the amendments and alterations of earlier scientific sources – especially from the Greek tradition – see George Saliba, *Islamic Science and the Making of the European Renaissance* (Cambridge, MA: The MIT Press, 2007), esp. 78–84; and Emilie Savage-Smith, 'Medicine', in *Encyclopedia of the History of Arabic Science*, ed. Roshdi Rashed (London: Routledge, 1996), Vol. 3, 903–62.

26 On Ibn al-'Adīm and his work, the most important modern study is David W. Morray, *An Ayyubid Notable and His World: Ibn al-'Adīm and Aleppo as Portrayed in his Biographical Dictionary of People Associated with the City* (Leiden: Brill, 1994).

27 Bernard Lewis, 'Ibn al-'Adīm', *EI*[2].

28 A city near the frontier in Anatolia known in Greek as Melitene and often caught in conflict between Muslim and Byzantine troops.

29 The title 'Commander of Believers' (*amīr al-mu'minīn*), as noted above, is omitted in Ibn al-'Adīm's text. This is the only difference in the Arabic sentences translated here.

30 *Futūḥ*, 173 (H 223-224); Ibn al-'Adīm, *Bughyat al-ṭalab fī ta'rīkh Ḥalab*, ed. Suhayl Zakkār (Damascus: Dār al-Ba'th, 1988), Vol. 1, 137–8.

31 Ibn al-'Adīm, *Bughyat*, Vol. 1, 562.

32 This includes, but is certainly not limited to, the English translation by D. S. Richards' for the Seljuq and crusading periods which appears in several volumes and is titled *The Annals of the Saljuq Turks: Selections from* al-Kāmil fi'l-ta'rīkh *of 'Izz al-Dīn Ibn al-Athīr* (London: Routledge, 2002) and *The Chronicle of Ibn al-Athīr for the Crusading Period from* al-Kāmil fi'l-ta'rīkh (Aldershot: Ashgate, 2006–2008).

33 Franz Rosenthal, 'Ibn al-Athīr', *EI*[2].

34 See, for instance, a brief discussion of Ibn al-Athīr's reuse and amendment of traditions which appeared in al-Ṭabarī's *History* and Ibn Hishām's *Sīra* concerning the early Islamic period in Mahmood ul-Hasan, *Ibn al-Athīr, An Arab Historian: A Critical Analysis of His* Tarikh-al-kamil *and* Tarikh-al-atabeca (New Delhi: Northern Book Centre, 2005), 93–117. The author does not seem fully aware of the form Ibn al-Athīr's reuse of material takes, but he is among the few to attempt a discussion of this overlapping material at all.

35 An exception to this is the work of Chase Robinson, who has discussed the relationship between al-Ṭabarī's *History*, Ibn al-Athīr's *History*, and Yazīd b. Muḥammad al-Azdī's *History of Mosul* (*Ta'rīkh al-Mawṣil*). See Chase F. Robinson, 'A Local Historian's Debt to al-Ṭabarī: The Case of al-Azdī's *Ta'rīkh al-Mawṣil*', *Journal of the American Oriental Society*, Vol. 126, No. 4 (2006), 521–35 and to a lesser extent in Robinson, *Empires and Elites*, esp. 141–6.

36 Al-Ṭabarī, for instance, is named as a source. For a brief discussion of Ibn al-Athīr's use and expansion of the traditions of al-Ṭabarī and al-Mas'ūdī, see Daniel König,

Arabic-Islamic Views of the Latin West: Tracing the Emergence of Medieval Europe (Oxford: Oxford University Press, 2015), 142–5.

37 *Futūḥ*, 79–80 (H 103).

38 Ibn al-Athīr, *al-Kāmil fi-l-ta'rīkh*, ed. 'Umar Tadmurī (Beirut: Dār al-Kitāb al-'Arabī, 1997), Vol. 2, 159.

39 *Futūḥ*, 531 (M 211); Ibn al-Athīr, *al-Kāmil*, Vol. 3, 35.

40 According to al-Balādhurī, Qīqān 'is part of the land of *al-Sind* where it borders on Khurāsān'. *Futūḥ*, 531 (M 210). Worth noting, too, is that Yāqūt's version is actually closer to al-Balādhurī's than Ibn al-Athīr's is, including the phrase 'the frontier of *al-Hind*' which Ibn al-Athīr's version omits, but a word in the first section of the included verse is different.

41 Yale MS Landberg 33, folio 88b. I believe the script in the British Library and Leiden manuscripts could easily be misread as علاته, which is what de Goeje and al-Munajjid have rendered in their editions, instead of عدانه, but the Yale MS which was not available to either editor strongly suggests the latter reading by both Ibn al-Athīr and Yāqūt. A mistake would have been easy to make when both editors were working with early facsimiles of one or both of the known manuscripts. The difference between al-Balādhurī's and Yāqūt's versions was noted by Murgotten on p. 211 n.1, but as he appears to have worked purely from de Goeje's edition of the Arabic, he would not have been able to recognize the truth of the text.

42 See the contributions in *Ibn 'Asākir and Early Islamic History*, but especially those by Fred Donner ("Uthmān and the Rāshidūn Caliphs in Ibn 'Asākir's *Ta'rīkh madīnat Dimashq*: A Study in Strategies of Compilation') and Steven Judd ('Ibn 'Asākir's Sources for the Late Umayyad Period'). Donner is especially effective in highlighting Ibn 'Asākir's 'strategies of compilation' and his role as an author. He spends only minimal time, however, speaking about the author's 'strategy of manipulation' of earlier sources he used in crafting the *Ta'rīkh*, which will be added to here.

43 Ibn 'Asākir, *Dimashq*, Vol. 1, 253.

44 Ibid., Vol. 9, 204.

45 *Futūḥ*, 132–3 (H 172).

46 Ibn 'Asākir, *Ta'rīkh*, Vol. 2, 344.

47 *Fa-aslama*, which can simply mean 'and he submitted.'

48 Ibn 'Asākir, *Ta'rīkh*, Vol. 9, 204; *Futūḥ*, 73–4 (H 96).

49 The tradition itself, which describes the Prophet sending Khālid b. al-Walīd to Dūmat al-Jandal to deal with the purported apostate Ukaydir b. 'Abd al-Malik al-Kindī, is located in the *Futūḥ's* section on Dūmat al-Jandal. In Ibn 'Asākir's text, it is found in the biographical entry on Ukaydir himself, and so his brother's inheritance was of little import there.

50 Ibn ʿAsākir, *Taʾrīkh*, Vol. 8, 281; al-Balādhurī, *Ansāb al-ashrāf*, ed. Suhayl Zakkār and Riyāḍ Ziriklī (Beirut: Dār al-Fikr, 1996), Vol. 4, 190.

51 The opening chapter of the *Futūḥ* does not have any formal chapter heading in any of the surviving manuscripts.

52 Similar to the *Futūḥ*, the opening chapter of this section is actually Qudāma's title for this entire section of the book (*Futūḥ al-nawāḥī wa-l-amṣār*) rather than the opening, which similarly concerns the Prophet's time in Medina.

53 See, for instance, Qudāma's section on 'the matter of the island of Cyprus', which contains only a single large tradition on the authority of 'al-Wāqidī and others' which similarly opens al-Balādhurī's much lengthier chapter on the same issue. The reuse in this section is not verbatim, however. *Futūḥ*, 181 (H 235); Qudāma b. Jaʿfar, *Kitāb al-Kharāj wa-ṣināʿat al-kitāba*, ed. Muḥammad Ḥusayn Zubaydī (Baghdad: Wizārat al-Thaqāfa wa-l-Iʿlām, 1981), 306.

54 Al-Dhahabī, *Siyar aʿlām al-nubalāʾ*, Vol. 13, 163.

55 Khaṭīb al-Baghdādī, *Taʾrīkh Baghdād*, ed. Aḥmad Ibn al-Ṣiddīq (Cairo: Maktabat al-Khānjī, 1931), Vol. 7, 205.

56 The relationship between Qudāma and his father is briefly discussed by S. A. Bonebakker, 'Ḳudāma', *EI*^{2} and Heck, *Construction of Knowledge*, 23.

57 See, for instance, A. Ben Shemesh, *Taxation in Islam*, Vol. 2, *Qudāma b. Jaʿfar's* Kitāb al-Kharāj, *Part Seven* (Leiden: E. J. Brill, 1965), 3.

58 See, for instance, Langarudī, 'al-Balādhurī', 3.

59 Especially if we consider Qudāma needing to have reached an age where he could have been competent as a student of high-level material. Al-Balādhurī is remembered – rightly or wrongly – as being incompetent due to his consumption of *al-Balādhur* at the end of his lifetime, with his latest date of death ca. 892/AH 279. Qudāma, on the other hand, has similarly problematic biographical details regarding his lifetime, but he seems to be alive until 948 CE/337AH according to Ibn al-Jawzī (d. 1201 CE/AH 597), although others such as Yāqūt argue for a late ninth-/third-century date. This is discussed in Heck, *Construction of Knowledge*, 24.

60 On the reuse without citation of the ninth-/third-century scholar ʿAlī b. Rabban al-Ṭabarī's material from his *Firdaws al-Ḥikma*, see J. T. Olsson, 'Design, Determinism, and Salvation in the *Firdaws al-Ḥikma* of ʿAlī Ibn Rabban al-Ṭabarī' (PhD diss., University of Cambridge, 2016), esp. 29–67.

61 *Futūḥ*, 485–6 (M 143); Ibn al-Athīr, *al-Kāmil*, Vol. 2, 498. This example in itself is noteworthy, however, and may have been the reason why it was included. Sijistān is one of the few conquered locations which is remembered by al-Balādhurī (via al-Madāʾinī) as having a non-standard conquest agreement, one which did not stipulate the regular payment of tax but a large, one-time payment.

62 Landau-Tasseron, 'Lost Sources'.

63 As Travis Zadeh has suggested concerning the content and construction of Ibn Khurradādhbih's *Masālik*, there may well have been bureaucratic materials and/or archives that were used and even circulated among these middle ʿAbbāsid scholars. See Zadeh, 'Of Mummies, Poets, and Water Nymphs', 8–75, esp. 33.

64 Sharīf al-Murtaḍā, *Kitāb al-Shāfī fi-l-imāma*, discussed and Arabic provided by Goitein, 'Introduction', 23–4.

Conclusion: A portrait of authority

For much of the opening two centuries of Islamic history, Islam and the Islamic state had proven to be a powerful imperial force. Whether it would have endurance or not, however, was another story entirely. The ninth/third century was a fascinating time for the Islamic world, and was a transitional period for nascent Islam. While it was in some aspects a challenging century for the ʿAbbāsid government, it was also a period of boundless intellectual development and the entrance into a new phase of scholarship in the Islamic Middle East. It was the period in which Islamic law began to be codified, and where we see the rise to prominence of a distinct religious class, the *ʿulamāʾ*. It was characterized by the trials of the caliphally organized *miḥna* over the createdness of the Qurʾān, and similarly, the patronization of a translation movement which brought the scholarly works of pre-Islamic antiquity into Arabic. It was also, of course, the period which defined what shape the early Arabic historical tradition would take in a written form. It was a time of experimentation and of great progress, and we see this firmly through the analysis of al-Balādhurī's *Futūḥ al-buldān*. Al-Balādhurī's text bears the imprint of a pushback against a trauma, even if it rarely addresses the problems faced by the Islamic world directly.

A different kind of history

There have been several modern scholars who have commented on the *Futūḥ* and its 'lack of artistic effect' or on its overall conciseness compared to other great early Arabic historical works. Many, however, seem to lack a full awareness of al-Balādhurī's authorial vision and what seems likely to have been his intention in creating his text. If we look to the *Futūḥ* to be merely a work of 'conquest literature', a narrative of the conquest period of the first two Islamic centuries, it fits imperfectly, and the comparison with other similarly classified texts betrays inconsistencies in style and content. The similarities with other conquest texts are certainly there, but differences abound. If al-Balādhurī was intending to simply commit a narrative of the conquests to writing, the surviving form of the *Futūḥ* would not have been the practical way one might imagine it, and his omissions of other available material support this. It finds some commonality with a number of genres of Islamic texts, and was designed to amalgamate the content of this variety of texts into a unique arrangement. We find this in the form of the text, but we also find it in the sources used in its creation. While the reader discovers material attributed to many of the great early *akhbārīs* within the *Futūḥ*, the analysis of the *Futūḥ's* sources shows that al-Balādhurī relied heavily on jurists for material in his work despite not being remembered as a jurist or a *muḥaddith* himself. Separately, when we analyse the content of that material, we can clearly identify goals the author must have held separate from merely crafting a narrative of the conquests.

Thematically, the analysis of the *Futūḥ* shows an author engaged in a very distinct process of arranging and cataloguing material directly relevant to the origins and development of the early Islamic state. This included the conquest context for legal and administrative traditions that concerned the practical affairs of governance, including issues of land ownership, taxation, personal possession, resource management, and public works projects. Perhaps most telling of all are his inclusions of such an ample amount of settlement agreements purporting to date back to a location's conquest, and apparently still of considerable relevance to an ʿAbbāsid administration reliant on the productivity of the provinces outside of Baghdad.

All of this provides the setting within which al-Balādhurī chose to create *Futūḥ al-buldān*, and the author's decision to pass over information directly discussing the disunity which characterized the ʿAbbāsid state during the century was a prescient choice for a project intended to project ʿAbbāsid authority. The bulk of al-Balādhurī's life was spent in and around an ʿAbbasid court with dwindling control, and yet still substantial responsibilities. The analysis of the content of the *Futūḥ* suggests that it would have served an important purpose for those bureaucrats working within the capital and on behalf of the state. Members of the bureaucracy were constantly faced with the challenges of administering such a sizeable empire, portions of which were now seeking new levels of autonomy not previously held and were, therefore, creating an additional barrier between the centre and the resources of the peripheral zones. Added to this is the high likelihood that al-Balādhurī was writing *Futūḥ al-buldān* during the later years of theʿ 'Anarchy at Samarrā" of the 860s CE, and a book which projects the legitimacy of the Islamic state while at the same time serving a practical purpose as a reference work for bureaucrats makes a great deal of sense.

Reinforcing the idea that al-Balādhurī was writing the *Futūḥ* with the crises of the 860s still not concluded is his total failure to mention the difficulties brought about by the Turkish military. The *Futūḥ* is not a traditional work of history in the same form as the early works of *taʾrīkh*, but its chosen content and the exclusion of other available material only reinforces this dating. Aside from the turmoil of the 860s, al-Balādhurī fails to mention other watershed moments in Islamic history that do not fit his purpose in representing a unified and strong caliphate.[1] But the realities of the era provided plenty of opportunities for a writer as skilled as al-Balādhurī to at least hint at the problems of the realm, and yet he never takes those opportunities. At the death of al-Mutawakkil in the *Futūḥ*, who was famously murdered by a member of his Turkish guard to plunge the realm into the period of 'anarchy', the assassination of the caliph goes completely unmentioned by al-Balādhurī, who writes simply that 'from the time he started [building] it (his city, *al-Mutawakkiliyya)* to the time he resided in it, only a few months [had passed] … he died in it in Shawwāl, [2]47'.[2]

That a text such as the *Futūḥ,* with an all-encompassing focus on the financial matters and possessions of the central Islamic state, would also choose to completely pass over any mention of the financial burden being placed on the state by the Turkish military seems suspect. This is even considering the focus of the text on precedent, which is overwhelmingly born from the seventh-/first-century conquest context. Al-Balādhurī may have had, quite understandably, apprehensions about providing too much detail in his text about the political turmoil of his time before the situation had been resolved – one way or the other. The fact remains, however, that other scholars writing in the period shortly following the Sāmarrān *intermezzo* – not least of which was al-Ṭabarī – show a willingness to spill a considerable amount of ink over the turmoil of the period. The most likely reason for this total silence, it could be posited, was that al-Balādhurī had concern not over the relevance of this historical material in the creation of his text, but over how this material would be received in an age where the Turks still maintained considerable influence around the 'Abbāsid court or, at the least, where the 'Abbāsid state was still attempting an authoritative recovery. As such, while the *Futūḥ* may not be explicit in its discussions of the financial burden plaguing the 'Abbāsid treasury during the 860s, its mere existence and thematic focus is, in fact, engaging with the political and administrative realities of the time in the way al-Balādhurī felt he was most able.

An administrator's handbook

In speaking of the challenges of this era, the concerns of collecting tax from distant and diverse locations of the Islamic world presented unique challenges for Muslim administrators. Not only were regions conquered at different times by different armies, but they often made unique terms for capitulation that they expected to be honoured even centuries later. Both Calder and Robinson have emphasized the importance of the memory of these agreements, even if the reliability of their information can be reasonably scrutinized.[3] That these settlement agreements made during the Arab-Islamic conquests of the seventh and eighth centuries CE find such a clear presence in a variety of early Arabic texts from centuries later is a testament to their importance for successive generations. The collective memory of these events was important in its own right, but its continued financial relevance for both the state and its protectorate made the collection and verification of this material increasingly important in this period. And yet, as was shown in Chapter 4, no other early Arabic text includes anywhere near as many of these settlement agreements as al-Balādhurī's *Futūḥ*.

The ʿAbbāsid state's rights in issues such as tax reform and land ownership were purported to have been challenged even in the time of Abū Yūsuf, and we return again to his writing about these challenges:

> You are now ignorant, as we are now ignorant, of how things were at the beginning (*wa-qad jahiltum wa-jahilnā kayfa kāna awwal al-amr*). How can you see fit to impose on us something for which you can provide no established precedent, and how can you break from this practice, which is verifiable in our records, and according to which we still operate?[4]

A work was needed that sat firmly at the crossroads between the historical contextualization that came along with narrative; the referential nature of recordkeeping that was so important to the secretaries; and yet was constructed with the concerns of precedent and authenticity so important to the jurists. What was needed was an 'administrator's handbook'. Al-Balādhurī's skill and training as a secretary, coupled with his opportunity to study under some of the most important jurists and *akhbāriyyūn* of his day and access to written materials of others, made him an ideal scholar to create a text that combined the needs of two separate professions into a single work. As ʿAbd al-Ḥamīd had written, the *kātib* was much more than just a scribe or low-level administrator; they were trained in the art of statecraft and governance, well versed in the history and traditions of both the state they now served and its historical predecessors.

With the devolution of the power of the ʿAbbāsids occurring within al-Balādhurī's lifetime, the need for the state to retain its revenue flow was essential. This was not just due to the commitments the state had long made to the infrastructure of the realm, the payment of soldiers and bureaucrats, and the protection of its borders, but for the very maintenance of the legitimacy of the caliph and the state more generally. As the turmoil of the 860s continued, the necessity of steady funding did not dissipate, while the growing autonomy of regions previously under the clear authority of the ʿAbbāsid caliph and his chosen agents directly challenged the authority of the centre. Al-Balādhurī's location at the court – working as a member of this bureaucracy among this commotion – would have made him aware of the challenges of his fellow administrators. It would have made him recognize the need for the creation of a reference handbook – an administrator's history – to be consulted whenever the need arose. To use the account of Abū Yūsuf: if the state was not ignorant of 'how things were at the beginning', they could reasonably require cities and regions to maintain their original agreements which, in most cases, should provide guaranteed benefit for the state.

There is a level of disconnection between the administrators working in the centre of the state, however, and those actually collecting resources on behalf of the state in peripheral zones. The administrators working at the court were not necessarily concerned with precisely how much of the surplus made by peasants in a particular territory was being paid in tax; they were only concerned that the payment making its way to the treasury was similar in level to the payment which had been historically promised, either in coin or in kind. The advancement in Arabic papyrological studies over the last several decades has significantly bolstered our understanding of the reality of tax payment/collection, for Egypt in particular. This continued analysis demonstrates the variation in the payment expectations of the narrative sources with local realities recorded in tax receipts and other agreements. A direct comparison between these papyri and the narrative sources, however, is problematic. There were a great many layers involved in the system of taxation between the payee's first transaction within the system (the payment of tax in some form, usually via tax farming) and the eventual arrival of a portion of that payment into the treasury of the central government. There also remains a great amount of research to be conducted on this complete financial apparatus, but current research advancing the understanding of both local collection and central expectation will play an important part in furthering our understanding of this entire system.

It is difficult to say with certainty precisely who al-Balādhurī's intended audience for *Futūḥ al-buldān* was. The author's surviving works offer disappointingly little direct evidence speaking to this question. That the *Futūḥ* was not a straightforwardly patronized endeavour seems clear, however, and is more fully evinced by how far removed al-Balādhurī places himself from the work. In addition to lacking any real introduction or conclusion,[5] the text also includes no panegyric praising the ruler or some other patron, and never provides any explicit comments on its *raison d'être* as the surviving works of Abū Yūsuf and Abū 'Ubayd do. The evidence provided by both the background of the author and, crucially, the context of the text itself, however, suggests that he intended the book for practical use by the high-level bureaucracy. The administrators needed a reference work to assist them with their roles at court and as a means to reassert the authority of the caliph throughout the entire *dār al-Islām*. Therefore, a member of the administration created the *Futūḥ*. It was not meant to sit on a patron's shelves; rather, it was intended for consultation by these administrators at court who could utilize it to provide evidence and support for demands of payment by regions increasingly resistant to the command of the caliph.

It seems also, however, to have been an important site of memory for these administrators, and the text's occasional stylistic flourishes and shared features with other works of *adab* also attest to this. These two characteristics – the practical and theoretical, the temporal and the historical – were not mutually exclusive, and the *Futūḥ*'s role as a *lieu de mémoire* and as a bureaucratic reference work would have served the same audience of contemporary 'Abbāsid administrators well. In this way, the *Futūḥ* recalled what had worked in the past in establishing the Islamic state, and why – when remembered and put to use – it could work once more. Thus, al-Balādhurī brought together traditions from multiple disciplines and countless scholars into a single, synthesized, and easily digestible work. There had been no Arabic text previously written which included both the *Futūḥ's* form and content, and there would never again be a need for another text that filled so precisely this niche.

The window of opportunity for a text in the form of the *Futūḥ* may have been small, but this did not mean that the text lost relevance as the century ended and regional dynasties continued to rise. The identification and analysis of the reuse of traditions from the *Futūḥ* in later medieval Arabic books shows that al-Balādhurī remained a trusted authority for historical information, and that his text maintained considerable relevance across centuries and genres. Later authors reused differing material in different ways for different reasons, but the significant amount of reuse which can be identified demonstrates that the *Futūḥ* was a crucial reference work of deep historical significance. Relying on the *Futūḥ* as a vital historical source detailing the seventh/first and eighth/second centuries proves to be a time-honoured custom carried on by modern scholars, as is the esteem al-Balādhurī has garnered over the centuries.

While it is hoped that the present research will have contributed to filling the significant lacunae which have existed concerning the author of two of the most important surviving early Arabic texts, it will no doubt have raised many more questions worth exploring in the future. With the publication of a strong edition of al-Balādhurī's *Ansāb al-ashrāf* not long completed, there is a great amount of opportunity for further research testing many of the hypotheses developed here, and for further direct comparisons to be made between the author's two works. The potential held within *Ansāb al-ashrāf* for historical and linguistic analysis is massive; I am hopeful that much of the research I have brought together here on al-Balādhurī and the hypotheses I have made about him and his authorial process will help to stimulate future work on his other text.

Finally, it is hoped that this research has demonstrated the value that studies on individual authors and/or individual texts can provide for our overall understanding of Arabic historical writing and Arabic historiography more generally, and that we will continue to see the revival of studies in this method concerning both well-known and lesser-known authors and their works. Our understanding of the earliest centuries of Islamic history is unlikely to be further augmented by the discovery of great lost historical works contemporary to these events. This makes it all the more important that we understand as much about the construction, intentions, and limitations of the earliest surviving sources as possible in order to make not just full use of them, but to understand more about the period, people, and politics that created and guided their construction.

Notes

1 As an example, al-Balādhurī almost completely passes over all four of the significant Islamic civil wars that had occurred up until his lifetime. We can be certain, especially in the case of the first two civil wars, that this was not because he lacked traditions detailing those events, as they are thoroughly covered in his *Ansāb al-ashrāf*.

2 *Futūḥ*, 364 (H 461).

3 Robinson, *Empires and Elites*, 1–4; Calder, *Early Muslim Jurisprudence*, 139.

4 Abū Yūsuf, *Kitāb al-Kharāj*, trans. Chase Robinson, *Empires and Elites*, 3.

5 The surviving manuscript of the *Ansāb* in Turkey bears a single line at the end of the work reading 'This is the end of the work of Aḥmad b. Yaḥyā', while the *Futūḥ opens* simply with the line 'Aḥmad b. Yaḥyā b. Jābir said…' *Futūḥ*, 1 (H 1); Langarudī, 'al-Balādhurī', 6.

Bibliography

Primary sources

‘Abd al-Ḥamīd b. Yaḥyā al-Kātib. ‘*Risāla ilā al-kuttāb*’. In *ʿAbd al-Ḥamīd ibn Yaḥyā al-Kātib wa-mā tabaqqā min rasāʾilihi wa-rasāʾil Sālim Abī al-ʿAlāʾ*. Edited by Iḥsān ʿAbbās. Amman: Dār al-Shurūq, 1988.

Abū ‘Ubayd al-Qāsim b. Sallām. *Kitāb al-Amwāl*. Edited by Muḥammad Ḥāmid Fiqī. Cairo: Maktabat al-Tijāriyya al-Kubrā, 1934.

Abū Yūsuf. *Kitāb al-Kharāj*. Būlāq: al-Maṭba‘a al-Mīriyya, 1884.

Al-Azdī. *Futūḥ al-Shām*. Edited by William Nassau Lees as *The Fotooh al-Sha‘m: Being an Account of the Moslim Conquests in Syria*. Calcutta: Baptist Mission Press, 1854.

Al-Balādhurī. *Ansāb al-ashrāf*. Edited by Suhayl Zakkār and Riyāḍ Ziriklī. Beirut: Dār al-Fikr, 1996.

Al-Balādhurī. *Kitāb Futūḥ al-buldān*. Edited by M. J. de Goeje as *Liber Expugnationis Regionum*. Leiden: E. J. Brill, 1866.

Al-Balādhurī. *Kitāb Futūḥ al-buldān*. Edited by Ṣalāḥ al-Dīn al-Munajjid. Cairo: Maktabat al-Nahḍa al-Miṣriyya, 1956–1957.

Al-Balādhurī. *Kitāb Futūḥ al-buldān*. Translated by Philip Khuri Hitti as *The Origins of the Islamic State: Being a Translation from the Arabic Accompanied with Annotations Geographic and Historic Notes of the Kitāb Futūḥ al-Buldān of al-Imām Abu-l ‘Abbās Aḥmad b. Jābir al-Balādhurī*, Vol. 1. New York: Columbia University Press, 1916.

Al-Balādhurī. *Kitāb Futūḥ al-buldān*. Translated by Francis Clark Murgotten as *The Origins of the Islamic State: Being a Translation from the Arabic Accompanied with Annotations Geographic and Historic Notes of the Kitāb Futūḥ al-Buldān of al-Imām Abu-l ‘Abbās Aḥmad b. Jābir al-Balādhurī*, Vol. 2. New York: Columbia University Press, 1924.

Al-Balawī. *Sīrat Aḥmad b. Ṭūlūn*. Edited by Muḥammad Kurd ‘Alī. Damascus: al-Maktabat al-‘Arabiyya fī Dimashq, 1939.

Al-Biqā‘ī, Ibrāhīm b. ‘Umar. *Naẓm al-durar fī tanāsub al-āyāt wa-l-suwar*. Hyderabad: Dār al-Ma‘ārif al-‘Uthmāniyya, 1969–1984.

Al-Dhahabī. *Siyar a‘lām al-nubalā’*. Edited by Shu‘ayb Arnā’ūṭ, Ḥusayn Asad, et al. Beirut: Mu’assasat al-Risāla, 1981–1988.

Al-Dhahabī. *Ta’rīkh al-Islām*. Edited by ‘Umar al-Tadmurī. Beirut: Dār al-Kitāb al-‘Arabī, 1987–1993.

Al-Iṣṭakhrī. *Kitāb al-Masālik wa-l-mamālik*. Edited by Muḥammad Jābir Ḥīnī. Cairo: al-Idāra al-'Āmma li-l-Thaqāfa, 1961.

Al-Jāḥiẓ. 'Portrait of a Secretary'. In *The Life and Works of Jāḥiẓ*. Translated by Charles Pellat and D. M. Hawke. London: Routledge, 1969.

Al-Jahshiyārī, Muḥammad b. 'Abdūs. *Kitāb al-Wuzarā' wa-l-kuttāb*. Edited by Muṣṭafā Saqqā, Ibrāhīm Ibyārī, and 'Abd al-Ḥafīẓ Shalabī. Cairo: Muṣṭafā al-Bābī al-Ḥalabī wa-Awlāduhu, 1938.

Al-Mas'ūdī, 'Alī b. al-Ḥusayn. *Murūj al-dhahab wa-ma'ādin al-jawhar*. Edited and translated by Charles Barbier de Meynard and Charles Pellat as *Les Prairies D'Or*. Paris: Société Asiatique, 1962–1997.

Al-Mizzī. Tahdhīb al-kamāl fī asmā' *al-rijāl*. Edited by Bashshār 'Awwād Ma'rūf. Beirut: Mu'assasat al-Risāla, 1980–1992.

Al-Sakhāwī. *Al-I'lān bi-t-tawbīkh li-man dhamma al-ta'rīkh*. Edited by Franz Rosenthal. Beirut: Dār al-Kutub al-'Illmiyya, 1986.

Al-Shaybānī, Ibrāhīm. *Al-Risāla al-'adhrā'*. In *Etude Critique sur la Lettre Vierge d'Ibn al-Mudabber*. Edited by Zaki Mubarak. Cairo: Imp. de la Bibliothèque Egyptienne, 1931.

Al-Ṭā'ī, Aḥmad b. Muḥammad. *Kitāb al-Wuzarā'*. Edited by H. F. Amedroz as *The Historical Remains of Hilâl al-Sâbi: First Part of His* Kitab al-Wuzara. Leiden: E. J. Brill, 1904.

Al-Ṭabarī, Muḥammad b. Jarīr. *The History of al-Ṭabarī*. Vol. 1, *General Introduction, and From the Creation to the Flood*. Translated by Franz Rosenthal. Albany: State University of New York Press, 1989.

Al-Ṭabarī, Muḥammad b. Jarīr. *The History of al-Ṭabarī*. Vol. 11, *The Challenge to the Empires*. Translated by Khalid Yahya Blankinship. Albany: State University of New York Press, 1993.

Al-Ṭabarī, Muḥammad b. Jarīr. *The History of al-Ṭabarī*. Vol. 14, *The Conquest of Iran*. Translated by G. Rex Smith. Albany: State University of New York Press, 1994.

Al-Ṭabarī, Muḥammad b. Jarīr. *The History of al-Ṭabarī*. Vol. 32, *The Reunification of the 'Abbasid Caliphate*. Translated by C. E. Bosworth. Albany: State University of New York Press, 1987.

Al-Ṭabarī, Muḥammad b. Jarīr. *The History of al-Ṭabarī*. Vol. 35, *The Crisis of the 'Abbāsid Caliphate*. Translated by George Saliba. Albany: State University of New York Press, 1985.

Al-Ṭabarī, Muḥammad b. Jarīr. *Ta'rīkh al-rusul wa-l-mulūk*. Edited by M. J. de Goeje as *Annales quos scripsit Abu Djafar Mohammed ibn Djarir at-Tabari*. Leiden: E. J. Brill, 1879–1901.

Al-Tanūkhī. *Kitāb al-Fara ba'd al-shiddaj*. Edited by 'Abbūd al-Shāljī. Beirut: Dār Ṣādir, 1978.

Al-Ya'qūbī, Aḥmad b. Abī Ya'qūb. *Kitāb al-Ta'rīkh*. Edited by M. Th. Houtsma as *Ibn-Wādhih qui Dicitur al-Ja'qubi Historiae*. Leiden: E. J. Brill, 1883.

Ibn al-Abbār. Kitāb al-Ḥulla al-siyarā'. Edited by M. J. Müller as *Beiträge zur Geschichte der westlichen Araber*. Munich, 1866.

Ibn 'Abd al-Ḥakam. *Kitāb Futūḥ Miṣr wa-akhbāruhā*. Edited by Charles Cutler Torrey. New Haven: Yale University Press, 1922.

Ibn al-'Adīm, Kamāl al-Dīn. *Bughyat al-ṭalab fī ta'rīkh Ḥalab*. Edited by Suhayl Zakkār. Damascus: Dār al-Ba'th, 1988.

Ibn al-Athīr, 'Izz al-Dīn 'Alī. *Al-Kāmil fi-l-ta'rīkh*. Edited by 'Umar Tadmurī. Beirut: Dār al-Kitāb al-'Arabī, 1997.

Ibn al-Faqīh al-Hamadhānī. *Kitāb al-Buldān*. Edited by Yūsuf al-Hādī. Beirut: 'Ālam al-Kutub, 1996.

Ibn al-Nadīm. *Kitāb al-Fihrist*. Edited by Riḍā Tajaddud. Tehran: Maṭba'at Dānishgāh, 1971.

Ibn al-Nadīm. *Kitāb al-Fihrist*. Translated by Bayard Dodge as *The Fihrist of Ibn al-Nadīm: A Tenth Century Survey of Muslim Culture*. New York: Columbia University Press, 1970.

Ibn 'Asākir. *Ta'rīkh madīnat Dimashq*. Edited by 'Umar al-'Amrawī and 'Alī Shīrī. Beirut: Dār al-Fikr, 1995–2001.

Ibn Hishām. *Sīrat al-nabī*. Edited by M. M. 'Abd al-Ḥamīd. Cairo: Maktabat Muḥammad 'Alī Ṣubayḥ, 1963.

Ibn Kathīr, 'Imād al-Dīn. *Al-Bidāya wa-l-nihāya fi-l-ta'rīkh*. Cairo: Maṭba'at al-Sa'āda, 1932.

Ibn Khaldūn. *Al-Muqaddima*. Translated by Franz Rosenthal as *The Muqaddimah: An Introduction to History*. Princeton: Princeton University Press, 1958.

Ibn Khurradādhbih. *Kitāb al-Masālik wa-l-mamālik*. Edited and translated by M. J. de Goeje as *Bibliotheca Geographorum Arabicorum*. Vol. 6. Leiden: E. J. Brill, 1889.

Ibn Qutayba. *Kitāb al-Ma'ārif*. Edited by Saroite Okacha. Cairo, 1960.

Ibn Qutayba. *'Uyūn al-akhbār*. Cairo: Dār al-Kutub al-Miṣriyya, 1925–1930.

Ibn Sa'īd al-Andalusī. *Al-Mughrib fī ḥulā al-Maghrib*. Edited by Shawqī Ḍayf. Cairo: Dār al-Ma'ārif, 1953–1955.

Khaṭīb al-Baghdādī. *Ta'rīkh Baghdād*. Edited by Aḥmad b. al-Ṣiddīq. Cairo: Maktabat al-Khānjī, 1931.

Niẓām al-Mulk. *Siyar al-mulūk*. Translated by Hubert Darke as *The Book of Government or Rules for Kings*. London: Routledge, 1960.

Qudāma b. Ja'far. *Kitāb al-Kharāj wa-ṣinā'at al-kitāba*. Edited by Muḥammad Ḥusayn Zubaydī. Baghdad: Wizārat al-Thaqāfa wa-l-I'lām, 1981.

Qudāma b. Ja'far. *Kitāb al-kharāj wa-ṣinā'at al-kitāba*. Translated by A. Ben Shemesh as *Taxation in Islam*. Vol. 2, *Qudāma b. Ja'far's* Kitāb al-Kharāj, *Part Seven*. Leiden: E. J. Brill, 1965.

Yaḥyā b. Ādam. *Kitāb al-Kharāj*. Edited by Th. W. Juynboll. Leiden: E. J. Brill, 1896.

Yaḥyā b. Ādam. *Kitāb al-Kharāj*. Translated by A. Ben Shemesh as *Taxation in Islam*. Vol. 1, *Yaḥyā ben Ādam's* Kitāb al-Kharāj. Leiden: E. J. Brill, 1958.

Yāqūt al-Ḥamāwī. *Irshād al-arīb ilā maʿrifat al-adīb*. Edited by D. S. Margoliouth. London: Luzac, 1923–1931.

Yāqūt al-Ḥamāwī. *Muʿjam al-buldān*. Edited by Ferdinand Wüstenfeld as *Jacut's Geographisches Wörterbuch*. Leipzig: F. A. Brockhaus, 1866–1873.

Secondary sources

Adams, Robert McCormick. *Land Behind Baghdad: A History of Settlement on the Diyala Plains*. Chicago: University of Chicago Press, 1965.

Adams, Robert McCormick. *Heartland of Cities: Surveys of Ancient Settlement and Land Use on the Central Floodplain of the Euphrates*. Chicago: Chicago University Press, 1981.

Afsaruddin, Asma. *Excellence and Precedence in Medieval Islamic Discourse on Legitimate Leadership*. Leiden: Brill, 2002.

Al-Naboodah, Hasan. 'Al-Balādhurī'. In *Encyclopedia of the Medieval Chronicle*. Edited by Graeme Dunphy et al. Leiden: Brill, 2010.

Al-Qadi, Wadad. 'The Names of Estates in State Registers Before and After the Arabization of the "Dīwāns"'. In *Umayyad Legacies: Medieval Memories from Syria to Spain*. Edited by Antoine Borrut and Paul M. Cobb. Leiden: Brill, 2010: 255–80.

Ali, Samer M. *Arabic Literary Salons in the Islamic Middle Ages: Poetry, Public Performance and the Presentation of the Past*. Notre Dame: University of Notre Dame Press, 2010.

Antrim, Zayde. *Routes & Realms: The Power of Place in the Early Islamic World*. Oxford: Oxford University Press, 2012.

Athamina, Khalil. 'Abū Mikhnaf'. In *Encyclopaedia of Islam*, Third Edition. Edited by Kate Fleet, Gudrun Krämer, Denis Matringe, John Nawas, and Everett Rowson. Leiden: Brill, 2009–Present.

Athamina, Khalil. 'The Historical Work of al-Ṭabarī and al-Balādhurī: The Author's Attitude Towards the Sources'. In *al-Ṭabarī: A Medieval Muslim Historian and His Work*. Edited by Hugh Kennedy. Princeton: The Darwin Press, 2008: 141–55.

Athamina, Khalil. 'Introduction.' In *Ansāb al-Ashrāf*, Vol. 6B. Edited by Khalil Athamina. Jerusalem: The Hebrew University of Jerusalem, 1993: 7–18.

Athamina, Khalil. 'The Sources of al-Balādhurī's *Ansāb al-Ashrāf*. *Jerusalem Studies in Arabic and Islam*. Vol. 5 (1984): 237–62.

Ayalon, David. 'The Military Reforms of Caliph al-Muʿtaṣim'. In *Islam and the Abode of War: Military Slaves and Islamic Adversaries*. Aldershot: Ashgate, 1994: 1–39.

Becker, Christopher H., and Franz Rosenthal. 'al-Balādhurī'. In *Encyclopaedia of Islam*, Second Edition. Edited by P. Bearman, Th. Bianquis, C. E. Bosworth, E. van Donzel, and W. P. Heinrichs. Leiden: Brill, 1960–2007.

Beckwith, Christopher I. 'Aspects of the Early History of the Central Asian Guard Corps in Islam'. In *The Turks in the Early Islamic World*. Edited by C. E. Bosworth. Aldershot: Ashgate, 2007: 275–90. Previously published in *Archivum Eurasiae Medii Aevi*. Vol. 4 (1984): 29–43.

Beeston, A. F. L., and Lawrence I. Conrad. 'On Some Umayyad Poetry in the *History* of al-Ṭabarī'. *Journal of the Royal Asiatic Society*. Vol. 3, No. 2 (1993): 191–206.

Behzadi, Lale, and Jaakko Hämeen-Anttila, editors. *Concepts of Authorship in Pre-Modern Arabic Texts*. Bamberg: University of Bamberg Press, 2015.

Berg, Herbert. 'Competing Paradigms in the Study of Islamic Origins: Qur'an 15: 89–91 and the Value of *Isnāds*'. In *Method and Theory in the Study of Islamic Origins*. Leiden: Brill, 2003: 259–90.

Bonebakker, S. A. 'Ḳudāma'. *Encyclopaedia of Islam*, Second Edition.

Bonner, Michael Richard Jackson. 'An Historiographical Study of Abū Ḥanīfa Aḥmad ibn Dāwūd ibn Wanand al-Dīnawarī's *Kitāb al-Akhbār al-ṭiwāl*'. PhD diss., University of Oxford, 2013.

Borrut, Antoine. *Entre mémoire et pouvoir: L'espace syrien sous les derniers Omeyyades et les premiers Abbassides (v. 72–193/692–809)*. Leiden: Brill, 2011.

Borrut, Antoine, and Paul M. Cobb, editors. *Umayyad Legacies: Medieval Memories from Syria to Spain*. Leiden: Brill, 2010.

Bos, Gerrit. '*Balādhur* (Marking Nut): A Popular Medieval Drug for Strengthening Memory'. *Bulletin of the School of Oriental and African Studies*. Vol. 59, No. 2 (1996): 229–36.

Bosworth, Clifford Edmund. 'Administrative Literature'. In *Religion, Learning, and Science in the 'Abbāsid Period*. Edited by M. J. L. Young, J. D. Latham, and R. B. Serjeant. Cambridge: Cambridge University Press, 1990: 155–67.

Bray, Julia. "Abbasid Myth and the Human Act: Ibn 'Abd Rabbih and Others'. In *On Fiction and Adab in Medieval Arabic Literature*. Edited by Philip F. Kennedy. Wiesbaden: Harrassowitz Verlag, 2005.

Bray, Julia. 'Lists and Memory: Ibn Qutayba and Muḥammad b. Ḥabīb'. In *Culture and Memory in Medieval Islam: Essays in Honour of Wilferd Madelung*. Edited by Farhard Daftary and Josef W. Meri. London: I. B. Tauris and the Institute of Ismaili Studies, 2003: 210–31.

Brown, Jonathan A. C. *Hadith: Muhammad's Legacy in the Medieval and Modern World*. Oxford: Oneworld, 2009.

Bulliet, Richard W. *Conversion to Islam in the Medieval Period: An Essay in Quantitative History*. Cambridge, MA: Harvard University Press, 1979.

Calder, Norman. *Studies in Early Muslim Jurisprudence*. Oxford: Clarendon Press, 1993.

Campopiano, Michele. 'State, Land Tax, and Agriculture in Iraq from the Arab Conquest to the Crisis of the Abbasid Caliphate (Seventh-Tenth Centuries)'. *Studia Islamica*. Vol. 3 (2012): 5–50.

Chejne, Anwar G. 'The Boon-Companion in Early 'Abbāsid Times'. *Journal of the American Oriental Society*. Vol. 85, No. 3 (1965): 327–35.

Clarke, Nicola. *The Muslim Conquest of Iberia: Medieval Arabic Narratives*. London: Routledge, 2012.

Cobb, Paul M. 'Al-Mutawakkil's Damascus: A New 'Abbāsid Capital?' *Journal of Near Eastern Studies*. Vol. 58, No. 4 (1999): 241–57.

Conrad, Lawrence I. 'Ibn A'tham and His History'. *Al–'Uṣūr al-Wusṭā*. Vol. 23 (2015): 87–125.

Conrad, Lawrence I. 'Theophanes and the Arabic Historical Tradition: Some Indications of Intercultural Transmission'. *Byzantinische Forschungen*. Vol. 15 (1990): 1–43.

Cook, Michael. *Early Muslim Dogma: A Source-Critical Study*. Cambridge: Cambridge University Press, 1981.

Cooperson, Michael. 'Al-Amīn, Muḥammad'. *Encyclopaedia of Islam*, Third Edition.

Cooperson, Michael. *Classical Arabic Biography: The Heirs of the Prophets in the Age of al-Ma'mūn*. Cambridge: Cambridge University Press, 2000.

Crone, Patricia. 'The 'Abbāsid Abnā' and Sasanid Cavalrymen'. *Journal of the Royal Asiatic Society*. Vol. 8 (1998): 1–19.

Crone, Patricia. *Meccan Trade and the Rise of Islam*. Princeton: Princeton University Press, 1987.

Crone, Patricia. *Slaves on Horses: The Evolution of the Islamic Polity*. Cambridge: Cambridge University Press, 1980.

Crone, Patricia, and Michael Cook. *Hagarism: The Making of the Islamic World*. Cambridge: Cambridge University Press, 1977.

Cubitt, Geoffrey. *History and Memory*. Manchester: Manchester University Press, 2007.

Cureton, William, and Charles Rieu. *Catalogus codicum manuscriptorum orientalium qui in Museo Britannico asservantur: Pars secunda, codices arabicos*. London: Impensis cutatorum Musei Britannici, 1846–1871.

De La Vaissière, Étienne. *Samarcande et Samarra: Élites d'Asie Centrale dans l'Empire Abbaside*. Leuven: Peeters Publishers, 2007.

Donner, Fred M. *The Early Islamic Conquests*. Princeton: Princeton University Press, 1981.

Donner, Fred M. *Narratives of Islamic Origins: The Beginnings of Islamic Historical Writing*. Princeton: The Darwin Press, 1998.

Donner, Fred M. "Uthmān and the *Rāshidūn* Caliphs in Ibn 'Asākir's *Ta'rīkh madīnat Dimashq*: A Study in Strategies of Compilation'. In *Ibn 'Asākir and Early Islamic History*. Edited by James E. Lindsay. Princeton: The Darwin Press, 2001: 44–61.

Dunlop, Douglas Morton. *The History of the Jewish Khazars*. Princeton: Princeton University Press, 1954.

Duri, 'Abd al-Aziz. *The Rise of Historical Writing Among the Arabs*. Translated by Lawrence I. Conrad. Princeton: Princeton University Press, 1983.

El-Hibri, Tayeb. 'Harūn al-Rashīd and the Mecca Protocol of 802: A Plan for Division or Succession?' *International Journal of Middle East Studies*. Vol. 24, No. 3 (1992): 461–80.

El-Hibri, Tayeb. *Parable and Politics in Early Islamic History: The Rashidun Caliphs*. New York: Columbia University Press, 2010.

El-Hibri, Tayeb. 'The Redemption of Umayyad Memory by the 'Abbāsids'. *Journal of Near Eastern Studies*. Vol. 61, No. 4 (2002): 241–65.

El-Hibri, Tayeb. *Reinterpreting Islamic Historiography: Hārūn al-Rashīd and the Narrative of the 'Abbāsid Caliphate.* Cambridge: Cambridge University Press, 1999.

Elad, Amikam. 'The Armies of al-Ma'mūn in Khurāsān (193–202/809 –817–18): Recruitment of its Contingents and their Commanders and their Social-Ethnic Composition'. *Oriens.* Vol. 38 (2010): 35–76.

Elad, Amikam. 'Al-Ma'mūn's Military Units and their Commanders up to the End of the Siege of Baghdad (195/810-198/813)'. In *'Abbāsid Studies.* Vol. 4, Occasional Papers *of the School of 'Abbāsid Studies.* Edited by Monique Bernards. Exeter: Gibb Memorial Trust, 2013: 245–84.

Fariq, K. Ahmad. 'A Remarkable Early Muslim Governor Zayīd b. Abīh'. *Islamic Quarterly.* Vol. 26, No. 4 (1952): 1–31.

Fattal, Antoine. *Le statut legal des non-musulmans en pays d'Islam.* Beirut: Impr. Catholique, 1958.

Fleischhammer, Manfred. 'Quellenuntersuchungen zum *Kitāb al-Aghānī*'. PhD diss., University of Halle/Saale, 1965.

Gibb, Hamilton Alexander Rosskeen. *Studies on the Civilization of Islam.* Edited by Stanford J. Shaw and William R. Polk. Princeton: Princeton University Press, 1962.

Gil, Moshe. 'The Earliest Waqf Foundations'. *Journal of Near Eastern Studies.* Vol. 57, No. 2 (1998): 125–40.

Goeje, Michael Jan de. *Mémoire sur la conquête de la Syrie.* Leiden: E. J. Brill, 1864.

Goitein, Shelomo Dov. 'Introduction'. In *Ansāb al-ashrāf.* Vol. 5. Edited by S. D. Goitein. Jerusalem: Hebrew University Press, 1936.

Goitein, Shelomo Dov. 'The Place of Balādhurī's *Ansāb al-Ashrāf* in Arabic Historiography'. In *Atti del XIX Congresso Internazionale degli Orientalisti.* Rome: Tipografia del Senato del Doit G. Bardi, 1938: 603–6.

Golden, Peter B. 'Khazar Turkic Ghulāms in Caliphal Service'. *Journal Asiatique.* Vol. 292 (2004): 279–309.

Goldziher, Ignaz. *Muhammedanische Studien.* Halle: a. S. Max Niemeyer, 1889.

Goldziher, Ignaz. *Muslim Studies.* Translated by Samuel Miklos Stern and Christa Renate Barber. Chicago: Aldine, 1967.

Gordon, Matthew S. 'Aḥmad b. Ṭūlūn'. *Encyclopaedia of Islam,* Third Edition.

Gordon, Matthew S. *The Breaking of a Thousand Swords: A History of the Turkish Military of Samarra (AH 200-275/815-889 C.E.).* Albany: State University of New York Press, 2001.

Görke, Andreas. *Das* Kitāb al-amwāl *des Abū 'Ubaid al-Qāsim b. Sallām: Entstehung und Überlieferung eines frühislamischen Rechtswerkes.* Princeton: The Darwin Press, 2003.

Görke, Andreas, and Konrad Hirschler, editors. *Manuscript Notes as Documentary Sources.* Beirut: Ergon Verlag Würzburg, 2011.

Gottschalk, H. L. 'Ibn al-Mudabbir'. *Encyclopaedia of Islam,* Second Edition.

Gruendler, Beatrice. 'Verse and Taxes: The Function of Poetry in Selected Literary *Akhbār* of the Third/Ninth Century'. In *On Fiction and Adab in Medieval Arabic Literature.* Edited by Philip F. Kennedy. Wiesbaden: Harrassowitz, 2005: 85–124.

Grundmann, Herbert. *Geschichtsshreibung im Mittelalter: Gattungen, Epochen, Eigenart*. Göttingen: Vandenhoeck and Ruprecht, 1978.

Günther, Sebastian. 'Assessing the Sources of Classical Arabic Compilations: The Issue of Categories and Methodologies'. *British Journal of Middle Eastern Studies*. Vol. 32, No. 1 (2005): 75–98.

Günther, Sebastian. 'Due Results in the Theory of Source-Criticism in Medieval Arabic Literature'. *Al-Abhath*. Vol. 42 (1994): 3–15.

Günther, Sebastian. *Quellenuntersuchungen zu den Maqātil aṭ-Ṭalibiyyin des Abū 'l-Farağ al-Isfahānī (gest. 356/967)*. Hildesheim: Olms, 1991.

Hakim, Avraham. "Umar b. al-Ḫaṭṭāb: L'autorité religieuse et morale'. *Arabica*. Vol. 55, No. 1 (2008): 1–34.

Hasson, Isaac. '*Ansāb al-ašrāf* d'al-Balāḏurī est-il un Livre de Ta'rīḫ ou D'Adab?' In *Israel Oriental Studies*. Vol. 19, *Compilation and Creation in Adab and* Luġa. Edited by Albert Arazi, Joseph Sadan, and David J. Wasserstein. Winona Lake: Eisenbrauns, 1999: 479–93.

Hasson, Isaac. 'L'affiliation (*di'wa*) de Ziyād b. Abīhi'. *Jerusalem Studies in Arabic and Islam*. Vol. 29 (2004): 413–25.

Hasson, Isaac. 'Ziyād b. Abīhi'. *Encyclopaedia of Islam*, Second Edition.

Heath, Peter. 'Some Functions of Poetry in Premodern Historical and Pseudo-Historical Texts: Comparing *Ayyām al-'Arab*, al-Ṭabarī's *History*, and *Sirāt 'Antar*'. In *Poetry and History: The Value of Poetry in Reconstructing Arab History*. Edited by Ramzi Baalbaki, Saleh Said Agha, and Tarif Khalidi. Beirut: American University of Beirut Press, 2011: 39–60.

Heck, Paul L. *The Construction of Knowledge in Islamic Civilization: Qudāma b. Ja'far and His* Kitāb al-Kharāj wa-ṣinā'at al-kitāba. Leiden: Brill, 2002.

Heinrichs, Wolfhart. 'Prosimentrical Genres in Classical Arabic Literature'. In *Prosimetrum: Cross Cultural Perspectives on Narrative in Prose and Verse*. Edited by Joseph Harris and Karl Reichl. Cambridge: D. S. Brewer, 1997: 249–75.

Hill, Donald Routledge. *The Termination of Hostilities in the Early Arab Conquests, A.D.* London: Luzac & Company, 1971: 634–56.

Hinds, Martin. 'The First Arab Conquests in Fārs'. *Iran*. Vol. 22 (1984): 39–53.

Hinds, Martin, and Hamdi Sakkout. 'A Letter From the Governor of Egypt to the King of Nubia and Muqurra Concerning Egyptian-Nubian Relations in 141/758'. In *Studia Arabica et Islamica: Festschrift for Ihsan 'Abbas on His Sixtieth Birthday*. Edited by Wadad al-Qadi. Beirut: American University of Beirut, 1981: 209–30.

Hirschler, Konrad. *Medieval Arabic Historiography: Authors as Actors*. London: Routledge, 2011.

Hirschler, Konrad. 'Reading Certificates (*samā'āt*) as a Prosopographical Source: Cultural and Social Practices of an Elite Family in Zangid and Ayyubid Damascus'. In *Manuscript Notes as Documentary Sources*. Edited by Andreas Görke and Konrad Hirschler. Beirut: Ergon Verlag Würzburg, 2011: 73–92.

Hirschler, Konrad. *The Written Word in the Medieval Arabic Lands: A Social and Cultural History of Reading Practices*. Edinburgh: Edinburgh University Press, 2012.

Hirschler, Konrad, and Sarah Bowen Savant. 'Introduction – What is in a Period? Arabic Historiography and Periodization'. *Der Islam*. Vol. 91, No. 1 (2014): 6–19.

Hoyland, Robert G. 'Epigraphy and the Emergence of Arab Identity'. In *From al-Andalus to Khurasan: Documents from the Medieval Muslim World*. Edited by Petra M. Sijpesteijn, Lennart Sundelin, Sofía Torallas Tovar, and Amalia Zomeño. Leiden: Brill, 2007: 219–42.

Hoyland, Robert G. *In God's Path: The Arab Conquests and the Creation of an Islamic Empire*. Oxford: Oxford University Press, 2015.

Hoyland, Robert G. 'History, Fiction, and Authorship in the First Centuries of Islam'. In *Writing and Representation in Medieval Islam*. Edited by Julia Bray. London: Routledge, 2006.

Hoyland, Robert G. *Seeing Islam as Others Saw It: A Survey and Evaluation of Christian, Jewish, and Zoroastrian Writings on Early Islam*. Princeton: The Darwin Press, 1997.

Hoyland, Robert G. *Theophilus of Edessa's Chronicle and the Circulation of Historical Knowledge in Late Antiquity and Early Islam*. Liverpool: Liverpool University Press, 2011.

Humphreys, R. Stephen. *Islamic History: A Framework for Inquiry*. London: I. B. Tauris, 1991.

Judd, Steven C. 'Ibn 'Asākir's Sources for the Late Umayyad Period'. In *Ibn 'Asākir and Early Islamic History*. Edited by James E. Lindsay. Princeton: The Darwin Press, 2001: 78–99.

Judd, Steven C. 'Narratives and Character Development: Al-Ṭabarī and al-Balādhurī on Late Umayyad History'. In *Ideas, Images, and Methods of Portrayal: Insights Into Classical Arabic Literature and Islam*. Edited by Sebastian Günther. Leiden: Brill, 2005: 209–26.

Juynboll, Gautier H. A. *Muslim Tradition: Studies in Chronology, Provenance, and Authorship of Early Ḥadīth*. Cambridge: Cambridge University Press, 1983.

Juynboll, Th. W. *Le Livre de L'impôt Foncier de Yahyā ibn Ādam*. Leiden: Brill, 1896.

Kallek, Cengiz. 'Yaḥyā ibn Ādam's *Kitāb al-Kharādj*: Religious Guidelines for Public Finance'. *Journal of the Economic and Social History of the Orient*. Vol. 44, No. 2 (2001): 103–22.

Kennedy, Hugh, editor. *Al-Ṭabarī: A Medieval Muslim Historian and His Work*. Princeton: The Darwin Press, 2008.

Kennedy, Hugh, editor. *The Armies of the Caliphs: Military and Society in the Early Islamic State*. London: Routledge, 2001.

Kennedy, Hugh, editor. 'The Decline and Fall of the First Muslim Empire'. *Der Islam*. Vol. 81, No. 1 (2004): 1–29.

Kennedy, Hugh, editor. 'The Feeding of the Five Hundred Thousand: Cities and Agriculture in Early Islamic Mesopotamia'. *Iraq*. Vol. 73 (2011): 177–99.

Kennedy, Hugh, editor. 'Landholding and Law in the Early Islamic State'. In *Diverging Paths? The Shapes of Power and Institutions in Medieval Christendom and Islam*. Edited by John Hudson and Ana Rodríguez. Leiden: E. J. Brill, 2014: 159–81.

Kennedy, Hugh, and Ihab el Sakkout. 'Book Review: The *Ansāb al-Ashrāf*, Vol. 6B, by Aḥmad b. Yaḥyā b. Jābir al-Balādhurī, edited and annotated by Khalil Athamina', *Journal of the Royal Asiatic Society of Great Britain & Ireland*. Vol. 5, No. 3 (1995): 410–13.

Khalek, Nancy. *Damascus After the Muslim Conquest: Text and Image in Early Islam*. Oxford: Oxford University Press, 2011.

Khalek, Nancy. '"He Was Tall and Slender, and His Virtues Were Numerous:" Byzantine Hagiographical Topoi and the Companions of Muḥammad in al-Azdī's *Futūḥ al-Shām*'. In *Writing True Stories: Historians and Hagiographers in the Late Antique and Medieval Near East*. Edited by Arietta Papaconstantinou. New York: Brepols Publishers, 2010: 105–23.

Khalidi, Tarif. *Arabic Historical Thought in the Classical Period*. Cambridge: Cambridge University Press, 1994.

Kilito, Abdelfattah. *The Author and His Doubles: Essays on Classical Arabic Culture*. Translated by Michael Cooperson. Syracuse: Syracuse University Press, 2001.

Kilpatrick, Hilary. '*Adab*'. In *Encyclopedia of Arabic Literature*. Edited by Julie Scott Meisami and Paul Starkey. London: Routledge, 1998.

Kilpatrick, Hilary. 'A Genre in Classical Arabic Literature: The *Adab* Encyclopedia'. In *Union Européenne des Arabisants et Islamisants 10th Congress Proceedings*. Edited by Robert Hillenbrand. Edinburgh: Union Européenne des Arabistants et Islamisants, 1982: 34–43.

Kilpatrick, Hilary. *Making the Great Book of Songs: Compilation and the Author's Craft in Abū l-Faraj al-Iṣbahānī's Kitāb al-aghānī*. London: Routledge, 2003.

König, Daniel. *Arabic-Islamic Views of the Latin West: Tracing the Emergence of Medieval Europe*. Oxford: Oxford University Press, 2015.

Kramers, Johannes Hendrik. 'The Military Colonization of the Caucasus and Armenia under the Sassanids'. *Bulletin of the School of Oriental and African Studies*. Vol. 8 (1936): 613–18.

Labidi, Mohamed Mokhtar. 'al-Shaybānī', *Encyclopaedia of Islam*, Second Edition.

Lake, Justin. 'Authorial Intention in Medieval Historiography'. *History Compass*. Vol. 12, No. 4 (2014): 244–360.

Landau-Tasseron, Ella. 'On the Reconstruction of Lost Sources'. *Al-Qanṭara*. Vol. 25 (2004): 45–91.

Landau-Tasseron, Ella. 'Sayf ibn 'Umar in Medieval and Modern Scholarship'. *Der Islam*. Vol. 67, No. 1 (1990): 1–26.

Langarudī, Riḍā Riḍāzādih. 'al-Balādhurī'. In *Historians of the Islamic World: Selected Entries from Encyclopaedia of the World of Islam*. Edited by Gholamali Haddad Adel, Mohammad Jafar Elmi, and Hassan Taromi-Rad. London: EWI Press, 2013.

Larsen, Curtis E. 'The Mesopotamian Delta Region: A Reconsideration of Lees and Falcon'. *Journal of the American Oriental Society*. Vol. 95, No. 1 (1975): 43–57.

Lecker, Michael. 'Tribes in Pre- and Early Islamic Arabia'. In *People, Tribes, and Society in Arabic Around the Time of Muḥammad*. Aldershot: Ashgate, 2005: 34–47.

Lecker, Michael. 'Wāqidī's Account on the Status of the Jews of Medina: A Study of a Combined Report'. *Journal of Near Eastern Studies*. Vol. 54, No. 1 (1995): 15–32.

Leder, Stefan. 'Conventions of Fictional Narration in Learned Literature'. In *Story-Telling in the Framework of Non-Fictional Arabic Literature*. Edited by Stefan Leder. Wiesbaden: Harrassowitz Verlag, 1998: 34–60.

Leder, Stefan. 'Features of the Novel in Early Historiography: The Downfall of Xālid al-Qasrī'. *Oriens*. Vol. 32 (1990): 72–96.

Leder, Stefan. 'The Literary Use of the *Khabar*: A Basic Form of Historical Writing'. In *The Byzantine and Early Islamic Near East*. Vol. 1, *Problems in the Literary Source Material*. Edited by Averil Cameron and Lawrence I. Conrad. Princeton: The Darwin Press, 1992: 277–315.

Leder, Stefan, and Hilary Kilpatrick. 'Classical Arabic Prose Literature: A Researchers' Sketch Map'. *Journal of Arabic Literature*. Vol. 23 (1992): 2–26.

Lev, Yaacov. 'Coptic Rebellions and the Islamization of Medieval Egypt (8th–10th century): Medieval and Modern Perceptions'. *Jerusalem Studies in Arabic and Islam*. Vol. 39 (2012): 303–44.

Levy-Rubin, Milka. *Non-Muslims in the Early Islamic Empire: From Surrender to Coexistence*. Cambridge: Cambridge University Press, 2011.

Levy-Rubin, Milka. '*Shurūṭ 'Umar* and Its Alternatives: The Legal Debate on the Status of the *Dhimmīs*'. *Jerusalem Studies in Arabic and Islam*. Vol. 30 (2005): 170–206.

Lewental, D. Gershon. 'Qādisiyyah, Then and Now: A Case Study of History and Memory, Religion, and Nationalism in Middle Eastern Discourse'. PhD diss., Brandeis Univeristy, 2011.

Lindsay, James E., editor. *Ibn 'Asākir and Early Islamic History*. Princeton: The Darwin Press, 2001.

Lindstedt, Ilkka. 'Al-Madā'inī's *Kitāb al-Dawla* and the Death of Ibrahim al-Imām'. In *Case Studies in Transmission*. Edited by Ilkka Lindstedt, Jaakko Hämeen-Anttila, Raija Mattila, and Robert Rollinger. Munster: Ugarit-Verlag, 2014: 103–30.

Lindstedt, Ilkka. 'The Transmission of al-Madā'inī's Historical Material to al-Balādhurī and al-Ṭabarī: A Comparison and Analysis of Two *Khabars*'. In *Studia Orientalia*. Vol. 114, *Travelling Through Time: Essays in Honour of Kaj Öhrnberg*. Edited by Sylvia Akar, Jaako Hämeen-Anttila, and Inka Nokso-Koivisto. Helsinki: Finnish Oriental Society, 2013: 41–59.

Lindstedt, Ilkka. 'The Transmission of al-Madā'inī's Material: Historiographical Studies'. PhD diss., University of Helsinki, 2013.

Lynch, Ryan J. 'Cyprus and Its Legal and Historiographical Significance in Early Islamic History'. *Journal of the American Oriental Society*. Vol. 136, No. 3 (2016): 535–50.

Lynch, Ryan J. 'Linking Information, Creating a Legend: The Desert March of Khālid b. al-Walīd'. *Lights: The MESSA Journal of the University of Chicago*. Vol. 2, No. 2 (2013): 28–41.

Lynch, Ryan J. '"The Wall of Rock and Lead": 'Abbāsid Reflections on Sasanian Caucasian Policy in Arrān.' In *From Albania to Arran: The East Caucasus between Antiquity and Medieval Islam*. Edited by Robert G. Hoyland. Piscataway: Gorgias Press, 2019.

Marlow, Louise. *Hierarchy and Egalitarianism in Islamic Thought*. Cambridge: Cambridge University Press, 1997.

Marsham, Andrew. 'Fay''. *Encyclopaedia of Islam*, Third Edition.

Marsham, Andrew. *Rituals of Islamic Monarchy: Accession and Succession in the First Muslim Empire*. Edinburgh: Edinburgh University Press, 2009.

Massé, Henri. 'Ibn al-Faḳīh'. *Encyclopaedia of Islam*, Second Edition.

Maqbul, Ahmad S. 'Djughrāfiyā'. *Encyclopaedia of Islam*, Second Edition.

Maqbul, Ahmad S. *A History of Arab-Islamic Geography (9th–16th Century A.D.)*. Amman: Al al-Bayt University, 1995.

McCoy, Roy Michael. '*Scriptura Scripturam Interpretatur*: An Analysis of the Arabic Bible as Used in the *Tafsīrs* of Ibn Barrajān and al-Biqā'ī'. PhD diss., University of Oxford, 2018.

Meisami, Julie Scott. *Persian Historiography to the End of the Twelfth Century*. Edinburgh: Edinburgh University Press, 1999.

Miquel, André. *Le géographie humaine du monde musulman jusqu'au milieu du 11e siècle: Les travaux et les jours*. Paris: Éditions de l'École des hautes études en sciences sociales, 1967–1987.

Montgomery, James E. 'Ibn Rusta's Lack of "Eloquence," the *Rūs*, and Samanid Cosmography'. *Edebiyāt*. Vol. 12 (2001): 73–93.

Montgomery, James E. 'Serendipity, Resistance, and Multivalency: Ibn Khurradādhbih and his *Kitāb al-Masālik wa-l-mamālik*'. In *On Fiction and Adab in Medieval Arabic Literature*. Edited by Philip F. Kennedy. Wiesbaden: Harrassowitz Verlag, 2005: 177–230.

Morimoto, Kosei. *The Fiscal Administration of Egypt in the Early Islamic Period*. Kyoto: Dohasha, 1981.

Morray, David W. *An Ayyubid Notable and His World: Ibn al-'Adīm and Aleppo as Portrayed in his Biographical Dictionary of People Associated with the City*. Leiden: Brill, 1994.

Motzki, Harold. 'The Author and His Work in the Islamic Literature of the First Centuries: The Case of 'Abd al-Razzāq's *Muṣannaf*. *Jerusalem Studies in Arabic and Islam*. Vol. 28 (2003): 171–201.

Mourad, Suleiman A. 'On Early Historiography: Abū Ismā'īl al-Azdī and His *Futūḥ al-Shām*'. *Journal of the American Oriental Society*. Vol. 120, No. 4 (2000): 577–93.

Mourad, Suleiman A. 'Poetry, History, and the Early Arab-Islamic Conquests of *al-Shām* (Greater Syria)'. In *Poetry and History: The Value of Poetry in Reconstructing Arab History*. Edited by Ramzi Baalbaki, Saleh Said Agha, and Tarif Khalidi. Beirut: American University of Beirut Press, 2011: 175–94.

Munt, Harry. 'Caliphal Estates and Properties Around Medina in the Umayyad Period'. In *Authority and Control in the Countryside: From Antiquity to Islam in the Mediterranean and Near East (Sixth-Tenth Century)*. Edited by Alain Delattre, Marie Legendre, and Petra Sijpesteijn. Leiden: Brill, 2018: 432–63.

Munt, Harry. 'Writing the History of an Arabian Holy City: Ibn Zabāla and the First Local History of Medina'. *Arabica*. Vol. 59 (2012): 1–34.

Nemoy, Leon. *Arabic Manuscripts in the Yale University Library*. New Haven: Yale University Press, 1956.

Nora, Pierre. 'Between Memory and History: *Les Lieux de Mémoire*'. *Representations Special Issue: Memory and Counter-Memory*. Vol. 26 (1989): 7–24.

Noth, Albrecht. 'Iṣfahān-Nihāwand: Eine quellenkritische Studie zur frühislamischen Historiographie'. *Zeitschrift der Deutschen Morgenländischen Gesellschaft*. Vol. 118 (1968): 274–96.

Noth, Albrecht. 'On the Relationship in the Caliphate Between Central Power and the Provinces: The '*Ṣulḥ*' – '*Anwa*' Traditions for Egypt and Iraq'. In *The Expansion of the Islamic State*. Edited by Fred M. Donner. Aldershot: Ashgate, 2008: 178–88. Previously published as 'Zum Verhältnis von Kalifaler Zentralgewalt und Provinzen in umayyadischer Zeit: Die 'Ṣulḥ' – 'Anwa'-Traditionen für Ägypten und den Iraq'. *Die Welt des Islams*. Vol. 14 (1973): 150–62.

Noth, Albrecht. 'Some Remarks on the Nationalization of Conquered Lands at the Time of the Umayyads'. In *Land Tenure and Social Transformation in the Middle East*. Edited by Tarif Khalidi. Beirut: American University of Beirut, 1984: 223–8.

Noth, Albrecht, and Lawrence I. Conrad. *The Early Arabic Historical Tradition: A Source-Critical Study*. Princeton: The Darwin Press, 1994.

Olsson, J. T. 'Design, Determinism, and Salvation in the *Firdaws al-Ḥikma* of 'Alī Ibn Rabban al-Ṭabarī'. PhD diss., University of Cambridge, 2016.

Øverby, Erlend. 'Problems with Linking, and Reuse of Text'. Accessed 19 February 2016. https://www.infoloom.com/media/gcaconfs/WEB/granada99/ove.HTM.

Paret, Rudi. 'The Legendary *Futūḥ* Literature'. In *The Expansion of the Early Islamic State*. Edited by Fred M. Donner. Aldershot: Ashgate, 2008: 163–75. Previously published as 'Die Legendäre *Futūḥ*-Literature'. In *La poesia epica e la sua formazione*. Rome: 1970: 735–49.

Petersen, Erling Ladewig. 'Alī and Mu'*āwiya in Early Arabic Tradition: Studies on the Genesis and Growth of Islamic Historical Writing Until the End of the Ninth Century*. Copenhagen: Munksgaard, 1964.

Popovic, Alexandre. *The Revolt of African Slaves in Iraq in the 3rd/9th Century*. Translated by Leon King. Princeton: Markus Wiener Publishers, 1999.

Pyrovolaki, Marina. '*Futūḥ al-Shām* and other *futūḥ* texts: A Study of the Perception of Marginal Conquest Narratives in Arabic in Medieval and Modern Times'. PhD diss., University of Oxford, 2008.

Randa, Ernest William. 'The Tulunid Dynasty in Egypt: Loyalty and State Formation During the Dissolution of the 'Abbasid Caliphate'. PhD diss., University of Utah, 1990.

Robinson, Chase F. 'Crone and the End of Orientalism'. In *Islamic Cultures, Islamic Contexts: Essays in Honor of Professor Patricia Crone*. Edited by Behnam Sadeghi, Asad Q. Ahmed, Adam Silverstein, and Robert Hoyland. Leiden: Brill, 2015: 597–620.

Robinson, Chase F. *Empires and Elites After the Muslim Conquest: The Transformation of Northern Mesopotamia*. Cambridge: Cambridge University Press, 2000.

Robinson, Chase F. 'Islamic Historical Writing, Eighth through the Tenth Centuries'. In *The Oxford History of Historical Writing*. Vol. 2, 400–1400. Edited by Sarah Foot and Chase Robinson. Oxford: Oxford University Press, 2012: 238–66.

Robinson, Chase F. *Islamic Historiography*. Cambridge: Cambridge University Press, 2003.

Robinson, Chase F. 'A Local Historian's Debt to al-Ṭabarī: The Case of al-Azdī's *Ta'rīkh al-Mawṣil*'. *Journal of the American Oriental Society*. Vol. 126, No. 4 (2006): 521–35.

Robinson, Chase F. 'Neck-Sealing in Early Islam'. *Journal of the Economic and Social History of the Orient*. Vol. 48, No. 3 (2005): 401–41.

Robinson, Chase F. 'The Study of Islamic Historiography: A Progress Report'. *Journal of the Royal Asiatic Society of Great Britain and Ireland*. Vol. 7, No. 2 (1997): 199–227.

Robson, James. 'The *Isnād* in Muslim Tradition'. In *The Ḥadīth*. Edited by Mustafa Shah. London: Routledge, 2010: 12–21.

Rosenthal, Franz. 'al-Farghānī'. *Encyclopaedia of Islam*, Second Edition.

Rosenthal, Franz. *A History of Muslim Historiography*. Leiden: E. J. Brill, 1952.

Rosenthal, Franz. 'Ibn al-Athīr'. *Encyclopaedia of Islam*, Second Edition.

Rotter, Gernot. 'Zur Überlieferung einiger historischer Werke Madā'inīs in Ṭabarīs *Annalen*'. *Oriens*. Vol. 23–4 (1974): 103–33.

Rydving, Håkan. *Al-Ṭabarī's History: Interpretation and Challenges*. Uppsala: Uppsala University, 2007.

Sahas, Daniel J. 'The Face to Face Encounter Between Patriarch Sophronius of Jerusalem and the Caliph 'Umar ibn al-Khaṭṭāb: Friends or Foes?' In *The Encounter of Eastern Christianity with Early Islam*. Edited by Emmanouela Grypeou, Mark Swanson, and David Thomas. Leiden: Brill, 2005: 33–44.

Savant, Sarah Bowen. *The New Muslims of Post-Conquest Iran: Tradition, Memory, and Conversion*. Cambridge: Cambridge University Press, 2013.

Schacht, Joseph. *An Introduction to Islamic Law*. Oxford: Clarendon Press, 1964.

Schacht, Joseph. *The Origins of Muhammadan Jurisprudence*. Oxford: Clarendon Press, 1950.

Schoeler, Gregor. *The Genesis of Literature in Islam: From the Aural to the Read*. Translated by Shawkat M. Toorawa. Edinburgh: Edinburgh University Press, 2009.

Schoeler, Gregor. *The Oral and the Written in Early Islam*. Translated by Uwe Vagelpohl. Edited by James E. Montgomery. London: Routledge, 2006.

Segovia, Carlos A. 'John Wansbrough and the Problem of Islamic Origins in Recent Scholarship: A Farewell to the Traditional Account'. In *The Coming of the Comforter: When, Where, and to Whom? Studies on the Rise of Islam and Various Other Topics in Memory of John Wansbrough*. Edited by Carlos A. Segovia and Basil Lourié. Piscataway: Gorgias Press, 2012: xv–xxiv.

Sellheim, R., and D. Sourdel, 'Kātib'. *Encyclopaedia of Islam*, Second Edition.

Semalty, Mona, Ajay Semalty, Ashutosh Badola, Geeta Pant Joshi, and M. S. M. Rawat. '*Semecarpus anacardium* Linn: A Review'. *Pharmacognosy Reviews*. Vol. 4, No. 7 (2010): 88–94.

Serjeant, Robert B. 'Review of Quranic Studies: Sources and Methods of Scriptural Interpretation and Hagarism: The Making of the Islamic World'. *Journal of the Royal Asiatic Society*. Vol. 110, No. 1 (1978): 76–8.

Sezgin, Fuat. *Geschichte des arabischen Schrifttums*. Leiden: E. J. Brill, 1967–2000.

Shaban, Muhammad A. *Islamic History, A New Interpretation*. Vol. 1, AD 600–750 *(AH 132)*. Cambridge: Cambridge University Press, 1971.

Shatzmiller, Maya. *Labour in the Medieval Islamic World*. Leiden: Brill, 1994.

Shboul, Ahmad. *Al-Masʿūdī and His World: A Muslim Humanist and His Interest in Non-Muslims*. London: Ithaca Press, 1979.

Shoshan, Boaz. *The Arabic Historical Tradition and the Early Islamic Conquests: Folklore, Tribal Lore, Holy War*. New York: Routledge, 2016.

Shoshan, Boaz. *Poetics of Islamic Historiography: Deconstructing Ṭabarī's History*. Leiden: Brill, 2004.

Sijpesteijn, Petra M. *Shaping a Muslim State: The World of a Mid-Eighth-Century Egyptian Official*. Oxford: Oxford University Press, 2013.

Simonsen, Jørgen Bæk. 'Deux Versions de *Futūḥ al-Buldān*?' In *Living Waters: Scandinavian Orientalistic Studies Presented to Frede Løkkegaard on His Seventy-Fifth Birthday*. Copenhagen: Museum Tusculanam Press, 1990: 339–45.

Toorawa, Shawkat M. *Ibn Abī Ṭāhir Ṭayfūr* and Arabic Writerly Culture: *A Ninth-Century Bookman in Baghdad*. London: Routledge, 2005.

Toral-Niehoff, Isabel. 'History in *Adab* Context: "The Book on Caliphal Histories" by Ibn ʿAbd Rabbih (246/860-328/940)'. *Journal of Abbasid Studies*. Vol. 2 (2015): 61–85.

Torrey, Charles Cutler. 'Special Collections in American Libraries: The Landberg Collection of Arabic Manuscripts at Yale University'. *The Library Journal* 28 (February 1903): 53–7.

Touati, Houari. *Islam & Travel in the Middle Ages*. Translated by Lydia G. Cochrane. Chicago: The University of Chicago Press, 2010.

Tritton, Arthur Stanley. *The Caliphs and Their Non-Muslim Subjects: A Critical Study of the Covenant of ʿUmar*. London: Oxford University Press, 1930.

Turner, John P. 'The *abnā' al-dawla*: The Definition and Legitimation of Identity in Response to the Fourth *Fitna*'. *Journal of the American Oriental Society*. Vol. 124, No. 1 (2004): 1–22.

Ul-Hasan, Mahmood. *Ibn al-Athīr, An Arab Historian: A Critical Analysis of His Tarikh-al-Kamil and Tarikh-al-Atabeca*. New Delhi: Northern Book Centre, 2005.

Vadet, J. C. 'Ibn Ḥādjib, ʿAlī b. ʿAbd al-ʿAzīz b. Ibrāhīm b. al- Nuʿmān, called Ibn Ḥādjib al- Nuʿmān'. *Encyclopaedia of Islam*, Second Edition.

Vajda, G. 'Quelques Certificats de Lecture dans les Manuscrits Arabes de la Bibliothèque Nationale de Paris: La Transmission du *Kitāb al-Ḫarāǧ* de Yaḥyā b. Ādam'. *Arabica*. Vol. 1, No. 3 (1954): 337–42.

Van Berkel, Maaike. 'The Bureaucracy'. In *Crisis and Continuity at the Abbasid Court: Formal and Informal Politics in the Caliphate of al-Muqtadir (295-320/908-32)*. Edited by Maaike van Berkel, Nadia Maria El Cheikh, Hugh Kennedy, and Letizia Osti. Leiden: Brill, 2013: 87–109.

Van Caenegem, Raoul Charles. *Guide to the Sources of Medieval History*. Amsterdam: North-Holland Publishing Co., 1978.

Van Gelder, Geert Jan. 'Poetry in Historiography: The Case of *al-Fakhrī* by Ibn Ṭiqṭaqā'. In *Poetry and History: The Value of Poetry in Reconstructing Arab History*. Edited by Ramzi Baalbaki, Saleh Said Agha, and Tarif Khalidi. Beirut: American University of Beirut Press, 2011: 61–94.

Voorhoeve, P. *Codices Manuscripti. Vol. 7, Handlist of Arabic Manuscripts in the Library of the University of Leiden and Other Collections in the Netherlands*. Leiden: In Bibliotheca Universitatis Lugduni Batavorum, 1957.

Waines, David. 'The Third Century Internal Crisis of the Abbasids'. *Journal of the Economic and Social History of the Orient*. Vol. 20, No. 3 (1977): 282–306.

Waldman, Marilyn Robinson. *Towards a Theory of Historical Narrative: A Case Study in Perso-Islamicate Historiography*. Columbus: Ohio State University Press, 1980.

Wansbrough, John E. *Quranic Studies: Sources and Methods of Scriptural Interpretation*. Oxford: Oxford University Press, 1977.

Wansbrough, John E. *The Sectarian Milieu: Content and Composition of Islamic Salvation History*. Oxford: Oxford University Press, 1978.

Webb, Peter. 'Poetry and the Early Islamic Historical Tradition: Poetry and Narrative of the Battle of Ṣiffīn'. In *Warfare and Poetry in the Middle East*. Edited by Hugh Kennedy. London: I. B. Tauris, 2013: 119–48.

Weipert, Reinhard. 'Abū 'Ubayd al-Qāsim b. Sallām'. *Encyclopaedia of Islam*, Third Edition.

Weipert, Reinhard. 'Abū 'Ubayda'. *Encyclopaedia of Islam*, Third Edition.

Wellhausen, Julius. *Das Arabische Reich und sein Sturz*. Berlin: De Gruyter, 1902.

Wellhausen, Julius. *Die religiös-politischen Oppositionsparteien im alten Islam*. Berlin: Weidmannsche Buchhandlung, 1901.

Witkam, Jan Just. 'Manuscripts & Manuscripts: The "Lost" Manuscripts of al-Balāduri's *Kitāb Futūḥ al-Buldān*'. *Manuscripts of the Middle East*, Vol. 1 (1986): 111–17.

Wood, Philip. *The Chronicle of Seert: Christian Historical Imagination in Late Antique Iraq*. Oxford: Oxford University Press, 2013.

Wurtzel, Karl. *Khalifa ibn Khayyat's History on the Umayyad Dynasty (660–750)*. Edited by Robert G. Hoyland. Liverpool: Liverpool University Press, 2015.

Yarshater, Ehsan. 'The Iranian Renaissance and the Rise of the National Language and Literature'. In *History of Humanity*. Vol. 4, *From the Seventh to the Sixteenth Century*. Edited by M. A. al-Bakhit, L. Bazin, and S. M. Cissoko. London: Routledge/UNESCO, 2000: 724–35.

Zadeh, Travis. *Mapping Frontiers Across Medieval Islam: Geography, Translation, and the 'Abbāsid Empire*. London: I. B. Tauris, 2011.

Zadeh, Travis. 'Of Mummies, Poets, and Water Nymphs: Tracing the Codicological Limits of Ibn Khurradādhbih's Geography'. In *'Abbasid Studies*. Vol. 4, Occasional Papers *of the School of 'Abbasid Studies*. Edited by Monique Bernards. Oxford: Gibb Memorial Trust, 2013: 8–75.

Zaman, Muhammad Qasim. 'al-Ya'ḳūbī'. *Encyclopaedia of Islam*, Second Edition.

Index

'Abbās b. Hishām al-Kalbī (*fl.* mid 800s CE/early 200s AH) 71, 76–7, 132, 205–8
'Abbāsid. *See* caliphate, 'Abbāsid
'Abd al-Ḥamīd (d. ca. 750 CE/AH 132) 42, 226
'Abd Allāh b. 'Āmir b. Kurayz 196
'Abd al-Malik b. Marwān, caliph (r. 685–705 CE/AH 65–86) 125, 146 n.80, 148 n.95
abnā' al-dawla (sons of the state) 35, 43–5
Abū Bakr al-Ṣiddīq, caliph (r. 632–634 CE/AH 11–13) 82, 136, 147 n.90, 199
Abū Hurayra (d. ca. 678–680 CE/AH 57–59) 132–3, 197–8
Abū Mas'ūd al-Kūfī (d. 803–804 CE/AH 207–213) 74–5, 78–80, 203–4
Abū Mikhnaf (d. 774 CE/AH 157) 54, 74–5, 77–8, 80, 93, 105–7, 197–9, 214
Abū Mūsā al-Ash'arī 71, 89–90
Abū 'Ubayda (d. ca. 822–828 CE/AH 207–213) 74–5, 80
Abū 'Ubayda b. al-Jarrāḥ 125–6, 159, 201
Abū 'Ubayd al-Qāsim b. Sallām (d. 838 CE/AH 224) 38–9, 47, 54, 67, 72, 87–92, 111, 161–2, 171, 228
Abū Yūsuf (d. 798 CE/AH 182) 46–7, 54, 69–71, 110–11, 171, 226–8
adab (*belles-lettres*) 15, 41–2, 130–1, 133–4, 151–2, 170, 193, 228
  mirrors for princes 130–1
administrators 15, 35, 39, 52, 55, 107, 117, 119–20, 123–5, 129–31, 133–4, 136, 139, 153, 166, 170, 172, 175, 177–8, 226–8
  handbook 8, 15, 55, 131, 164, 175, 226–8
Aghlabid dynasty (r. 800–909 CE/AH 184–297) 51
agriculture. *See* produce of land
'Ahd Ardashīr 42
Aḥmad b. al-Mudabbir (d. 892–893/AH 279) 53, 170
Aḥmad b. Ṭūlūn 50–3
al-Ahwāz 107
aides-mémoire. *See under* memory
'ajā'ib (wonder) 165
akhbār (narrative historical accounts) 5, 13, 27, 71, 105, 109, 129, 134–7, 161, 189, 198, 211
  akhbāriyyūn (transmitters) 8, 108–9, 141 n.18, 161, 198, 224, 226
'Alī b. Abī Ṭālib, caliph (r. 656–661 CE/AH 35–40) 62 n.64, 121, 132, 202–3
'Alī b. Muḥammad al-Zanjī 53
'Alids 50–1, 119
'Amr b. al-'Āṣ 84, 88, 100 n.98, 106, 186 n.97
amwāl (wealth, possessions) 9, 16, 48, 54, 117, 161, 163, 177, 209
Ansāb al-ashrāf 1, 6–8, 10, 12, 35, 40–2, 54, 65–6, 68, 80, 104, 119, 124–5, 127, 130, 137, 154, 158, 174, 190, 194, 200, 207–8, 229
  content 6–8, 40–2, 54, 68, 118–21, 123–5, 127, 130, 137, 158
  manuscripts (*see under* manuscripts)
  sources 6–8, 10, 65–6, 72–3, 75, 80–1, 108–9
Antrim, Zayde 123
'anwatan (without treaty) 87, 111, 162, 174. *See also* settlement agreements
'appendices' 41, 73, 170–3
Arabic historiography. *See under* historiography
Arabs 44, 50, 79, 107, 123–4, 172, 206
  rule 123–4
archival material 43, 79, 105, 110, 114–16, 166–7, 221 n.63

Ibn Aʿtham al-Kūfī (*fl.* late 800s CE/mid-200s AH) 69, 130, 157–9, 174
Ibn al-Athīr, ʿIzz al-Dīn (d. 1233 CE/AH 630) 192, 201–5, 212–14
Ibn al-Faqīh al-Hamadhānī (*fl.* late 800s CE/AH late 200s) 12, 167–9, 192–5, 214–15
Ibn al-Jawzī (d. 1201 CE/AH 597) 151, 156
Ibn al-Kalbī, Hishām (d. ca. 819–821/AH 204–206) 66, 74–7, 80, 132
Ibn al-Muddabir, Aḥmad (d. ca. 883 CE/AH 270) 53, 170
Ibn al-Nadīm (d. 987–988 CE/AH 377) 12, 36–8, 41–2, 78, 106–8, 129–30, 154–5, 160–1, 194
Ibn al-Zubayr, ʿAbd Allāh 146 n.80, 158, 181 n.32
Ibn Isḥāq, Muḥammad (d. ca. 767 CE/AH 150) 68
Ibn Kathīr, ʿImād al-Dīn (d. 1373 CE/AH 774) 42
Ibn Khayyāṭ. *See* Khalīfa b. Khayyāṭ
Ibn Khurradādhbih 12, 164, 166–9, 175
Ibn Qutayba (d. 889 CE/AH 286) 130, 170–1
Ibn Rabban al-Ṭabarī. *See* al-Ṭabarī, ʿAlī b. Rabban
Ibn Saʿd, Muḥammad (d. 845 CE/AH 230) 38, 41, 54, 66, 73, 75–7, 85, 93, 106, 161, 164, 201
Ibn Zanjawayh (d. between 861–866 CE/AH 247–251) 54
Ibrāhīm al-Shaybānī (d. 911 CE/AH 298) 170–1, 173
Idrīsid dynasty (r. 788–985 CE/AH 172–375) 51
Ifrīqiyya 5, 50–1, 53, 60 n.49, 116, 133, 157
ikhtiṣār. *See* collective *isnād*
imperial history 41, 103–5, 109, 138–9
India. *See* al-Sind
inheritance 87–8, 163–4
  land 61 n.58, 87–8, 163
introductory phrase 15, 27, 67, 72–80, 86, 91, 93, 109
iqṭāʿ 47. *See also* land grant
irrigation 46–7, 49, 83, 115–16
isnād (chain of transmission) 15, 24, 67–74, 80, 84, 89, 91, 108, 161, 191, 200, 202–3
al-Iṣṭakhrī (*fl.* 900s CE/AH 300s) 164, 166–7

al-Jāḥiẓ (d. 868–869 CE/AH 255) 42, 195
al-Jahshiyārī (d. 942 CE/AH 331) 37–9
Jazīra 126, 133, 158
Jerusalem, surrender of 127
Jews 126, 136, 163, 209
jizya (poll tax) 71, 87, 91, 128
Jordan 158–9

al-Kāmil fī-l-taʾrīkh 192, 201–5, 214
Kathīr b. Shihāb 71, 131–2
kātib. *See* secretary
Kennedy, Hugh 46, 48, 116–17, 138
khabar. *See akhbār*
Khālid b. al-Walīd 82, 84, 125–7, 159, 206–7
Khalidi, Tarif 103, 138, 152–3
Khalīfa b. Khayyāṭ (d. 854 CE/AH 239) 14, 106, 119, 164
kharāj (tax, land tax) 9, 16, 35, 42, 47–9, 52, 54, 71, 87, 114–15, 117, 161, 163, 177
  office of 42, 52, 115
Khārijites 50, 119
Khaybar 48, 88–9, 162–3, 209
Khazars 168–9
Khumārawayh b. Aḥmad b. Ṭūlūn 53
Khurāsān 43–5, 50, 53, 75, 81, 106, 194
Khusrau Anūshirwān, Sasanian *shāhanshāh* (r. 531–579 CE) 167–9
Khūzistān 53
Kilito, Abdelfattah 155–6, 176–7
Kilpatrick, Hilary 130, 134
Kitāb al-Amwāl
  of Abū ʿUbayd 72, 87–91, 161, 171, 191
  of Ibn Zanjawayh 54
Kitāb al-Buldān
  of al-Balādhurī 8, 154, 200
  of Ibn al-Faqīh 167–9, 192–5, 214
  of al-Yaʿqūbī 165, 175
Kitāb al-Futūḥ
  of al-Balādhurī 154
  of Ibn Aʿtham 157, 174

www.ingramcontent.com/pod-product-compliance
Lightning Source LLC
Chambersburg PA
CBHW070026010526
44117CB00011B/1719

* 9 7 8 0 7 5 5 6 4 4 6 8 1 *